902 E McKissack

693-2243

# Marketing the Restaurant as a Total Graphic Environment

by

Judi Radice

**Marketing the Restaurant as a Total Graphic Environment**

by
Judi Radice
with
Jackie Comerford



**PBC** International, Inc.

*Distributor to the book trade in the United States and Canada:*

Rizzoli International Publications Inc.
597 Fifth Avenue
New York, NY 10017

*Distributor to the art trade in the United States:*

Letraset USA
40 Eisenhower Drive
Paramus, NJ 07653

*Distributor in Canada:*

Letraset Canada Limited
555 Alden Road
Markham, Ontario L3R 3L5, Canada

*Distributed throughout the rest of the world by:*

Hearst Books International
105 Madison Avenue
New York, NY 10016



**Library of Congress Cataloging-in-Publication Data**

Radice, Judi.
Menu design 3.

Bibliography: p.
Includes index.
1. Menus. I. Title. II. Title: Menu design three.
TX911.3.M45R329 1988 642'.5 87-43305
ISBN 0-86636-059-X

**Cover:**
art direction: David Bartels
design: Mark Illig
illustration: Frank Fruzyna

interior illustration: William P. Mack

Color separation, printing, and binding by
Toppan Printing Co. (H.K.) Ltd. Hong Kong

Printed in Hong Kong

10 9 8 7 6 5 4 3 2 1

## STAFF


| | |
|---|---|
| Pulisher: | *Penny Sibal-Samonte* |
| Creative Director: | *Richard Liu* |
| Associate Art Director: | *Daniel Kouw* |
| Editorial Manager: | *Kevin Clark* |
| Artists: | *William Mack* |
| | *Stacy Levy* |
| | *Kim McCormick* |
| Comptroller: | *Pamela McCormick* |

# ACKNOWLEDGMENTS

Successful completion of a project as large as a book demands the dedication and enthusiasm of a great many people. Not all of them can be personally thanked but a few were so generous with their time and expertise on this project that they must be mentioned by name.

Ron Schmidt not only created our call for entries, he turned our battered sheets of scribbled notes into a real, live data base. Beatriz Coll was kind enough to take time from a busy professional schedule to shoot working photos of each menu for us. Gertie, our faithful (mechanical) servant and Baron, our equally faithful sidewalk superintendent were critical to the tone of the book.

Our thanks also to those who graciously agreed to be interviewed, those who tracked down (and sent!) exciting menus and those who translated, interpreted and otherwise made clear the artist's intent. Last, but by no means least, we wish to express our heart-felt gratitude to "The Judges," Deborah Case and David Magennis. Their enthusiasm, constructive commentary, artistic acumen and insistence that even people working to deadline must eat, made this book what it is ... 'thanks' will never be enough to say.

*Dedication*

The point of traveling through life is not the arrival, but the journey itself. Our gratitude for the chance offered cannot be expressed by mere words. Nonetheless, this volume is dedicated, with our thanks, to the memory of Herb and Cora Taylor. *Vale.*

# CONTENTS

# INTRODUCTION

One of the people interviewed for this book said that operating a restaurant is "creating not merely a meal or a drink, but a form of theater." The analogy is a good one. Like a play, a restaurant must have sets, props and a program; each must be appropriate to the overall theme. You wouldn't find a telephone on stage if the play being presented were a Shakespearean drama; neither should a soda fountain have menus secured with gold cord. In both these cases, the anachronism would destroy the ambience.

The atmosphere in a restaurant is based on a variety of factors. The serving staff, their uniforms, the architecture, interior decor, lighting and graphics all play a part. If properly orchestrated, each of these elements will fit together into a seamless whole, creating a pleasant illusion for the diner. If the dining experience is viewed as a play, it becomes clear that most of these elements move on and off the stage during the course of a meal. The menu has a "cameo" part, since it appears only briefly at the beginning of the meal, before being whisked away to another table. But for the few minutes when a diner holds it, the menu becomes the main focus of attention.

The graphic designer's task is to make the most of the menu's bit part, using it to reinforce the main themes already established by the decor and the staff. Planned properly, a menu can be a powerful merchandising tool.

Many of the menus in this book, for example, incorporate wine and beer lists into the main menu. Some offer suggestions as to which wines to have with given selections. In a bow to the trend toward lighter drinking, many bar menus offer low-alcohol and non-alcoholic versions of popular concoctions.

The restaurants whose menus are featured run the gamut from a legendary dinner house through a Yugoslavian take-out place. The emphasis throughout has been on fresh, wholesome ingredients. This has led to a growing use of adaptable menus. At one time, menu inserts were usually hand-written and tacked into the menu somewhat haphazardly. Now, special insert pockets and highly-textured insert sheets have made this category both interesting and innovative.

Designers have shown great imagination in making many of the menus an extension of the restaurants themselves. Colors are drawn from the decor; in one case, the fiberglass used for privacy in the booths has been used for the menu cover. The interaction between designer and restaurateur reveals better communication than ever before.

As you read this book, bear in mind that the same process of trial and error and adjustment to the changing requirements imposed by a fluid design environment were faced — and solved — by each designer/restaurant team. Their common goal was to create an illusion. The magic may be fleeting, but it lasts until the curtain falls.

# CHAPTER 1

Creating an identity is one of the toughest tests for a graphic designer. A logo must provide instant identification on a non-verbal level; it must also be sufficiently flexible to be used in a variety of media — which can range from menus through billboards through T-shirts and postcards.

At its best, a logo will recall a restaurant in the same way that an image from a film — a child bicycling across the moon for *E.T.,* for example — recalls that film. In both cases, an attempt to sum up a variegated whole in one simple picture has been made.

If we continue our image of restaurant as theater, the logo may be thought of as the masthead on the playbill.

# ESTABLISHING AN IDENTITY: LOGOS

Designer: *Brian Barclay*
*Bartels & Carstens, Inc.*
Restaurant: *Pantera's Pizzas*
*Express Buffet*

This logo embodies the speed and freshness implicit in a pizza buffet. The way this works is that a diner pays for the buffet, then helps himself to pieces of whichever pizzas offered he chooses. The logo appeared not only within the various outlets but also on outdoor signage, delivery trucks and as a symbol on television.

Designer: *John Casado*
*Bartels & Carstens, Inc.*
Restaurant: *Park West*
*Chicago, IL*

Chic and "classy," Park West is probably Chicago's premier restaurant/night club. Big name stars appear here. The illustrator decided that a high-energy image was needed to underline the theme of the place. The Art Deco illustration recalls Chicago of the 1920's.

Designer: *Don Strandell*
*Bartels & Carstens, Inc.*
Restaurant: *Fischer's*
*Belleville, IL*

This project began as a prototype for a letterhead and eventually evolved into a logo for the whole restaurant. The owner wanted a Maxfield Parrish-type feeling. The dwarves carrying cutlery embodied the desired effect.

Designer: *Keith Anderson*
*Bartels & Carstens, Inc.*
Restaurant: *Othello's*
*Atlanta, GA*

This award-winning logo was created for a private club in an Art Deco building. Since the club's primary audience is black, the choice of Othello, the title character from Shakespeare's play, made sense. The elegant and streamlined female figures pay tribute to the building's architecture.

AMBROSIA

AMBROSIA

AMBROSIA

AMBROSIA

AMBROSIA

Jamaica Rum Fruitcake
Bourbon Pecan Fruitcake
Christmas Plum Pudding
Christmas Plum Pudding
Christmas Plum Pudding
Walnut Butter Toffee
Walnut Butter Toffee

AMBROSIA

Designer: *Bruce Yelaska*
*Bruce Yelaska Design*

Restaurant: *Ambrosia*
*Woodacre, CA*

Though this bakery is new, the owners wanted to establish a traditional feeling. The designer's response was to use a traditional, serif typeface and a rather ornate capital 'A' as the focus of the design.

These elements, together with the strong red in which they are executed, provide an inexpensive solution to a classic design problem.

AMBROSIA

Great

American

Food

**Designer:** *Bruce Yelaska*
*Bruce Yelaska Design*
**Restaurant:** *Great American Food*
*San Francisco, CA*

For this bakery, which was moving from a strictly wholesale operation to a retail format, the designer wanted to achieve an American look without being too obvious. To quote the designer himself, "By taking two obvious icons, the star and pie, and combining them in a unique manner, I've created a rebus which describes the product and its origins. The handmade look of the logo helps reinforce the handmade quality (of the product)."

573 Hayes

San Francisco

California 94102

415-863-0312

Great American Food

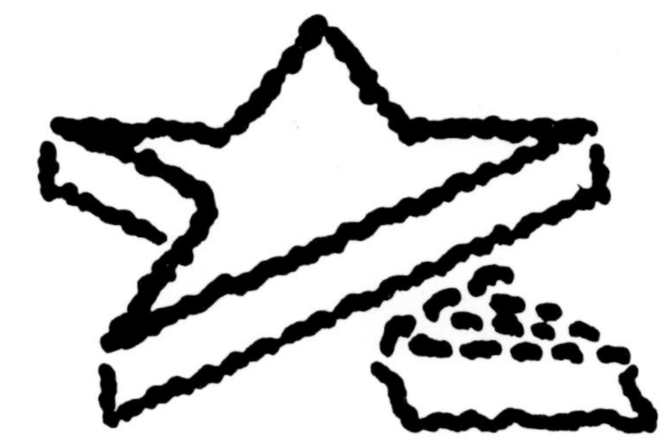

Great American Food

Great American Food

**Designer:** *Paula Richards*
*Rees Thompson Designers*
**Restaurant:** *Caffe Pasta*
*Seattle, WA*

The house specialty is pasta so a strand of spaghetti separates the red and green halves of the logo. Along with the white used for the reversed type, these are the national colors of Italy. The colors are repeated on the two large blackboards which serve as the menus.

The semicircular logo lends a note of formality to the blackboard format. The two boards, located in the two main traffic areas of the restaurant, replace an earlier, rather haphazard collection of signs that, like Topsy, weren't planned, "they just grew." Response to the new format has been very positive.

CAFFE PASTA

CAFFE PASTA
DELI
LUNCH-11-3:30
HOT SANDWICHES
MEATBALL — 4.20
ITALIAN SAUSAGE — 4.20
SALADS
GREEN SALAD 1.75

| | |
|---|---|
| Designer: | *Bruce Yelaska* |
| | *Bruce Yelaska Design* |
| Restaurant: | *Little City* |
| | *San Francisco, CA* |

The key element in all of the designer's work is the violation of spacial integrity. He begins with a compact, coherent design and deliberately shifts one small element outside the congruity of the whole. In the case of "Little City," he has chosen to take a dot and move it from its proper place above the 'i' to a space over the double 't'.

The dot is also used in the same manner as a bus transfer. In the case of a bus transfer, the date is punched to show it has been used. On the menu, this provides a unifying element to the entire design.

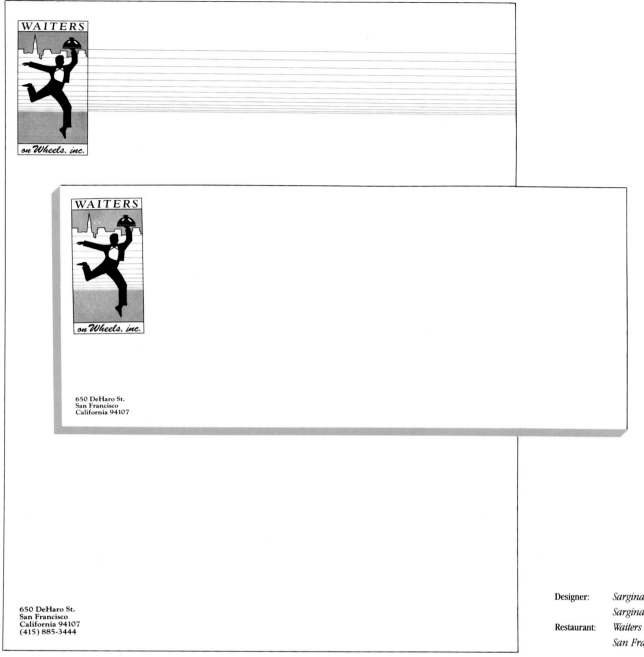

650 DeHaro St.
San Francisco
California 94107

650 DeHaro St.
San Francisco
California 94107
(415) 885-3444

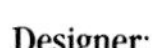

Designer: *Sargina A. Tamimi*
*Sargina A. Tamimi Design*
Restaurant: *Waiters on Wheels*
*San Francisco, CA*

TAKIS ZARIKOS
*Vice President*

650 DeHaro Street
San Francisco, CA 94107
(415) 885-3444

For San Francisco's first non-restaurant-specific meal delivery service, the designer has created an imaginative logo. Since the service's strong points include speed, a sophisticated style and computer technology, all of these elements were incorporated, at least by inference, into the design.

W.O.W. delivery people wear bright red waiter's jackets and bow ties. Food delivery is coordinated by computer. And the service is available only in San Francisco proper. Therefore, an elegantly clad, running waiter is silhouetted against the City's skyline. The design is executed in black and white with a tint, both to control the expense and to lend the design an austere beauty.

**DONUT**
**EXCHANGE**

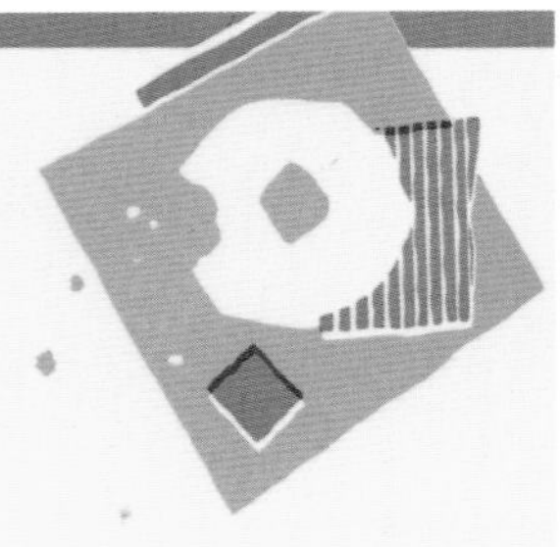

**AND A SHARE OF MUFFINS**
163 WEST SANTA CLARA STREET
SAN JOSE, CALIFORNIA 95113

DANNY Y. KIKUCHI
408.293.2244

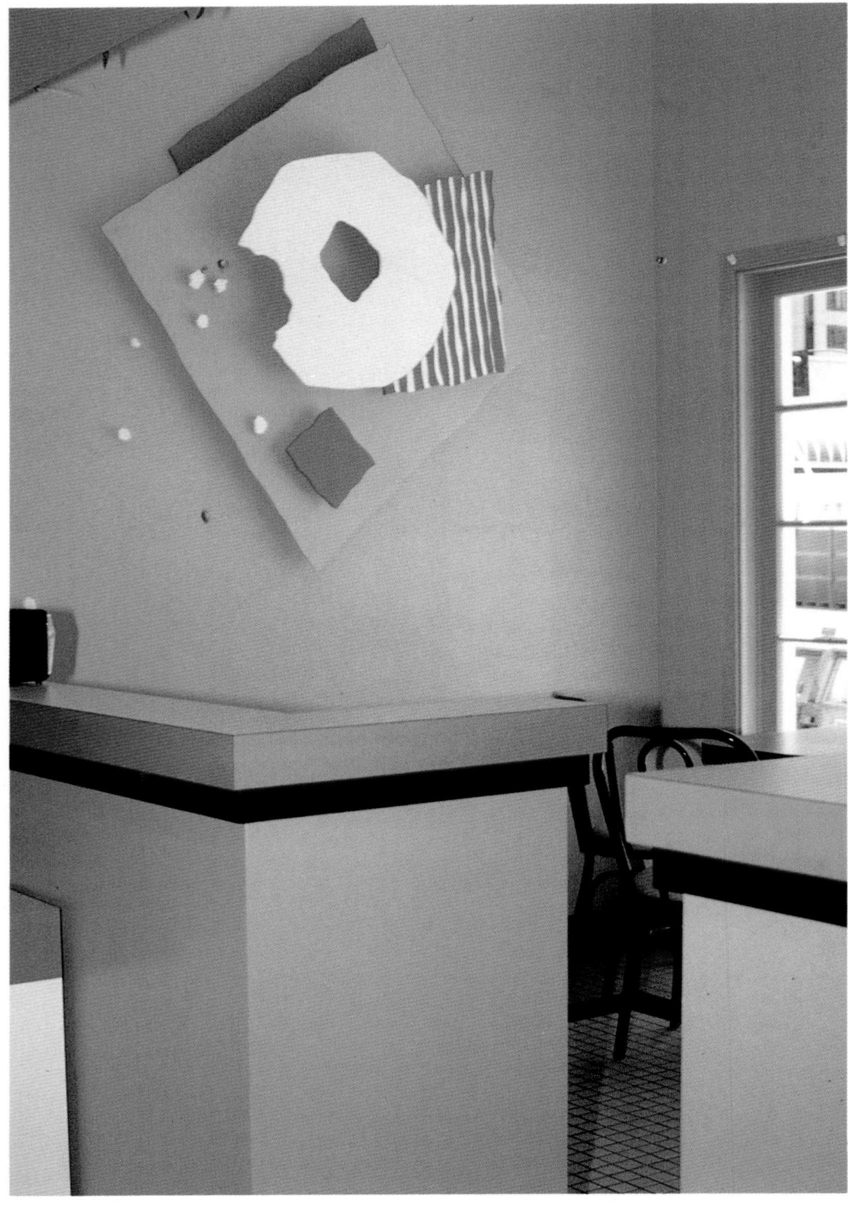

| | |
|---|---|
| Designer: | *Rich Tharp* |
| | *Tharp Did It* |
| Restaurant: | *The Donut Exchange* |
| | *San Jose, CA* |

Situated in the heart of the city's financial district, this doughnut (and muffin) shop caters to bankers and stockbrokers. Recognizing the primary audience, the shop positioned itself as a playful take-off on the stock market. Take-out orders are accompanied by "share" certificates and the signage features an endless mix of product descriptions and prices intermingled, reminiscent of a ticker tape.

The humor in the concept is supported by the use of vivid colors for the various applications. While recognizing the surrounding serious business atmosphere, the shop is a respite from that strain. As a result, the share certificates are somehow more like Monopoly than the real thing, providing tense business people with a chance to relax.

SHARES
SHARES
DONUT EXCHANGE
AND A SHARE OF MUFFINS
This certificate verifies that you are the shareholder
of the freshest shares made of
the finest and tastiest ingredients available.
Daniel Y. Kikuchi President
163 W. SANTA CLARA ST. SAN JOSE, CALIFORNIA 408.293.2244

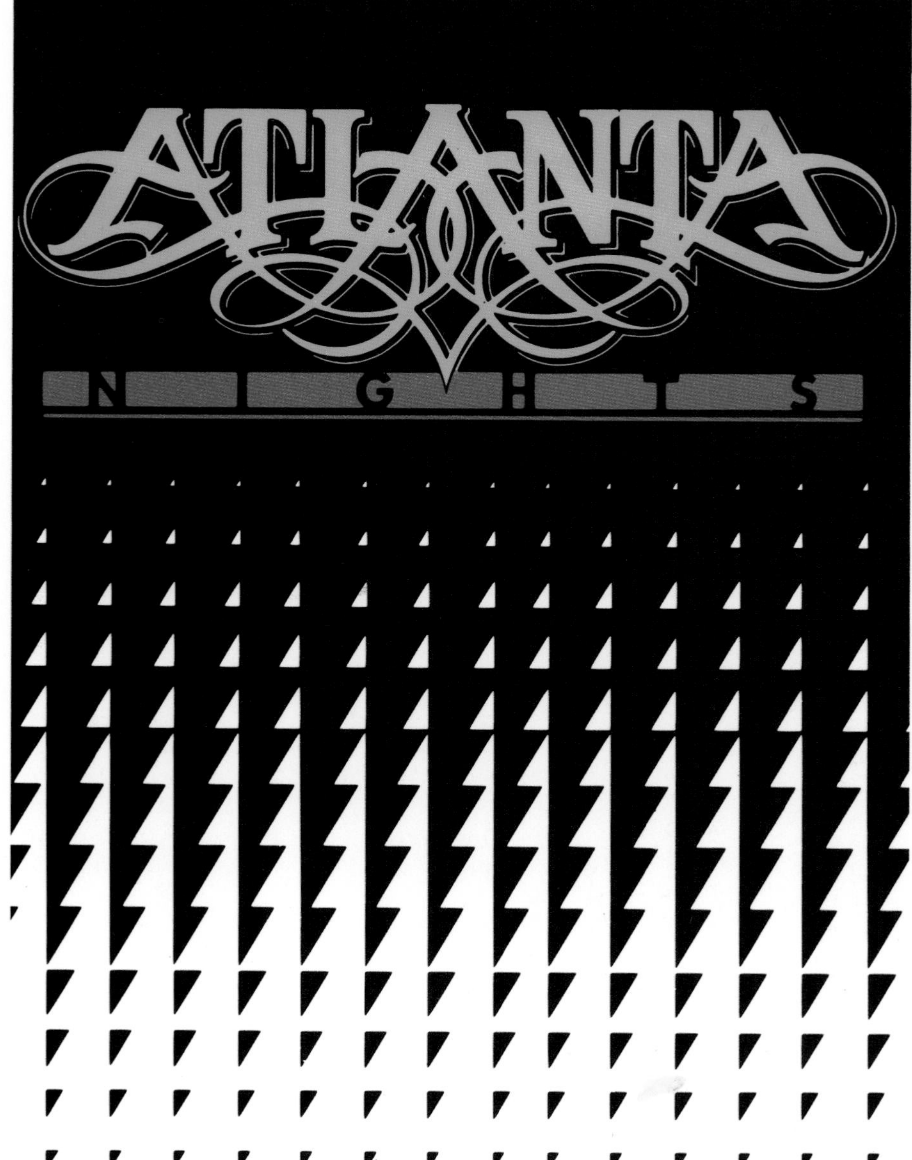


**Designer:** *Brian Barclay*
*Bartels & Carstens, Inc.*
**Restaurant:** *Atlanta Nights*
*Atlanta, GA*

The designer was struck by the beauty of the city's — and restaurant's — name, 'Atlanta.' From his point of view, the word itself is perfectly balanced. Three 'A's', interspersed with two consonants, presented the opportunity to make the word *itself* a part of the design. The balance of the design decisions was dictated by the fact that the restaurant itself is modern but it is located in an Art Deco building. Note that the strength of the design is apparent, whether considered in its black-and-white or colored treatments.

# CHAPTER 2

*Lisa Edson*
Royal Viking Line, San Francisco, CA

*Ric Tombari*
Small Business Entrepreneur

*Tom Hinkel*
Kenyon Press

*Dwight Clark*
Clark's By-the-Bay, Redwood City, CA

*Peter Garin*
Consultant, San Francisco, CA

A number of different professions are involved in the creation of a successful restaurant. Not only the owner and an architect but color consultants, lighting designers, kitchen designers and, yes, graphic designers each play a part. To continue the theatrical motif mentioned earlier, the owner may be seen as the playwright, anxious to see his dream take on substance. The architect is rather like the stage manager, ensuring that each detail has been placed correctly. The graphic designer prepares the program. Lighting and interior designers play much the same roles as they would in a theatrical setting.

In this chapter, you will hear from a few people who have been involved in the creative process of a restaurant opening. A graphic designer, an architect, a printer specializing in menus and collateral restaurant pieces, a celebrity-turned-restaurateur and someone who can best be described as a "restaurant midwife" have each contributed some insights into the ongoing process of restaurant creation. Their comments provide a valuable look at how others view restaurant creation.

# INTERVIEWS

*"The room should show off the people and the food. In my opinion, the restaurant is only as good as the food and service. The funny part is that, of all the little details in a restaurant, the vast majority are never noticed by the diner ... but the experience would be substantially different if any of those details were missing."*

**RIC TOMBARI**
Small Business Entrepreneur

Ric Tombari is a man of many and varied interests. He has, at one time or another, served as the architectural consultant for a law firm, operated his own restaurant and, as an undergraduate, organized major parties for the Architecture Department at the University of California, Berkeley. "I've also designed the concepts for a number of food service establishments and restaurants including two of the San Francisco branches of Oh La La Bakery and Firehouse No. 1, a restaurant specializing in barbecue in Larkspur, California."

"As a result of my work with the law firm, I was able to save the money to start a small cafe. I opened the cafe on impulse. While standing in line, I noticed the space was available, decided it was the perfect location and took it. It was about six weeks from the time the lease was signed until the cafe opened. Starting a cafe was very naive. I had the idea I could come in to my own cafe and have a good time and walk away from it when I wanted to leave. Obviously, I learned differently. Running a restaurant can be great fun, if you like that sort of thing, but it can require as much as 17 to 20 hours a day, seven days a week."

In terms of the restaurant projects he has handled as an architect, Tombari states, "The first thing you have to be aware of is that you're not making *your* dream, you're making the *owner's* dream. The best thing the architect or designer can do is to listen. The architect's role is minute by comparison to the role of the people who are going to be operating the restaurant — basically *living* there, seven days a week. When considering the design, I like to keep things as simple as possible so that there are clues for the diners as they enter; if I've planned correctly, they can use those clues to get an idea of the restaurant's goals and approach as they go through the dining experience. The key to the success of any of the restaurants and food service operations I've designed is the special relationship between the equipment and the staff who work there and what their needs are."

"When I approach a restaurant design project, how involved I get with such decisions as lighting, selection of equipment and kitchen placement, and the like depends on the budget. If the budget permits, I prefer to retain the services of both a lighting designer and a color consultant. I *always* insist on a graphic designer for the menu, the logo and other graphics. Sometimes, particularly with a large project, I have enough just to coordinate everyone else's work."

"Cafe Americain (Tombari's own restaurant) was built on a very limited budget. In a way, that was good because we learned how to fix things as we built them. Most of the materials used in construction were salvaged and we upgraded the cafe to a restaurant in just 16 weeks. Sometimes, friends helped with labor, which helped defer costs. I will always remember that we opened on the night we selected but, as a group of long-time customers, drinks in hand, stood in the restaurant lobby, the bus boys and waiters finished applying the last coat of wax to the floors as the carpenters were leaving by the fire door. I still remember that one of my customers took the broom from my hands as I tried to sweep away the last of the sawdust and, like magic, we were opened."

"Building the cafe ourselves enabled the owners to achieve a much higher-quality product than we could otherwise have afforded. Even though we supplied most of the manual labor, we still had to hire certain professionals — electricians, plumbers and finish carpenters, just to name a few. Some of their work we *could* have done, but it would have taken much longer. We spent about $54 per square foot (including all the equipment, fees and permits), while the industry average is about $125 per square foot."

"I like to hire the graphic designer at an early stage of the design. Depending upon how convinced the owner is of his (or her) own ideas, the graphic designer can sometimes provide a focus for the interior at a stage when it's still feasible to implement the idea. Sometimes a subtle use of painted details can provide an identity for the room. The graphic designer may see the need for this where someone else might miss the possibilities."

"It's really easy to spend money on a restaurant. The critical factor is how *little* you can spend and still achieve great results. When a restaurateur sets out to create a new restaurant, it's important for him to trust the professionals he has hired to create it for him. He should be willing to react on a gut level but should have done his homework so he can react logically to suggestions offered by the professionals. If the restaurateur understands managing money and keeping track of the details, he'll do all right. Sadly, most restaurants fail during the first year because they're undercapitalized and/or the business was not managed properly. Understanding how much money will be required for the start-up and knowing how best to apply it are critical to the success of a new venture."

As far as the future of restaurant design is concerned, Tombari sees "a trend toward exhibition-style kitchens, not so much the smells and sounds as at least a window or aperture to bring the experience a little closer to the diner. Better use of lighting is another trend which improves the overall ambience. The new successful restaurants are

noisier, to provide a sense of excitement, yet this can backfire by driving away older customers, if not handled properly. As far as decorative motifs are concerned, *trompe* l'oeil has been very popular for the last year or two, especially when it's used to "bring the outdoors inside."

"Part of the charm of *trompe l'oeil* effects is that, using sponges, paint and rags, one can achieve a textural interest that can literally, as the name implies, 'fool the eye.' Theatrical lighting, another current trend, can enhance the effect."

In conclusion, Tombari says, "Without restaurants, the world wouldn't be half as interesting a place because people wouldn't have the opportunity to get together at 'great little spots.' For that, architects are owed a vote of thanks for their input into this process. Owners of restaurants should be thanked even more, for their ability to put up with architects. The restaurateur breathes life into a restaurant with the force of his own personality. If breath runs out, the restaurant suffers. Most people who open restaurants are very naive about what is involved. Yet

that naivete is part of the charm; without it, the restaurant world would be a very dull and calculated place. People who are already involved in running a restaurant might not choose to enter that world again, but having dived in, continue to provide a party for the rest of us."

*"Royal Viking Line has provided me with a real challenge as a designer. I've had to return to the basics I learned in design school and find a way to express the essential elegance of classic design."*

**LISA EDSON**
ROYAL VIKING LINE
San Francisco, CA

Lisa Edson is one designer whose employers would like her to take a cruise — at their expense — just as soon as she has time. Of course, the idea is for Edson to experience the environment for which she designs not only menus but also signage, special invitations and any other graphics needed for use aboard or to promote any of Royal Viking's three luxurious cruise ships.

One reason Royal Viking's menus are unique is that both the luncheon and dinner menus are typeset and printed on board every day. Menu shells are printed ashore and stored ready for use on each ship. Over twenty different shells are available and, on shorter cruises, are never repeated. The content of the menus — that is, the individual dishes — is never repeated on a cruise, not even the 100-day cruise offered each January. The same shells, designed and printed in Norway, have been in use for at least the past five years.

Within the past year, Royal Viking decided that its graphics needs had grown to the point where retaining an in-house designer made fiscal sense. They also wanted to ensure that the graphics were as consistent as the balance of the services the Line provides. Edson, its new designer, handles a variety of graphic assignments of which menus are only a part. Signage, creation of special logos for theme cruises and graphic needs for various in-house events are also part of her work.

Among her first assignments for the Line was the creation of two menus for special events held on board. Edson noted that "there isn't always time to go through the full development process of thumbnails, comps and finished piece. Sometimes I skip the thumbnail entirely and simply 'talk my way through' until I find an idea on which everyone can agree and we move directly to finished production."

The 'everybody' referred to is a committee which approves all of Edson's work. In the case of menus, the decision makers are Becky Brown, Director of Marketing Communications, Daniel Durand, Culinary Director, and Erling Frydenberg, Vice President of Hotel Operations. When the menu is for a special event, George Cruys, Manager of Public Relations is also involved.

According to Durand, "No one of us makes the final decision. The menus are a way for all of us to focus our creativity on something outside the mainstream of our daily activities." Frydenberg adds "somehow we all manage to agree ... we know when we are comfortable with a menu design."

Edson frequently "recycles" ideas. She maintains a file of "comps that didn't fly. When I'm stalled, I go back to the file and, frequently, find something I can use as a starting point for a new design." She has found, though, that certain ideas are inappropriate for Royal Viking. "As a designer, I'd like to be able to use some of the more modern type applications and play with unusual treatments. It took me a couple of months to realize that just wouldn't work here. The ships themselves are classically elegant. In keeping with the decor on the ships and in consideration of the mature outlook of our clientele clean, classic presentations are needed."

The advent of an in-house designer, one who, as Durand noted, "knows the corporate identity and doesn't have to have a lot of things explained to her," has opened up a broad variety of graphic possibilities for the Line. Cruys added "It would be foolish to have a graphic designer available in-house and not take advantage of the fact by giving her as many opportunities to use her talents as possible."

One of the ways that creativity will be tapped is in redesigning all of the menu shells. Frydenberg noted "Historically, we have many repeat passengers. We did not want them to get bored with too many repetitions of the same menus. Also, we are refurbishing the ships and getting one new one. It seemed like a good time for a change." Since the menus are reprinted daily, passengers are encouraged to collect the set from an entire cruise as a souvenir. In fact, the waiters are trained to offer to set aside a full set to be collected the last day of the cruise. Some of the menus are suitable for framing. With so much repeat business, it makes sense for the line to vary its menus as much as possible.

Edson is certainly game to try. "I'm really looking forward to the challenge of the new menus. You know, I spent the last ten years in the broadcast media, where I seemed to have all the money I would ever need for a graphic project. Here, my work is just one of many considerations that establish an identity. Royal Viking tries to create a total gracious environment for its passengers. Menus and signage are a part of a harmonious whole."

Both the Line and Edson are embarking on a creative adventure. Whatever happens, watching the development of the new menus and a new feeling about the role of graphics in the cruise industry should be exciting. And yes, eventually Lisa Edson may get her cruise ... when there's time.

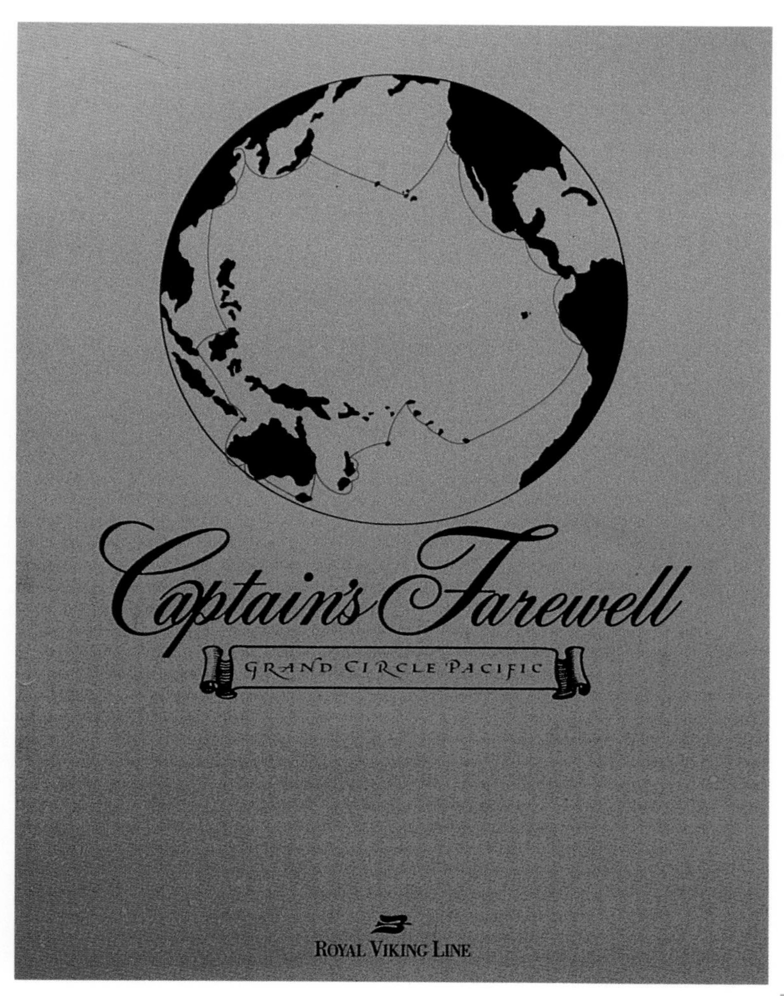

**"Grand Circle Pacific Cruise" menus**

Because most people do not have time to take a full 100-day cruise, the designer created special "Welcome Aboard" menus for each of four segments, in addition to the one for the official start of the cruise and a formal "Captain's Farewell" menu. What distinguishes the segment menus is that the appropriate leg of the cruise is highlighted in red foil, with the balance of the trip executed in gold foil on the menu covers. This technique gives each menu an added excitement for the diner. All of the menus were designed to be imprinted aboard except the first "Welcome Aboard;" this dinner was executed with foodstuffs available in the ship's home port, San Francisco, from which it departed, therefore the menu was preprinted.

*"We strive to listen to the client and be flexible."*

**TOM HINKLE**
General Manager
Kenyon Press
Los Angeles, CA

The stated aim of Kenyon Press is "to provide quality products with excellent service to our customers." A less obvious goal is to educate those customers in how best to implement their ideas. This secondary goal is exemplified by the "Menu Workbook." "The Workbook is a tool Kenyon Press developed to educate clients who are involved in ordering menus. With input from Kenyon's sales staff, a restaurateur can make intelligent, informed selections."

"We can't have as personal a relationship with many of our clients as we'd like. Hotel Food and Beverage Directors simply don't have the time. For hotels, menus are based on a variety of photographs and very little personal discussion. The Workbook provides a way for us to bridge that 'information gap.' You get a lot closer to an individual owner or restaurant chain ... with a chain, there's always someone whose main job is coordinating the menu development."

Interestingly, Kenyon Press draws its sales force not from the printing industry, as one might expect, but from the hotel/catering restaurant management field. "It's easier for us to teach them the printing business than for a printing professional to learn the ins and outs of the restaurant business."

"When we design a new menu, we have a form our sales staff completes, telling us the color of the carpets and noting details about the general decor. This is useful in reinforcing memory when the salesperson returns to the plant."

Hinkle grew up with the business. His father ran Kenyon Press when it still specialized in pharmaceutical printing. During the sixties, a local menu printer fell on hard times. Many of its personnel gravitated to Kenyon and, bit by bit, menus became the primary focus of Kenyon's business. "I ran a press after school when I was still in high school," notes Hinkle. "When I joined the sales force, I worked on commission ... I couldn't *afford* to take a long view. Now that I'm in management, I can."

As far as peripheral menus are concerned, Hinkle feels that "any kind of direct mail advertising would help anybody. The problem is, they don't have the time and knowledge to really set it up and produce it properly." Wine menus, on the other hand "are often subsidized by the wine companies. They offer the menus at a low price; they're standardized, of course, and often the restaurateur doesn't want to pay for anything more."

"I never like putting anything on the back page of a menu. It's better to integrate the wines with the menu selections or, at least, to feature them on one of the interior pages; it's better merchandising."

As far as trends in the industry are concerned, Hinkle feels "fresh produce has been important for several years. As far as word processing or desk-top publishing menus are concerned, they're fooling themselves ... they forget just how labor-intensive it is." Instead, he suggests, "Having a special card or insert can make the menu appear just as 'fresh' without all that extra typing." "The use of inserts requires more creativity on our part. We try to develop creative die cuts and unusual pockets as holders for the insert sheets."

"There are a lot of merchandising 'tricks' we can bring to bear for a client — boxes, inserts or clip-ons can make an item 'pop.' It's all a question of what someone wants." "We can do just about anything a client wants, in terms of a menu ... we just need to know what is wanted. A lot of our back-up paperwork is aimed at that ... identifying what someone wants."

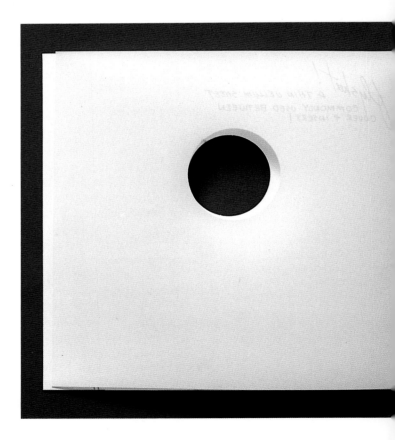

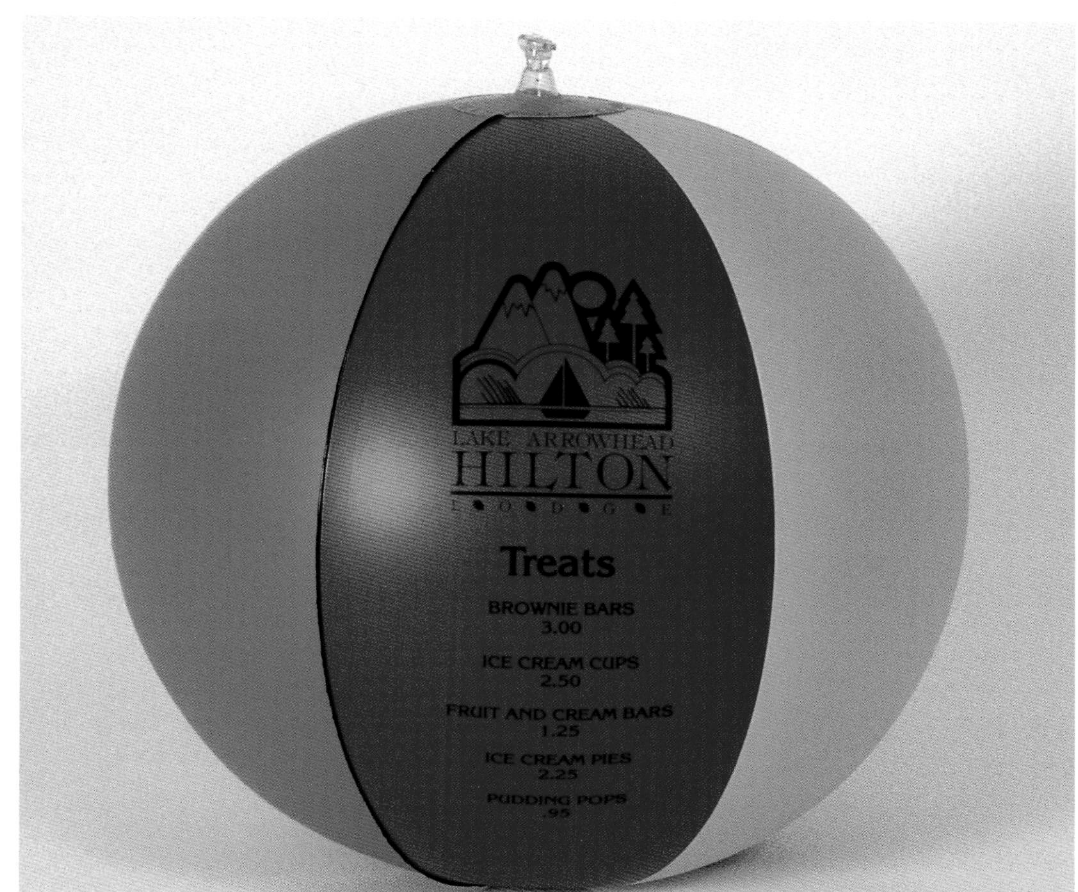


Restaurant: Arrowhead Hilton
Pool Menu
Lake Arrowhead, CA

This resort has long been a chic vacation destination for Californians. Using an inflatable beach ball as the vehicle for a menu is in perfect keeping with the atmosphere. The beach ball can also serve as a souvenir of a lovely holiday.

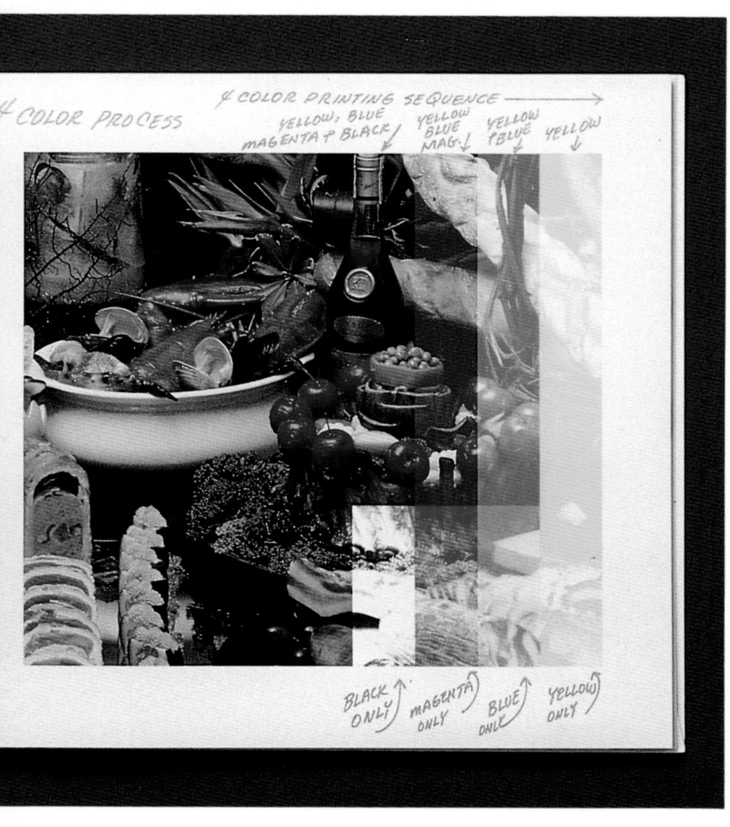


**Menu Workbook**

The menu workbook provides prospective menu buyers with a guide to the ins and outs of the printing industry. Such esoterica as four-color process printing, screens, foil stamping and holding lines are explained with both words and pictures in terms easy enough for the layman to understand.

*"I have a passion for trivia ... especially when it relates to food and drink, and I love the theatrical nature of bars, clubs, and restaurants. The two interests made my present business an obvious choice."*

**PETER GARIN**
Restaurant Strategies

Garin has been called a "restaurant midwife." As he explains it, this means "finding the right style for a restaurant's audience, geographical location and price range." He applies 'sociobiology' to achieve this. One example is "the meat test." In essence, it amounts to getting a raw steak from a restaurant kitchen and "walking through the restaurant with it. If the appearance of the meat is enhanced by the ambient lighting and color in the surrounding decor, the environment is a hospitable one. The more relaxed and comfortable a customer is, the less subconscious resistance to spending he retains."

Garin lards his conversation with trivia relating to restaurant and bar design. "The use of mirrors behind a bar dates back to the time when the bartender — more often than not the owner — as well as the patrons were more than just a little leery of being shot in the back. The mirrors forestalled any nasty surprises." "The difference between bar customs in the East and in the West — in the East, you run a tab; on the West Coast, you put your money in front of you on the bar — dates to the Gold Rush, when less than honorable men had to prove they could afford their liquor. An added incentive was that many were suddenly inspired to leave when their past attempted to catch up with them." Garin's point is that "there's a logical reason behind many of the customs and practices you see in bars and restaurants."

"The difference between a successful restaurant and its less-successful imitators is attention to detail. A restaurant is probably the toughest kind of business to run because everything is so closely intertwined. You aren't simply responsible for the food, you're manufacturing an environment, a total atmosphere. From sound systems to graphics, no matter how much money has been spent, it all boils down to the impression you leave with your patron." "It helps to be an absolute *fanatic* about detail. For example, if you're opening an Italian restaurant, you might ensure all the managers speak Italian. This fastidiousness and the attitude displayed by the whole staff provide the opportunity for *your* business to distance itself from its competitors."

"A restaurant," contends Garin, "is one of the three places you really see what a person is like. The other two are when an individual is sleeping and immediately after physical intimacy." "Because of constant scrutiny by the customers and management, pressure on restaurant staff is intense and the turnover rate, high. Restaurant work is demanding and not for everyone. Statistics show the average length of employment nationally is only ninety days. The successful restaurateur will find a way to make his staff sufficiently happy that *his* staff will exceed the national average in staying power."

"An obnoxious or just plain unhappy staff member can upset every person he comes into contact with; in a restaurant, this can be lethal. Impressions are what it's all about ... the waiter with tomato on his shirt, the greasy or illegible menu, lighting so poor that the diner calls for a flashlight ... all of these can ruin the impression. You're selling a respite from that when you create a pleasant atmosphere in a restaurant."

The lesson in all of this for the budding restaurateur is that there's a lot of competition out there. "If you don't pay attention to the details, if you aren't aware that what you are creating is not merely a meal or a drink, but a form of theater, then your business will suffer. After all, what's so enviable or special about having paid to see a bad movie?"

*"I knew it was almost time for me to retire from football. I love the interaction with the fans and didn't want to give up all the contact with the public. In some ways, this is better ... there's no helmet, I'm not out there on the field while they're in the stands, there's no* barrier *there anymore ... I have the opportunity to really talk to people. I enjoy that very much."*

**DWIGHT CLARK** and **PAUL BOUCHARD**
Clark's by the Bay
Redwood City, CA

Dwight Clark is the perfect restaurateur. He's personable, gracious and genuinely interested in providing his customers with good value and a pleasant time. Clark's By-the-Bay is his second venture into operating a restaurant. "We started with a little burger place in the City (San Francisco), Time Out. That space is very bright and light, with lots of blond wood and brass. For 'Clark's,' we wanted something more homey. I've been in restaurants so bright that the lights glared off the walls at you. We wanted an atmosphere that would feel softer than that." "We started with the shell of the building, which included the shafts for the fireplaces, and went from there."

(Clark's By-the-Bay had been open for little more than a month at the time this interview was conducted.) "Our biggest problem," says Clark, "is the wait at the front door. We hadn't anticipated that business would grow this much this fast. We're still short of banquet facilities and office space ... we hope to find something in one of the adjacent buildings."

Clark selected restaurants as a second career partly because of the experience of friends who retired from professional sports and opened restaurants. Another factor was that his father introduced him to Paul Bouchard, currently the managing general partner of Clark's.

Bouchard's expertise in the retail sector became the impetus for, first, Time Out and, later, Clark's By-the-Bay. Says Clark, "What we learned from Time Out is that, in order to make a profit, you have to sell a whole lot of $4.00 hamburgers ... it's easier with more upscale food. There isn't that much difference in the operating costs from one food genre to another." Bouchard notes that "We got into fast foods at exactly the wrong point. All the "big boys" were cutting back, becoming nervous about their profit margins. We had initially planned on a chain of Time Outs. At this point, we're satisfied with the one. We learned a lot from the experience."

Part of the rationale behind Clark's By-the-Bay is the marketability of Clark himself. He has a name, and, more importantly, has the right personality for an "image" restaurant. No-one who comes to Clark's and meets Clark himself will be disappointed by the experience. He, Bouchard and the third general partner, Lloyd Canton, have definite ideas about what makes a successful restaurant. "We didn't want anything trendy and weren't interested in fads. We felt that, if we charged, say $15.00 for dinner and provided what people perceived as a $30.00 experience, both in terms of food and service, we would do well."

In the future, the partners in Clark's envision opening other branches of the restaurant. For this first location, 'By-the-Bay' seemed a logical choice as a tag. "We always want to retain a sense of place. Most cities have some symbol that, more than any other, characterizes the place. Here, it happened to be San Francisco Bay. In other cities, the symbol might be a river or a tree or a silhouette of the skyline ... it's a matter of placement. The logotype was designed so that it could be incorporated with a variety of different symbols, depending on where it was used."

"The theater aspect of dining in a restaurant was really important in the design, not only of the logo, but of the restaurant as a whole. We realized that not everybody could have a view of the Bay, so we decided on an exhibition kitchen to provide some entertainment for those tables which couldn't be next to a window." "We learned from building this restaurant. It's really a business of sometimes painful details ... everything, including the graphics, has *got* to be right or it just doesn't work together."

**Restaurant:** Clark's By-the-Bay Collateral

The basic restaurant logo appears on a variety of collateral pieces. These range from t-shirts through sweatshirts, caps and even the house line of wines. The softball t-shirt was designed for a charity softball game. Clark captained one team; the other was led by Huey Lewis of the rock group, Huey Lewis and the News (which explains the guitar in the hands of one batter). The quality of the shirts is evident when you realize that the sweatshirts are manufactured by the same company that produces them for professional football teams. Here, as with the food, quality is the underlying theme.

# CHAPTER 3

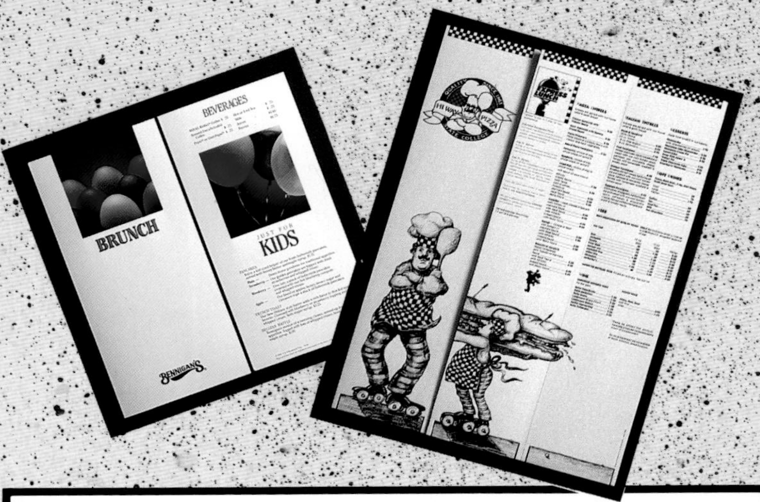


Nobody really likes a commercial. And nobody goes to a restaurant expecting to see one. Yet a well-planned menu can be exactly that — a commercial not only for the food items offered but for peripheral products and services provided by the organization.

The peripherals may include an associate's market or bakery, gift items that will provide a secondary "sell," long after the details of the meal are forgotten or simply catering services. If these are to be marketed via the medium of the menu, the sales pitch must be so soft as to slip past the diner's sales resistance without his noticing it.

Similarly, the restaurant can choose to highlight high-profit items by carefully choosing their placement on the menu. Sales of alcoholic beverages may be increased by suggesting wine and food pairings the restaurant has found suitable. Someone who is normally timid about ordering wine in public because he is afraid of appearing ignorant of the proper choices may be more inclined to do so when it is made easy for him.

Successful menu-based merchandising is never solely the product of a brilliant designer. Input from the restaurant's management and kitchen staff, who are better-equipped to know which items are most profitable and what goals the restaurant has for the menu, is critical to the success of the project.

Color, copywriting, typography and placement on the menus are among the techniques which can be used to highlight certain selections. Graphic devices such as checkmarks, boxes and use of contrasting colors also come into play. Insert sheets for the daily specials are a popular method of either highlighting profitable items or of testing new recipes before including them on the permanent menu. Many of these techniques are explored on the following pages.

# MERCHANDISING POWER

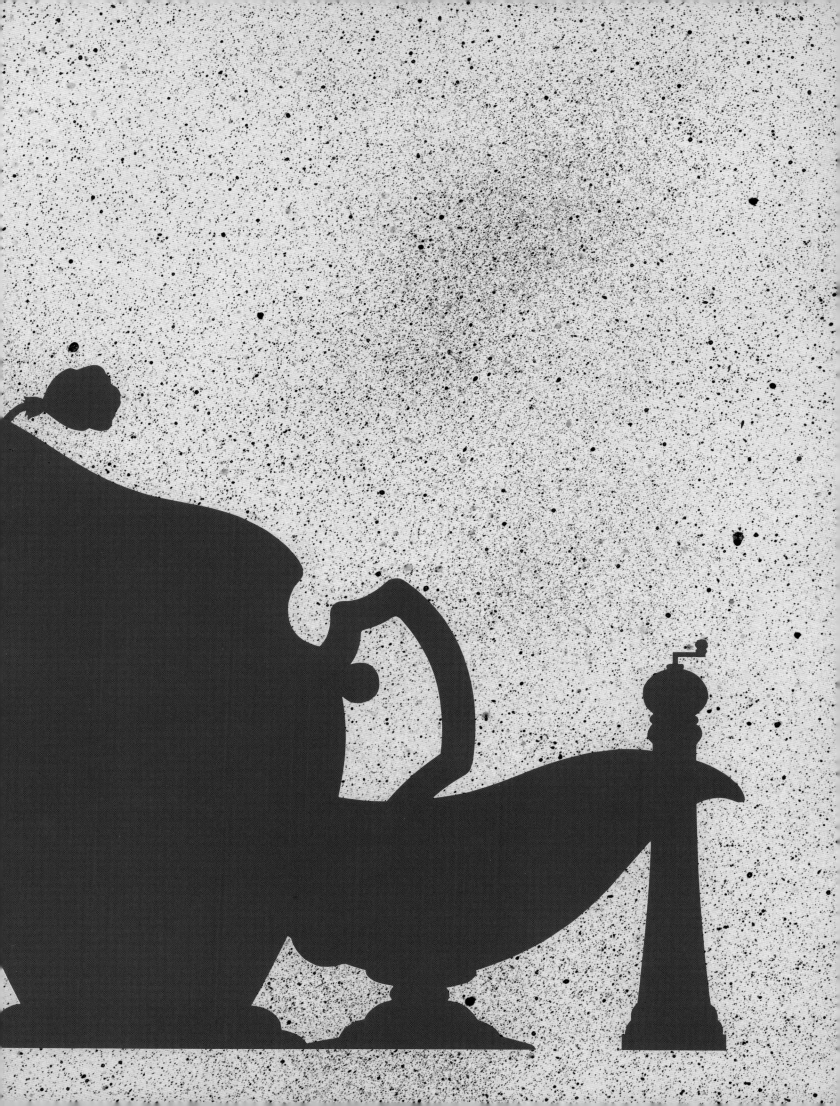

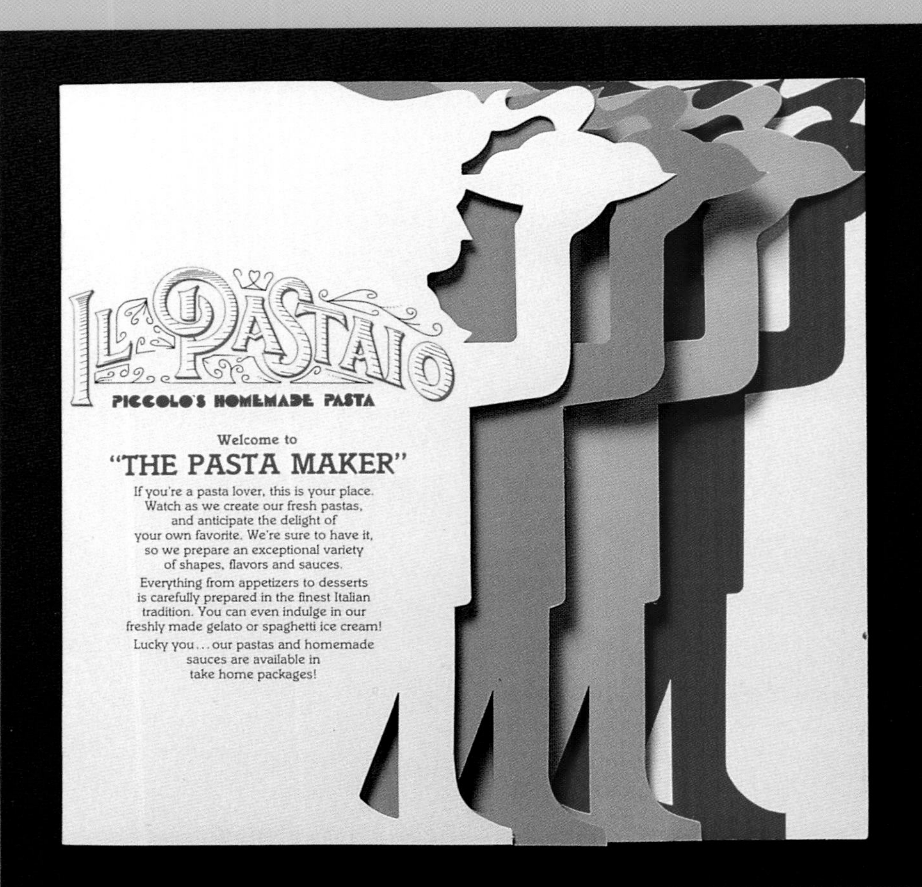
IL PASTAIO
PICCOLO'S HOMEMADE PASTA
Welcome to
"THE PASTA MAKER"
If you're a pasta lover, this is your place.
Watch as we create our fresh pastas,
and anticipate the delight of
your own favorite. We're sure to have it,
so we prepare an exceptional variety
of shapes, flavors and sauces.
Everything from appetizers to desserts
is carefully prepared in the finest Italian
tradition. You can even indulge in our
freshly made gelato or spaghetti ice cream!
Lucky you... our pastas and homemade
sauces are available in
take home packages!

Designer: *John McCormick*
*Studio 2*

Restaurant: *Il Pastaio/Piccolo's*
*Homemade Pasta*
*Philadelphia, PA*

**1987 GREAT MENUS CONTEST WINNER:**
**THIRD PLACE, GRAND PRIZE**

A line of die-cut pasta chefs, each imprinted in a different color, leads the diner through this pleasant and informative menu. As you might suspect,

IL PASTAIO'S
PASTAS
Spaghetti and Meatballs
The old favorite 6.90
Spaghetti and Italian Sweet Sausage 7.90
Cheese Ravioli
Ricotta-stuffed pasta squares 6.50
Meat Ravioli
Beef filled pasta squares 7.50
Meat Lasagne
Wide ribbons of pasta layered with
tomato sauce, ricotta, mozzarella,
meat, and parmesan cheese 7.50
Pasta Parmasano
Oven-baked spaghetti with tomato sauce
with mozzarella cheese 5.90
Fettuccini Alfredo
In creamy parmesan sauce 7.90
Straw & Hay
A mixture of egg and spinach pasta
in a parmesan cream sauce with
peas and prosciutto 8.50
Linguine Carbonara
With a sauce of egg yolks, cream, parmesan
cheese and bits of Italian bacon 8.50
Tortellini Bolognese
Meat-filled pasta rings topped
with tomato meat sauce 7.50
Tortellini Pesto Genovese
Topped with pesto sauce - fresh garlic,
fresh basil and parmesan cheese 8.50
Cheese Tortellini Alfredo
Cheese filled pasta doughnuts in
creamy parmesan cheese sauce 8.90
Tortellini Pomodori
With tomato sauce 6.90

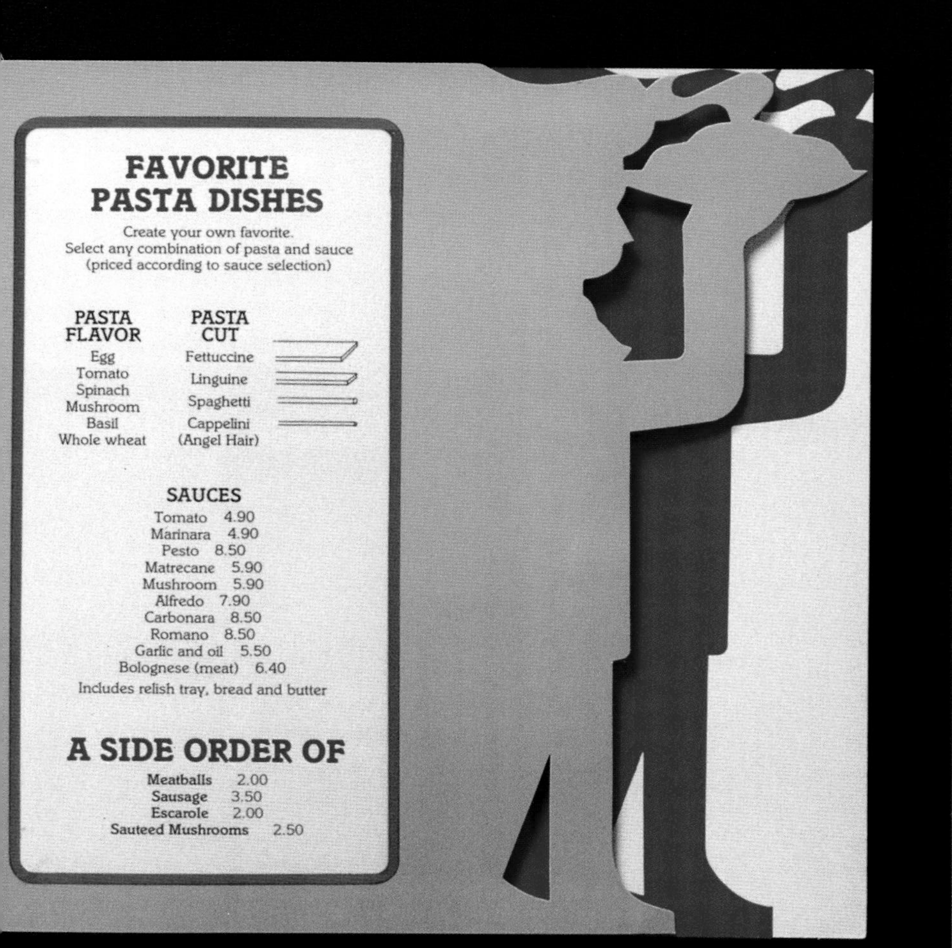


fresh pasta is the specialty; it is made daily in full view of the diners.

FAVORITE PASTA DISHES
Create your own favorite.
Select any combination of pasta and sauce
(priced according to sauce selection)
PASTA FLAVOR
Egg
Tomato
Spinach
Mushroom
Basil
Whole wheat
PASTA CUT
Fettuccine
Linguine
Spaghetti
Cappelini (Angel Hair)
SAUCES
Tomato 4.90
Marinara 4.90
Pesto 8.50
Matrecane 5.90
Mushroom 5.90
Alfredo 7.90
Carbonara 8.50
Romano 8.50
Garlic and oil 5.50
Bolognese (meat) 6.40
Includes relish tray, bread and butter
A SIDE ORDER OF
Meatballs 2.00
Sausage 3.50
Escarole 2.00
Sauteed Mushrooms 2.50

Menu headings are listed in green, in Italian, on the left and in red, in English, on the right side of the menu. There is also a guide to the different sizes and shapes of pasta offered. Fortunately, since the range of pastas routinely served in Italy is immense, the restaurant has limited itself to producing only two flat and two round varieties. Each is available in any one of six different flavors.

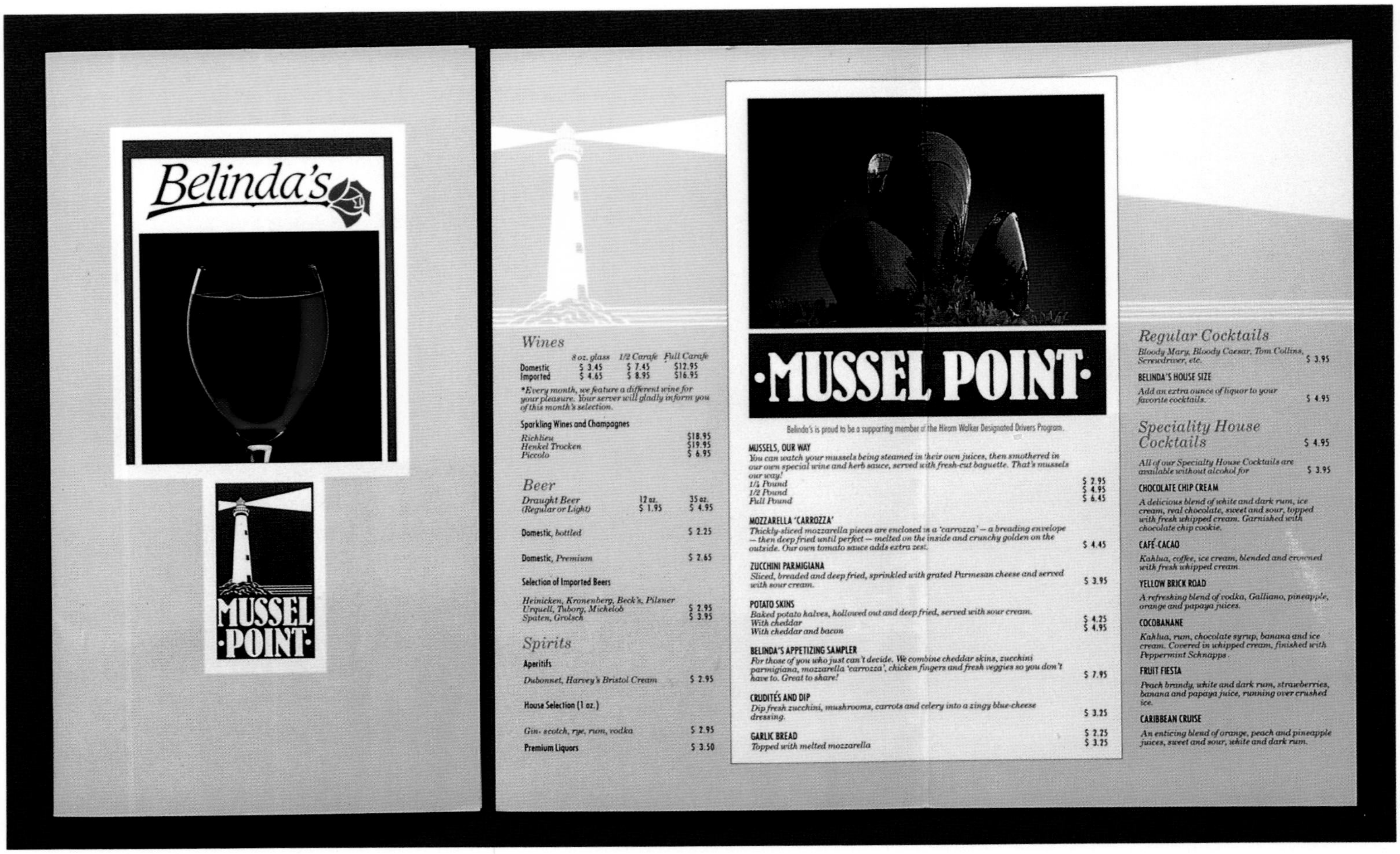

Belinda's
MUSSEL POINT
Wines
8 oz. glass 1/2 Carafe Full Carafe
Domestic $ 3.45 $ 7.45 $12.95
Imported $ 4.65 $ 8.95 $16.95
*Every month, we feature a different wine for your pleasure. Your server will gladly inform you of this month's selection.
Sparkling Wines and Champagnes
Richlieu $18.95
Henkel Trocken $19.95
Piccolo $ 6.95
Beer
Draught Beer (Regular or Light) 12 oz. $ 1.95 35 oz. $ 4.95
Domestic, bottled $ 2.25
Domestic, Premium $ 2.65
Selection of Imported Beers
Heinicken, Kronenberg, Beck's, Pilsner Urquell, Tuborg, Michelob $ 2.95
Spaten, Grolsch $ 3.95
Spirits
Aperitifs
Dubonnet, Harvey's Bristol Cream $ 2.95
House Selection (1 oz.)
Gin, scotch, rye, rum, vodka $ 2.95
Premium Liquors $ 3.50
·MUSSEL POINT·
Belinda's is proud to be a supporting member of the Hiram Walker Designated Drivers Program.
MUSSELS, OUR WAY
You can watch your mussels being steamed in their own juices, then smothered in our own special wine and herb sauce, served with fresh-cut baguette. That's mussels our way!
1/4 Pound $ 2.95
1/2 Pound $ 4.95
Full Pound $ 6.45
MOZZARELLA 'CARROZZA'
Thickly-sliced mozzarella pieces are enclosed in a 'carrozza' — a breading envelope — then deep fried until perfect — melted on the inside and crunchy golden on the outside. Our own tomato sauce adds extra zest. $ 4.45
ZUCCHINI PARMIGIANA
Sliced, breaded and deep fried, sprinkled with grated Parmesan cheese and served with sour cream. $ 3.95
POTATO SKINS
Baked potato halves, hollowed out and deep fried, served with sour cream.
With cheddar $ 4.25
With cheddar and bacon $ 4.95
BELINDA'S APPETIZING SAMPLER
For those of you who just can't decide. We combine cheddar skins, zucchini parmigiana, mozzarella 'carrozza', chicken fingers and fresh veggies so you don't have to. Great to share! $ 7.95
CRUDITÉS AND DIP
Dip fresh zucchini, mushrooms, carrots and celery into a zingy blue-cheese dressing. $ 3.25
GARLIC BREAD $ 2.25
Topped with melted mozzarella $ 3.25
Regular Cocktails
Bloody Mary, Bloody Caesar, Tom Collins, Screwdriver, etc. $ 3.95
BELINDA'S HOUSE SIZE
Add an extra ounce of liquor to your favorite cocktails. $ 4.95
Speciality House Cocktails $ 4.95
All of our Specialty House Cocktails are available without alcohol for $ 3.95
CHOCOLATE CHIP CREAM
A delicious blend of white and dark rum, ice cream, real chocolate, sweet and sour, topped with fresh whipped cream. Garnished with chocolate chip cookie.
CAFÉ-CACAO
Kahlua, coffee, ice cream, blended and crowned with fresh whipped cream.
YELLOW BRICK ROAD
A refreshing blend of vodka, Galliano, pineapple, orange and papaya juices.
COCOBANANE
Kahlua, rum, chocolate syrup, banana and ice cream. Covered in whipped cream, finished with Peppermint Schnapps.
FRUIT FIESTA
Peach brandy, white and dark rum, strawberries, banana and papaya juice, running over crushed ice.
CARIBBEAN CRUISE
An enticing blend of orange, peach and pineapple juices, sweet and sour, white and dark rum.

Restaurant: *Belinda's Restaurant*
*Thornhill, Ontario, Canada*

**1987 GREAT MENUS CONTEST WINNER:**
**FIRST PLACE, DESIGN**

The restaurant's signature rose appears in a discreet screen at the bottom of the page for each separate menu section, as well as on the cover of this attractive spiral-bound menu. Printed on Kimdura™, a durable and grease-resistant synthetic paper, the menu is both inviting and easy to read.

Catherine de Medici, a queen of France in the 16th century, came from a long line of patrons and promoters of the arts. She also popularized ice cream, made by the cooks she brought with her from Florence, Italy.

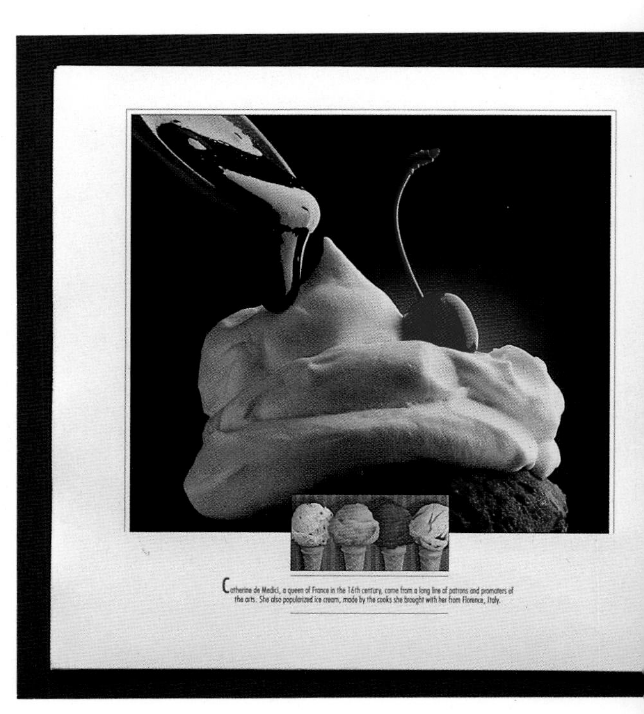

Creative copywriting and a combination of luscious food photography and illustration combine to give this menu its merchandising punch. A spirit of genuine friendliness and concern for the comfort of the customer pervades the writing. A note on the inside front cover, for example, mentions that "Babies eat free." The restaurant will provide free baby food to patrons who bring their children who are too young for the general menu. This is a marvelous technique for capturing the business of couples who might otherwise not dine out.

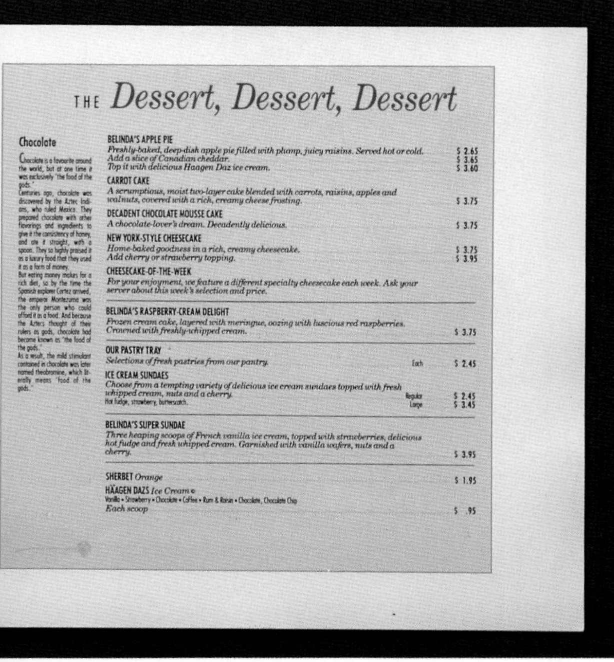

THE *Dessert, Dessert, Dessert*

**Chocolate**

Chocolate is a favourite around the world, but at one time it was exclusively "the food of the gods."
Centuries ago, chocolate was discovered by the Aztec Indians, who ruled Mexico. They prepared chocolate with other flavorings and ingredients to give it the consistency of honey, and ate it straight, with a spoon. They so highly praised it as a luxury food that they used it as a form of money.
But eating money makes for a rich diet, so by the time the Spanish explorer Cortez arrived, the emperor Montezuma was the only person who could afford it as a food. And because the Aztecs thought of their rulers as gods, chocolate had become known as "the food of the gods."
As a result, the mild stimulant contained in chocolate was later named theobromine, which literally means "food of the gods."

BELINDA'S APPLE PIE
*Freshly-baked, deep-dish apple pie filled with plump, juicy raisins. Served hot or cold.* $ 2.65
*Add a slice of Canadian cheddar.* $ 3.65
*Top it with delicious Haagen Daz ice cream.* $ 3.60

CARROT CAKE
*A scrumptious, moist two-layer cake blended with carrots, raisins, apples and walnuts, covered with a rich, creamy cheese frosting.* $ 3.75

DECADENT CHOCOLATE MOUSSE CAKE
*A chocolate-lover's dream. Decadently delicious.* $ 3.75

NEW YORK-STYLE CHEESECAKE
*Home-baked goodness in a rich, creamy cheesecake.* $ 3.75
*Add cherry or strawberry topping.* $ 3.95

CHEESECAKE-OF-THE-WEEK
*For your enjoyment, we feature a different specialty cheesecake each week. Ask your server about this week's selection and price.*

BELINDA'S RASPBERRY-CREAM DELIGHT
*Frozen cream cake, layered with meringue, oozing with luscious red raspberries. Crowned with freshly-whipped cream.* $ 3.75

OUR PASTRY TRAY
*Selections of fresh pastries from our pantry.* Each $ 2.45

ICE CREAM SUNDAES
*Choose from a tempting variety of delicious ice cream sundaes topped with fresh whipped cream, nuts and a cherry.*
Hot fudge, strawberry, butterscotch. Regular $ 2.45
Large $ 3.45

BELINDA'S SUPER SUNDAE
*Three heaping scoops of French vanilla ice cream, topped with strawberries, delicious hot fudge and fresh whipped cream. Garnished with vanilla wafers, nuts and a cherry.* $ 3.95

SHERBET *Orange* $ 1.95

HÄAGEN DAZS *Ice Cream©*
Vanilla • Strawberry • Chocolate • Coffee • Rum & Raisin • Chocolate, Chocolate Chip
*Each scoop* $ .95

| | |
|---|---|
| **Designer:** | *Lanny Sommese* |
| | *Lanny Sommese Design* |
| **Restaurant:** | *Hi Way Pizza Pub* |
| | *Dante's Restaurants, Inc.* |
| | *State College, PA* |

Catering to college students and other "on-the-go" pizza lovers, this restaurant wanted to emphasize speedy service and a playful atmosphere. Menu items are simple, mostly pizzas, salads and "grinders," which appear to be a kind of hearty sandwich. The pizza chefs on roller skates provide the perfect support for the theme.

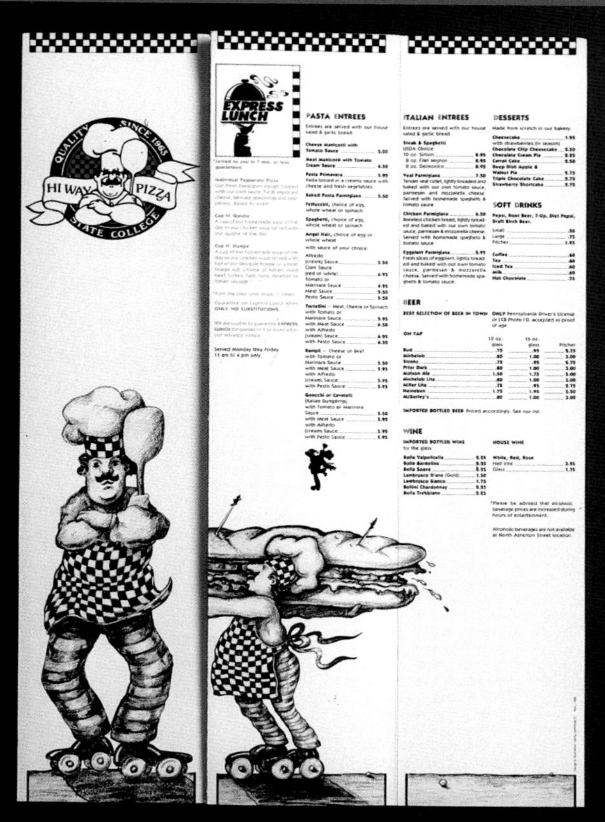

Stock for the menus was chosen for its durability and imperviousness to dirt. The two-color execution makes for relatively inexpensive updates. In a nice touch, the designer is credited on the menu.

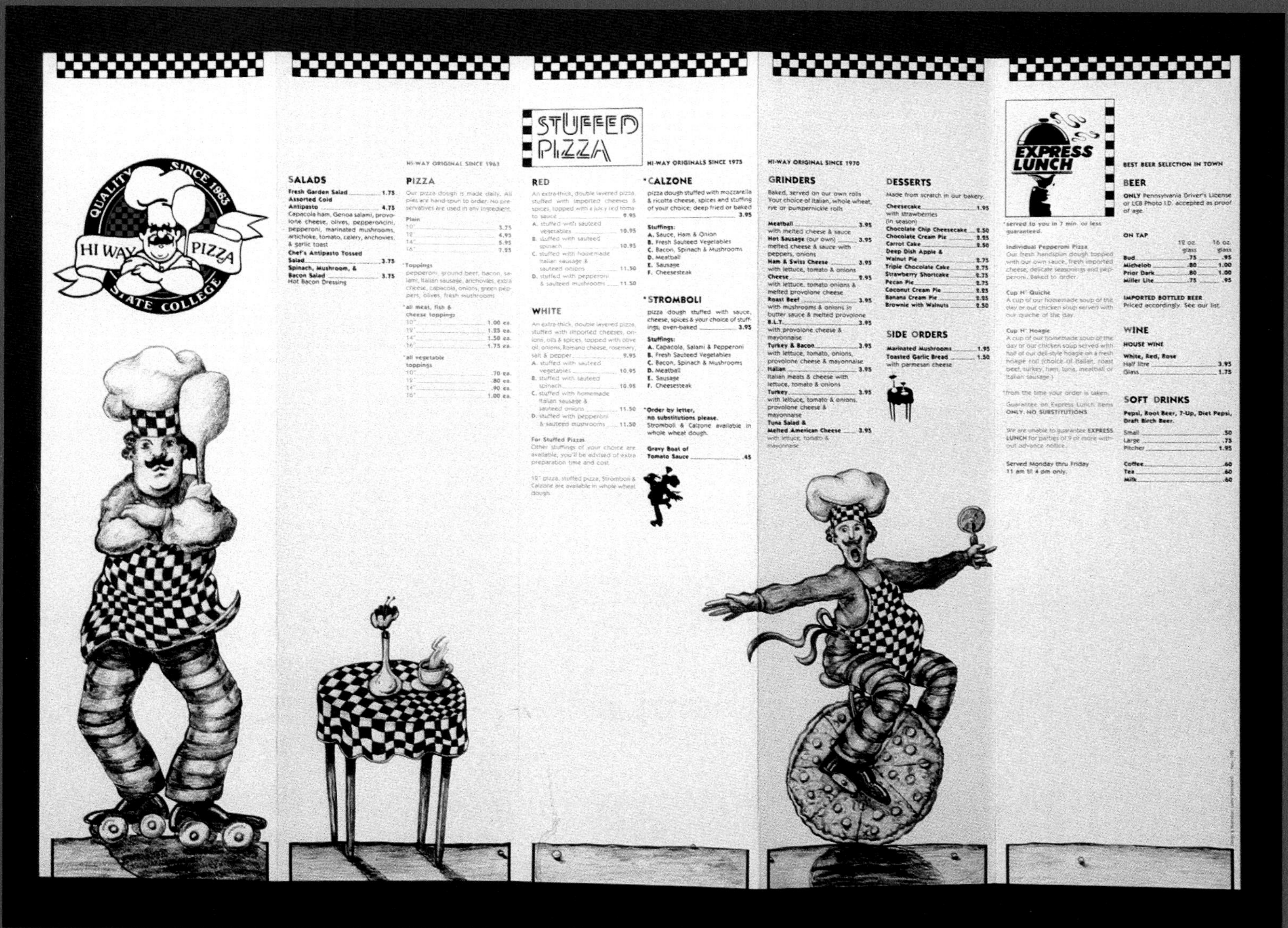

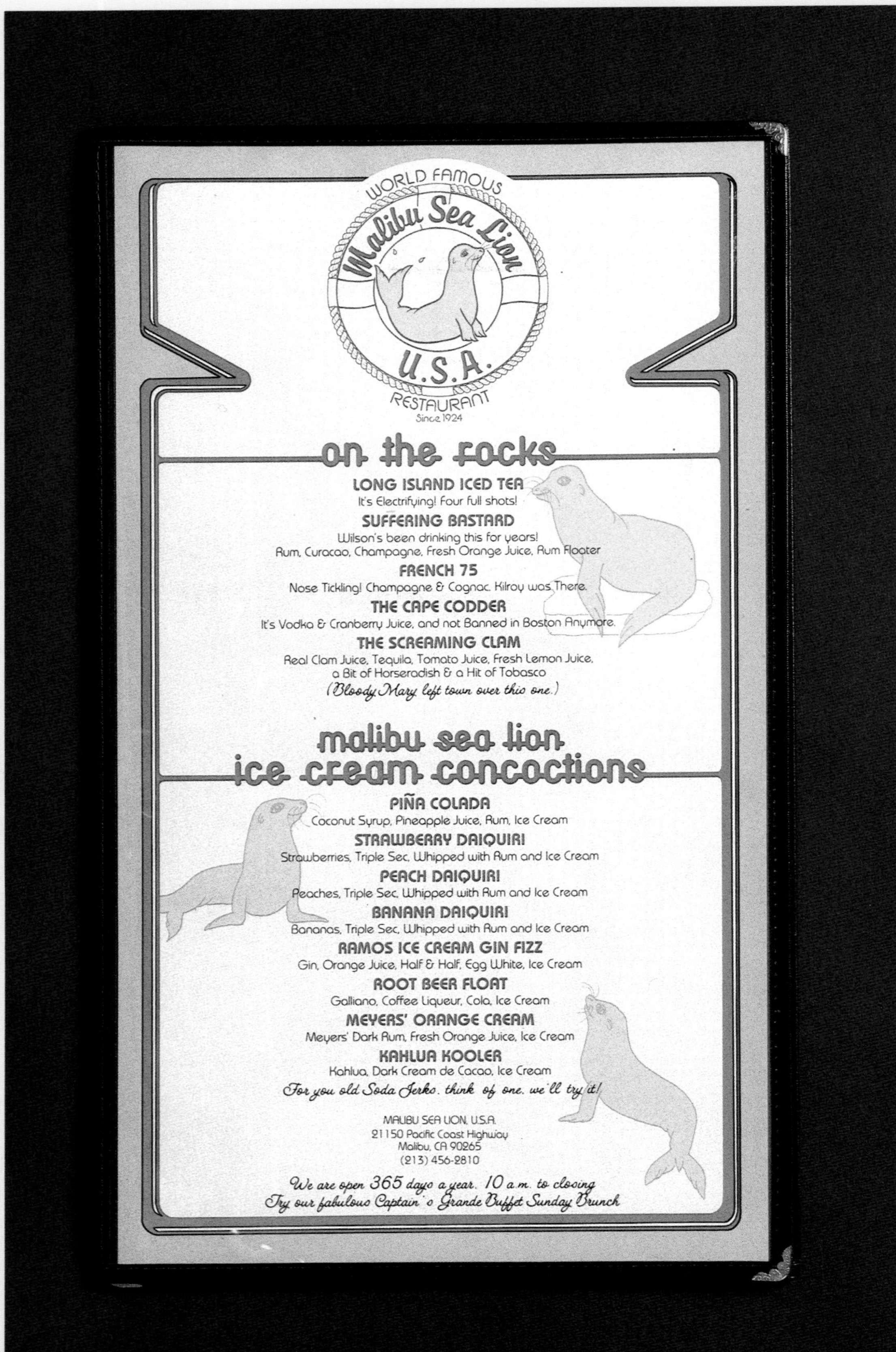


Designer: *Lori J. Rand*
*Grace Restaurant Co.*

Restaurant: *The Malibu Sea Lion USA/*
*Mor Food 'N Fun*
*Santa Monica, CA*

**1987 GREAT MENUS CONTEST WINNER: FIRST PLACE, MERCHANDISING POWER**

This two-color menu in cafe covers uses a combination of snappy copywriting and illustrations of playful sea lions to sell its message. And, just in case you didn't realize this was a seafood house, the dorsal fins on each insert will tell you without words.

Everything from wines to salad bar to buffet to house specials is marketed via the same menu. Specialty drinks are listed on the front (before dinner) and back (after) of the menu. This is an inexpensive and creative way to market a broad menu of both food and drink.

Designer: *Associates Printing Service, Inc.*
Restaurant: *The Other Place ... The Place for Steaks*
*Hyatt Regency O'Hare*
*Rosemont, IL*

This two-color brochure and "Frequent Eaters Program" card is an innovative marketing concept. To encourage diners to more frequently choose this restaurant over others, the diner is offered the opportunity to earn bonus meals or hotel stays by having his card "validated" each time he dines at The Other Place. The program not only increases business at the restaurant, but, by limiting the time by which all bonuses must be redeemed, ensures higher occupancy at the hotel during off-peak travel season.

Graphically, the card and brochure are a nice example of the fine effects obtainable using only two colors. A speckle-pattern background screen of the deep green provides the interior of the brochure and the card with textural interest. Stamping the front cover with the words "Top Secret" is creative copywriting. How can you resist opening it to learn the secret?

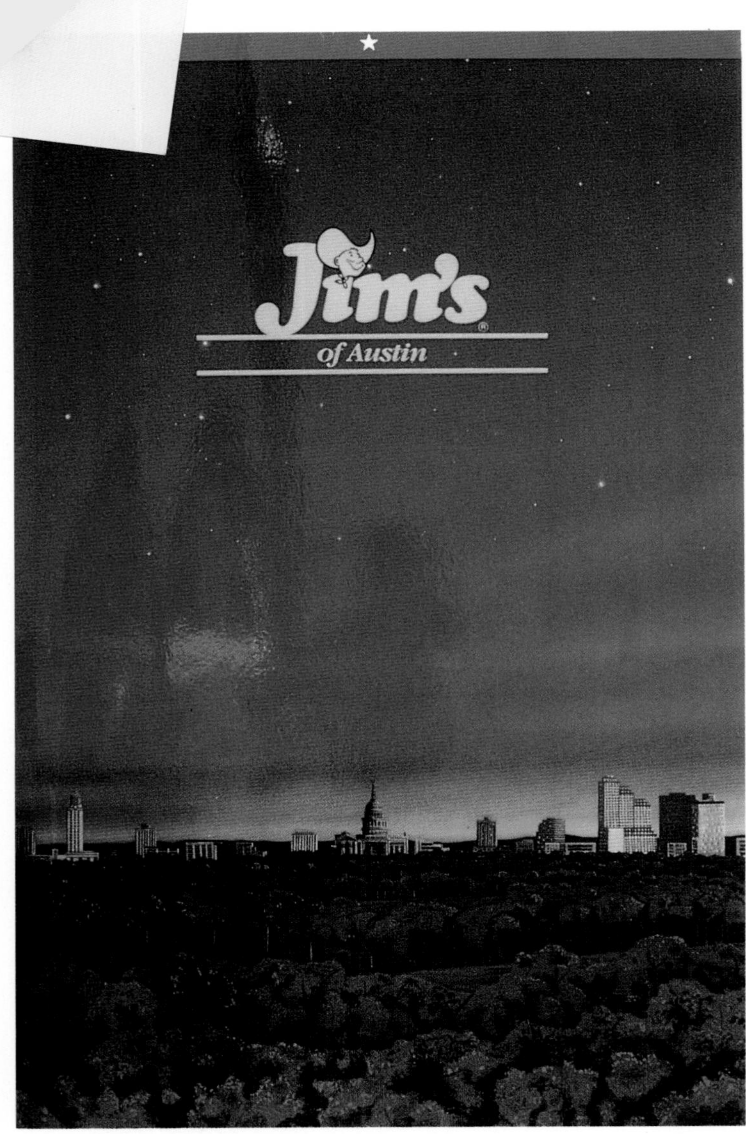


Designer: *Various freelance artists*
*Tuck & Company*

Restaurant: *Jim's of Austin*
*Frontier Enterprises*
*Austin, TX*

**1987 GREAT MENUS CONTEST WINNER:**
**FIRST PLACE, UNDER $5 PER PERSON**

This menu has a definite sense of its geographical location. Austin, as well as being the state capital, may, indeed, be described as being "in the heart of Texas," and the "big and bright stars" featured in the song adorn the menu's cover above the skyline of Austin at sunset.

A playful mix of illustrations, photographs, line drawings and even the city limits sign enlivens the menu interior. The menu items and copywriting reflect the Mexican and Deep South influences which make Texas unique. Clever copywriting invites the diner to explore the menu. The dessert category, located on the back inside flap, appears under the Texas star.

AUSTIN
CITY LIMIT
POP. 345496

RIVER CITY
APPETEASERS
*A River City Welcome to Jim's Loyal Friends and New Acquaintances*

Crazy Cheese Skins .......... 2.95
Potato skins crowned with glorious melted cheese, sour cream, and bacon bits.
Veggie Beauties .......... 1.95
Tender fried mushrooms, zucchini, and onion rings. Served with ranch dressing or cream gravy.
Sombrero Nachos (serves two) .......... 3.95
Chips covered with chili, melted cheese, and jalapeños.
Chicken Lickens' .......... 2.95
Fried Chicken fingers with hot creamy gravy.
Homestyle Soup .......... Cup 1.25 Bowl 1.55
Made fresh daily.
Jim's Capital Fries .......... .95
Garden-Fresh Salad .......... 1.35
Jim's Famous Onion Rings .......... 1.35
River City Chili .......... Cup 1.95 Bowl 2.95

SANDWICHES
AROUND THE CLOCK

All sandwiches served with Capital fries.
Chicken Fried Steak Sandwich .......... 3.95
Mayonnaise, lettuce, tomato.
Catfish Sam .......... 3.95
A sourdough Po' Boy catfish sandwich with tartar sauce.
French Dip Sandwich .......... 3.95
Thinly sliced roast beef on a sourdough roll. Served with au jus.
Clubhouse Sandwich .......... 4.25
Triple deckered with sliced turkey, crisp bacon, lettuce, tomato and mayonnaise.
Grilled Colorado Club Sandwich .......... 4.25
Triple deckered with ham, bacon, cheese, lettuce, tomato, and mayonnaise.
Bacon, Lettuce & Tomato .......... 2.95
Grilled Cheese .......... 2.25
Turkey Sandwich .......... 2.95
Tuna Salad Sandwich .......... 2.95
Ham and Swiss .......... 3.35
Patty Melt on Rye .......... 3.95

★BURGERS★
Big enough to satisfy the hungriest lobbyist.

Great ol' Austin Burger .......... 3.50
Lettuce, tomato, pickles, onions, mayonnaise or mustard.
With cheese add .......... .20
Bacon & Swiss Burger .......... 3.95
Swiss cheese, bacon, lettuce, tomato, pickles, onions and mayonnaise.
With guacamole add .......... .75
Mushroom and Swiss Burger .......... 3.95
A burger with swiss cheese, sauteed onions and mushrooms, lettuce, tomato and mayonnaise.
California Harvest Burger .......... 4.35
6-oz. beef patty on a toasted bun with avocado slices, tomato, onion, lettuce and special dressing.
All Rotunda burgers served with Jim's Capital Fries.
Soup or salad an additional .......... 1.00

Stingy Burgers
Stingy on the cost but not on the serving.
Jim's Original Burger .......... 1.95
¼ pound patty, mayonnaise, tomato, pickles, onions, and lettuce.
With cheese add .......... .20
Ol' Smokey—A Great Favorite .......... 1.95
¼ pound patty, smoked sauce, onions and pickles.
The Frontier Burger .......... 3.25
Two ¼ pound patties, melted cheese, tomato, onions, lettuce, and special dressing.
Combo Special
Any Stingy Burger with Capital fries and garden salad.
Add .......... 1.40

HOOK 'EM
Fried Gulf Shrimp .......... 6.95
Hand breaded and deep fried. Served with garden-fresh salad or soup of the day, vegetable, choice of potato and hot roll.
Broiled Fish .......... 4.95
A treasure from the deep. Served with vegetable, choice of potato and hot roll.
With garden-fresh salad or soup .......... 5.95
Grandpa's Fried Catfish .......... 4.95
Served with tartar sauce, vegetable, choice of potato and hot roll.
With garden-fresh salad or soup .......... 5.95
Hot Baked Potato served from 5pm to midnight.

AUSTIN'S ALL-TIME FAVORITES
The Unlegislated Chicken Fried Steak .......... 3.95
Specially seasoned golden crust, tasty gravy, mashed potatoes, vegetable and, for good sopping, our home-style rolls.
Char-Broiled Chicken .......... 4.95
Marinated and charbroiled chicken breast, topped with swiss cheese. Served with mashed potatoes, vegetable and hot roll.
Hot Roast Beef Sandwich .......... 3.95
Open-faced with mashed potatoes, gravy and vegetable.
The Light Lure .......... 3.95
Two strips of fried catfish served with tartar sauce, lemon wedge, Capital fries, vegetable and hot roll.

THE LIGHTER SIDE
Waistwatcher Special .......... 4.95
Choice of broiled chicken, chopped steak, or fish filet. Served with cottage cheese, tomatoes, and strawberries.
Chef's Choice Salad .......... 3.95
Lettuce, tomato, diced ham, cheese, and hard-boiled egg. Served with dressing and crackers.
Avocado-Turkey Salad .......... 4.25
Lettuce, tomato and sliced turkey topped with avocado slices and grated cheese. Served with dressing and crackers.
Springtime Tuna Salad .......... 4.25
Tuna salad served with cottage cheese, pineapple, a peach half, tomato slices and strawberries.

DINNER
Served with garden-fresh salad or soup of the day, vegetable, choice of potato and hot roll.
*When you see the lights of D. E. Crumley's, you know you're almost home.*
Chicken Fried Steak .......... 4.95
Cream or brown gravy.
7 oz. Chopped Sirloin .......... 4.95
Broiled Breast of Chicken .......... 5.95
Marinated in our special sauce.
Choice Top Sirloin 8 oz. .......... 5.95
Austin's best buy!
Ribeye Steak—8 oz. .......... 6.95
Top of the line
One Great Texas Steak .......... 7.95
A T-Bone for Texas sized appetites.

late night date

For the Young and Young at Heart
For Juniors (12 and under) and Senior Citizens.
Sandwiches
Served with french fries.
Grilled Cheese .......... 1.35
Jim's Burger .......... 1.75
With cheese add .......... .20
Lunch or Dinner
Served with mashed potatoes or french fries, vegetable and hot roll.
Golden Fried Fish .......... 2.95
Char-Broiled Chopped Steak .......... 3.25
Jim's Chicken Fried Steak .......... 3.25

Ay! Chihuahua
FOOD FIESTA
Fajita Platter .......... 5.95
Marinated beef or chicken, sauteed onions, guacamole, diced tomato, refried beans, sour cream, cheese, hot sauce and flour tortillas. Delicioso!
Tres Enchiladas and Chili .......... 3.95
Three enchiladas covered with Frontier Chili and cheddar cheese. (Onions optional.) Served with hot roll.
Mexican Chicken Fried Steak .......... 4.25
Refried beans, guacamole, flour tortillas. Topped with spicy ranchero sauce.
Soft Tacos .......... 3.95
Three flour tortillas with spicy beef, grated cheese, lettuce, tomatoes and guacamole.
The Piñata Taco Salad .......... 4.25
Crispy flour tortilla filled with lettuce, spicy beef, pinto beans, diced tomato, cheddar cheese, guacamole, sour cream and hot sauce or Ranch dressing.

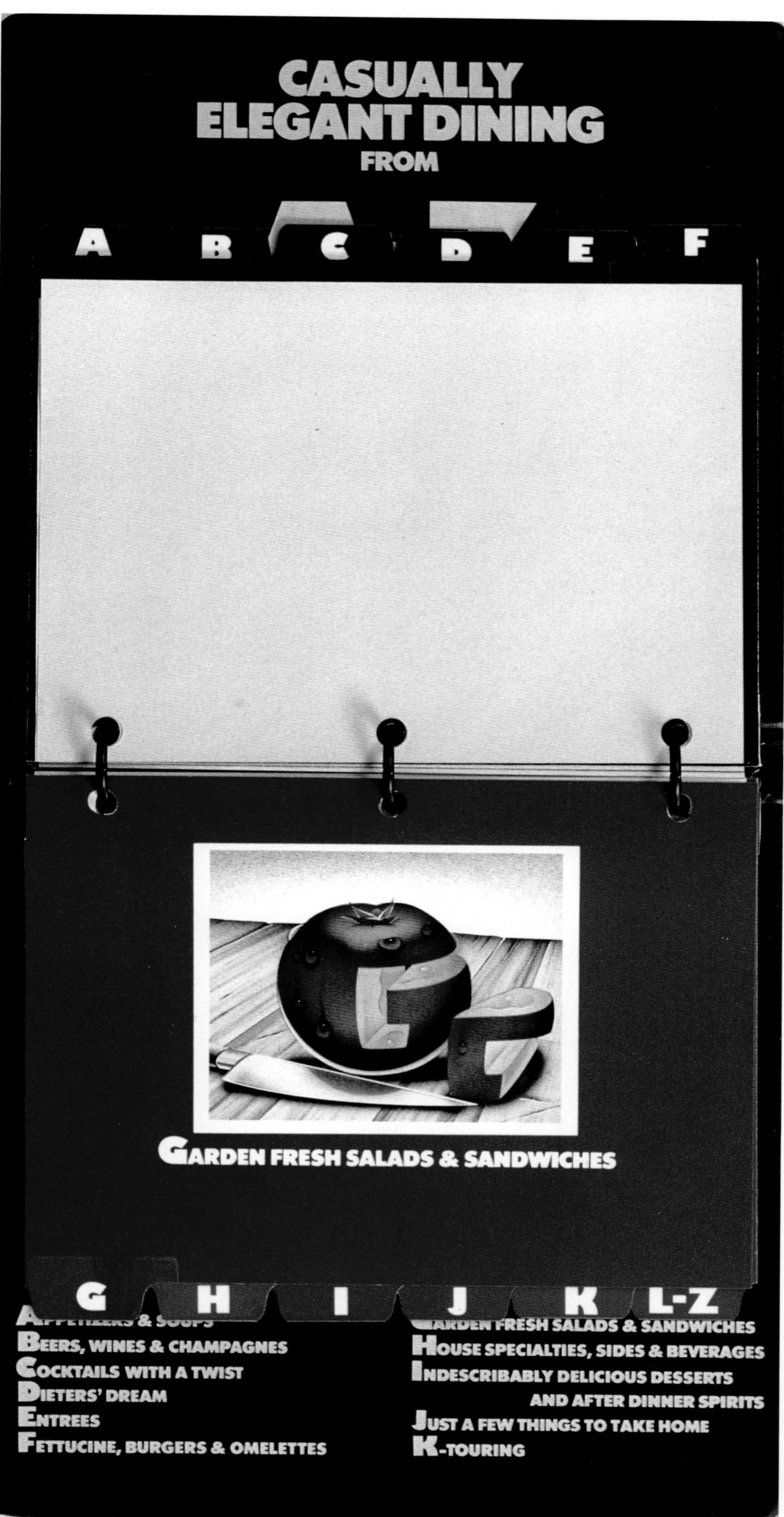


Designer: *Scott Mahr*
*Great Scott Graphics*
Restaurant: *Harvey's Restaurant*
*Lutherville, MD*

**1987 GREAT MENUS CONTEST WINNER: SECOND PLACE, $5-$15 CHECK AVERAGE**

Creative and humorous graphics appear on the bright red tabs that head each section of the menu in this sturdy black plastic-covered binder. The theme of the menu is "Casual Dining from A to Z." Reversed type on the inside back cover identifies each alphabetical section for the diner in a hurry. The copywriting is so descriptive throughout — even to the wine and beer choices — that further clarification from the server should not be needed.

The "Dieter's Dream" section features a puffy capital 'D', waist cinched in with a tape measure. The menu cards are simply printed in black to permit inexpensive updates. A clear plastic pocket on the inside front cover allows the restaurant to market seasonal specialties; in this case, Spring, catered wedding receptions and graduation gift certificates are featured.

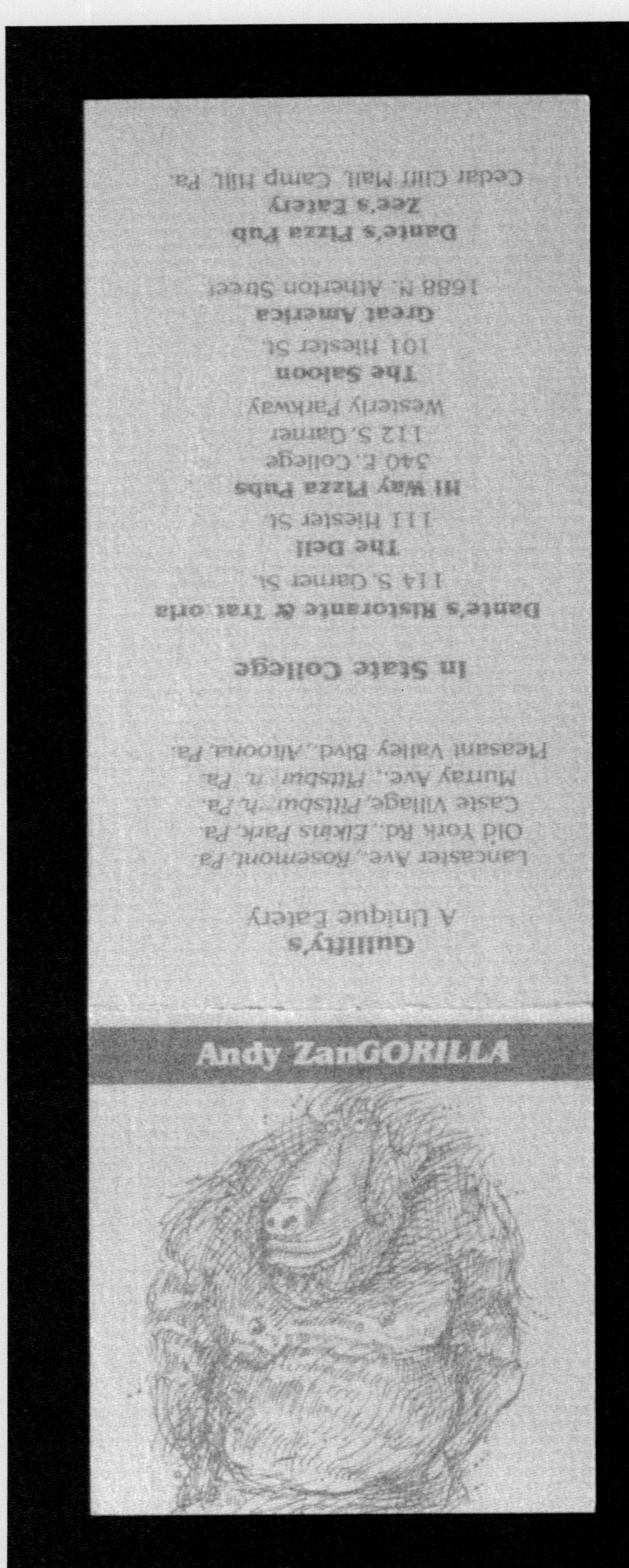


**Designer:** *Lanny Sommese*
*Lanny Sommese Design*
**Restaurant:** *Dante's Restaurants, Inc.*
*State College, PA*

Dante's Restaurants, Inc., which operates a number of restaurants, is owned and operated by Andy Zangrilli, affectionately known to his friends as "Andy Zangorilla." This business card conveys both the nickname and, with the top flap unfolded, his business.

The fanciful line drawing of the gorilla bearing a covered dish and champagne flute makes words superfluous. Only the standard business information — address and phone number are needed. This playful approach probably ensures that Mr. Zangrilli will not be forgotten, even by someone who has half a dozen business appointments in a day.

| | |
|---|---|
| Designer: | *Mike Wagner* |
| | *The Menu Workshop* |
| Restaurant: | *Pogacha* |
| | *Seattle, WA* |

This piece is one of the most effective uses of the marketing dollar we've seen. It works as a menu for use in the restaurant, a direct mail promotional piece and a take-out menu. The menu was designed at the restaurant's inception so the piece needed to be sufficiently dramatic to create an audience from scratch. The image of the pizza dough being tossed into the air demands that the reader at least look inside to see if disaster will follow. In fact, the hands are there, ready to catch it . . . we think.

The vivid colors and playful copywriting convey a lively atmosphere. A broad menu selection, even though not many items are featured, would make the place appealing to a group with varied tastes — if you don't want a pizza, maybe the duck liver paté sounds good. In the dessert section, the associated bakery is also mentioned.

The design is very well thought-out. On the self-mailing side, the hours of operation are noted to ensure the diner won't be disappointed by arriving to find the restaurant closed.

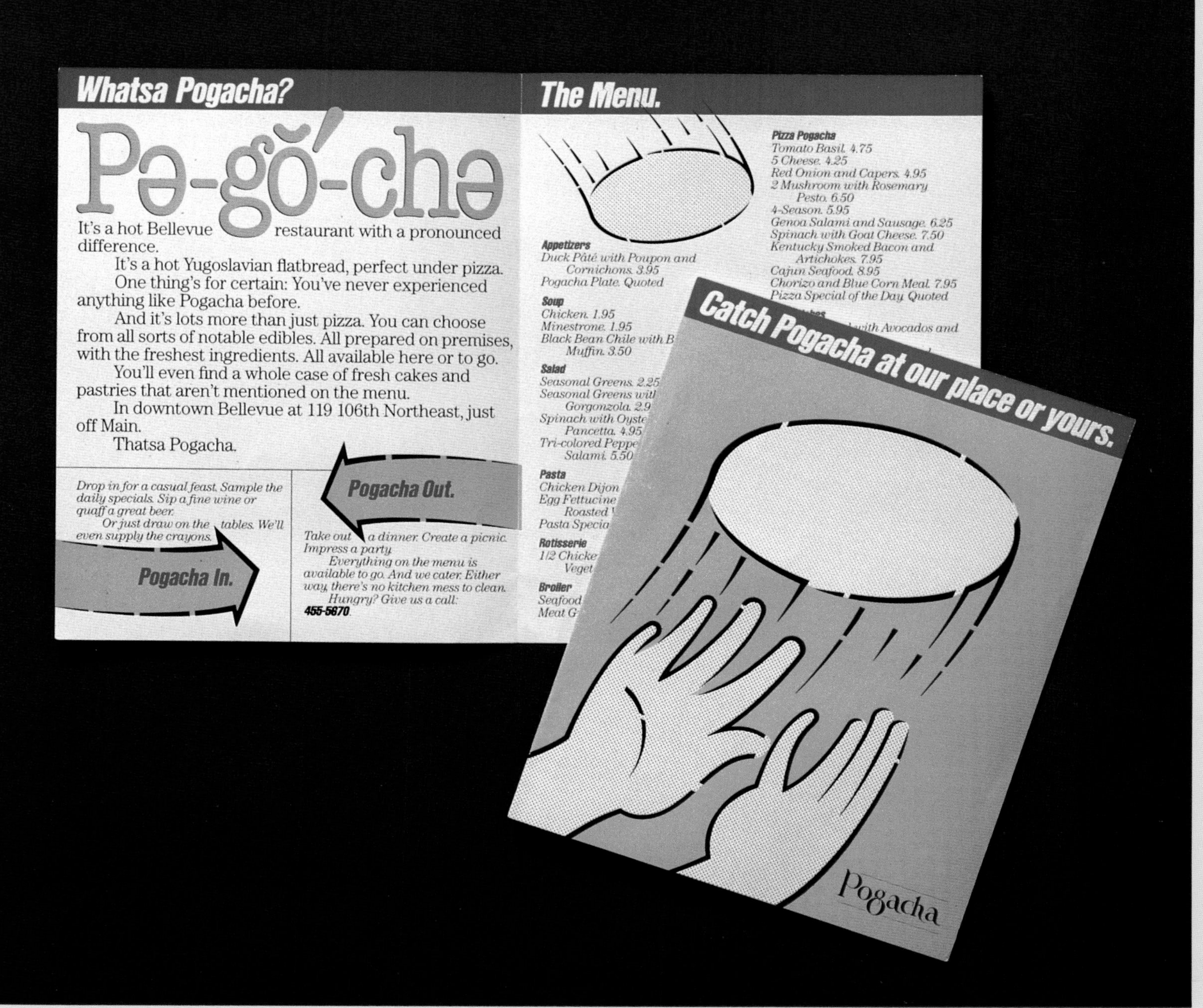

Whatsa Pogacha?
Pə-gŏ́-chə
It's a hot Bellevue restaurant with a pronounced difference.
It's a hot Yugoslavian flatbread, perfect under pizza.
One thing's for certain: You've never experienced anything like Pogacha before.
And it's lots more than just pizza. You can choose from all sorts of notable edibles. All prepared on premises, with the freshest ingredients. All available here or to go.
You'll even find a whole case of fresh cakes and pastries that aren't mentioned on the menu.
In downtown Bellevue at 119 106th Northeast, just off Main.
Thatsa Pogacha.
Drop in for a casual feast. Sample the daily specials. Sip a fine wine or quaff a great beer.
Or just draw on the tables. We'll even supply the crayons.
Pogacha In.
Pogacha Out.
Take out a dinner. Create a picnic. Impress a party.
Everything on the menu is available to go. And we cater. Either way, there's no kitchen mess to clean.
Hungry? Give us a call:
455-5870.
The Menu.
Appetizers
Duck Pâté with Poupon and Cornichons. 3.95
Pogacha Plate. Quoted
Soup
Chicken. 1.95
Minestrone. 1.95
Salad
Pasta
Rotisserie
Broiler
Pizza Pogacha
Tomato Basil. 4.75
5 Cheese. 4.25
Red Onion and Capers. 4.95
2 Mushroom with Rosemary Pesto. 6.50
4-Season. 5.95
Genoa Salami and Sausage. 6.25
Spinach with Goat Cheese. 7.50
Kentucky Smoked Bacon and Artichokes. 7.95
Cajun Seafood. 8.95
Chorizo and Blue Corn Meal. 7.95
Pizza Special of the Day. Quoted
Catch Pogacha at our place or yours.
Pogacha

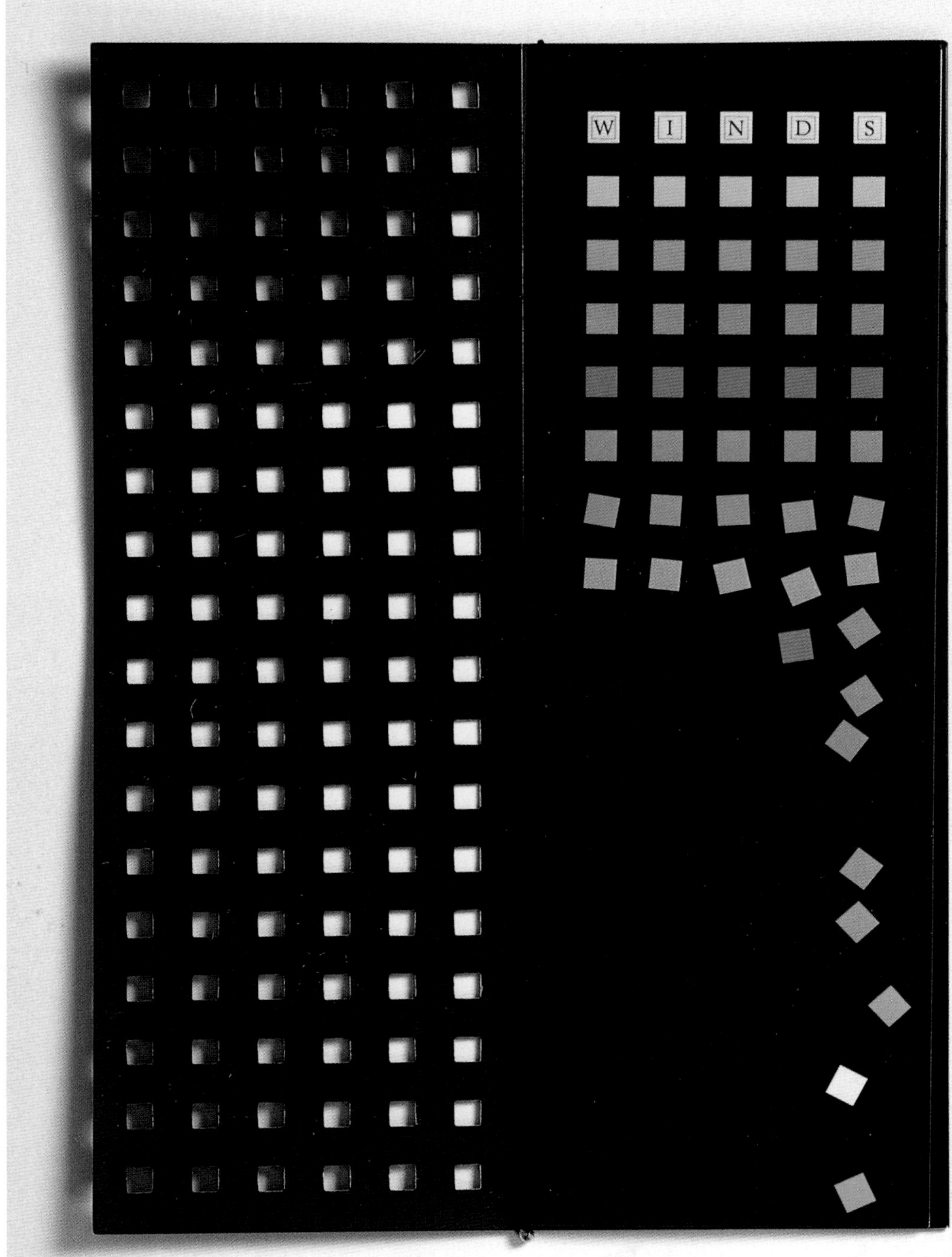


Designer: *James Gohl*

Restaurant: *Winds Bar & Grill*
*Southwind Restaurant, Inc.*
*Lenexa, KS*

**1987 GREAT MENUS CONTEST WINNER: FIRST PLACE, GRAND PRIZE**

The dramatic die-cut cover of the menu announces that this restaurant will be something a little different from the norm. The first inside page announces the kitchen's commitment to freshness and the explanation behind the restaurant's name. Located in eastern Kansas, Winds remembers the natives of the area, who called themselves the "People of the South Wind."

The readily-modified interior pages specify "Castroville" artichokes and "Maryland" blue crab, a sure sign to the cognoscenti that the restaurant will serve only the best available fresh foods. Menu sections are divided into "Light Breezes," for appetizers and "Evening Breezes," for main course selections. These headings are both descriptive and a nice play on the restaurant's name.

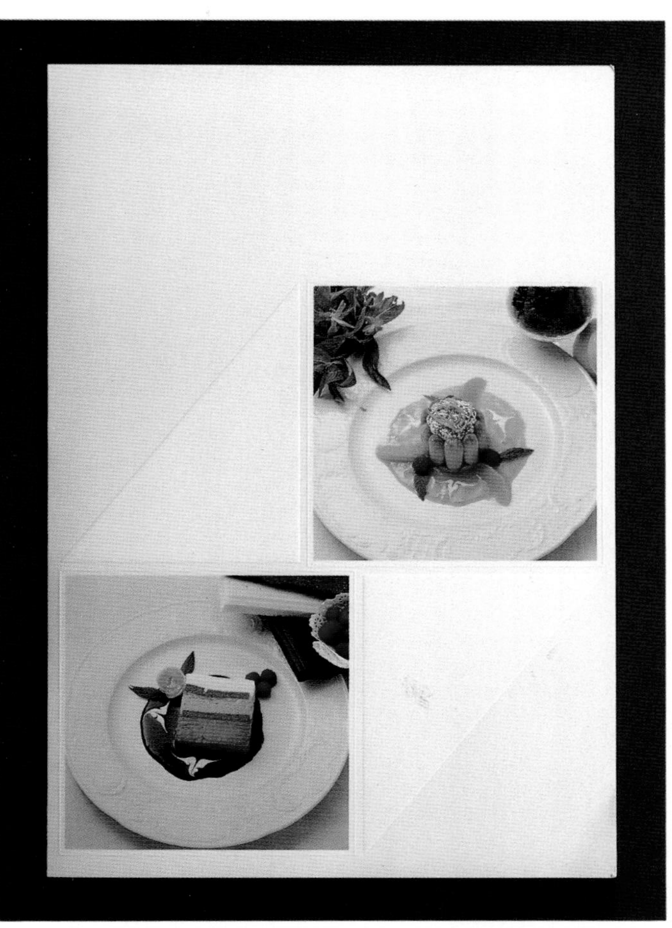

Designer: *Sky Kwan*
*Hilton International Sydney*
Restaurant: *San Francisco Grill*
*Hilton International Sydney*
*Sydney, Australia*

The dishes on which these tempting desserts were photographed are those actually in use in the restaurant throughout the meal. This reinforces the diner's belief that *his* dessert will, indeed, look and taste as good as the photography would have one believe.

The white coated stock, brightly-lit shots and pale grey type were chosen to give the menu a feeling of lightness. Most of the desserts offered are fruit-based and, while rich, are not too heavy.

Breaking with the tradition of listing all wines on a separate wine list together, the restaurant has chosen to present its dessert wines in the logical place — on the dessert menu. Diners who might balk at calling for the wine list again at the end of a meal might be tempted when confronted with them here.

Designer: *Georgia Korzenowski*
*Associates Printing Service, Inc.*
Restaurant: *Captain Streeter's Outdoor Cafe*
*Hyatt Regency Chicago*
*Chicago, IL*

The cover's cheerful umbrella, set against the backdrop of the Chicago skyline, invites the diner to sit for a while in the sunshine. The bright red initial capital letters of the restaurant's name are repeated in the fanciful names of the food items in the interior. Detailed descriptions of the ingredients in each dish might prove a boon to those with dietary sensitivities. The skyline peeps from behind the menu items, echoing the cover, as does a bit of brightly striped awning.

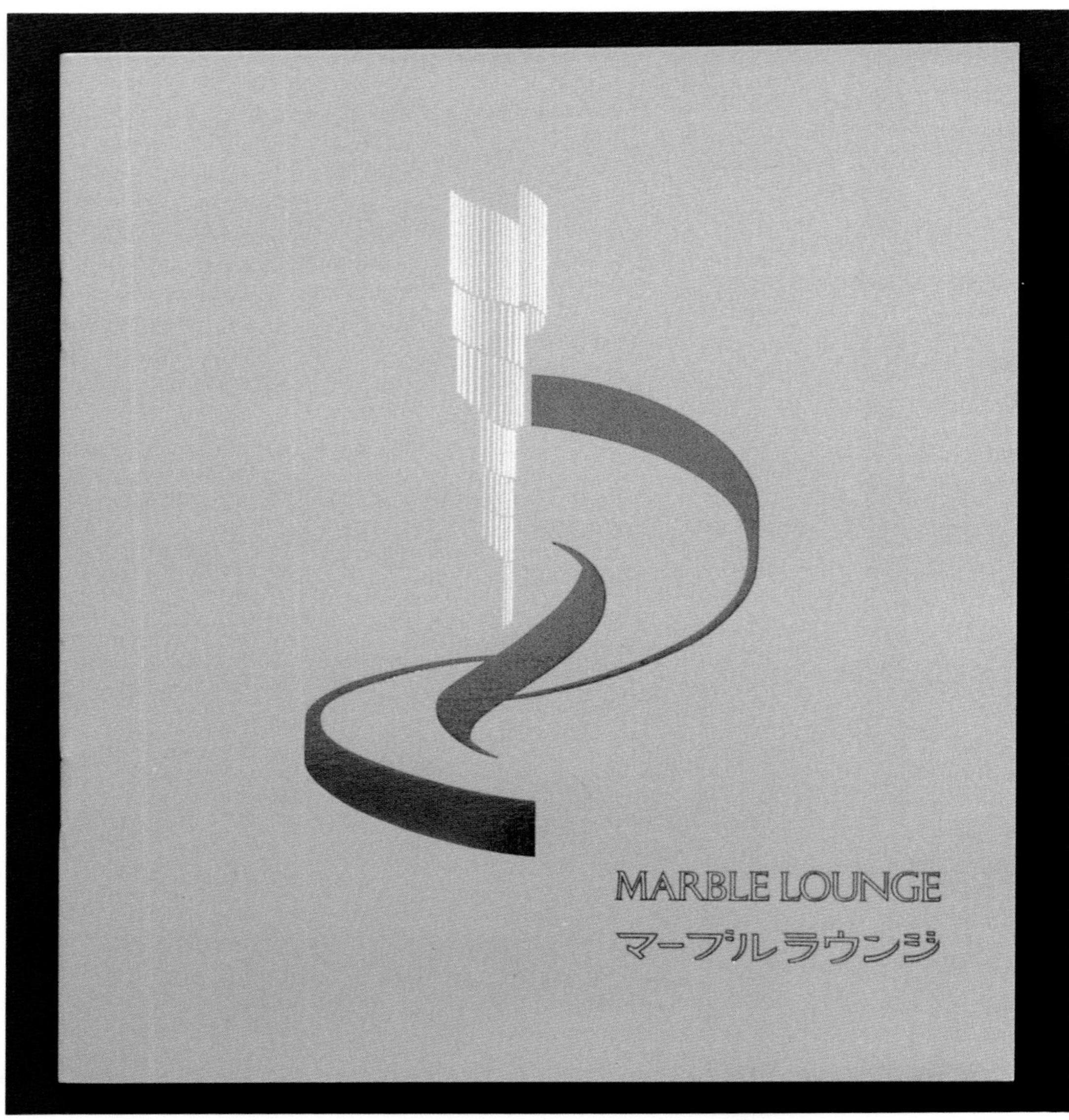


Designer: *Design Studio, Ltd.*
Restaurant: *Marble Lounge*
*Tokyo Hilton International*
*Tokyo, Japan*

**1987 GREAT MENUS CONTEST WINNER: THIRD PLACE, MERCHANDISING POWER**

Abstract gold foil swirls highlight the cover of this international snack menu. Recognizing that its clientele comes from all over the world, choices range from the Japanese items you might expect — sashimi and yakitori — to bundnerfleisch, steak tartare and potatoes stuffed with chili. Liquor suggestions accompany many of the food items.

Each item is beautifully photographed so that, even if the diner reads neither English nor Japanese, the two languages used in the brief copy, he need not go hungry. The picture will permit him to choose. This technique derives from the Japanese custom of using plastic models of food items in sushi bars.

The menu interior is further distinguished by the gold foil holding line which separates the photograph from the description.

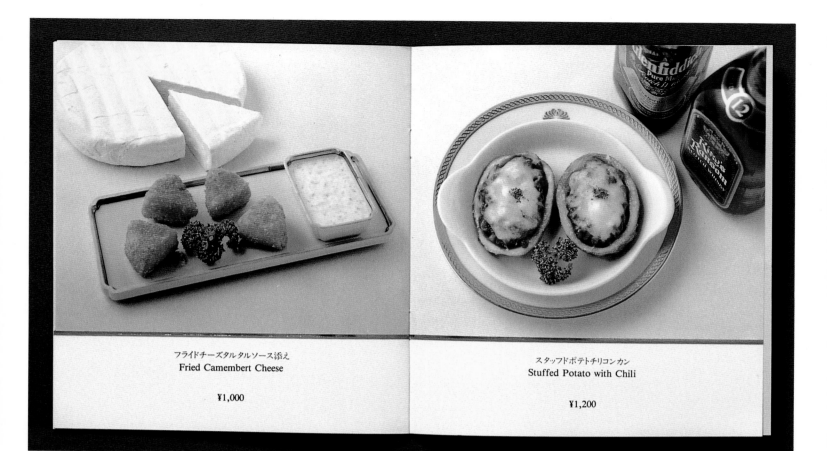

フライドチーズタルタルソース添え
Fried Camembert Cheese

¥1,000

スタッフドポテトチリコンカン
Stuffed Potato with Chili

¥1,200

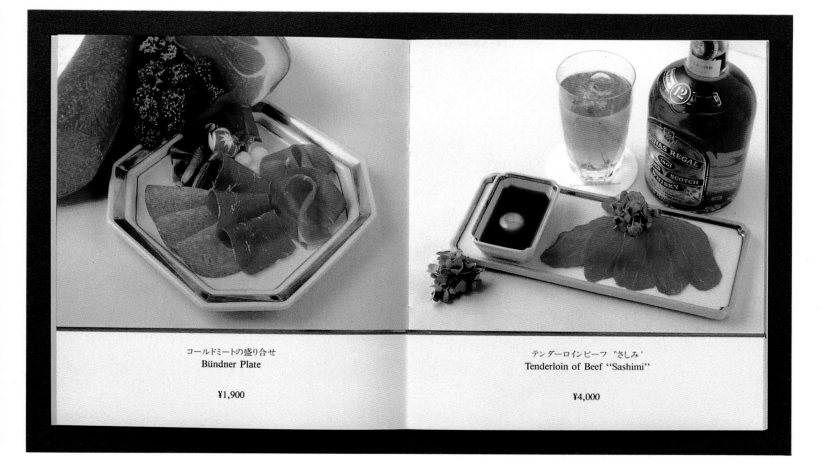

コールドミートの盛り合せ
Bündner Plate

¥1,900

テンダーロインビーフ "さしみ"
Tenderloin of Beef "Sashimi"

¥4,000

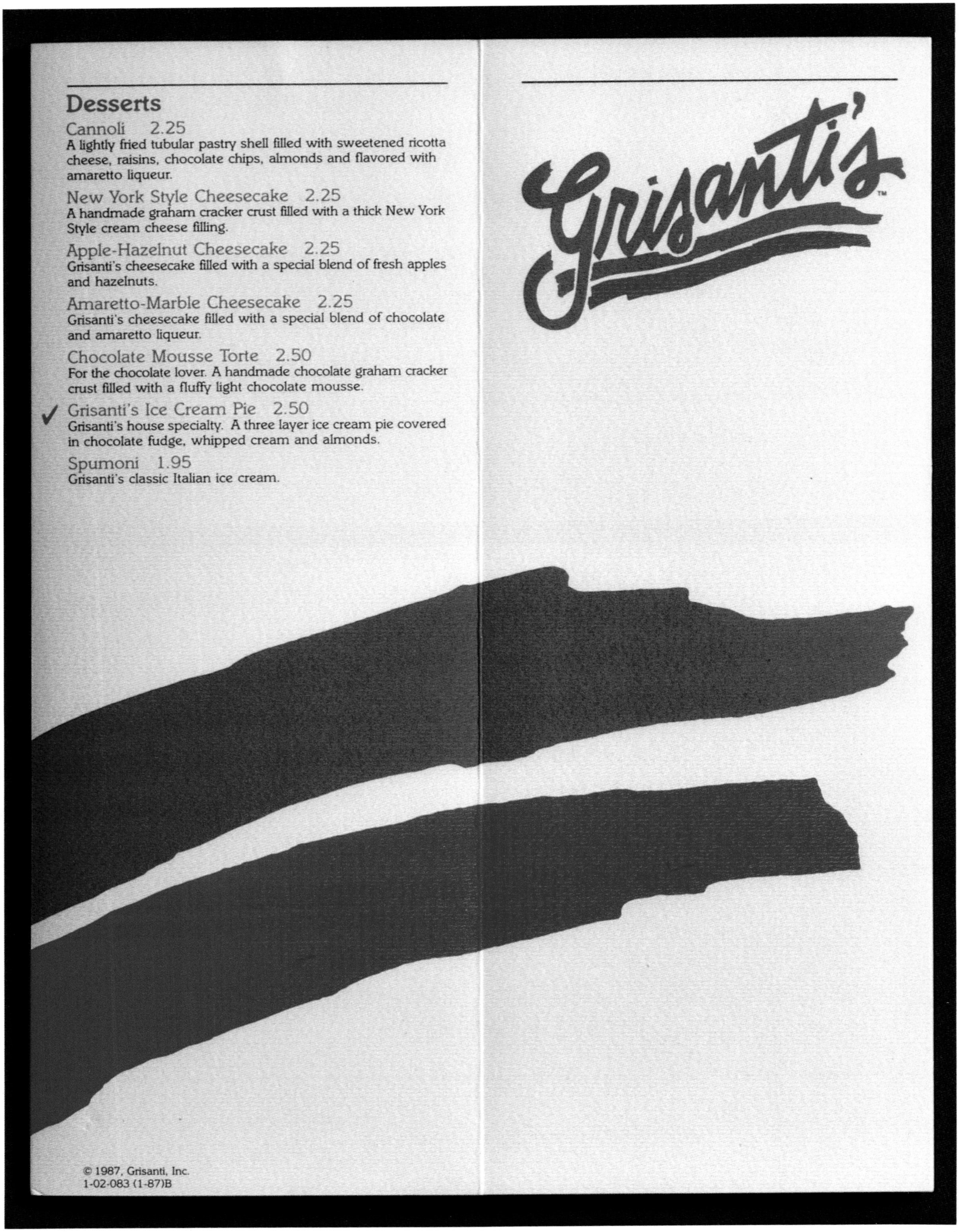

## Desserts

**Cannoli 2.25**
A lightly fried tubular pastry shell filled with sweetened ricotta cheese, raisins, chocolate chips, almonds and flavored with amaretto liqueur.

**New York Style Cheesecake 2.25**
A handmade graham cracker crust filled with a thick New York Style cream cheese filling.

**Apple-Hazelnut Cheesecake 2.25**
Grisanti's cheesecake filled with a special blend of fresh apples and hazelnuts.

**Amaretto-Marble Cheesecake 2.25**
Grisanti's cheesecake filled with a special blend of chocolate and amaretto liqueur.

**Chocolate Mousse Torte 2.50**
For the chocolate lover. A handmade chocolate graham cracker crust filled with a fluffy light chocolate mousse.

✓ **Grisanti's Ice Cream Pie 2.50**
Grisanti's house specialty. A three layer ice cream pie covered in chocolate fudge, whipped cream and almonds.

**Spumoni 1.95**
Grisanti's classic Italian ice cream.

© 1987, Grisanti, Inc.
1-02-083 (1-87)B

Grisanti's™

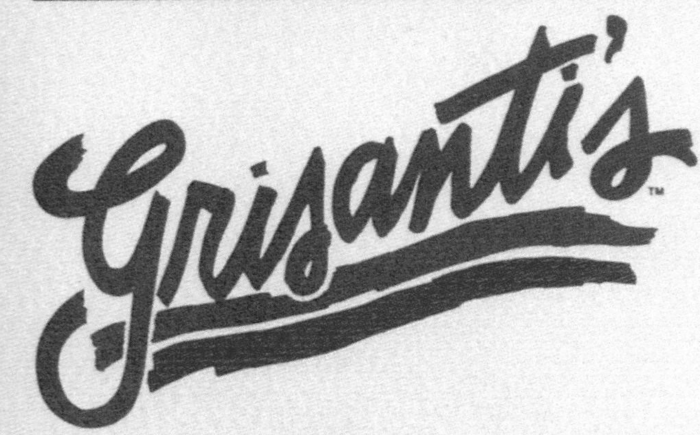

Designer: *Concepts Marketing Design*
Restaurant: *Grisanti's*
*Louisville, KY*

**1987 GREAT MENUS CONTEST WINNER: SECOND PLACE, MERCHANDISING POWER**

Grisanti's features Italian cuisine matched to Italian wines. If this weren't evident from the name, the vivid brush strokes of green and red on the off-white cover would make it clear. In deference to American sensibilities, any items listed in Italian are clearly explained in the copy. Wines are identified as to type and level of sweetness; phonetic pronunciations of their names are also provided.

The first inside flap markets catering, gift certificates and the associated market, as well as providing the "Grisanti's Promise" — if the diner is not satisfied, his meal will be replaced or refunded cheerfully.

Red checkmarks in the margin identify house specialties, a nice way to more aggressively market high-profit items.

Tycoons

BOCARATON

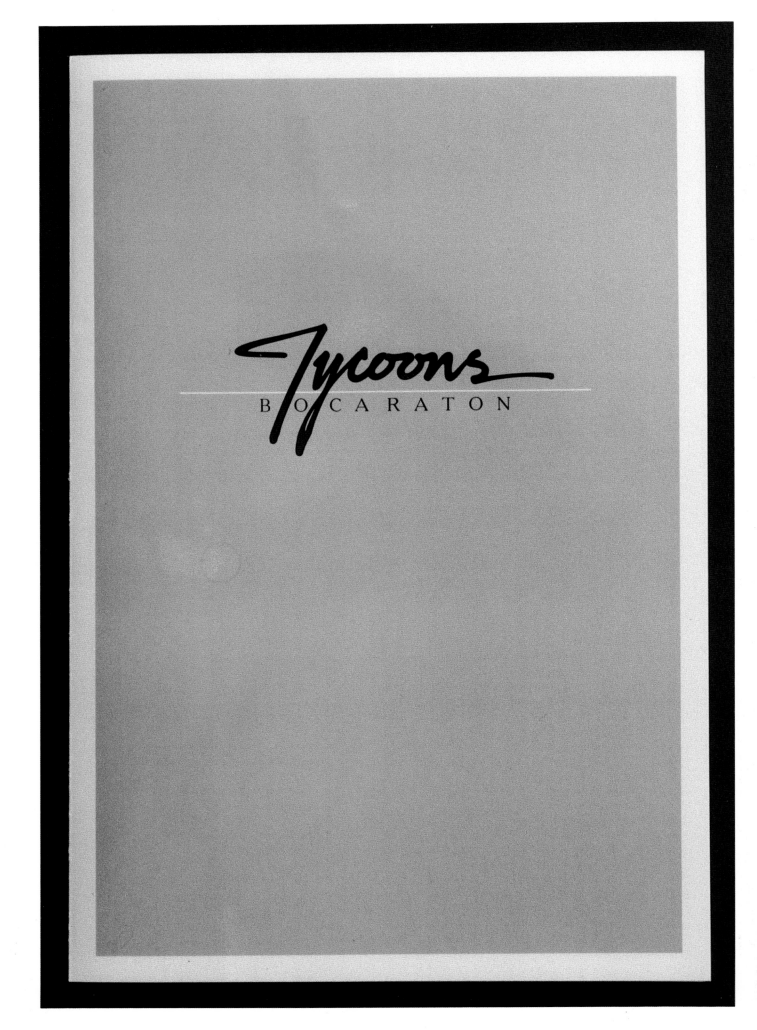

**Designer:** *David Savage*
*David Savage/Art & Design*
**Restaurant:** *Tycoons*
*Boca Raton, FL*

The menu cover, like the design of the restaurant itself, is understated. Inside, the menu resembles a poster more than a menu. Oversized type and large illustrations, executed in brilliant colors, further this impression. The type size and the layout were deliberately selected to encourage customer involvement. A copywriter was retained to make the copy as readable and pleasant as the illustrations.

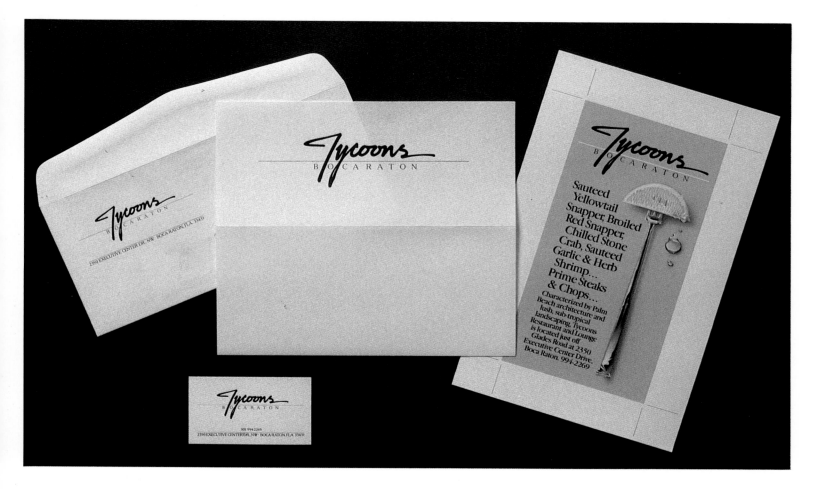

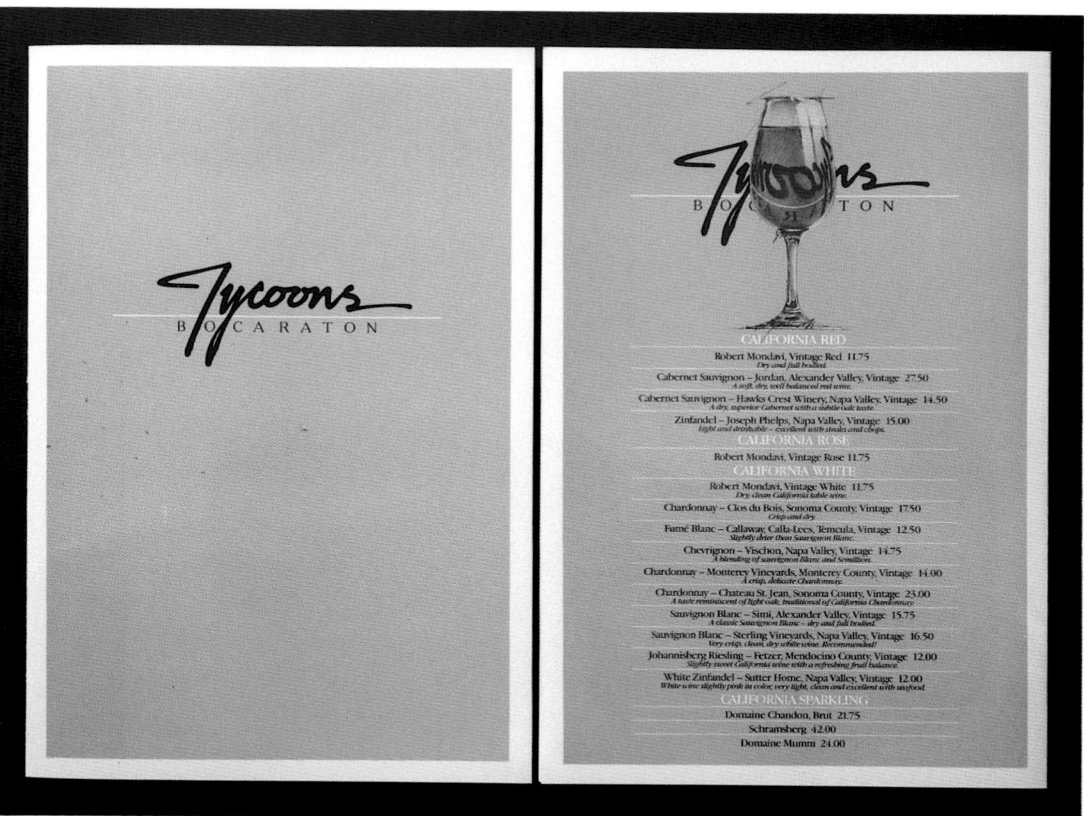

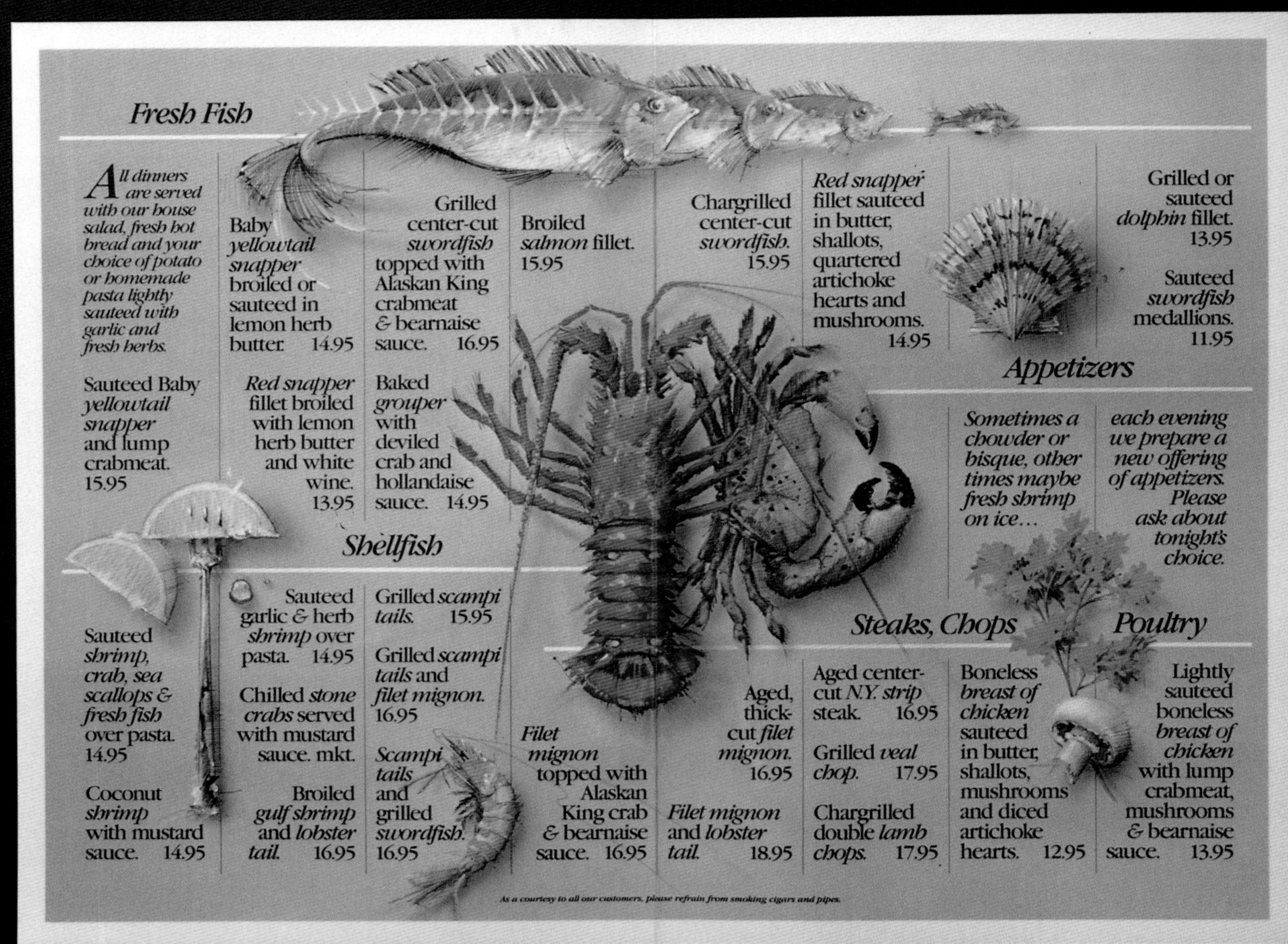

## Fresh Fish

*All dinners are served with our house salad, fresh hot bread and your choice of potato or homemade pasta lightly sauteed with garlic and fresh herbs.*

Sauteed Baby *yellowtail snapper* and lump crabmeat. 15.95

Baby *yellowtail snapper* broiled or sauteed in lemon herb butter. 14.95

*Red snapper* fillet broiled with lemon herb butter and white wine. 13.95

Grilled center-cut *swordfish* topped with Alaskan King crabmeat & bearnaise sauce. 16.95

Baked *grouper* with deviled crab and hollandaise sauce. 14.95

Broiled *salmon* fillet. 15.95

Chargrilled center-cut *swordfish.* 15.95

*Red snapper* fillet sauteed in butter, shallots, quartered artichoke hearts and mushrooms. 14.95

Grilled or sauteed *dolphin* fillet. 13.95

Sauteed *swordfish* medallions. 11.95

## Appetizers

*Sometimes a chowder or bisque, other times maybe fresh shrimp on ice… each evening we prepare a new offering of appetizers. Please ask about tonight's choice.*

## Shellfish

Sauteed *shrimp, crab, sea scallops & fresh fish* over pasta. 14.95

Coconut *shrimp* with mustard sauce. 14.95

Sauteed garlic & herb *shrimp* over pasta. 14.95

Chilled *stone crabs* served with mustard sauce. mkt.

Broiled *gulf shrimp* and *lobster tail.* 16.95

Grilled *scampi tails.* 15.95

Grilled *scampi tails* and *filet mignon.* 16.95

*Scampi tails* and grilled *swordfish.* 16.95

## Steaks, Chops

*Filet mignon* topped with Alaskan King crab & bearnaise sauce. 16.95

Aged, thick-cut *filet mignon.* 16.95

*Filet mignon* and *lobster tail.* 18.95

Aged center-cut *N.Y. strip* steak. 16.95

Grilled *veal chop.* 17.95

Chargrilled double *lamb chops.* 17.95

## Poultry

Boneless *breast of chicken* sauteed in butter, shallots, mushrooms and diced artichoke hearts. 12.95

Lightly sauteed boneless *breast of chicken* with lump crabmeat, mushrooms & bearnaise sauce. 13.95

*As a courtesy to all our customers, please refrain from smoking cigars and pipes.*

A drop of lemon juice incorporated into the illustration and the shadows behind the fish and other raw foodstuffs pictured lend a note of realism to the piece.

On the associated lunch menu, the sections have been arranged to overlap in a staggered fashion, reminiscent of fish scales. The wine list is incorporated on the back of the menu, which is laminated for durability.

Coconut Shrimp
HAND DIPPED AND LIGHTLY FRIED 6.50

Swordfish Medallions
FRANCAIS, SERVED OVER FRESH PASTA 6.25

Hot Crabmeat, Melted Cheddar,
BACON AND TOMATOES, SERVED OVER ENGLISH MUFFINS 5.95

Garlic & Herb Shrimp
SAUTEED, SERVED OVER FRESH PASTA 6.50

Sauteed Shrimp, Crab,
BAY SCALLOPS AND FRESH FISH OVER PASTA 6.50

Shrimp Salad Sandwich
SERVED WITH TODAY'S CUP OF SOUP 5.95

Sauteed Red Snapper
BUTTER, SHALLOTS, ARTICHOKE HEARTS AND MUSHROOMS 7.25

Grilled Center-cut Swordfish
TOPPED WITH ALASKAN KING CRABMEAT AND BEARNAISE 7.50

Tycoons
BOCA RATON

Shrimp & Crabmeat Salad
TOSSED WITH ICEBERG, BIBB AND ROMAINE—LOUIS DRESSING 6.50

Pasta, Shrimp & Crab Salad
SERVED WITH HOUSE DRESSING AND GRATED CHEESE 6.50

Bacon, Lettuce & Tomato Salad
ICEBERG, BIBB AND ROMAINE WITH BLEU CHEESE 6.25

Chicken Salad Sandwich
SERVED WITH TODAY'S CUP OF SOUP 5.95

Chicken & Vegetable Sautee
SERVED OVER FRESH PASTA 5.95

Sauteed Boneless Breast of Chicken
WITH LUMP CRABMEAT, MUSHROOMS AND BEARNAISE 6.50

Chicken Salad Platter
SERVED WITH TODAY'S CUP OF SOUP 5.95

Grilled Hamburger
AND FRIES 4.95 CHEESEBURGER 5.25

6 Ounce Filet Mignon
SERVED WITH FRESH PASTA OR POTATO 6.95

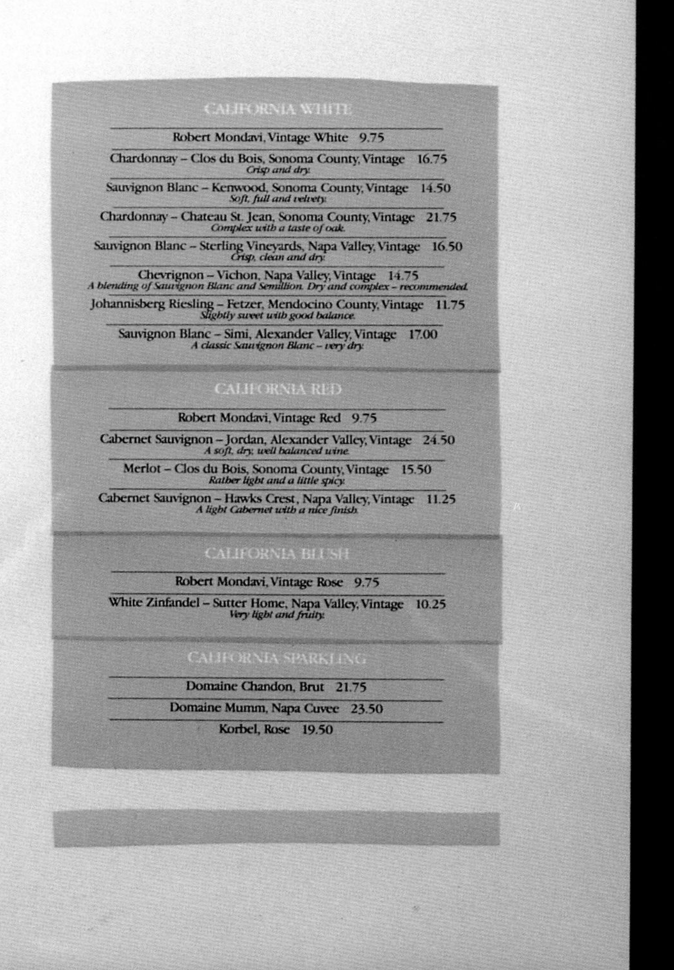

CALIFORNIA WHITE

Robert Mondavi, Vintage White 9.75

Chardonnay – Clos du Bois, Sonoma County, Vintage 16.75
*Crisp and dry.*

Sauvignon Blanc – Kenwood, Sonoma County, Vintage 14.50
*Soft, full and velvety.*

Chardonnay – Chateau St. Jean, Sonoma County, Vintage 21.75
*Complex with a taste of oak.*

Sauvignon Blanc – Sterling Vineyards, Napa Valley, Vintage 16.50
*Crisp, clean and dry.*

Chevrignon – Vichon, Napa Valley, Vintage 14.75
*A blending of Sauvignon Blanc and Semillion. Dry and complex – recommended.*

Johannisberg Riesling – Fetzer, Mendocino County, Vintage 11.75
*Slightly sweet with good balance.*

Sauvignon Blanc – Simi, Alexander Valley, Vintage 17.00
*A classic Sauvignon Blanc – very dry.*

CALIFORNIA RED

Robert Mondavi, Vintage Red 9.75

Cabernet Sauvignon – Jordan, Alexander Valley, Vintage 24.50
*A soft, dry, well balanced wine.*

Merlot – Clos du Bois, Sonoma County, Vintage 15.50
*Rather light and a little spicy.*

Cabernet Sauvignon – Hawks Crest, Napa Valley, Vintage 11.25
*A light Cabernet with a nice finish.*

CALIFORNIA BLUSH

Robert Mondavi, Vintage Rose 9.75

White Zinfandel – Sutter Home, Napa Valley, Vintage 10.25
*Very light and fruity.*

CALIFORNIA SPARKLING

Domaine Chandon, Brut 21.75

Domaine Mumm, Napa Cuvee 23.50

Korbel, Rose 19.50

# BRUNCH

BENNIGAN'S®

BRUNCH

BENNIGAN'S®

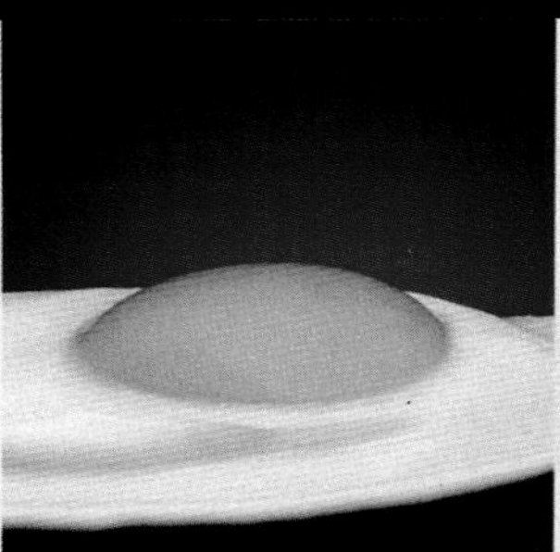

## EGGS
BENEDICTS

**PHILLY STEAK BENEDICT**
Wake up to two English muffins topped with thinly sliced beef, grilled onions and mushrooms, poached eggs and Hollandaise sauce. $6.95

**EGGS BENEDICT**
A brunch tradition. Two English muffins with lean Canadian bacon and poached eggs, topped with Hollandaise sauce. $5.95

**SHRIMPER'S BENEDICT**
A Bennigan's seaside favorite. Poached eggs served over succulent sautéed shrimp, seasoned with a wisp of garlic and lemon, then highlighted with Hollandaise sauce. $7.45

**FLORENTINE BENEDICT**
Creamed spinach and poached eggs, layered atop two English muffins. With Hollandaise sauce, it's a brunch delight! $5.75

## CREPES

**CAJUN CREPES**
Our secret recipe, straight from the bayou. Tasty crepes are stuffed with spicy crawfish and cheese, then covered with a spicy cheese sauce. A Bennigan's original! $6.45

**CREPES FLORENTINE**
Spinach and bacon come together with a medley of riccotta cheese and spices to create a brunch classic. Topped with Hollandaise sauce. $5.95

**APPLE CREPES**
Sliced apples blended with cinnamon and sweet brown sugar, all crowned with whipped cream. Just what the doctor ordered. $5.25

# BEVERAGES

| | | | |
|---|---|---|---|
| ROYAL KONA® Coffee | $ .75 | Hot or Iced Tea | $ .75 |
| Brewed Decaffeinated Coffee | $ .75 | Milk | $ .75 |
| Pepsi® or Diet Pepsi® | $ .75 | Juices | $1.00 |
| | | Perrier | $1.75 |

JUST FOR

# KIDS

PANCAKES
Enjoy a kid-sized helpin' of our fresh buttermilk pancakes, served with honey butter and maple syrup. $1.75

**Plain** — Down-home goodness for traditional appetites.
**Strawberry** — Our golden pancakes are topped with fresh strawberries and whipped cream.
**Blueberry** — Dive into a stack of buttermilk pancakes crowned with our hot blueberry compote and whipped cream.
**Apple** — Our blend of apples, honey, brown sugar and cinnamon tops a stack of buttermilk pancakes.

FRENCH TOAST
Our New Orleans style batter adds a rich flavor to this kid-sized favorite. Crowned with blueberry or strawberry topping and whipped cream. With maple syrup. $2.25

BELGIAN WAFFLE
Bennigan's version of a morning classic, served up for smaller appetites. Topped with lots of whipped cream, honey butter and maple syrup. $1.95

# EYE-OPENERS

RAMOS GIN FIZZ
Gin, lemon, half and half, vanilla and orange flower water create a good sippin', lemon zippy, tangy treat.

BRANDY MILK PUNCH
Start your day with a smile as you sip our magical blend of brandy, vanilla ice cream, dark cream de cocoa and milk.

BLUEBERRY FREEZE
Vodka, ice cream, pineapple, coconut cream and blueberries, topped with whipped cream. A delicious way to kick-off brunch!

MIMOSA
Wake up with a glass of sunshine! Champagne and fresh orange juice.

KIR ROYALE
The perfect celebration of champagne and creme de cassis. Say cheers with Bennigan's special touch of elegance.

# STARTERS

BRUNCH QUESADILLAS
Enjoy flour tortillas, filled with scrambled eggs, Jack cheese, bacon and mushrooms. Served grilled with creamy guacamole, sour cream and snappy salsa for dipping. Dig in! $4.95

BRUNCH SKINS
Our crispy, fried potato skins are loaded with cheeses, scrambled eggs and green onions. Topped with bacon, tomatoes and Hollandaise sauce and served with picante for dipping. They'll get you going! $5.95

BEVERAGES

ROYAL KONA® Coffee $ .75 Hot or Iced Tea $ .75
Brewed Decaffeinated Coffee $ .75 Milk $ .75
Pepsi® or Diet Pepsi® $ .75 Juices $1.00
Perrier $1.75

JUST FOR
KIDS

PANCAKES
Enjoy a kid-sized helpin' of our fresh buttermilk pancakes, served with honey butter and maple syrup. $1.75
Plain — Down-home goodness for traditional appetites.
Strawberry — Our golden pancakes are topped with fresh strawberries and whipped cream.
Blueberry — Dive into a stack of buttermilk pancakes crowned with our hot blueberry compote and whipped cream.
Apple — Our blend of apples, honey, brown sugar and cinnamon tops a stack of buttermilk pancakes.
FRENCH TOAST
Our New Orleans style batter adds a rich flavor to this kid-sized favorite. Crowned with blueberry or strawberry topping and whipped cream. With maple syrup. $2.25
BELGIAN WAFFLE
Bennigan's version of a morning classic, served up for smaller appetites. Topped with lots of whipped cream, honey butter and maple syrup. $1.95

© 1986, S & A Restaurant Corp. 9/86
Pepsi and Diet Pepsi are registered trademarks of the Pepsi Cola Co., Purchase, N.Y.

# BRUNCH

BENNIGAN'S®

Designer: *Ted J. Karch*
*The Beaird Agency*
Restaurant: *Bennigan's*
*Dallas, TX*

This menu is the result of thoughtful interaction among the Agency, top restaurant management and the operations staff of the restaurant. Both illustration and photography were considered for the design. The luminous colors of the Easter eggs on the cover and balloons on the back are echoed in the surreal presentations in the interior. Pancakes so fluffy they seem to float make the diner's mouth water in anticipation. The copywriting uses adjectives and associations with tradition to enhance the marketing work begun by the pictures.

# PANCAKES

TRAWBERRY PANCAKES
You'll love our buttermilk pancakes, topped with fresh strawberries and strawberry compote, along with your choice of sour cream or whipped cream. $4.95

LUEBERRY PANCAKES
Enjoy a stack of our buttermilk pancakes, crowned with our hot blueberry compote. $4.95

PPLE PANCAKES
Just like Mom used to make. Our secret blend of apples, honey, brown sugar and cinnamon tops a mouthwatering stack of buttermilk pancakes. $4.95

UTTERMILK PANCAKES
A Bennigan's brunch tradition. Three pancakes, served with lots of our honey butter and maple syrup. $4.25

# SPECIALTIES

ELGIAN WAFFLES
Bennigan's breakfast sensation! Two waffles with lots of honey butter, maple syrup, and blueberry and strawberry compotes. Topped with whipped cream. $4.95

RENCH TOAST
Our New Orleans style batter adds rich flavor to a brunch classic. Topped with blueberry and strawberry compotes, and served with maple syrup and honey butter. $5.45

EAFOOD QUICHE
Our combination of crabmeat, shrimp and mild cheese, together with our special egg mixture. Baked individually in our crust and topped with creamy Hollandaise sauce. The perfect cure for your seafood cravings! $5.75

UICHE LORRAINE
A traditional favorite. Our delicate blend of onions, bacon and Swiss cheese, together with our creamy egg mixture, baked individually in our crispy crust. Even real men will enjoy our quiche classic. $4.95

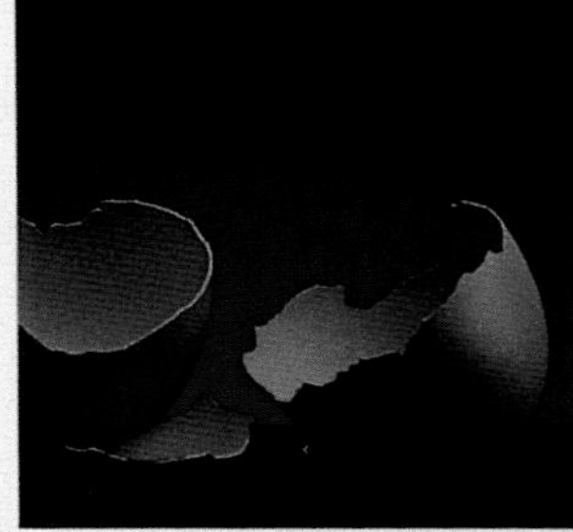

# OMELETTES

SEAFOOD
Our deep-sea brunch treasure features the perfect blend of shrimp and crab, topped with Hollandaise sauce. $6.95

SPANISH
This one's hot n' spicy! Filled with lots of colby cheese and sour cream, then topped with our secret Spanish sauce. $5.95

FLORENTINE
Our three egg omelette is filled with creamy spinach, mushrooms and Jack cheese, then topped with Hollandaise sauce. You'll savor every bite. $6.45

NAME YOUR OWN
Here's a breakfast for the creatively inclined. Choose any three favorites from our list of fresh, delicious ingredients. $5.95

| | |
|---|---|
| Sautéed Mushrooms | Bacon |
| Green Onions | Ham |
| Green Peppers | Tomatoes |
| Jack Cheese | Guacamole |
| Colby Cheese | Hollandaise Sauce |
| Sour Cream | Spanish Sauce |

# BUTCHER'S BLOCK

BACON STRIPS
Enjoy three strips of crispy, golden bacon with your meal. $.95

LINK SAUSAGE
Complement your brunch with two links of our sizzlin' sausage. $1.25

BREAKFAST STEAK
Dig into Bennigan's six-ounce top sirloin, cooked just the way you like it. $2.95

# EGGS
BENEDICTS

PHILLY STEAK BENEDICT
Wake up to two English muffins topped with thinly sliced beef, grilled onions and mushrooms, poached eggs and Hollandaise sauce. $6.95

EGGS BENEDICT
A brunch tradition. Two English muffins with lean Canadian bacon and poached eggs, topped with Hollandaise sauce. $5.95

SHRIMPER'S BENEDICT
A Bennigan's seaside favorite. Poached eggs served over succulent sautéed shrimp, seasoned with a wisp of garlic and lemon, then highlighted with Hollandaise sauce. $7.45

FLORENTINE BENEDICT
Creamed spinach and poached eggs, layered atop two English muffins. With Hollandaise sauce, it's a brunch delight! $5.75

# CREPES

CAJUN CREPES
Our secret recipe, straight from the bayou. Tasty crepes are stuffed with spicy crawfish and cheese, then covered with a spicy cheese sauce. A Bennigan's original! $6.45

CREPES FLORENTINE
Spinach and bacon come together with a medley of riccotta cheese and spices to create a brunch classic. Topped with Hollandaise sauce. $5.95

APPLE CREPES
Sliced apples blended with cinnamon and sweet brown sugar, all crowned with whipped cream. Just what the doctor ordered. $5.25

EYE-OPENERS

RAMOS GIN FIZZ
Gin, lemon, half and half, vanilla and orange flower water create a good sippin', lemon zippy, tangy treat.
BRANDY MILK PUNCH
Start your day with a smile as you sip our magical blend of brandy, vanilla ice cream, dark cream de cocoa and milk.
BLUEBERRY FREEZE
Vodka, ice cream, pineapple, coconut cream and blueberries, topped with whipped cream. A delicious way to kick-off brunch!
MIMOSA
Wake up with a glass of sunshine! Champagne and fresh orange juice.
KIR ROYALE
The perfect celebration of champagne and creme de cassis. Say cheers with Bennigan's special touch of elegance.

STARTERS

BRUNCH QUESADILLAS
Enjoy flour tortillas, filled with scrambled eggs, Jack cheese, bacon and mushrooms. Served grilled with creamy guacamole, sour cream and snappy salsa for dipping. Dig in! $4.95
BRUNCH SKINS
Our crispy, fried potato skins are loaded with cheeses, scrambled eggs and green onions. Topped with bacon, tomatoes and Hollandaise sauce and served with picante for dipping. They'll get you going! $5.95

LA FIESTA

Designer: *Claude Prettyman, Joy Pagara*
*El Torito Restaurants, Inc.*
Restaurant: *La Fiesta*
*Irvine, CA*

These laminated menus feature brightly-colored, Aztec-inspired graphics set against a speckled background reminiscent of tortillas. Designed for use throughout the day, the menus cover everything from Margaritas to desserts.

Most of the headings are in Spanish, but one unique featured section, the "Peso Power Platters™," is in English. This section is only available between the hours of 2:00 p.m. and 6:00 p.m., Monday through Saturday. Designed as a sort of light lunch, the Platters not only offer the diner good value for the money, they also ensure the restaurant will get at least some business during the slack period of the day. Suburban shoppers might well choose to stop at the restaurant for a quick break in the course of a busy afternoon.

## PESO POWER PLATTERS™ 3.95

**Served from 2 pm to 6 pm, Monday through Saturday.**
These complete dinner platters come with your choice of beverage*, black bean soup or salad, sweet corn cake and Flan for dessert. And all are specially priced to save you muchos pesos! (No Substitutions Please.)
*Beverage choices include soft drinks, coffee, milk or tea.

**Sonora**
Choice of black bean soup or fresh garden salad
Two cheese enchiladas, Rancheras and Suizas
Mexican-style rice, refried beans and sweet corn cake
Flan and beverage

**Baja**
Choice of black bean soup or fresh garden salad
Two soft picadillo tacos
Mexican-style rice, refried beans and sweet corn cake
Flan and beverage

**Cabo**
Choice of black bean soup or fresh garden salad
Bean and cheese burrito
Mexican-style rice and sweet corn cake
Flan and beverage

## PLATILLOS MEXICANOS

Served with black bean soup or garden salad, Mexican-style rice, refried beans and sweet corn cake.

1. **Enchilada** . . . . . 4.95
Your choice of a cheese, chicken or beef enchilada, topped with piping hot sauce and cheese.
2. **Taco** . . . . . . 4.95
A crisp corn tortilla filled with your choice of chicken or beef, shredded cheddar cheese, lettuce and mild taco sauce.
3. **Chile Relleno** . . . . 4.95
A mild chile stuffed with Jack cheese, then dipped in our special batter and fried to a golden puff.
4. **Tamale** . . . . . . 4.95
Freshly ground corn meal filled with chunky beef, steamed until tender and served with enchilada sauce.
5. **Enchilada, Taco** . . . 5.95
Our special cheese, beef or chicken enchilada and a beef or chicken taco.
6. **Two Enchiladas** . . . 5.95
Two of our famous cheese, beef or chicken enchiladas topped with sauce and melted cheese.
7. **Chile Relleno, Taco** . . 5.95
A mild chile relleno and a beef or chicken taco.
8. **Two Tacos** . . . . 5.95
Crispy twin beef or chicken tacos, loaded with all the trimmings.
9. **Chile Relleno, Tostada** . . 5.95
A cheese filled chile relleno teamed with our mini beef or chicken tostada.
10. **Enchilada, Chile Relleno** 5.95
Our special cheese enchilada and a chile relleno.

## BURRITOS Y CHIMICHANGAS

Served with black bean soup or garden salad and sweet corn cake.

**Burrito Especial** . . . . 4.95
Spicy shredded beef, melted cheese and refried beans in a grilled flour tortilla. Topped with ranchera sauce, melted cheese and sour cream.

**Burrito Colorado** . . . 4.95
Tender chunks of beef simmered in a red chile sauce, rolled in a soft flour tortilla with refried beans. Topped with enchilada sauce and melted cheeses. Served with sour cream.

**Taco Burrito** . . . . . 4.95
Seasoned ground beef, refried beans, tomatoes, shredded lettuce and melted cheese in a grilled flour tortilla covered with Spanish sauce. Served with guacamole and sour cream.

**Burrito Verde** . . . . 4.95
Lean pork simmered in a green chile sauce, rolled in a fresh flour tortilla with refried beans. Topped with verde sauce and melted cheese. Served with sour cream.

**Burrito de Pollo** . . . . 4.95
Tender chicken and refried beans in a flour tortilla smothered with enchilada sauce and melted cheeses. Served with sour cream.

**Macho Chimichanga** . . . 5.25
Shredded beef, Mexican-style rice and cheeses in a crisp flour tortilla. Garnished with avocado sauce, fresh tomatoes and sour cream.

**Cancun Chimi** . . . . 5.75
A flour tortilla filled with shrimp, crab and rice simmered in our white wine cream sauce then rolled and fried. Topped with sour cream sauce. Served with avocado and sour cream.

**Outrageous Chimichanga** . . 6.75
A one and a half pound feast for chimi lovers. Shredded beef, chicken, our special beans and mixed cheeses in a flour tortilla, fried to a golden brown. Garnished with guacamole and sour cream.

## MACHO COMBOS™

Huge platters featuring our most popular items: enchiladas, chimichangas and more. All guaranteed to fill you up without emptying your pockets! Can't eat it all? We'll gladly package any items you aren't able to finish.
Served with black bean soup or garden salad and sweet corn cake.

**El Patrón** . . . . . . 6.95
Chile relleno, mini-chimichanga and two enchiladas. Served with refried beans.

**El Conquistador** . . . . 6.95
Beef or chicken taco, chile relleno, bean and cheese burrito and an Enchilada Suiza. Served with Mexican-style rice.

**El Dueño** . . . . . . 6.95
Burrito Especial, beef or chicken taco and a cheese enchilada. Served with Mexican-style rice.

**El Fundador** . . . . . 6.95
A beef or chicken taco and a trio of enchiladas. Served with rice and beans.

**El Presidente** . . . . . 6.95
A Macho Chimichanga, chile relleno and a cheese enchilada. Served with refried beans.

Designer: *Larry McAdams*
*Larry McAdams Design, Inc.*

Restaurant: *California Place*
*Los Angeles International Airport*
*Los Angeles, CA*

California Place is the third iteration of this restaurant. Moving from an upscale, French cuisine to a more moderately priced, casual California-style approach necessitated a complete redesign of the restaurant interior, the menu and collateral pieces.

Detailed copywriting, conveyed in a clean, legible typeface, makes the menu comprehensible even to the weary traveler suffering from jet lag. A broad selection of salads and appetizers will be kind to his stomach.

In addition to the menu itself, table tents, a guest check and even a mailable complimentary dinner certificate were developed. All use cheerful pastels and a subdued pattern, which is different on the lunch and dinner menus. The dinner menu includes a die-cut panel where a card listing daily specials can be slipped into place.

California
PLACE
RESTAURANT
California
PLACE
California
PLACE

California
PLACE
California
PLACE
California
PLACE
California
PLACE
RESTAURANT
Host International cordially invites
to enjoy a complimentary
at California Place Restaurant located atop the Los Angeles International Airport Theme Building. Our restaurant features a combination of traditional and contemporary California cuisine creating a dining experience for you, that will be as unique as the landmark building we occupy. Please call us at your convenience at (213) 646-5471 and indicate that you are a guest of Roger Gigling, General Manager. We will be pleased to make all the arrangements, including free valet parking.

# CHAPTER 4

A restaurant's theme can be based on any one of a variety of premises. It may feature ethnic or regional cuisine. It may be sports-oriented, or an opera-lover's homage to the art form he loves best. A theme can be based on paintings hung on its walls or the vistas beyond its windows. Whatever else it is, a theme restaurant is a tangible and distinct embodiment of a single vision.

How well that vision is realized is what separates the effective theme restaurant from its ineffective brethren. When the menu design team is involved in the development of a restaurant, or in its redesign, the menu often enhances the vision.

What follows is a collection of menus that transport the reader into the fantasy of the restaurant's personality. Copywriting has been extensively used to support the ideas of the restaurateur. Creative typography selection and imaginative production techniques have made these menus practical. In each case, the designer, working in tandem with the restaurant's representative, has created a menu that works *with*, not against, the theme.

# VARIATIONS ON A THEME

Monterey
BAY CANNERS
FRESH SEAFOOD
RESTAURANT
OYSTER BAR • COCKTAILS

| | |
|---|---|
| Designer: | *Bob Bates* |
| | *Bates/Lee Design* |
| Restaurant: | *Monterey Bay Canners* |
| | *Various locations in California and Hawaii* |

Although most of its restaurants are located inland, the Monterey Bay Canners takes its inspiration from Cannery Row in Monterey. Emphasis is on mesquite-grilled fresh fish. There is an insert listing the "Catch of the Day." These are the first menus in the restaurant's more than ten-year history to feature such inserts.

The laminated menu covers depict the actual architecture of the restaurants, transposed into a waterside setting reminiscent of the company's restaurant in Monterey. The fishing boat underlines the freshness of the fish offered.

The wine list wraps around a large can which also serves as the ice bucket.

**California White Wines**

| Bin No. | | By the Glass | Full Bottle |
|---|---|---|---|
| 100 | Calif. Sauvignon Blanc, Robert Mondavi (NAPA VALLEY) "V" | 2.75 | 8.95 |
| 101 | Blanc de Blanc, Fetzer (MENDOCINO COUNTY) "V" | | 8.95 |
| 102 | Chenin Blanc, Beringer (NAPA VALLEY) "V" | 3.00 | 10.95 |
| 103 | Monterey Riesling, Mirassou (MONTEREY COUNTY) "V" | | 10.50 |
| 104 | Johannisberg Riesling, Jekel (MONTEREY COUNTY) "V" | 3.25 | 11.95 |
| 105 | Sauvignon Blanc, Callaway (TEMECULA, CALIFORNIA) "V" | | 12.50 |
| 106 | Fume Blanc, Robert Mondavi (NAPA VALLEY) "V" | | 14.50 |
| 107 | Chardonnay, Stone Creek (SONOMA COUNTY) "V" | 3.25 | 11.50 |
| 108 | Chardonnay, Kendall Jackson (LAKE COUNTY) "V" | 4.00 | 15.50 |
| 109 | Chardonnay, Jekel (MONTEREY COUNTY) "V" | | 16.50 |

**Premium Wines By The Glass**

WE'RE PLEASED TO PRESENT A DAILY SELECTION OF OTHER FEATURED PREMIUM WINES BY THE GLASS.

**California Blush Wines**

| Bin No. | | By the Glass | Full Bottle |
|---|---|---|---|
| 201 | Steelhead Run, Buena Vista (SONOMA COUNTY) "V" | | 8.95 |
| 202 | White Zinfandel, Sutter Home (NAPA VALLEY) "V" | 2.75 | 9.95 |
| 203 | White Zinfandel, Beringer (NAPA VALLEY) "V" | 3.25 | 11.50 |

**California Red Wines**

| Bin No. | | By the Glass | Full Bottle |
|---|---|---|---|
| 301 | Calif. Cabernet, Robert Mondavi (NAPA VALLEY) "V" | 2.75 | 8.95 |
| 302 | Cabernet Sauvignon, Firestone (SANTA YNEZ VALLEY) "V" | 3.75 | 14.50 |

**California Champagnes**

| Bin No. | | By the Glass | Full Bottle |
|---|---|---|---|
| 401 | Le Domaine, Extra Dry (MONTEREY COUNTY) | | 8.50<br>Caddy 3.00 |
| 402 | Domaine Chandon, Blanc de Noirs (NAPA VALLEY, CALIFORNIA) "V" | 4.25 | 16.50 |

**House Wines**

STONE CREEK CELLARS

| | Glass | Half Carafe | Carafe |
|---|---|---|---|
| Chablis & Chablis Blush (NAPA VALLEY, CALIFORNIA) | 2.25 | 3.75 | 6.50 |

# Wine List

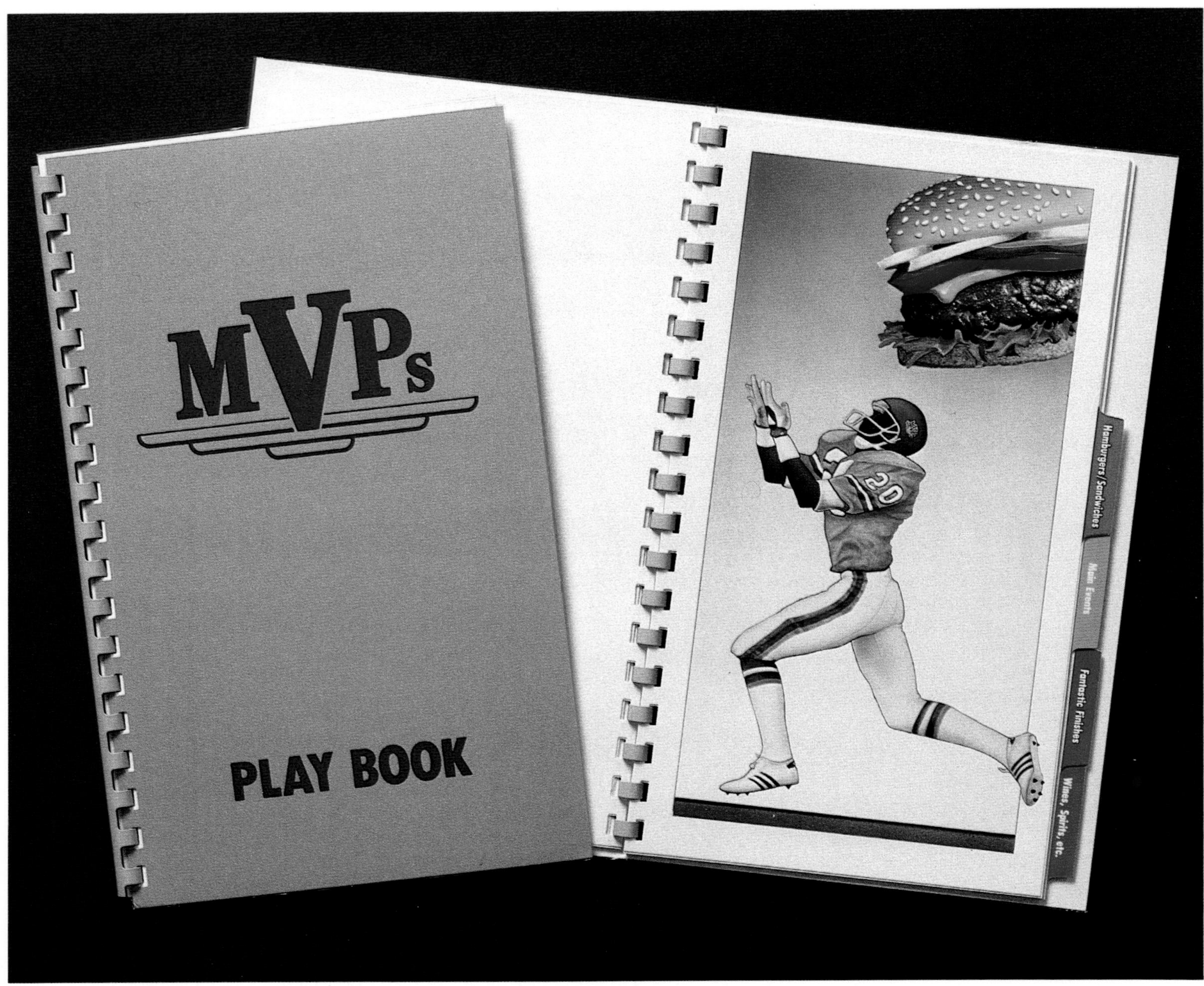


**Designer:** *Julie Patricio-Block*
*Julie Patricio-Block Graphic Design*
**Restaurant:** *MVPs*
*Santa Maria, CA*

The menu for this contemporary sports theme restaurant uses imaginative copywriting, full color illustrations and a carefully-planned production concept to realize its goals.

The main logo was designed to look like the type style used on trophies. The colored illustrations are on a sturdy laminated stock and serve as tabbed dividers for each menu section. The interior pages are printed in one color to permit inexpensive updates. Each color illustration features a different sport and integrates the image of the food section it precedes. Our favorite, for "Pre-Game Warm-Ups," is set off by a die-cut mountainside. This opens to reveal the climber scaling a mountain of nachos.

Copywriting incorporates the names of sports figures and techniques into the names of the dishes offered. Anecdotes and sports trivia questions are sprinkled throughout the menu.

Of course, the menu is only one element in the overall theme. Football field carpeting, baseball diamond tile and "dugout" booths, as well as local and national sports memorabilia also contribute. The servers and bar staff all wear golf shirts with the restaurant logo where an alligator might otherwise appear. The mood throughout is light-hearted without being too cute.

Designer: *Jan Wilson*
*Dennard Creative, Inc.*
Restaurant: *Key West Grill*
*Clearwater, FL and Arlington, TX*

If you aren't ready to run away to Key West after seeing the fluorescent-inked sunset on the cover of this menu, you will be after reading the copy on the first inside flap. "Jasmine-perfumed air" and "the taste of Paradise" ought to be enough to convince anybody.

The restaurant is designed as a casual beach house, incorporating traditional architectural elements from the Key itself. The menu design needed to achieve that same feeling. Accordingly, the designer tried to imagine what a beach bum artist might come up with to pay for a meal and tried to reproduce it. The main design problem was not to "overdesign." Anything too slick would have felt wrong.

The menu interior uses only two colors — a soft reddish brown suggesting tan skin and the famous aqua of the waters off the Keys. Both are set against a light sand color to complete the mood.

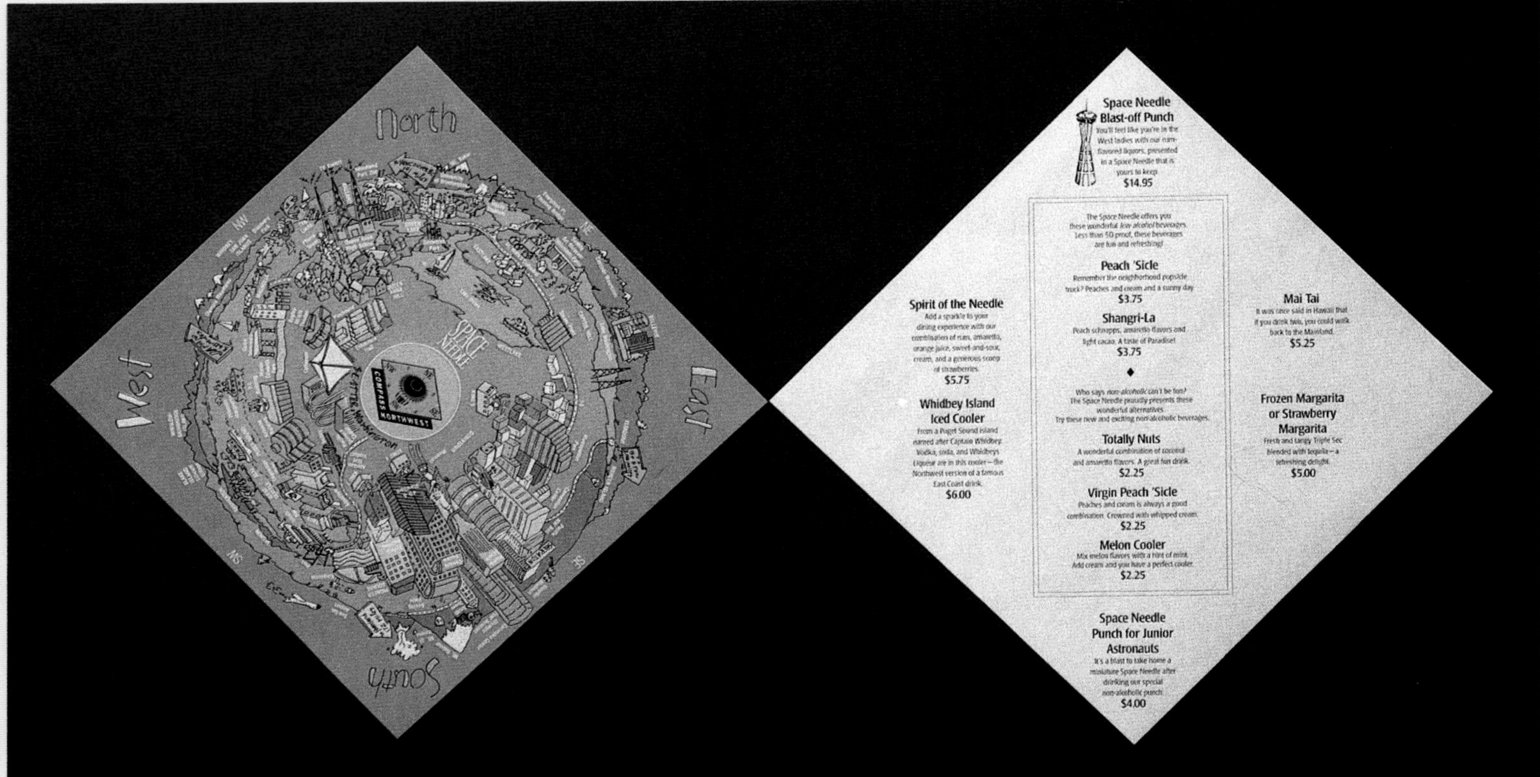


Designer: *Paula Rees*
*Rees Thompson Designers*
*Drink Menu*
Restaurant: *Space Needle*
*Seattle, WA*

The original purpose of this menu was to sell more specialty drinks — both alcoholic and non-alcoholic. The menu was also to be a give-away. The actual design as implemented produced some surprising dividends.

The Space Needle, constructed for the 1964 World's Fair, is a major landmark in Seattle. Many tourists visit the restaurant at the top, which rotates 360° each hour, providing a spectacular view of the entire city. Busy servers were constantly being stopped and questioned about what the visitors were actually seeing. This menu is designed to tell them.

To produce this stylized "map" of the views from the Space Needle, the art director and illustrator rotated for three hours, frantically taking notes all the way. Not only are important buildings, mountains and islands marked, they have also provided the distance and direction of several other locations — Japan, for example, is 3,627 miles west by northwest from the Space Needle.

When a customer arrives, the menu is placed in front of him, oriented in the direction he is facing. Not only have the questions become less repetitive, drink sales rose 20% overnight, once this menu came into use. Demand has been so great, they have had to reprint several times.

|  |  |
|---|---|
| **Designer:** | *Rick Tharp, Karen Nomura* |
|  | *Miller, Morton, Caillet & Nevis* |
| **Restaurant:** | *Eli McFly's* |
|  | *Cupertino, CA* |

For this Southwestern style restaurant, a theme character, "Eli McFly, time traveler," was invented. His "legend" appears on the first unfold. There is a hint that Eli himself will make an appearance at least once each evening in his time machine. Menu items are named to continue the time travel theme and are sufficiently varied in origin to suggest that Eli must have traveled across the globe as well as across time.

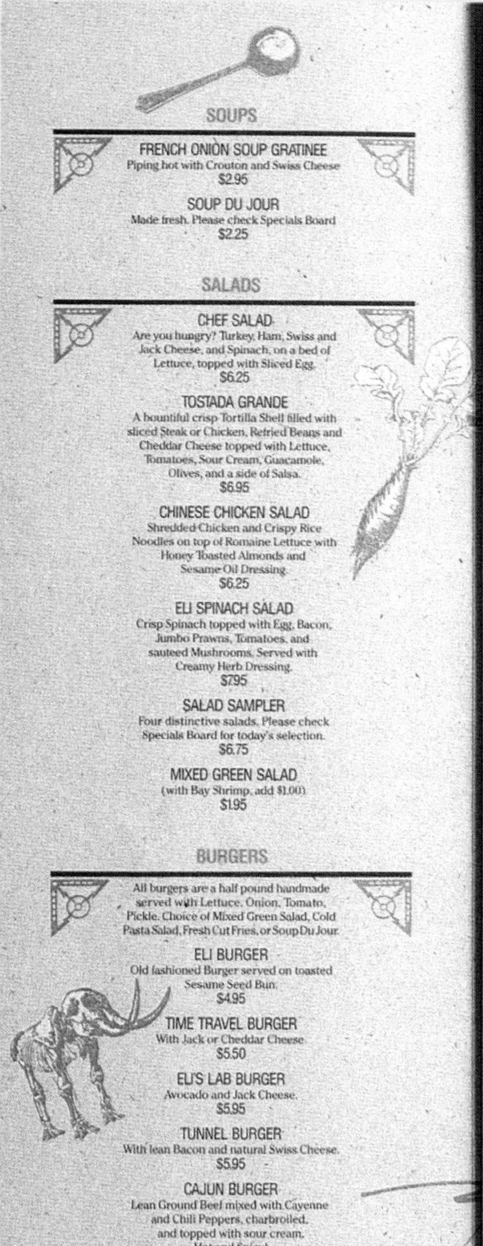

SOUPS

FRENCH ONION SOUP GRATINEE
Piping hot with Crouton and Swiss Cheese
$2.95

SOUP DU JOUR
Made fresh. Please check Specials Board
$2.25

SALADS

CHEF SALAD
Are you hungry? Turkey, Ham, Swiss and Jack Cheese, and Spinach, on a bed of Lettuce, topped with Sliced Egg.
$6.25

TOSTADA GRANDE
A bountiful crisp Tortilla Shell filled with sliced Steak or Chicken, Refried Beans and Cheddar Cheese topped with Lettuce, Tomatoes, Sour Cream, Guacamole, Olives, and a side of Salsa.
$6.95

CHINESE CHICKEN SALAD
Shredded Chicken and Crispy Rice Noodles on top of Romaine Lettuce with Honey Toasted Almonds and Sesame Oil Dressing.
$6.25

ELI SPINACH SALAD
Crisp Spinach topped with Egg, Bacon, Jumbo Prawns, Tomatoes, and sauteed Mushrooms. Served with Creamy Herb Dressing.
$7.95

SALAD SAMPLER
Four distinctive salads. Please check Specials Board for today's selection.
$6.75

MIXED GREEN SALAD
(with Bay Shrimp, add $1.00)
$1.95

BURGERS

All burgers are a half pound handmade served with Lettuce, Onion, Tomato, Pickle. Choice of Mixed Green Salad, Cold Pasta Salad, Fresh Cut Fries, or Soup Du Jour.

ELI BURGER
Old fashioned Burger served on toasted Sesame Seed Bun.
$4.95

TIME TRAVEL BURGER
With Jack or Cheddar Cheese
$5.50

ELI'S LAB BURGER
Avocado and Jack Cheese.
$5.95

TUNNEL BURGER
With lean Bacon and natural Swiss Cheese.
$5.95

CAJUN BURGER
Lean Ground Beef mixed with Cayenne and Chili Peppers, charbroiled, and topped with sour cream. Hot and Spicy!
$5.50

THE LEGEND OF ELI

*Imagine an age before the '60's, when traveling through time had a whole different meaning. This was the age of Eli McFly—internationally renowned inventor. Rumor had it that before the accident, ol' Eli was hard at work on some kind of time contraption. Call him brilliant. Call him eccentric. But Eli was certainly nobody's fool. Even though he, his laboratory, and his barn disappeared April 1, 1932.*

*His whereabouts? Well, this is where things get a bit strange. A stone mural exhumed from the Meroe pyramids, circa 832 BC, depicts a distracted, bespectacled gentleman that bears a striking resemblance to our friend Eli. Writings recently unearthed in a pre-Renaissance Italian abbey talk about an Englishman bearing the same characteristics. There's even some mention of a "Monk Fly" in an obscure Shakespearean sonnet.*

*The McFly clan has faithfully and painstakingly reproduced Eli's laboratory and many of his inventions—including an exact replica of his notorious time contraption—in what is now known as Cupertino, California.*

*It is anticipated that at some point each evening the lights will dim, sparks of color will vibrate and hum, and the time machine will come alive. Eli, on his flight through time is expected to reappear in the glass chamber of his making. He will impart a poignant message to those who witness his presence. Then he will continue his sojourn through eons of time and space.*

The theme is enhanced by playful use of old engravings fancifully colored and amended. For example, Benjamin Franklin is recognizable but why is his key so large and his kite so small. . .simply to underscore the light-hearted mood of the place.

The designer has used a 20% silver screen over the entire interior of the menu with selected areas knocked out and silver, purple and pink imprinting on this lively menu. The effect is subtle and somehow mysterious.

Prix-Fixe

All Dinners are Served with Hors d'Oeuvre Platter, Salade, An Entrée with Tumeric Rice, Raisins and Almonds, and Grilled Fresh Vegetable "Americain."

Hors d'Oeuvre

Fresh Vegetable Crudité, Marinated Eggplant, Meatballs in Spicy Sauce, Cheese, Dates, Olives and Figs, Pita and Peasant Bread.

Rick's Salade

Romaine and Boston Lettuce, Radish, Olives, Peppers, Green Onions, Cucumber, Tomato and Walnuts, Minted Lemon Oil Vinaigrette.

Dinner

Grilled Sea Bass, Moroccan Spice and Pine Nuts 20.00
Swordfish Shashlick with Citron Verte 21.00
Grilled Chicken Breast with Kumquats, Chilis and Walnuts 19.50
Broiled Top Sirloin Steak with Grilled Eggplant and Tomato 22.00
Grilled Lamb Chops with Lemon, Garlic and Coriander 23.50

Rick's Café Has Been Designed and Built By
Glen Lyon, The Finishing Touch, Tucson, Arizona.

Designer: *Donna Milord*
*Associates Printing Service, Inc.*
Restaurant: *Rick's Cafe Americain*
*Westin La Paloma*
*Tucson, AZ*

The theme of the restaurant is based on "Rick's Cafe Americain" in the film *Casablanca.* The logo at the top of the menu is similar to that used in the film and the stars and crescent moon featured suggest a desert location, which is also appropriate for Arizona.

The menu is printed on only one side but is a real "attention grabber." The black background is unusual. The reversed type is quite legible despite being "hand writen." Only five *prix-fixe* dinners are offered but there is something for every taste.

Interestingly, the architect/designer of the restaurant is credited at the bottom of the printed menu.

Designer: *Larry McAdams/John Patterson/ Phil Buck*
*Larry McAdams Design, Inc.*
Restaurant: *Elephant Bar & Restaurant*
*Santa Barbara, CA*

The sturdy look and feel of tropical luggage is recreated on the covers of the menus for this safari-theme restaurant. The paper is a linen stock and is accented with illustrations of leather corner reinforcements and an applique of the elephant in the center. To reinforce the image, the applique is actually raised under the laminated coating.

The menu interior, printed on a light screen of one of its two ink colors, leads the diner on a journey to various parts of the world. Whimsical journal entries, illustrations and photographs support the safari theme.

Slightly deeper screen blocks highlight various selections on each page. These are probably either the house specialties or high-profit items.

The typeface selected for the heads has a distinct safari flavor. Sans-serif and bold in outline, it makes the menu feel adventurous. This sentiment is further reinforced by the copywriting.

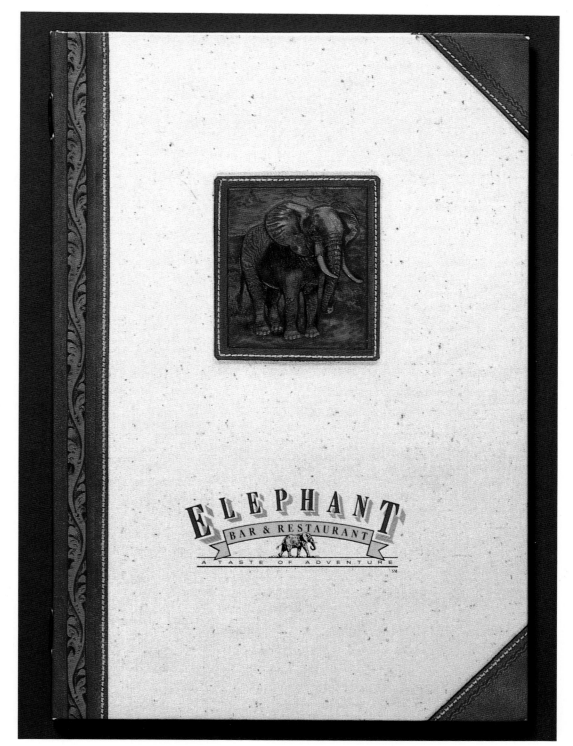

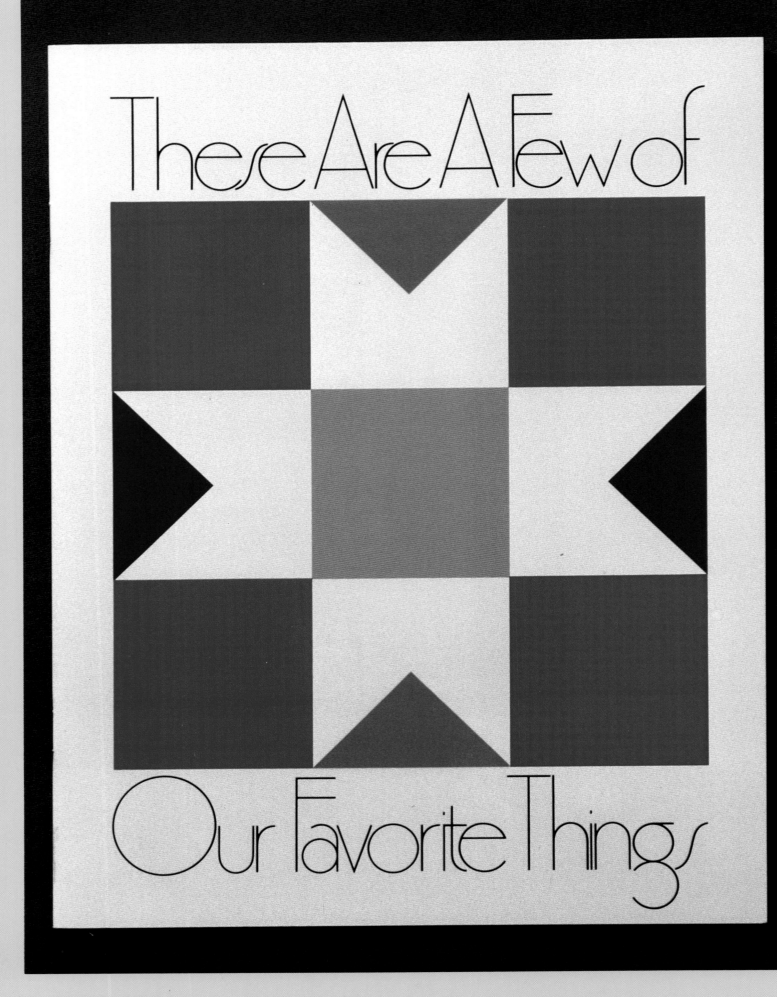

# These Are A Few of Our Favorite Things

**Designer:** *Nut Tree Design*

**Restaurant:** *These Are A Few of Our Favorite Things*
*Nut Tree Restaurant*
*Nut Tree, CA*

Believe it or not, this is a holiday menu, designed for use during the month of December. Using the stylized image of a quilt pattern, the restaurant suggests home and family without getting too specific about *which* holiday it had in mind.

The brilliant squares and triangles of the front cover are repeated in various combinations throughout the interior of the menu. Big, clear type is used for the menu listings. Descriptive copywriting, imprinted in a smaller size of the same clear typeface, heads each menu division.

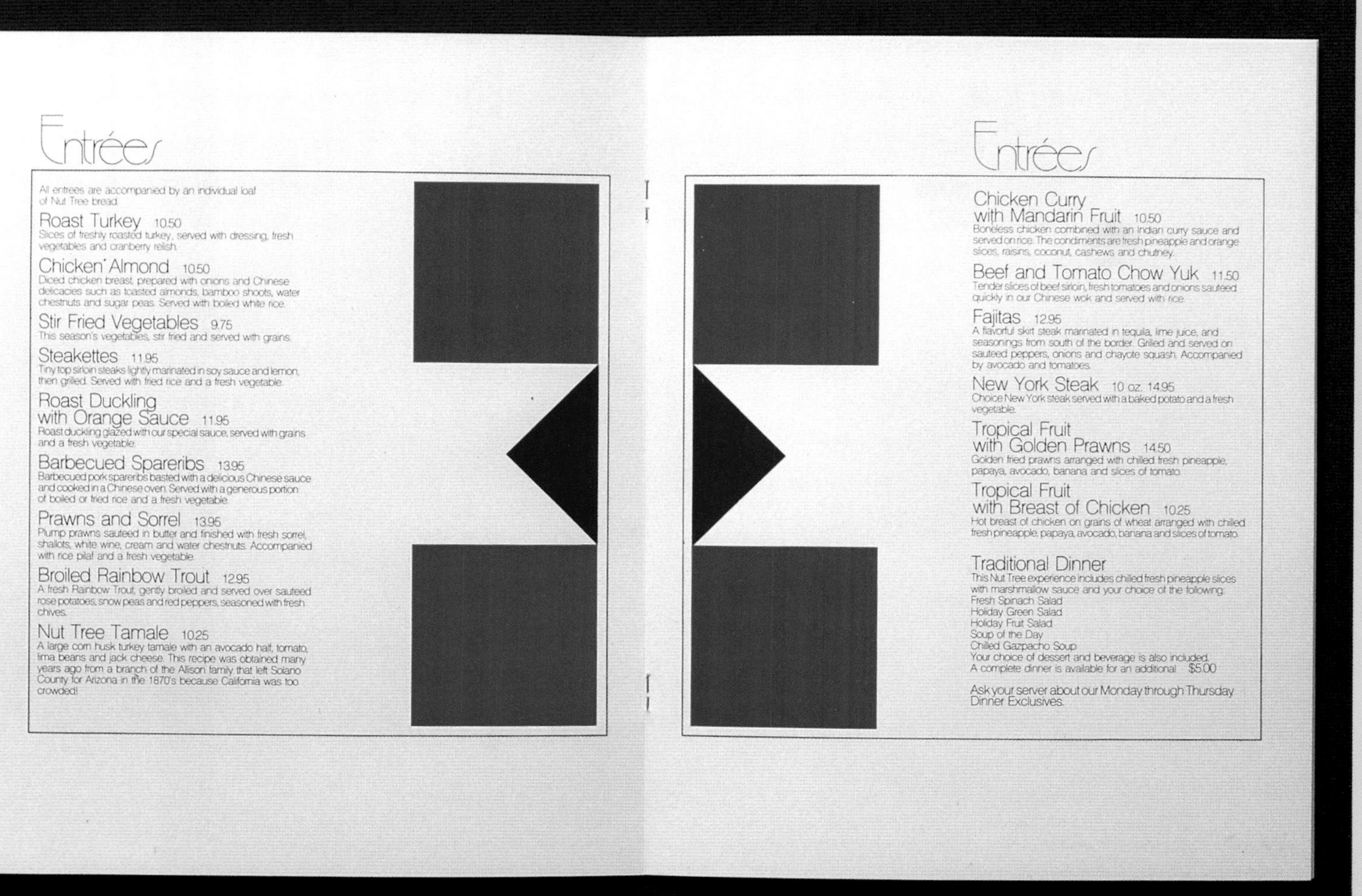

Entrées

All entrees are accompanied by an individual loaf of Nut Tree bread.

Roast Turkey 10.50
Slices of freshly roasted turkey, served with dressing, fresh vegetables and cranberry relish.

Chicken Almond 10.50
Diced chicken breast, prepared with onions and Chinese delicacies such as toasted almonds, bamboo shoots, water chestnuts and sugar peas. Served with boiled white rice.

Stir Fried Vegetables 9.75
This season's vegetables, stir fried and served with grains.

Steakettes 11.95
Tiny top sirloin steaks lightly marinated in soy sauce and lemon, then grilled. Served with fried rice and a fresh vegetable.

Roast Duckling with Orange Sauce 11.95
Roast duckling glazed with our special sauce, served with grains and a fresh vegetable.

Barbecued Spareribs 13.95
Barbecued pork spareribs basted with a delicious Chinese sauce and cooked in a Chinese oven. Served with a generous portion of boiled or fried rice and a fresh vegetable.

Prawns and Sorrel 13.95
Plump prawns sauteed in butter and finished with fresh sorrel, shallots, white wine, cream and water chestnuts. Accompanied with rice pilaf and a fresh vegetable.

Broiled Rainbow Trout 12.95
A fresh Rainbow Trout, gently broiled and served over sauteed rose potatoes, snow peas and red peppers, seasoned with fresh chives.

Nut Tree Tamale 10.25
A large corn husk turkey tamale with an avocado half, tomato, lima beans and jack cheese. This recipe was obtained many years ago from a branch of the Allison family that left Solano County for Arizona in the 1870's because California was too crowded!

Entrées

Chicken Curry with Mandarin Fruit 10.50
Boneless chicken combined with an Indian curry sauce and served on rice. The condiments are fresh pineapple and orange slices, raisins, coconut, cashews and chutney.

Beef and Tomato Chow Yuk 11.50
Tender slices of beef sirloin, fresh tomatoes and onions sauteed quickly in our Chinese wok and served with rice.

Fajitas 12.95
A flavorful skirt steak marinated in tequila, lime juice, and seasonings from south of the border. Grilled and served on sauteed peppers, onions and chayote squash. Accompanied by avocado and tomatoes.

New York Steak 10 oz. 14.95
Choice New York steak served with a baked potato and a fresh vegetable.

Tropical Fruit with Golden Prawns 14.50
Golden fried prawns arranged with chilled fresh pineapple, papaya, avocado, banana and slices of tomato.

Tropical Fruit with Breast of Chicken 10.25
Hot breast of chicken on grains of wheat arranged with chilled fresh pineapple, papaya, avocado, banana and slices of tomato.

Traditional Dinner
This Nut Tree experience includes chilled fresh pineapple slices with marshmallow sauce and your choice of the following:
Fresh Spinach Salad
Holiday Green Salad
Holiday Fruit Salad
Soup of the Day
Chilled Gazpacho Soup
Your choice of dessert and beverage is also included.
A complete dinner is available for an additional $5.00

Ask your server about our Monday through Thursday Dinner Exclusives.

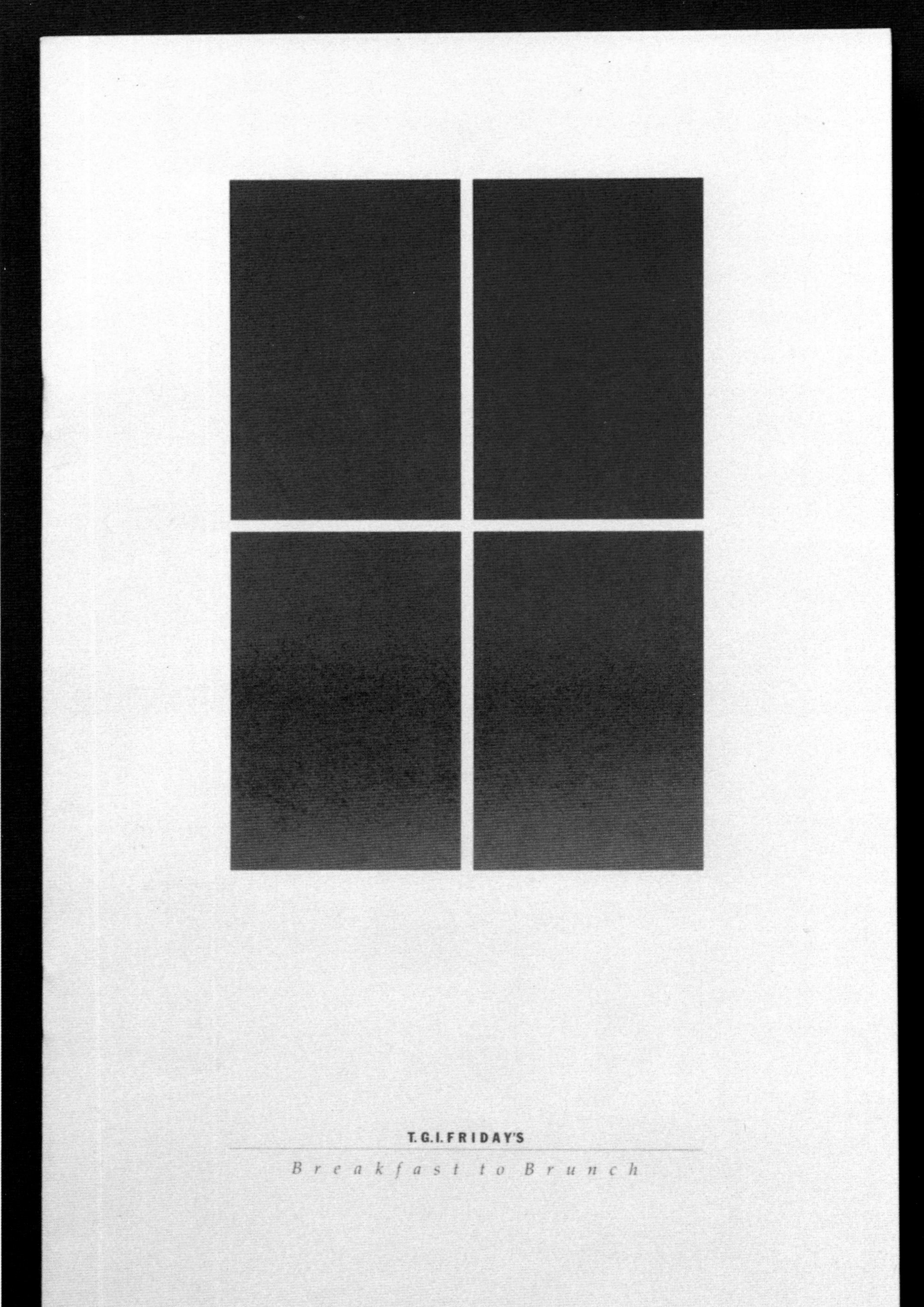
T.G.I.FRIDAY'S
Breakfast to Brunch

B r e a k f a s t

**BREAKFAST EYE OPENERS**

JUICES *Orange and grapefruit, both freshly-squeezed, and apple, cranberry, grape, papaya, pineapple, tomato and V-8. Small $.75 Large $.95*

FRESH BREWED "HILLS BROS" COFFEE *Regular and Decaffeinated. $.80*

HOT TEA *Orange Spice or English Breakfast. $.90*

MILK *White or Chocolate. Small $.75 Large $.95*

HOT CHOCOLATE *$.95*

FRIDAY'S SMOOTHIES™ *Healthful concoctions of juices, fruits, yogurt and, in some cases, ice cream or orange sherbet.*

FRIDAY'S FLINGS™ *Refreshing combinations of fruit juices and sparkling waters.*

**BREAKFAST FRUITS AND CEREALS**

FRIDAY'S BREAKFAST PARFAIT *A healthful breakfast salad prepared with layers of strawberries, peaches, blueberries, yogurt and granola. $3.50*

BREAKFAST FRUIT PLATE *Large cuts of fresh melon, pineapple, strawberries, bananas and grapes. $3.50*

CEREAL AND MILK *Choice of Corn Flakes, Rice Krispies, Raisin Bran, Frosted Flakes or Granola; served with a pitcher of milk. $1.50 With fresh strawberries and bananas. $1.95*

**BREAKFAST PLATES**

NUMBER ONE *Three eggs with choice of country ham, bacon or link sausage. Served with Friday's Hash Browns and choice of toast, English muffin or bagel. $4.45*

NUMBER TWO *Three eggs and Friday's Hash Browns, served with choice of toast, English muffin or bagel. $2.95*

NUMBER THREE *One egg with choice of country ham, bacon or link sausage. Served with Friday's Hash Browns and choice of toast, English muffin or bagel. $3.95*

NUMBER FOUR *Choice of three-egg omelette served with Friday's Hash Browns with toast, English muffin or bagel. Cheddar Cheese $3.95 Bacon and Cheddar Cheese $4.45 Ham and Cheese $4.45 Western Style $4.45 Ham, Cheese and Onion $4.45*

NUMBER FIVE *Three light and fluffy buttermilk pancakes served with butter and warm syrup. $2.75 Short Stack $2.50*

NUMBER SIX *Our Belgian-style granola waffle served with butter and warm syrup. $2.95*

NUMBER SEVEN *Baguette French Toast – slices of French baguette bread, grilled with egg custard batter and served with butter, warm syrup and fresh fruit salad. $3.25*

NUMBER EIGHT *Eggs Benedict – poached or scrambled eggs on toasted English muffin halves with Canadian bacon and hollandaise sauce. Served with Friday's Hash Browns and fresh fruit salad. $6.75*

**BREAKFAST SPECIALTIES**

LOX AND BAGEL *Slices of smoked Nova salmon lox served with sliced tomato, red onion, black olives, toasted bagel, cream cheese and butter. $5.95*

BREAKFAST NACHOS *Crisp corn tortillas, topped with layers of refried beans, scrambled eggs with ham, onions and green chilies, colby and jack cheeses and slices of jalapeño. $3.95*

FRIDAY'S BREAKFAST SANDWICH *Two fried eggs with crisp bacon and melted Swiss cheese on our special, toasted English muffin bun. Served with Friday's Hash Browns and fresh fruit salad. $4.45*
*IN A HURRY?... LET US MAKE YOU ONE TO GO*

*HEARTY BREAKFASTS Served with Friday's Hash Browns, country gravy, fresh fruit salad and choice of toast, English muffin or bagel.*

- STEAK AND EGGS *Three eggs, any style, with charbroiled New York strip steak. $7.95*
- CHICKEN-FRIED STEAK AND EGGS *Three eggs, any style, served with our golden chicken-fried steak. $5.95*
- WHITEFISH AND EGGS *Three eggs, any style, with a crisply-fried filet of whitefish. $6.95*

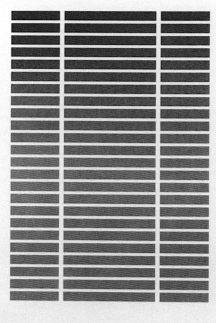

**Designer:** *Robin Ayers*
*Richards, Brock, Miller, Mitchell & Associates*
**Restaurant:** *"Breakfast to Lunch"*
*TGI Friday's Inc.*
*Addison, TX*

This menu uses the image of a light-filled window to take the diner from dawn to noon. Beginning with a deep indigo sky, barely tinted with rose at the horizon, the light gradually changes to deeper rose, then gold shot with rose and, finally, full sun to suggest the passage of time. To prevent the image from being too obvious, the "window treatments" vary from one panel to the next.

The copywriting subtly supports this theme, as do the menu selections. The selections listed for the "breakfast" section of the menu are fairly traditional. The first listing under "brunch" is a wide selection of fancy drinks, with the names imprinted in orange, descriptions in black type, for graeter appeal.

Designer: *Lanny Sommese*
*Lanny Sommese Design*

Restaurant: *Tussey Mountain Inn*
*Dante's Restaurants, Inc.*
*State College, PA*

This ski lodge, nestled in a forested area at the base of a slope, wanted a simple graphic that would reflect its surroundings. The lodge already possessed a stuffed deer head and many of the restaurant's windows look out into clearings in the forest which are frequented by deer.

The designer made the antlered deer head the focal point of the logo but showed the live deer on the menu cover. Because the light in a forest has a green tinge, he chose to depict them in green, set against a slightly lighter screen of the same color. Even holding the menu in your hands, you must look closely to see them, just as you would need to look closely to see them in their natural surroundings.

The menu interior is set against a very light screen of the same green to promote legibility.

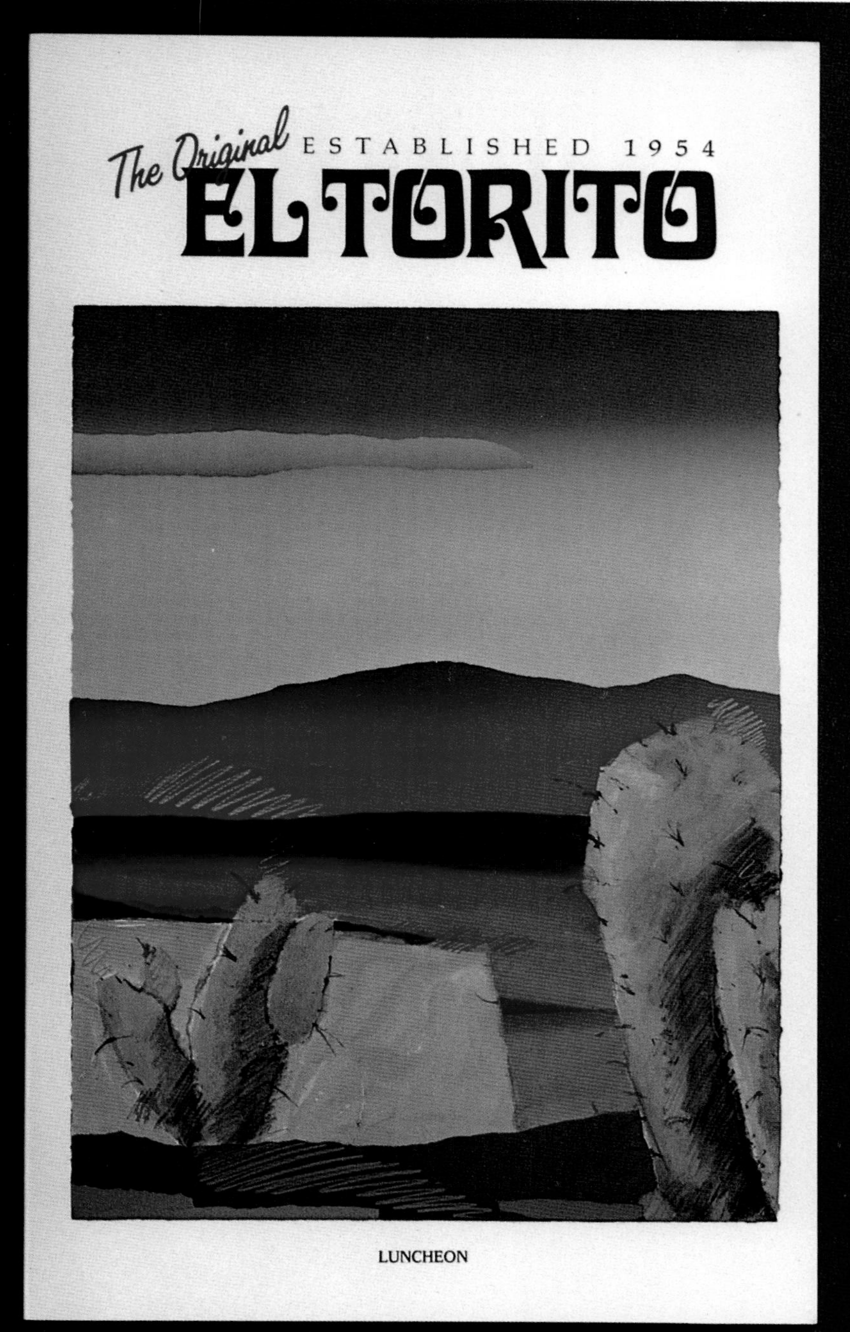


Designer: *Diane Richards & Claude Prettyman*
*El Torito Restaurants, Inc.*
Restaurant: *El Torito Restaurants*
*Irvine, CA*

**1987 N.R.A. GREAT MENUS CONTEST WINNER: THIRD PLACE, CHECKS AVERAGE UNDER $5**

Southwestern images and colors highlight this laminated luncheon menu. The interior features torn paper "mountain ranges" along the top and bottom edges.

The copywriting supports the restaurant's Mexican theme with lots of adjectives and thorough descriptions. The type has been set in blocks with price location varying sufficiently to merchandise the food offered, rather than the prices themselves.

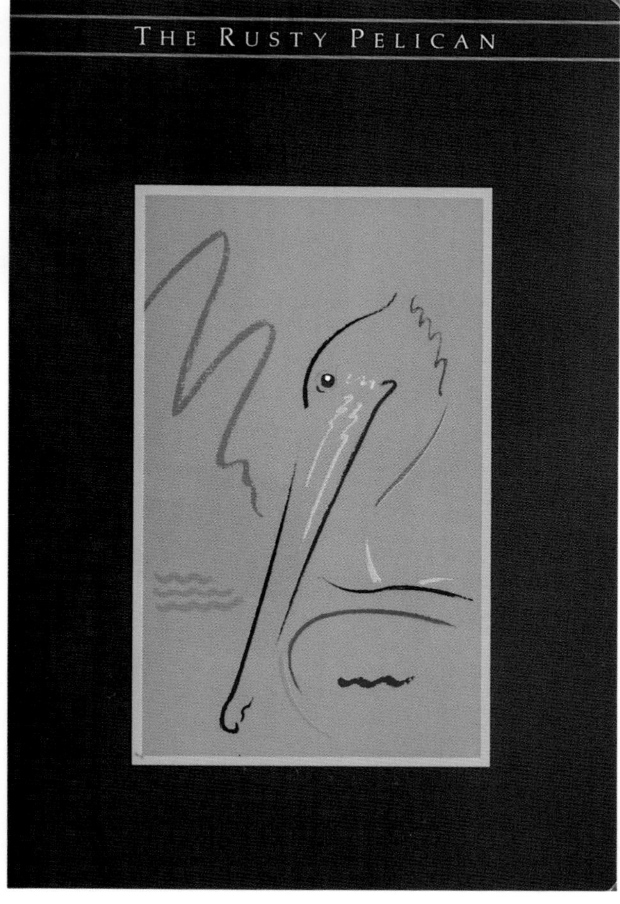


Restaurant: *Rusty Pelican Restaurant*
*Irvine, CA*

The pelican has appeared in various guises on most of the restaurant's menus and collaterals. Here, it is set against an aqua background, with a wave or two suggested on the left side of the illustrations. The wave is repeated both on the interior of the cover, which is laminated, and on the menu insert, which features the day's fresh catch.

Using the wave on the insert as well as on the permanent part of the menu pulls the piece together, giving it a finished look.

In micetype at the bottom of the inside cover, coding identifies which version of the menu this is.

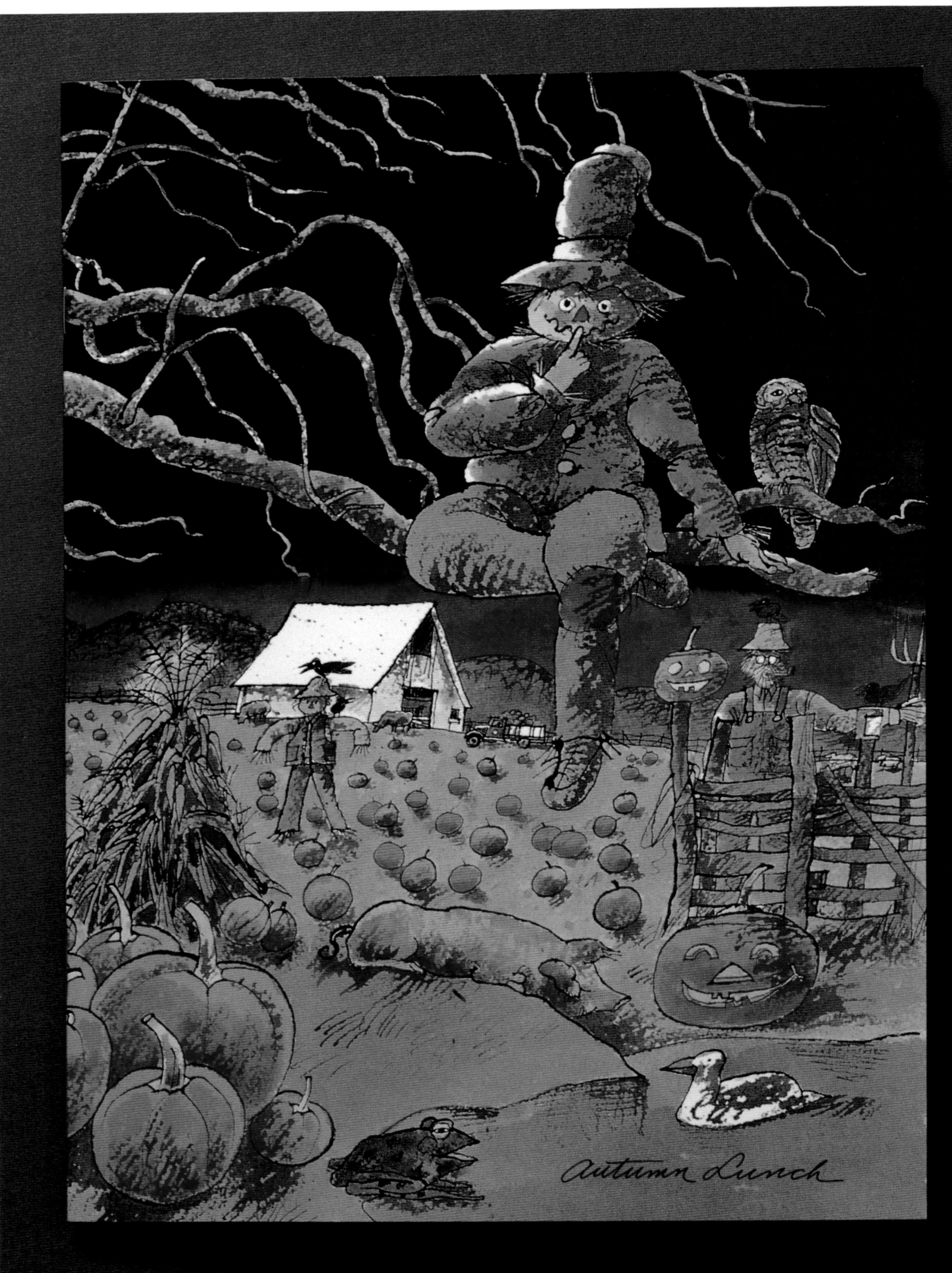
Autumn Lunch

Designer: *Earl Mollander*
*Nut Tree Design*
Restaurant: *Autumn Lunch*
*Nut Tree Restaurant*
*Nut Tree, CA*

Timed to coincide with the restaurant's annual "Great Scarecrow Contest," the playful cover illustration establishes the theme. Inside cover copy explains the origins of the contest and the rules. The menu copy, in two colors on Gainsborough, features seasonal fruits and vegetables as well as the favorite foods on which this restaurant built its reputation.

Both a beer list and a wine list are contained in the saddle-stitched menu. The wine list includes wines bottled for the Nut Tree under its own label. Having an extensive beer list makes good marketing sense as anyone who has crossed the Sacramento Valley in summer or early autumn can tell you.

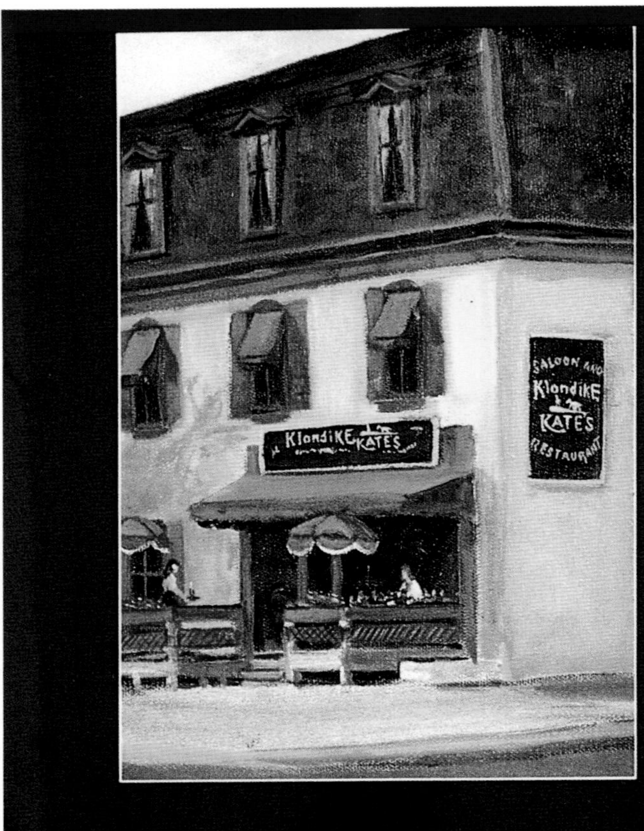


WELCOME

TO

KLONDIKE

KATE

COUNTRY

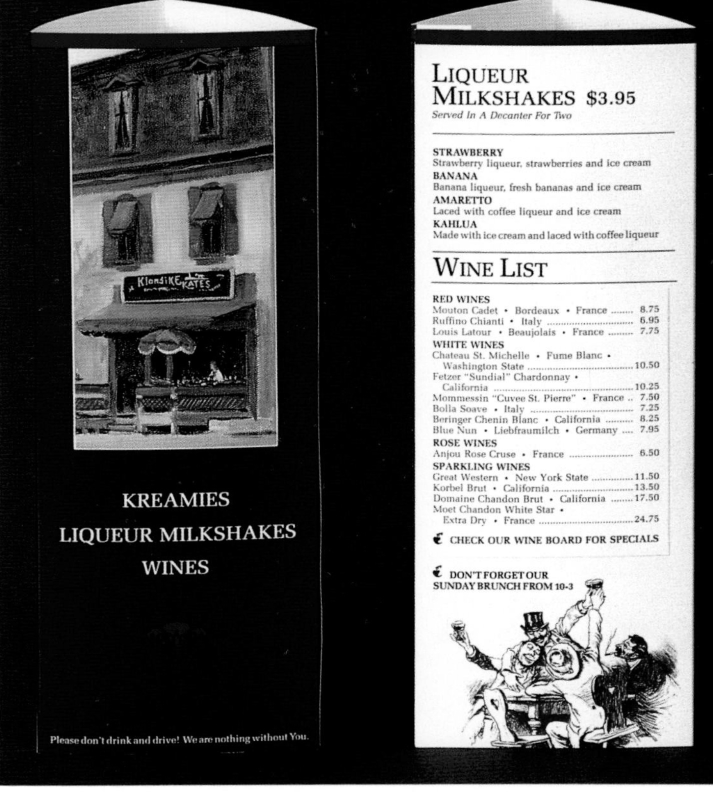


KREAMIES

LIQUEUR MILKSHAKES

WINES

Please don't drink and drive! We are nothing without You.

LIQUEUR MILKSHAKES $3.95

*Served In A Decanter For Two*

**STRAWBERRY**
Strawberry liqueur, strawberries and ice cream

**BANANA**
Banana liqueur, fresh bananas and ice cream

**AMARETTO**
Laced with coffee liqueur and ice cream

**KAHLUA**
Made with ice cream and laced with coffee liqueur

WINE LIST

**RED WINES**
Mouton Cadet • Bordeaux • France ........ 8.75
Ruffino Chianti • Italy ........ 6.95
Louis Latour • Beaujolais • France ........ 7.75

**WHITE WINES**
Chateau St. Michelle • Fume Blanc • Washington State ........ 10.50
Fetzer "Sundial" Chardonnay • California ........ 10.25
Mommessin "Cuvee St. Pierre" • France .. 7.50
Bolla Soave • Italy ........ 7.25
Beringer Chenin Blanc • California ........ 8.25
Blue Nun • Liebfraumilch • Germany .... 7.95

**ROSE WINES**
Anjou Rose Cruse • France ........ 6.50

**SPARKLING WINES**
Great Western • New York State ........ 11.50
Korbel Brut • California ........ 13.50
Domaine Chandon Brut • California ........ 17.50
Moet Chandon White Star • Extra Dry • France ........ 24.75

**CHECK OUR WINE BOARD FOR SPECIALS**

**DON'T FORGET OUR SUNDAY BRUNCH FROM 10-3**

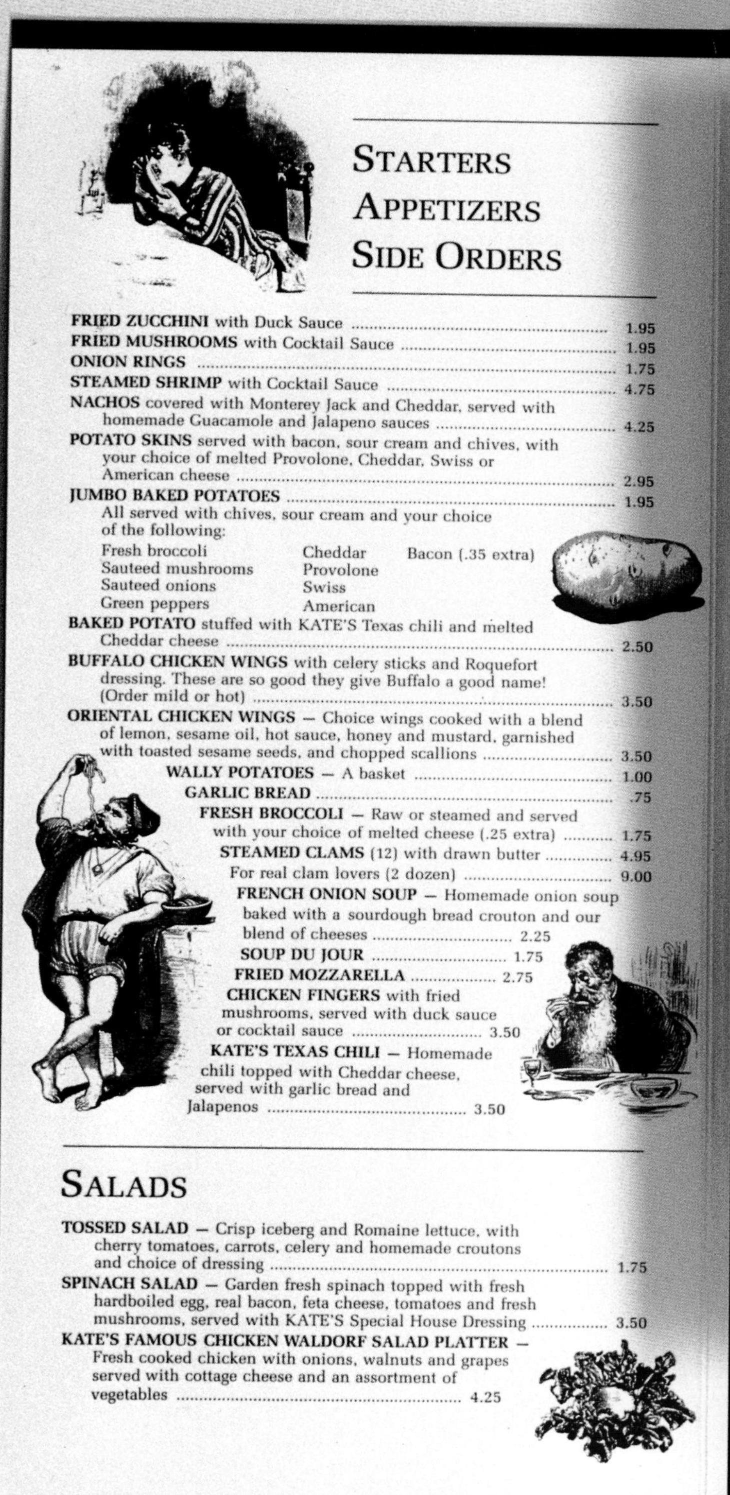

STARTERS
APPETIZERS
SIDE ORDERS

**FRIED ZUCCHINI** with Duck Sauce .......... 1.95
**FRIED MUSHROOMS** with Cocktail Sauce .......... 1.95
**ONION RINGS** .......... 1.75
**STEAMED SHRIMP** with Cocktail Sauce .......... 4.75
**NACHOS** covered with Monterey Jack and Cheddar, served with homemade Guacamole and Jalapeno sauces .......... 4.25
**POTATO SKINS** served with bacon, sour cream and chives, with your choice of melted Provolone, Cheddar, Swiss or American cheese .......... 2.95
**JUMBO BAKED POTATOES** .......... 1.95
All served with chives, sour cream and your choice of the following:
Fresh broccoli, Sauteed mushrooms, Sauteed onions, Green peppers, Cheddar, Provolone, Swiss, American, Bacon (.35 extra)
**BAKED POTATO** stuffed with KATE'S Texas chili and melted Cheddar cheese .......... 2.50
**BUFFALO CHICKEN WINGS** with celery sticks and Roquefort dressing. These are so good they give Buffalo a good name! (Order mild or hot) .......... 3.50
**ORIENTAL CHICKEN WINGS** — Choice wings cooked with a blend of lemon, sesame oil, hot sauce, honey and mustard, garnished with toasted sesame seeds, and chopped scallions .......... 3.50
**WALLY POTATOES** — A basket .......... 1.00
**GARLIC BREAD** .......... .75
**FRESH BROCCOLI** — Raw or steamed and served with your choice of melted cheese (.25 extra) .......... 1.75
**STEAMED CLAMS** (12) with drawn butter .......... 4.95
For real clam lovers (2 dozen) .......... 9.00
**FRENCH ONION SOUP** — Homemade onion soup baked with a sourdough bread crouton and our blend of cheeses .......... 2.25
**SOUP DU JOUR** .......... 1.75
**FRIED MOZZARELLA** .......... 2.75
**CHICKEN FINGERS** with fried mushrooms, served with duck sauce or cocktail sauce .......... 3.50
**KATE'S TEXAS CHILI** — Homemade chili topped with Cheddar cheese, served with garlic bread and Jalapenos .......... 3.50

SALADS

**TOSSED SALAD** — Crisp iceberg and Romaine lettuce, with cherry tomatoes, carrots, celery and homemade croutons and choice of dressing .......... 1.75
**SPINACH SALAD** — Garden fresh spinach topped with fresh hardboiled egg, real bacon, feta cheese, tomatoes and fresh mushrooms, served with KATE'S Special House Dressing .......... 3.50
**KATE'S FAMOUS CHICKEN WALDORF SALAD PLATTER** — Fresh cooked chicken with onions, walnuts and grapes served with cottage cheese and an assortment of vegetables .......... 4.25

THE
HISTORY OF
KLONDIKE KATE'S

Klondike Kate's is one of the oldest business locations on Newark's Main Street. For more than 242 years, it's been furnishing entertainment in a variety of ways.

The establishment was called "Three Hearts Tavern" on a map from 1757. In 1797 it became "Hossinger's Tavern." A map was published in 1860 which cites B. F. Herman as the proprieter of the "Newark Hotel." In 1880 the hotel became the "Exchange Building" and had shops, office space and apartments. Around the turn of the century, it was used as a furniture store. Everett C. Johnson took this over to begin publication of the "Newark Post." From 1905 to 1915 it was used as a courtroom and a jail cell in the basement which still exists today. Thus, the locattion came to be known as "Squire Lovett's Courthouse and Jail." Some people recall when it was used as Newark's roller skating rink.

In the twenties, the building became identified with the "Horseless Carriage." Joseph Brown opened a replacement parts business in 1929 and sold the property in 1977. In March of 1981, Davis Sezna became the new owner and remodeled it extensively. The lights are from the original Wilmington train station. The door behind the bar was one of the original doors from the Gold Ballroom in the Hotel Du Pont. In 1983 the upstairs was remodeled as a banquet facility which holds its own collection of historical pieces. The banquet bar is from a hotel in New York around the turn of the century.

And thanks to you, the history continues!

Designer: *Tony Ross*
*Ross Design*
Restaurant: *Klondike Kate's*
*Newark, DE*

Klondike Kate's is located in an eighteenth century building in a college town. The theme of the restaurant is derived from an Alaska-based madam, who also ran a bar and restaurant in Dawson City, Alaska during the gold rush of the late nineteenth century. The colorful history of the building is explained in detail on the first unfold of the laminated menu.

The menu's cover features a four-color illustration of the building itself, set against the burgundy and blue used as accents to compliment the brass and natural wood featured in the restaurant itself.

Coordinated table tents feature the same type style as the main menu and an affixed sticker listing the wines available. The sticker, together with a "wine specials" board permits the restaurant to offer its patrons a broad variety of wines without investing too heavily in any one varietal.

THE ROSE ROOM

**Designer:** *Kelly Brandon*
*TRA Graphic Design*
**Restaurant:** *The Rose Room*
*Sheraton Tacoma Hotel*
*Tacoma, WA*

The rose paintings featured in the restaurant and the sketch for the menu, by artist David Haidle, inspired the name of the room. Reproduced in a sepia screen on vellum, the rose has a softness that blends beautifully with the beige menu cover, die cut to reveal the rose beneath. The name of the restaurant, in its signature logotype, is blind-embossed below the die cut.

The two-color menu inserts are saddle-stitched into the covers and feature not only the rose but also the calligraphic patterns established in the logotype. The understated elegance of the room is complimented by the use of real roses in the decor.

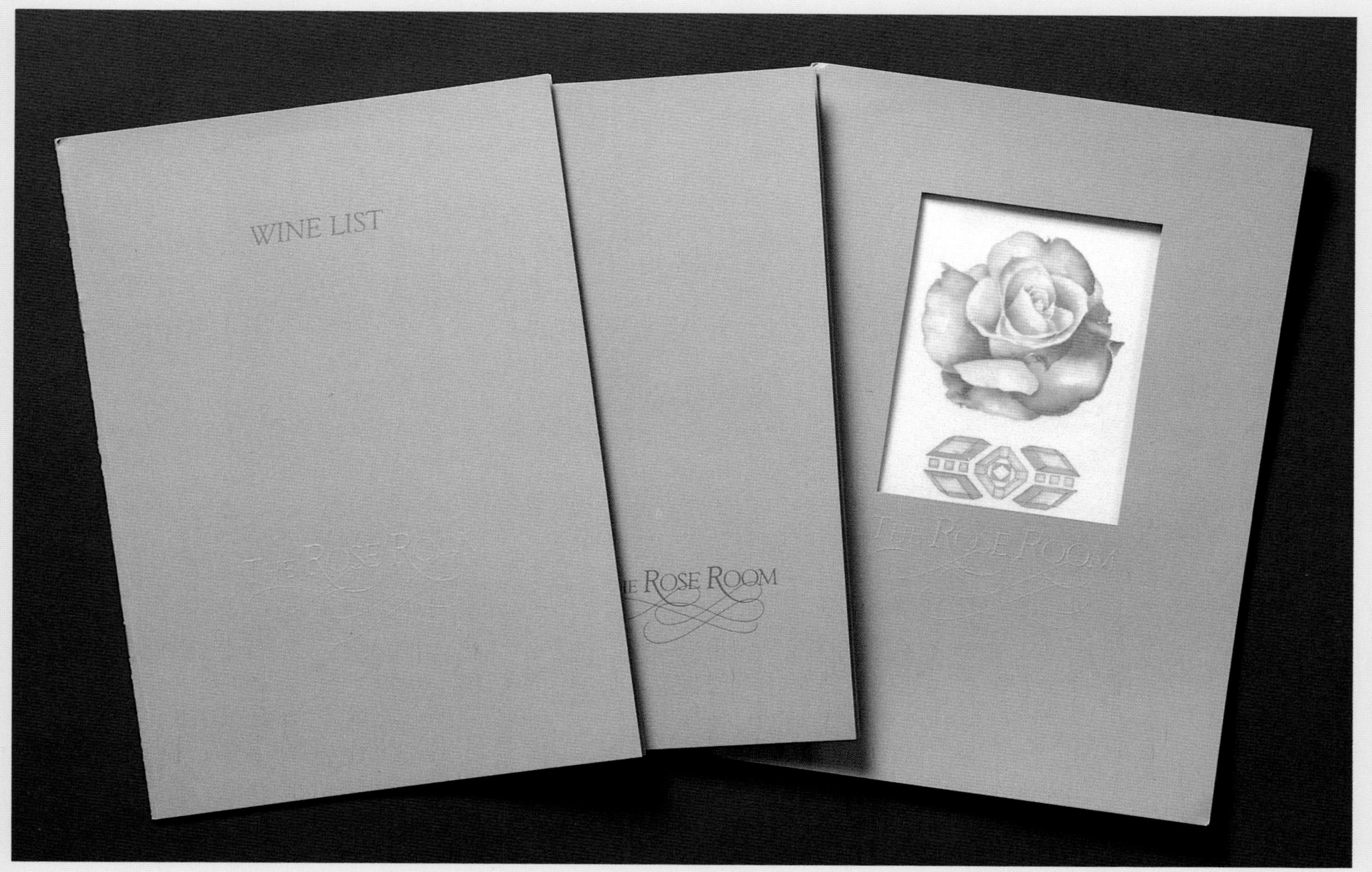

| | |
|---|---|
| Designer: | *Michael W. Green* |
| | *Nut Tree Design* |
| Restaurant: | *Winter Enchantment at Nut Tree* |
| | *Nut Tree Restaurant* |
| | *Nut Tree, CA* |

**1987 N.R.A. GREAT MENUS CONTEST WINNER: THIRD PLACE, DESIGN**

The Nut Tree has been an oasis along what is now U.S. Interstate 80 for generations of Californians en route from San Francisco to Lake Tahoe and other vacation destinations in the Sierra Nevada Mountains. Set amid groves of the walnut trees which gave the restaurant its name and one of its specialties — nut bread — the restaurant offers milkshakes and beer to cool the throat in summer, hearty soups and hot entrees to ward off winter's chill.

This beautiful menu shows the tracery of the nut tree's leafless branches embossed on a matte film coated cover. The cover is a duplex stock, with a light sand on the interior side. The same sand-colored paper is used for the two-color insert pages. More screened images of the trees grace each two-page spread. Big, readable type set in blocks further contributes to the lovely and functional design.

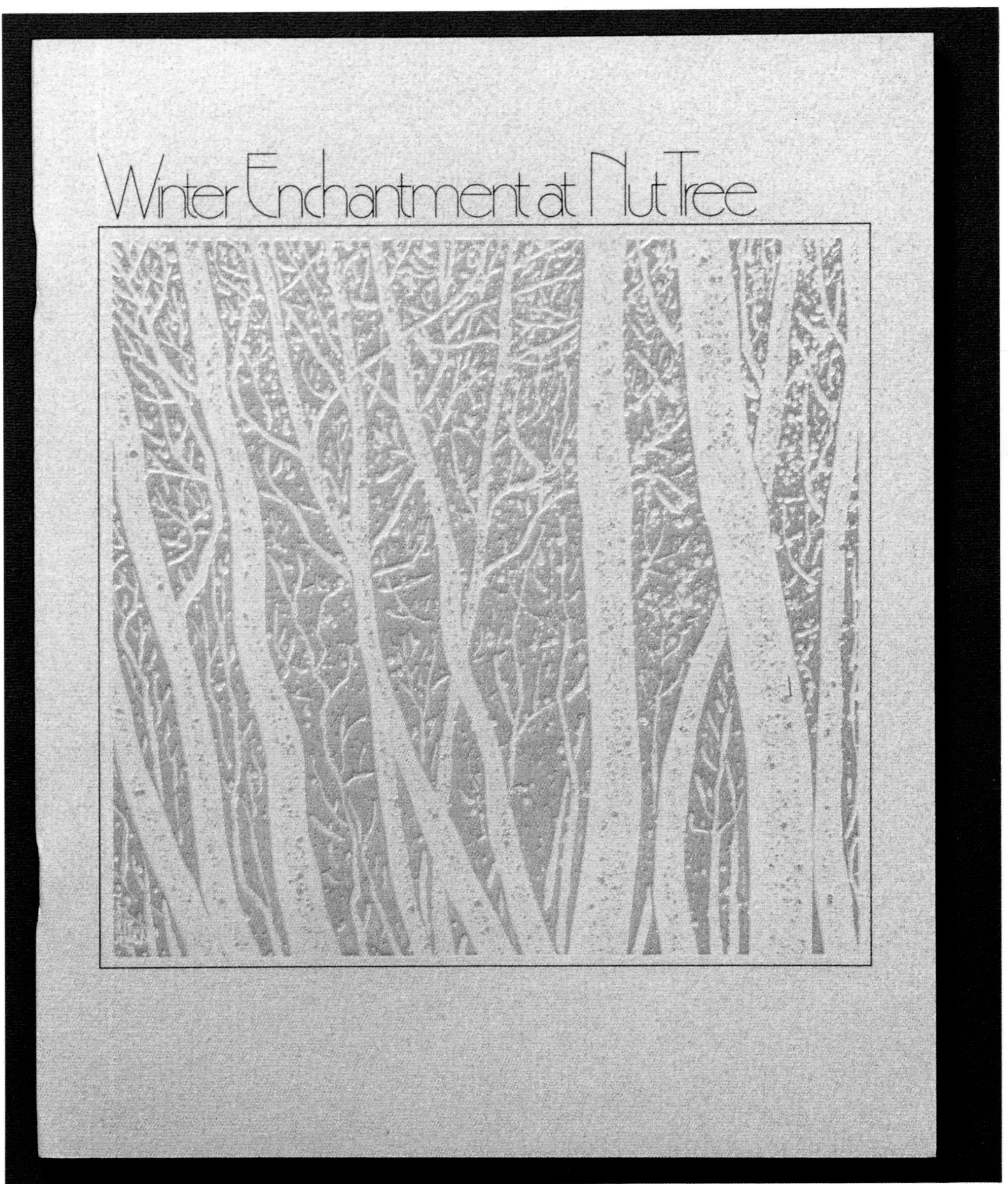

## Desserts

**Fresh Apple Pie** 3.25
Fresh apples in a flaky pastry crust, served with a wedge of sharp cheddar cheese or a mound of vanilla ice cream.

**Chocolate Truffle Torte** 4.75
A sinfully delicious chocolate cake with a creamy truffle center, subtly laced with Grand Marnier and generously topped with whipped cream.

**Coconut Joy** 3.50
A large, warm coconut macaroon, topped with vanilla ice cream and warm fudge sauce.

**Cherry-Berry Deep Dish Pie** 3.75
A delicious combination of cherries and blueberries, served warm with a flaky pastry and topped with a generous scoop of vanilla ice cream.

**Flan** 2.50
A delightfully smooth custard with a caramel glaze.

**Angel Cheesecake** 3.50
A light, deliciously creamy cheesecake.

**Chess Pie** 2.75
A Nut Tree favorite for nearly 50 years. A deliciously rich pie with California walnuts and raisins in a butterscotch filling, slowly baked to a golden brown.

**Banana Praline Sundae** 3.50
A pitcher of diced bananas in a hot praline sauce, served with a bowl of pecan-topped ice cream.

**Rocky Road Sundae** 3.25
Heated chocolate sauce with marshmallows and almonds, served over a scoop of ice cream.

**Ice Cream or Sherbet** 2.50

## Winter 1987

## Winter Lunch at Nut Tree

## Appetizers

Barbecued Spareribs 5.25
Chilled Pineapple Slices with Marshmallow Sauce 2.75
Mini Tamales (enough for two) 4.50
Chicken Flautas (enough for two) 5.25
Oriental Sampler (enough for two) 6.25

**Party Favorites**
A few suggestions to enhance this special occasion. Enough for 4 to 6 persons.

Barbecued Spareribs 8.95
Chilled Hawaiian Pineapple in the Shell 6.50
Seasonal Fresh Fruit Platter 9.50

6% sales tax will be added to the price of all food and beverages served. We welcome MasterCard, Visa and American Express cards.
Nut Tree is open every day of the year except Christmas from 7am to 9pm. For reservations and celebrations, please call 707/448 1818.

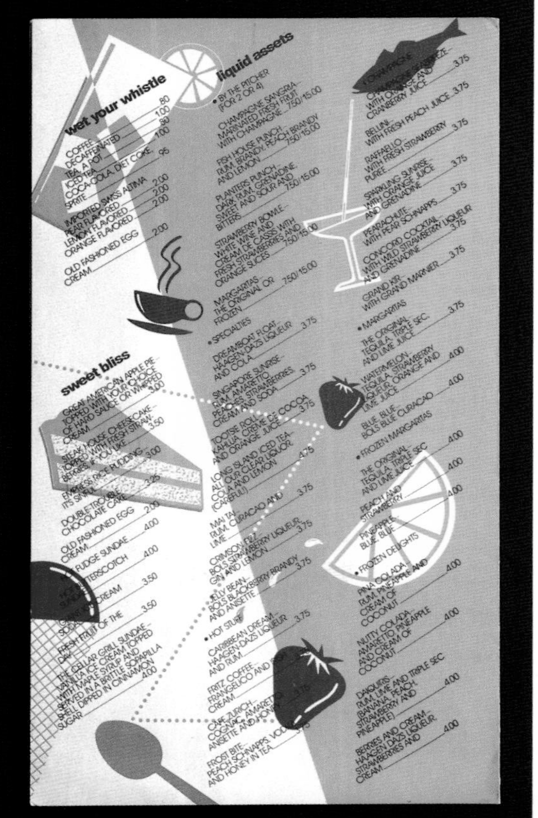


| | |
|---|---|
| Designer: | *David Antonuccio*<br>*Macy's Herald Square* |
| Restaurant: | *Cellar Grill, Macy's Herald Square*<br>*New York, NY* |

This colorful and eclectic menu reflects the atmosphere of the restaurant. Designed as a haven for shoppers in the midst of a busy day, the menu offers a selection of both hot and cold light meals, as well as ice cream-based and alcoholic beverages.

The menu sections use creative copywriting as a selling device. For example, "cool, calm and collected" is the head for composed and tossed salads; "egg it on" perfectly describes the egg-based dishes. A pot pourri of visual images — food, serving pieces and even a shark — enliven the background of the menu.

The graphic mood of the piece is borne out in the signage, an associated t-shirt and the pictures on the walls of the restaurant. The different graphic elements combine to make a coherent graphic whole.

Designer: *Paula Rees*
*Rees Thompson Designers*
Restaurant: *Space Needle*
*Seattle, WA*

Using the familiar image of the Space Needle to highlight the chef's suggestions, this menu is extremely well planned. A clear, legible typeface is set in blocks. Each menu item, set in italic type and separated from the description by a faint peach-colored holding line, is beautifully described. The descriptions themselves are rich in adjectives and thorough. In a nice merchandising touch, each entree has an accompanying suggested wine.

The insert is held into the laminated menu cover with a gold elasticized cord and imprinted on an embossed finish grooved paper. The colors used on the menu were drawn from those in the interior design scheme.

# CHAPTER 5

The elements in a coordinated packaging program can range from two or three menu covers, with perhaps a table tent or wine list, all the way up to gift items. This chapter includes at least one program with over one hundred different applications. Obviously, this scale is inappropriate for most operations. A few extras, such as matchbooks and business cards do, however, pay off as secondary marketing devices.

To understand the value of matches and business cards which use the restaurant's logo and signature colors, it is only necessary to put oneself in the diner's place. If the experience in the restaurant has been pleasant, the diner will take one or both of the items home. The next time a similar occasion arises, a reminder is there, without recourse to either memory or a phone directory.

For restaurants whose main focus is primarily business entertainment, a coordinated guest check is also a good idea. That check will show up at the end of the month when an expense report is prepared as yet another reminder.

As with any other menu application, deciding how many elements to incorporate into a program is a matter of identifying the audience and the applications for which pieces will be used. To a greater extent than perhaps any other instance of menu design, the final decision should be based upon serious discussions between designer and restaurant representative.

# COORDINATED PACKAGING

Designer: *Carol Denison*
*Denison Design Associates*
Restaurant: *John Ash & Co.*
*Santa Rosa, CA*

The unusual topography of Sonoma County, California prompted John Ash to develop seasonal menus to take advantage of the bounty of local vegetables, fruits, seafood and poultry. His restaurant is a reflection of his commitment to his cuisine. The menus had to be an accurate reflection of this vision. They also needed to be flexible to permit weekly changes.

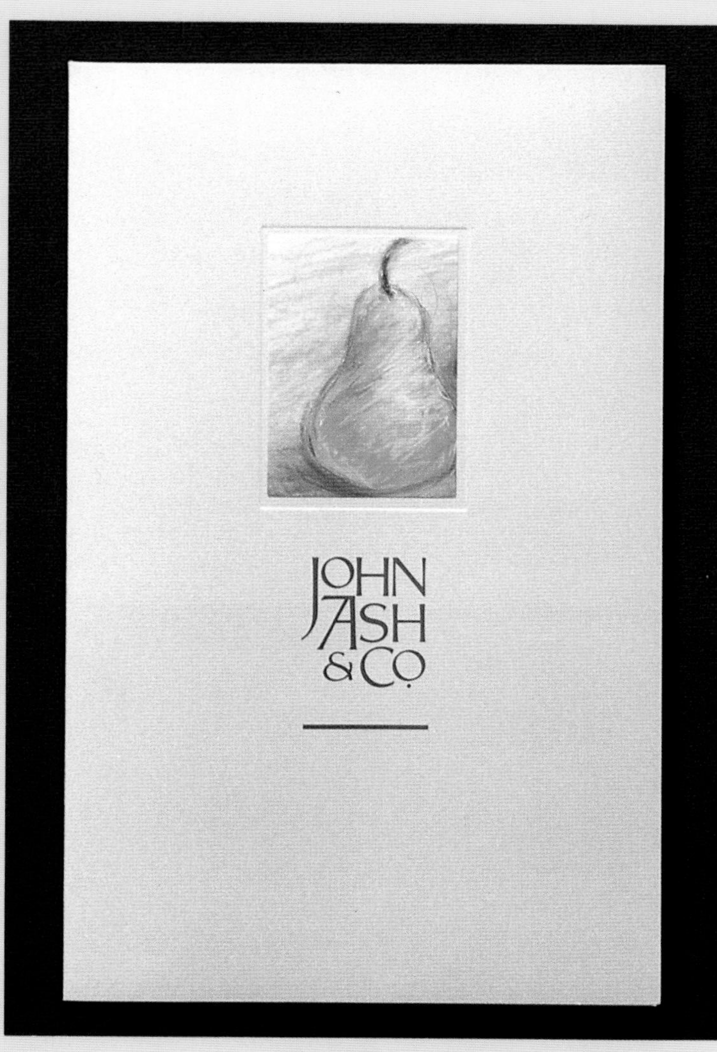


The design began with the logo, which is contemporary without being trendy. Indeed, there is an almost "bookish" feeling. The colors used in both the logo and the menu illustrations are drawn from the restaurant's interior; these were, in turn, drawn from the colors of the surrounding countryside. The menu covers are a simple coated stock.

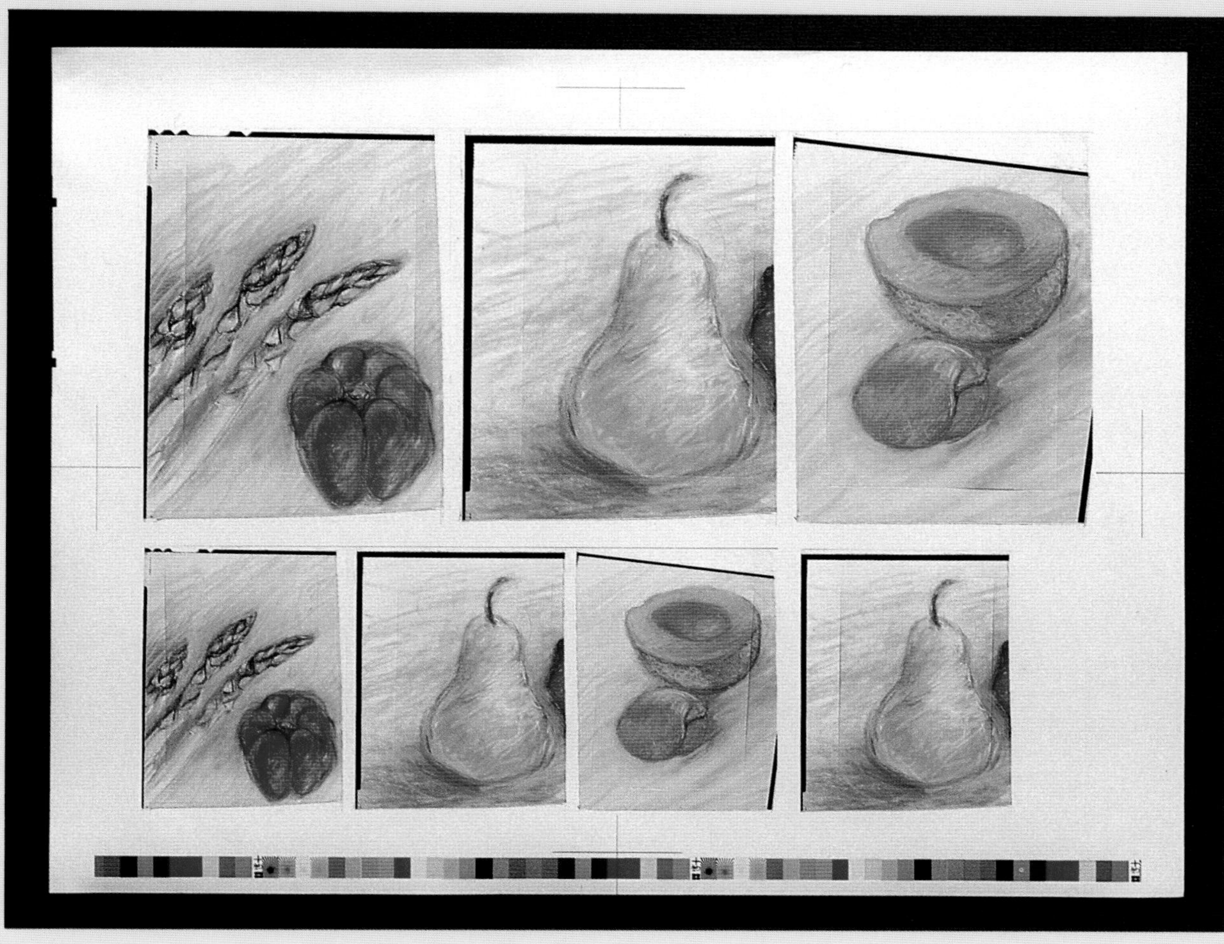

The cover illustrations were achieved through the use of applied full-color stickers. These are printed separately and affixed within the debossed frame as needed. Printing the various designs all at once on adhesive sheets is far less expensive than reprinting the entire menu cover would be.

Menu inserts are held in the covers by means of pre-drilled holes and studs. These are located in a turned-down edge at the top of the cover for a more finished look.

JOHN ASH & CO.
REGIONAL CUISINE IN SONOMA COUNTY
There are few places that manifest the natural abundance of Sonoma County. Diverse microclimates allow practically every type of fruit and vegetable to thrive. Goat cheese, camembert, other cheeses and butter are made from Sonoma's rich milk. Baby lamb, veal, duck, quail and free range chickens are raised on nearby farms and, only twenty-five miles away, the Pacific Ocean is home to every major
"The restaurant has earned a reputation as one of Northern California's finest. It was founded on Ash's sensitivities to ecology, beauty, innovation and seasonality of food products grown in Sonoma County . . ."
Rose Dosti, Los Angeles Times
"John Ash definitely reflects the new restaurant consciousness that seeks out quality local and homegrown products."
Patricia Unterman, S.F. Chronicle

Designer: *Rick Tharp*
*Tharp Did It*
Restaurant: *Brookside Cafe*
*Newark, CA*

The designer has chosen to echo the surrounding foothills in a "torn paper" design for the menu and collateral pieces. The earthy colors he has chosen are appropriate to the arid California climate; for much of the year, the foothills are a soft gold, touched with the reddish hues of the earth.

The torn paper motif appears as a stylized "squiggle" to highlight each section of the main menu. This same squiggle is used on each of the collateral pieces.

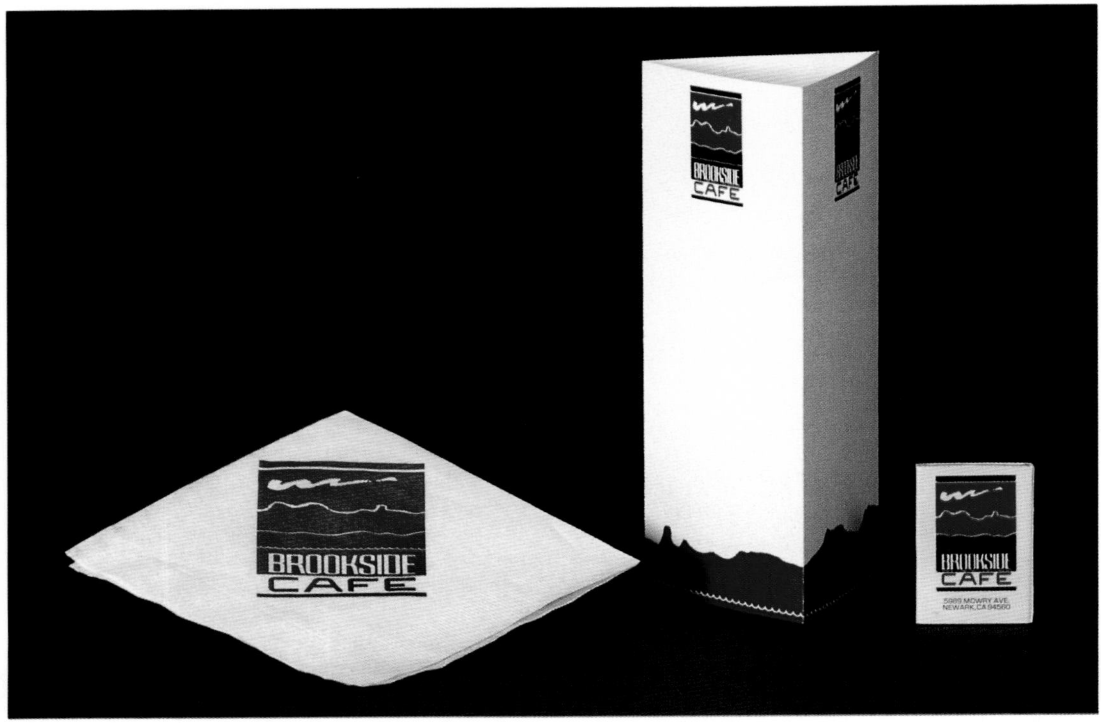

Designer: *Pamela Linsley*
*Quinlan Advertising*
Restaurant: *Left Bank*
*Columbus, IN*

The loose artist's brushstrokes imprinted in a bleed at the left side of the menu are meant to suggest the left bank of Paris. This theme is supported by the colors used, which are drawn from the Impressionist prints hung in the restaurant.

Both the restaurant logo and the corporate logo (not shown) were part of the design project. An existing restaurant and the name were purchased and the designer was retained to create a new identity. The Parisian, arty feeling is suggested in the logo, which is thermographically reproduced on the menu covers. To underline this, a canvas-textured paper was selected for the menus. Only the lounge menu is plastic-coated, a sensible choice as it is subjected to move spillage than either the lunch or dinner menu.

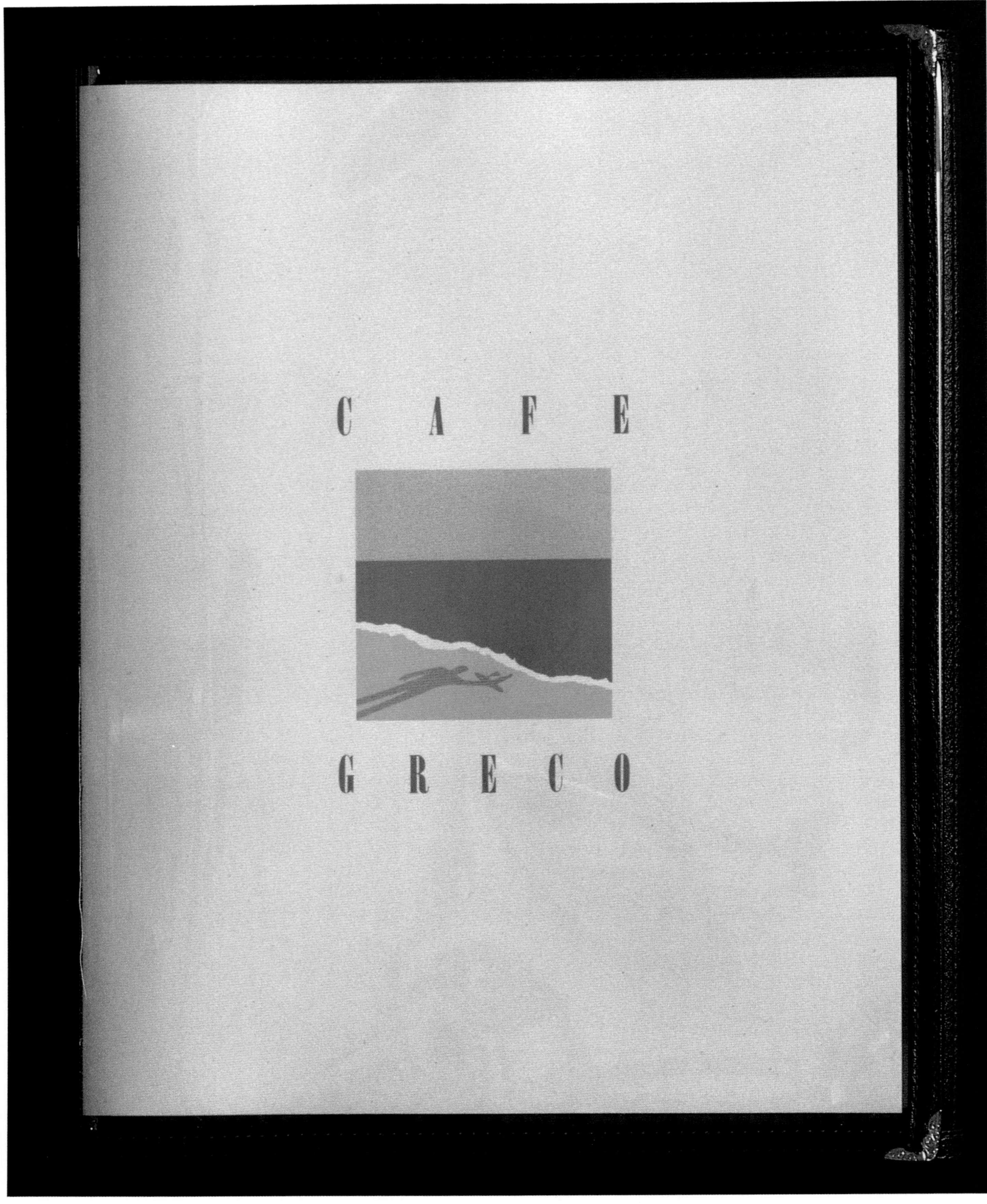


Designer: *Patricia Kovic*
*Dale Glasser Graphics*
Restaurant: *Cafe Greco*
*New York, NY*

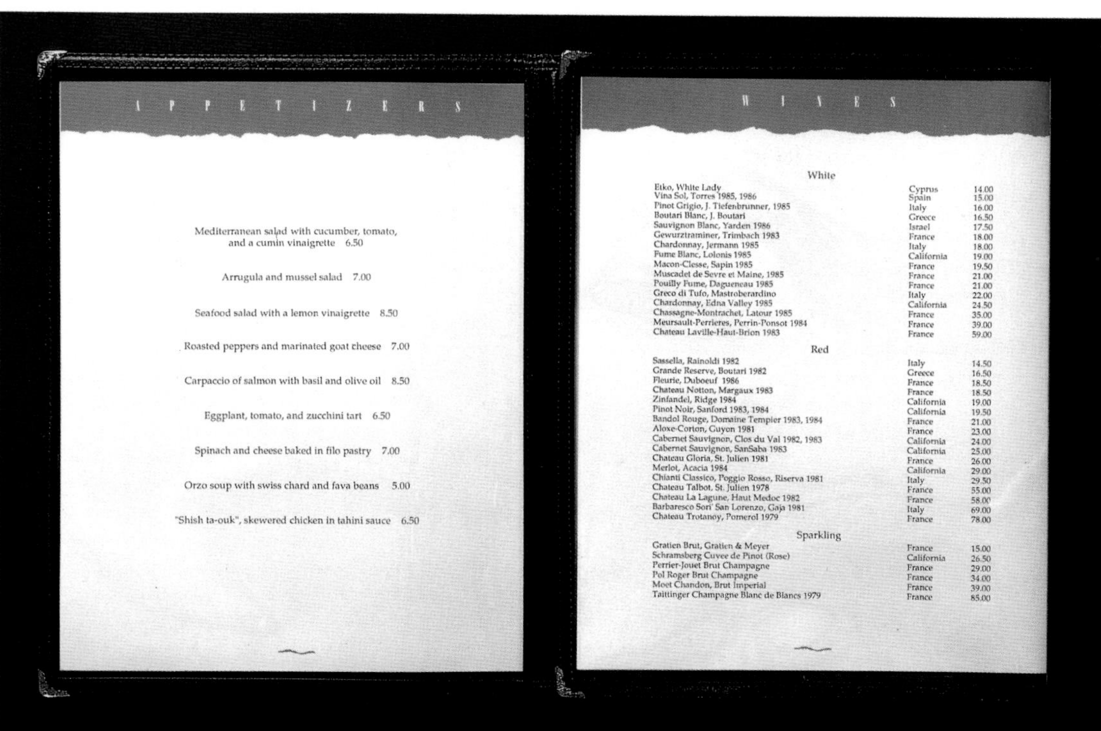


Working with the architect, the menu consultant and the owners, the designer developed a menu that conveyed a Mediterranean feeling without pinning down the geography too closely.

The tranquil blue, aqua and sand used in the "torn paper" beach scene were selected by the above-mentioned group, as well. The subtle shadow of a waiter, which appears on each of the main pieces, is only apparent after a moment's study.

Color-coordinated cafe covers permit easy updates to the elegant menu. Other pieces in the program include the wine list, which uses the same design in a different color, a postcard and stationery. A small wave at the bottom of each sheet provides a unifying element.

| | |
|---|---|
| Designer: | *Susan Hochbaum* |
| | *Pentagram* |
| Restaurant: | *The '21' Club* |
| | *New York, NY* |

How do you "improve upon" a legend ... particularly when that legend has been the favored gathering spot of the world's movers and shakers for three-quarters of a century? That was the design challenge, not just for the graphic arts team, but for the interior designers and restaurateurs involved in the recent refurbishing of The '21' Club.

Any such project must be approached with both caution and affection to ensure success. The interior designer, for example, promised in one gossip column that the interiors would be "the same, only restored." The graphics end of the project involved the commissioning of a new painting, featuring the signature jockey and his horse, whose blanket features the '21' logo.

A marbled-paper effect is used as border and background for many of the over 100 different items in the program. The effect is subtly modified by using coated and uncoated stocks of the finest papers. The inserts, which also have the marbled border, are held into the main menu with rawhide thongs. The thongs both underline the "horsey" theme and pick up one of the main colors in the marbled paper pattern.

No element of the program — not even the house wine labels — is flashy. Every piece has the feeling of a private club, which is exactly as it should be.

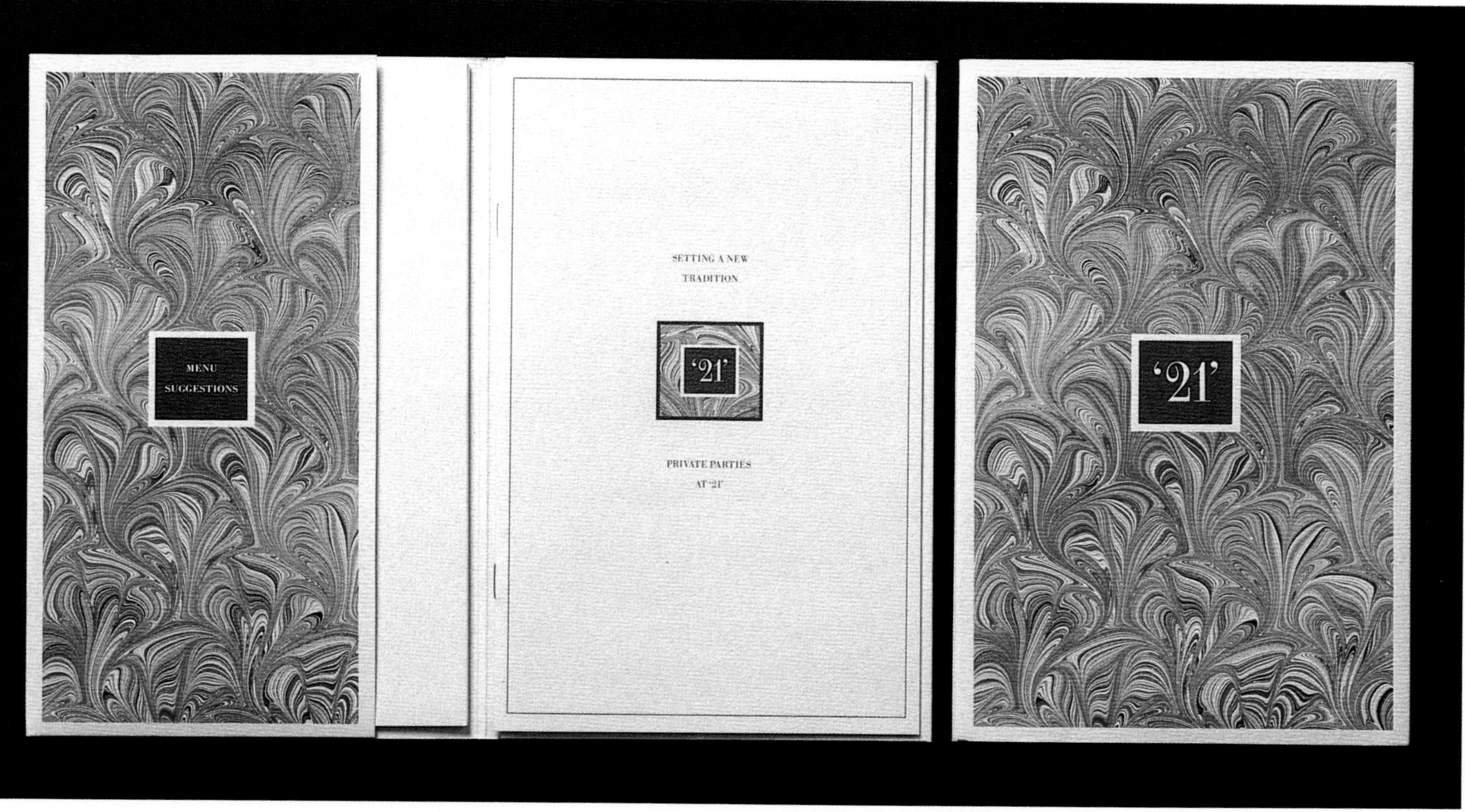
MENU
SUGGESTIONS
SETTING A NEW
TRADITION
'21'
PRIVATE PARTIES
AT '21'
'21'

THE '21' CLUB
21 WEST 52 STREET · NEW YORK
'21'
1983
MERLOT
MONTEREY
PRODUCED AND BOTTLED
BY SAN SABA VINEYARDS
SOLEDAD, CALIFORNIA 93960
ALCOHOL 13.5 BY VOLUME
CONTAINS SULFITES
'21'
'21'
'21'
The '21' Club
21 West 52 Street, New York, New York 10019, Telephone (212) 582-7200
THE '21' CLUB
21 WEST 52 STREET · NEW YORK

| | |
|---|---|
| **Designer:** | *Karla Buchinskas* |
| | *Vignelli Associates* |
| **Restaurant:** | *Palio* |
| | *New York, NY* |

This restaurant specializing in northern Italian cuisine uses the famed Sienese horse race, the Palio, as its theme. The Palio, held annually since the thirteenth century, still uses medieval heraldry and costumes in its pageantry, so the restaurant's graphics have a distinctly heraldic flavor.

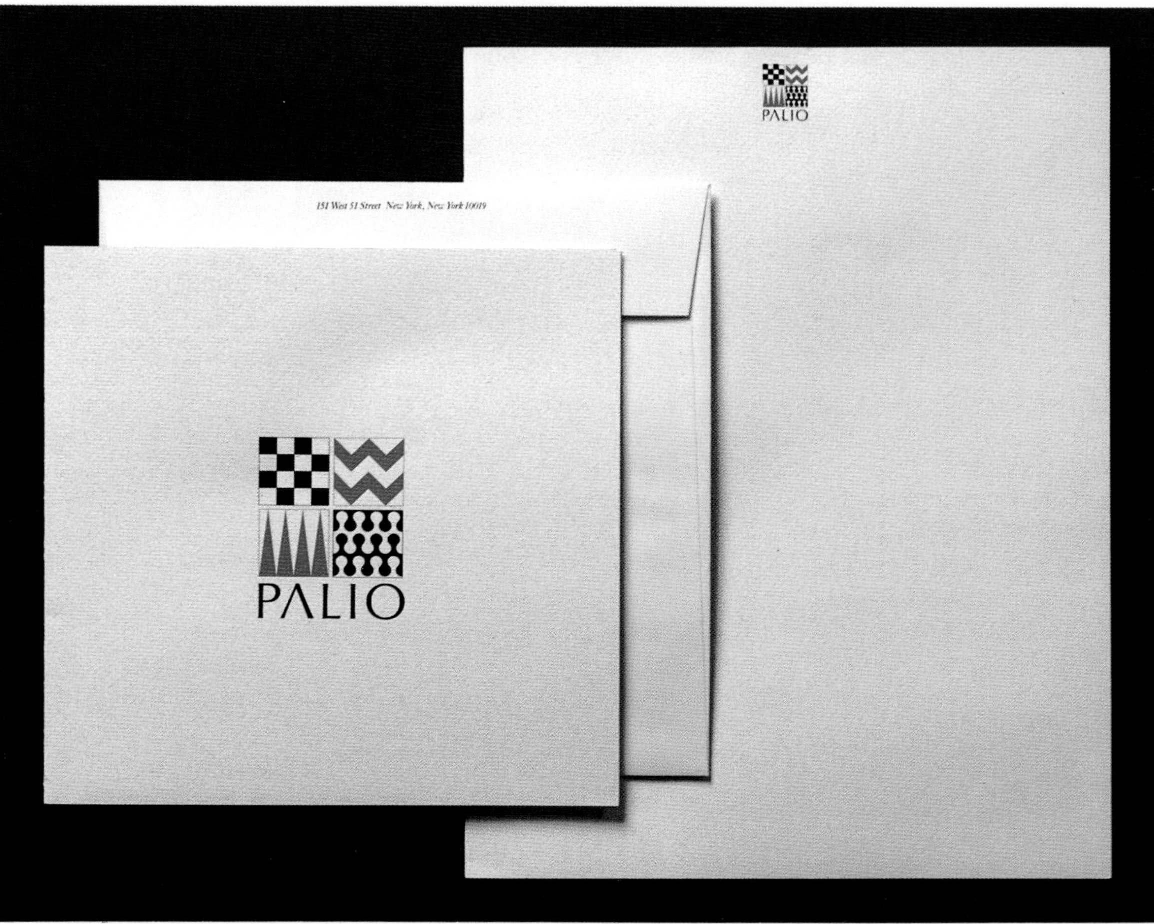

The elements of the fantastic in the Palio are embodied in the huge (54 ft. by 123 ft.) mural which hangs in the bar. Details of this mural are reproduced as end papers in the menu and wine list, as well as on a postcard. The heraldic theme is featured in four separate motifs which are used singly on coasters and bar napkins and together in the enameled metal squares inset on the leather menu and wine list covers. The signature typeface is based on engravings from the Roman Empire, yet retains a modern feeling.

A tremendous amount of research into Italian heraldry went into this design. Every detail, down to the napery, checks and match boxes, is consistent. To ensure that the diner understands the scope of the restaurant's vision, a brief history of the race and background on the artist, Sandro Chia, who painted the mural, are included in the menu. Menu inserts are designed for easy replacement. The wine list is tabbed for easy reference.

PALIO
PALIO
PALIO
PALIO
151 West 51 Street
New York, New York 10019
212/245 4850
151 West 51 Street
New York, New York 10019
212/245 4850
PALIO
063010
PALIO
PALIO
Name
Account

PALIO

**Designer:** *David Savage*
*David Savage/Art & Design*
**Restaurant:** *Khaki's Raw Bar & Grill*
*Boca Raton, FL*

The owners of this clubby restaurant are transplanted Midwesterners, as is the bulk of the clientele. The atmosphere sought in the restaurant design was casual and homey. The graphics used on the menu and associated collateral convey a geographical location — the hibiscus flower symbolizes Florida. More importantly, the number and variety of peripherals available support the sense of belonging. Regular customers can choose from a T-shirt, a khaki shirt, a cap and bumper stickers (which could easily double as coasters) to announce their loyalty.

While a line of products this extensive might not be appropriate everywhere, it works well for any restaurant which depends on a loyal clientele for the backbone of its business.

KHAKI'S
RAW BAR & GRILL

KHAKI'S
RAW BAR & GRILL
Boca Raton
Preferred Customer
305 3944644
DAVID SAVAGE

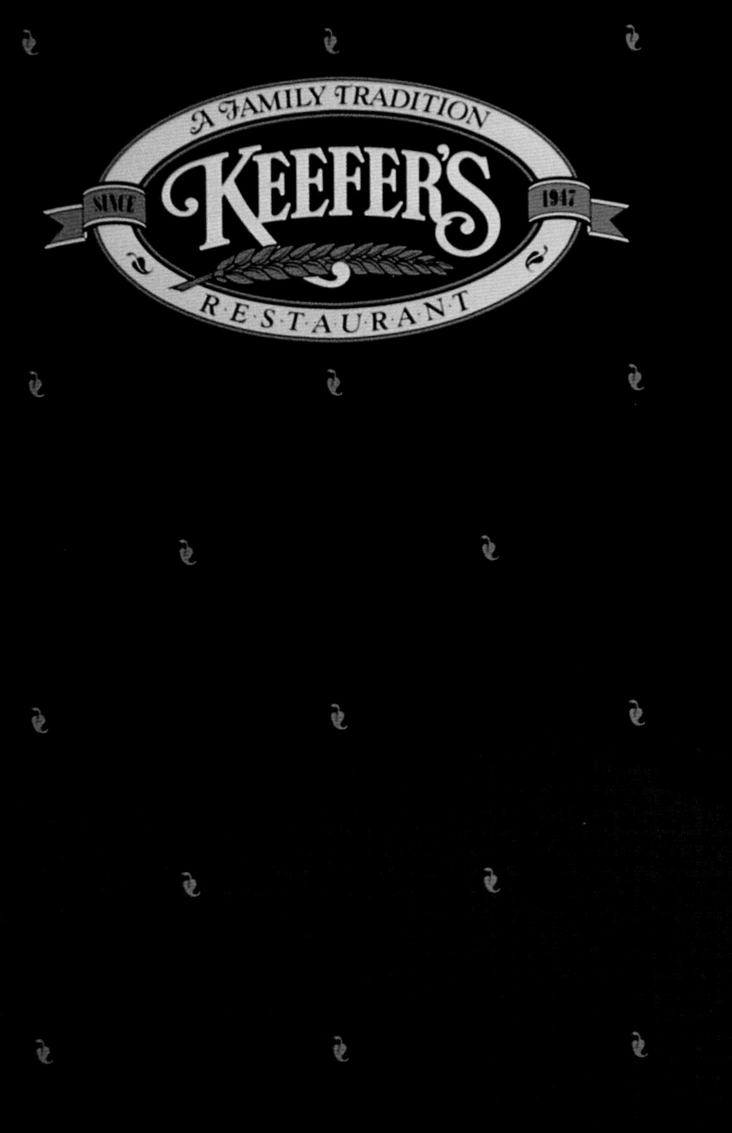
A FAMILY TRADITION
SINCE
KEEFER'S
1947
RESTAURANT

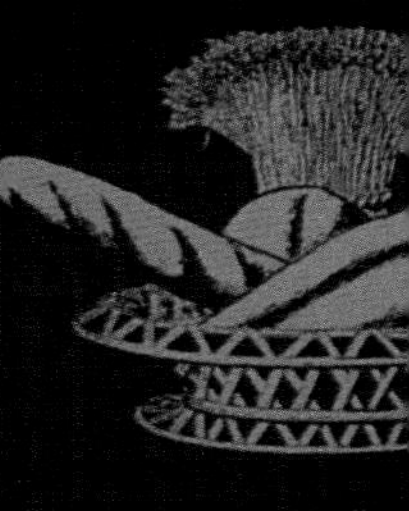

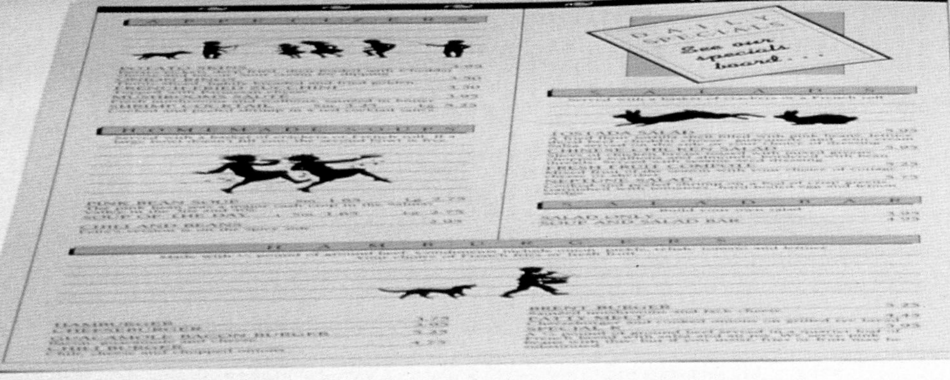

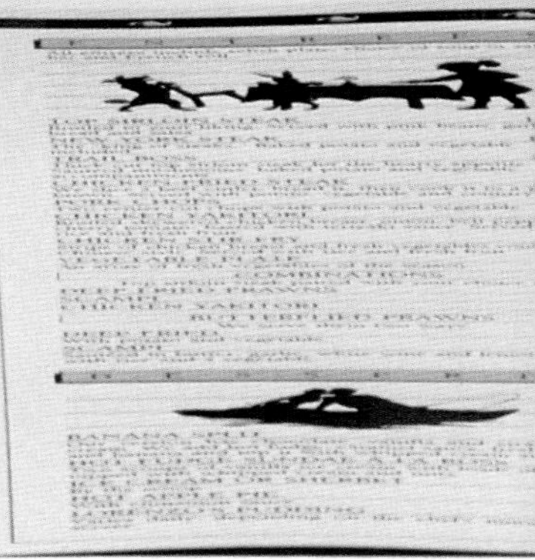

**Designer:** *Jack Biesek*
*Biesek Design*
**Restaurant:** *Keefer's*
*King City, CA*

Situated on one of the three major highways that traverse California fro north to south, Keefer's wanted to up its image to differentiate itself from t plethora of fast-food take-out places have sprung up as its competitors ov past ten years. This design goal was accomplished not merely by redoing menus but also by changing the sig and the architecture of the building.

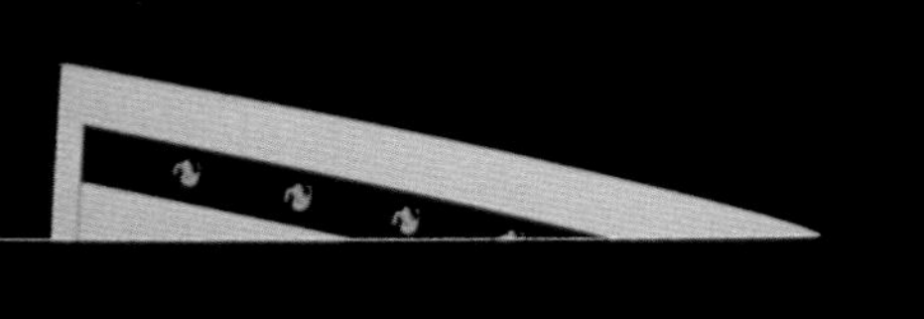

)ME to the garden heartland that
: once described as "East of Eden."
, you'll see that the Salinas Valley
dth and scope of locally produced
bounty that
might be better
described as a *feast* of
Eden. Our region's rolling hills
picturesque farmland create a
dible landscape, brimming with
bles, grains,
it's this rich
ie inspiration for
d menu features the
from a wealth of indigenous
ect wines from our
nd-coming vineyards) to
sh fish from the Monterey Bay.
Keefer's invites you to sample the
bounty and natural beauty of
the Salinas Valley – and to
discover the hearty heartland
oking that's a Keefer family
dition!
NG CITY, CALIFORNIA 93930
efer's Restaurant


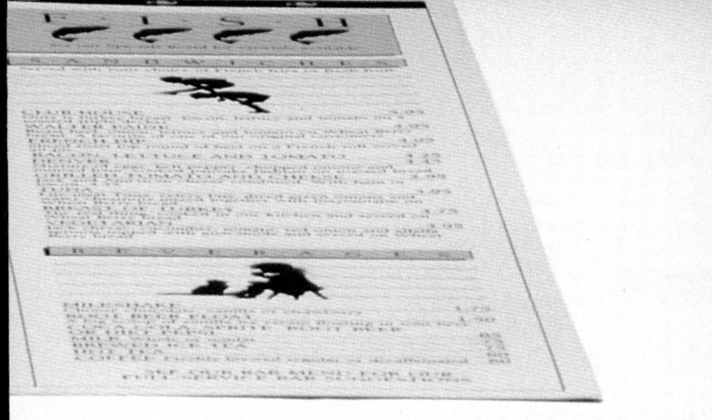

A FAMILY TRADITION
SINCE
KEEFER'S
1947
INN AND RESTAURANT
JIM SARGENT
HEATH AND COMPANY

A FAMILY TRADITION
KEEFER'S
1947
R·E·S·T·A·U·R·A·N·T

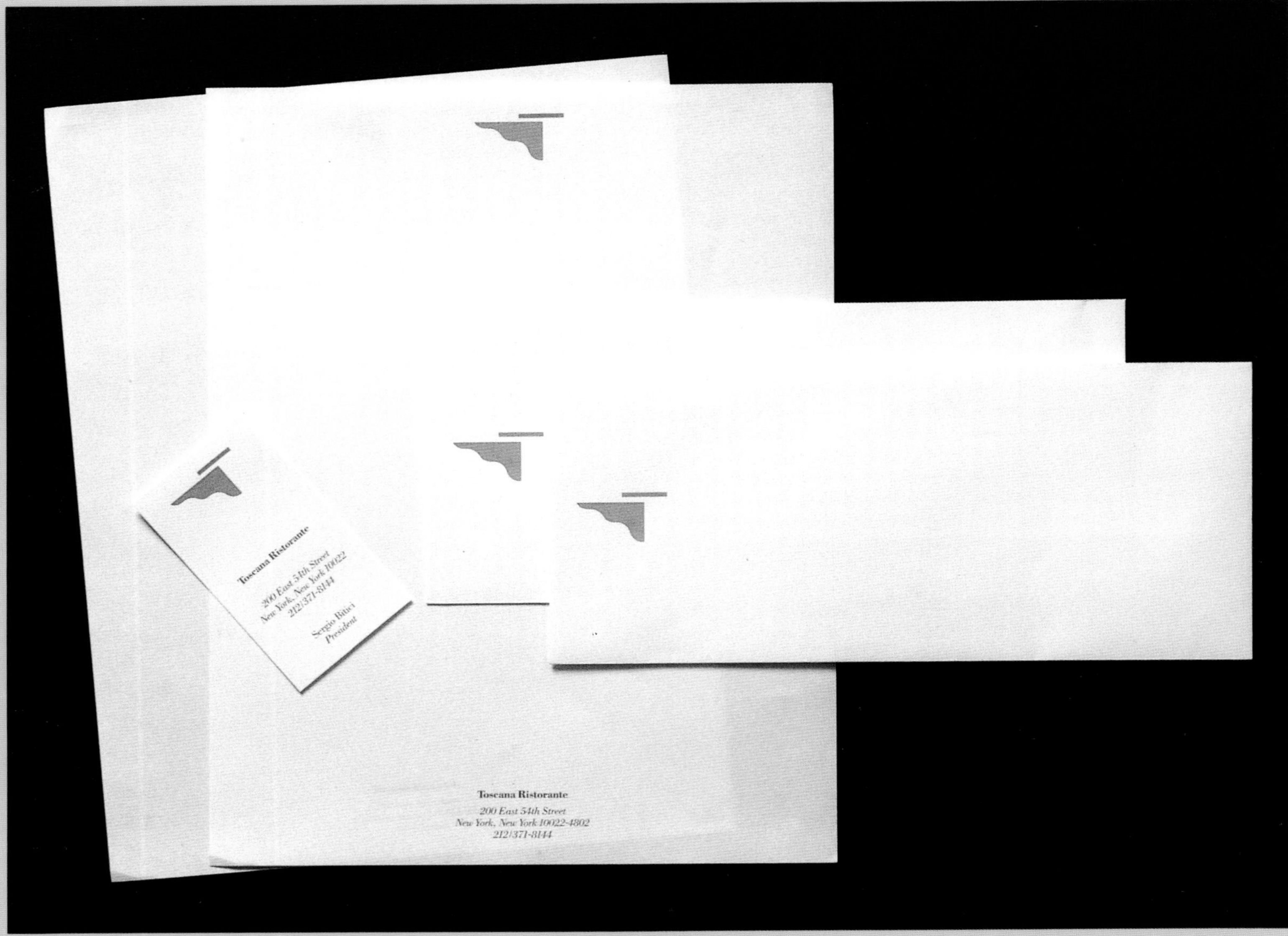


**Designer:** *Mark Randall*
*Vignelli Associates*
**Restaurant:** *Toscana Ristorante*
*New York, NY*

This menu package was designed as an integral part of the restaurant. The marble pattern on the covers and bill folder was drawn from the marble used in the interior. The curvilinear motif, repeated on each of these and on the stationery, is based on the shape of the bar.

The most serious item, the food, is presented simply and clearly in black, clean type on the cream-colored menu inserts, held into the covers with fabric tassel-finished cords. The inserts change seasonally. The prices are entered by hand, depending upon market price. The overall effect is of a serious "eater's restaurant," yet one where comfort and elegance are not neglected. Use of metallic inks throughout lends a note of luxury, as does the paper used for the changing inserts.

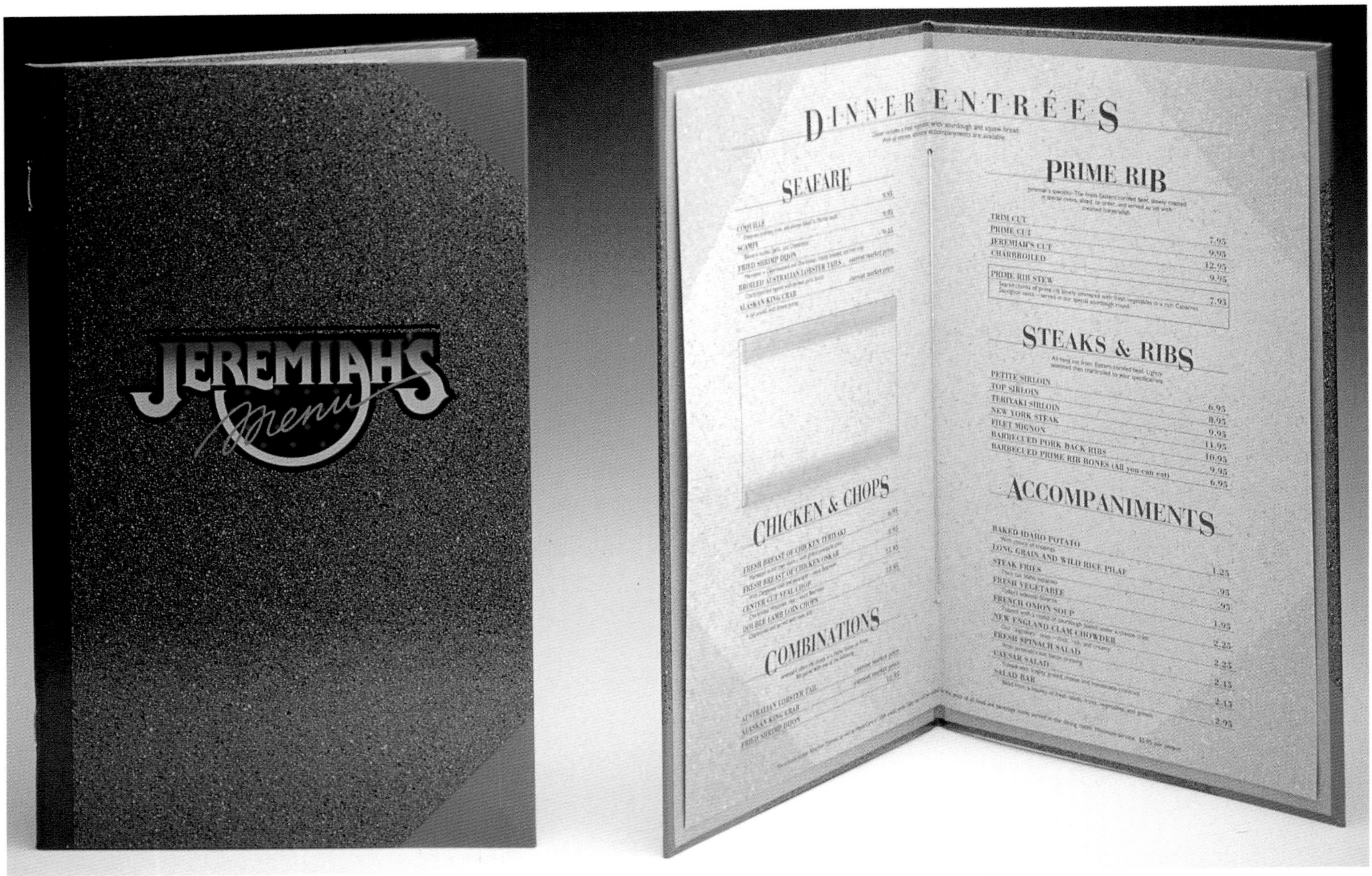

Designer: *Jack Biesek*
*Biesek Design*

Restaurant: *Jeremiah's*
*12 locations from Palm Springs to Houston*

Book cover finishing makes the menus for this restaurant special. The granite screen of the cover is repeated on the menu inserts, as well as on the match boxes.

This project was initiated as simply a redesign of the logo; it eventually evolved into a totally revamped corporate identity program, extending even to the billboards. The consistency of the image throughout all the associated pieces is a tribute to the owners' determination to distance these restaurants from other "chains."

Special marketing devices used in the menus include an affixed plastic cardholder for a specials card and the proud assertion that only U.S.D.A. Prime beef is served. The accompanying wine list reflects an adventurous spirit. Many of the selections are from boutique wineries and this section of the menu is divided into varietals, not merely "red, white and rose."

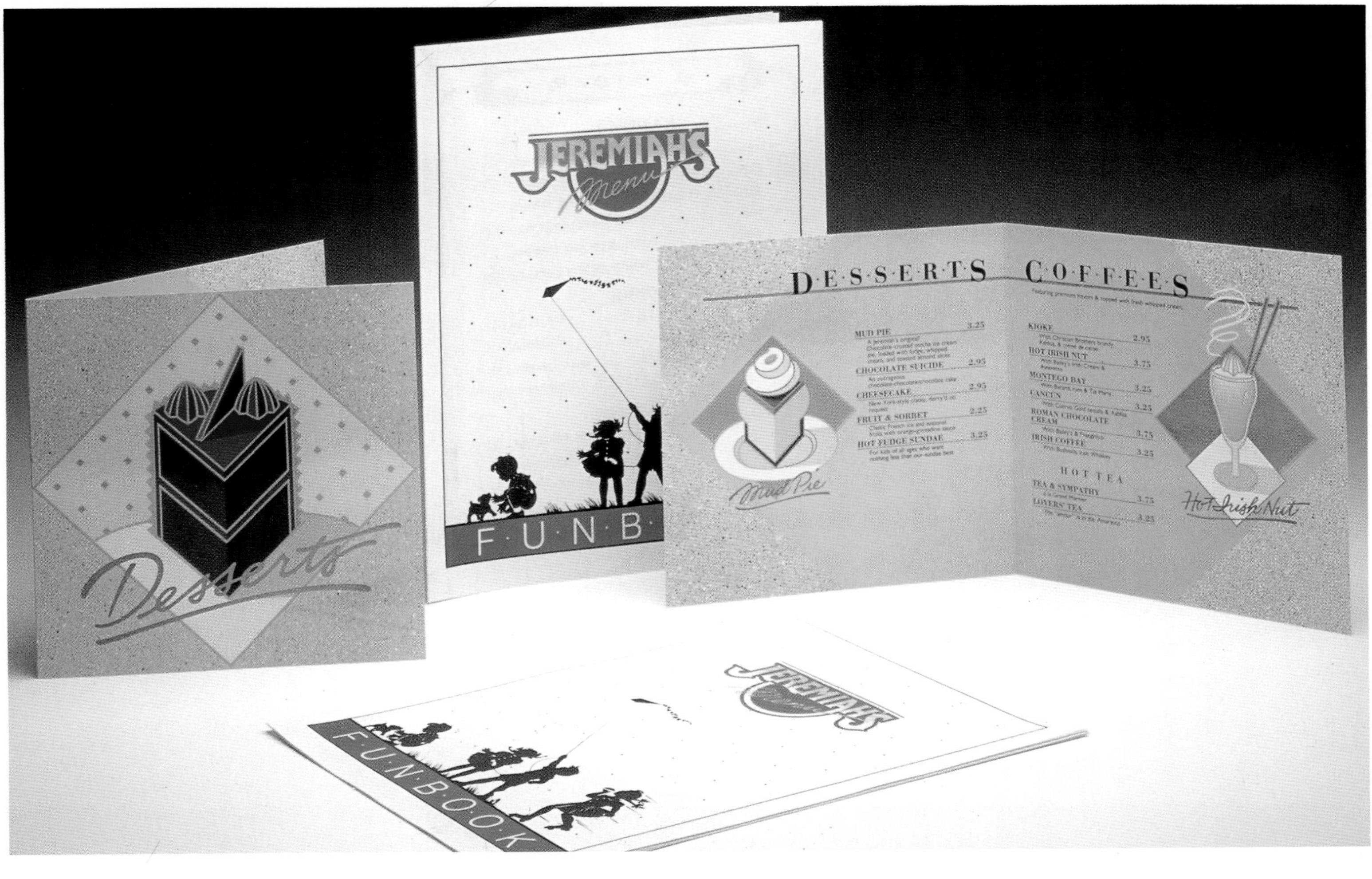

| | |
|---|---|
| Designer: | *Mike Wagner* |
| | *The Menu Workshop* |
| Restaurant: | *701 East West* |
| | *Seattle, WA* |

This menu packaging program is a classic example of an "architectural extension." It is directly derived from the architectural design of the restaurant. The grid pattern is taken both from the table tops and from the design of the building in which the restaurant is located — the tallest in Seattle.

The teal and black are drawn from the restaurant's color scheme. A modern typeface is used throughout, as befits a restaurant in a thoroughly modern building.

The program is particularly effective, in that it is very thorough. The basic theme appears even on the matches and on a special adhesive strip, designed to be wrapped around soda cans for the restaurant's take-out trade.

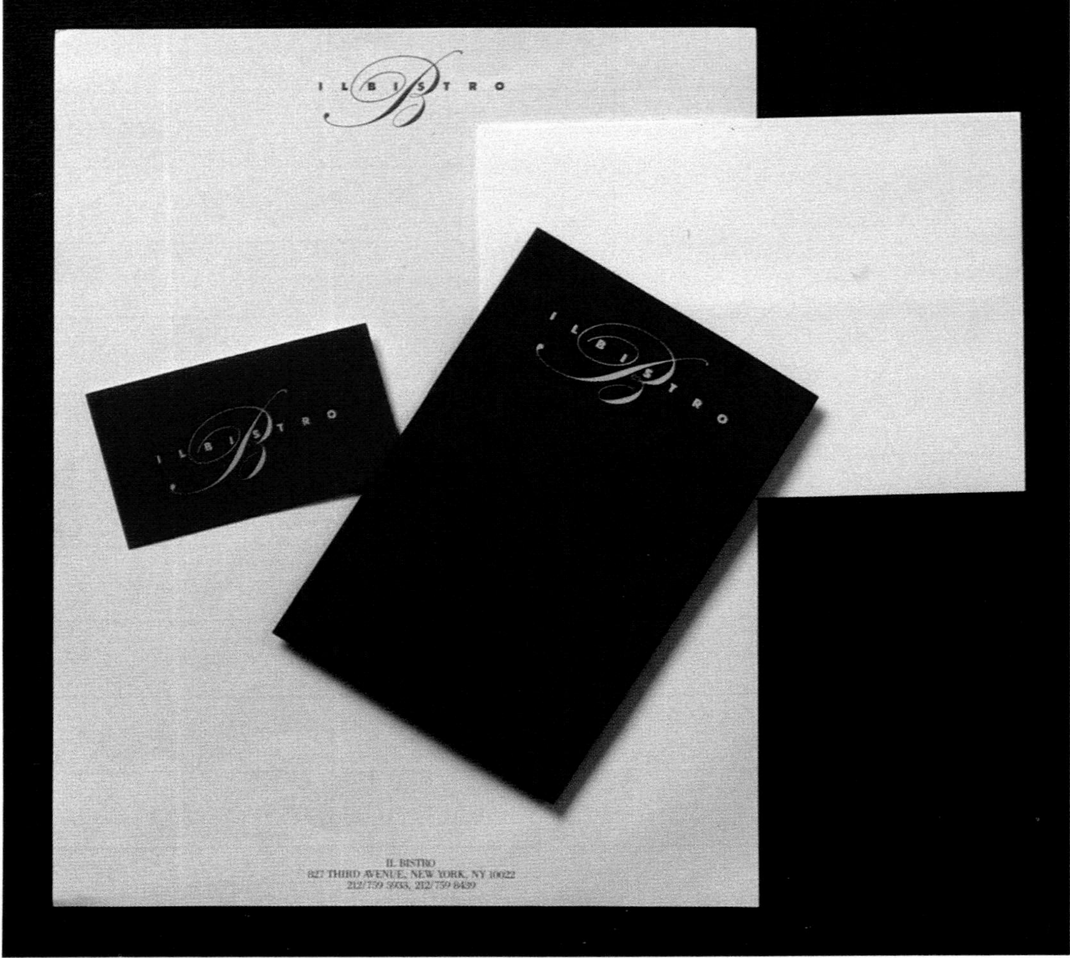


| | |
|---|---|
| Designer: | *Karla Buchinskas* |
| | *Vignelli Associates* |
| Restaurant: | *Il Bistro* |
| | *New York, NY* |

In an earlier incarnation, as 'Le Bistro,' this restaurant was French. Following extensive renovation and a minor modification to its name, it emerged as an elegantly simple Italian restaurant.

The existing rich red-brown wood paneling was retained and is reflected in the unusual menu cover material. Opaque inks would not have worked well on such a dark background. Bearing this in mind, the designer has instead chosen to silkscreen the logo and restaurant name in a pale turquoise. Both the logo and the color choice are intended to emphasize the rustic warmth of the food offered. A duplex business card uses the warm brown on one side, a white background on the other for legibility.

In developing the design concept, the graphic arts team exchanged ideas with the restaurant designers. The resulting program is a harmonious blend of the two points of view.

**Designer:** *Tony Ross and Nancy Northwood*
*Ross Design*
**Restaurant:** *Kid Shelleen's*
*Wilmington, DE*

The theme of this casual restaurant is based on the character played by Lee Marvin in the film Cat Ballou. The interior features natural woods and brass, accented with the burgundy and green used in the menu program.

The unifying element in the graphic design is a triangle. It appears as a tiny pattern on the green menu cover and serves as a backdrop for some of the menu heads; a whole line of triangles is centered at the top of each piece. Suggesting a mountain range or a line of tepees, this device subtly enhances the Western theme of the restaurant.

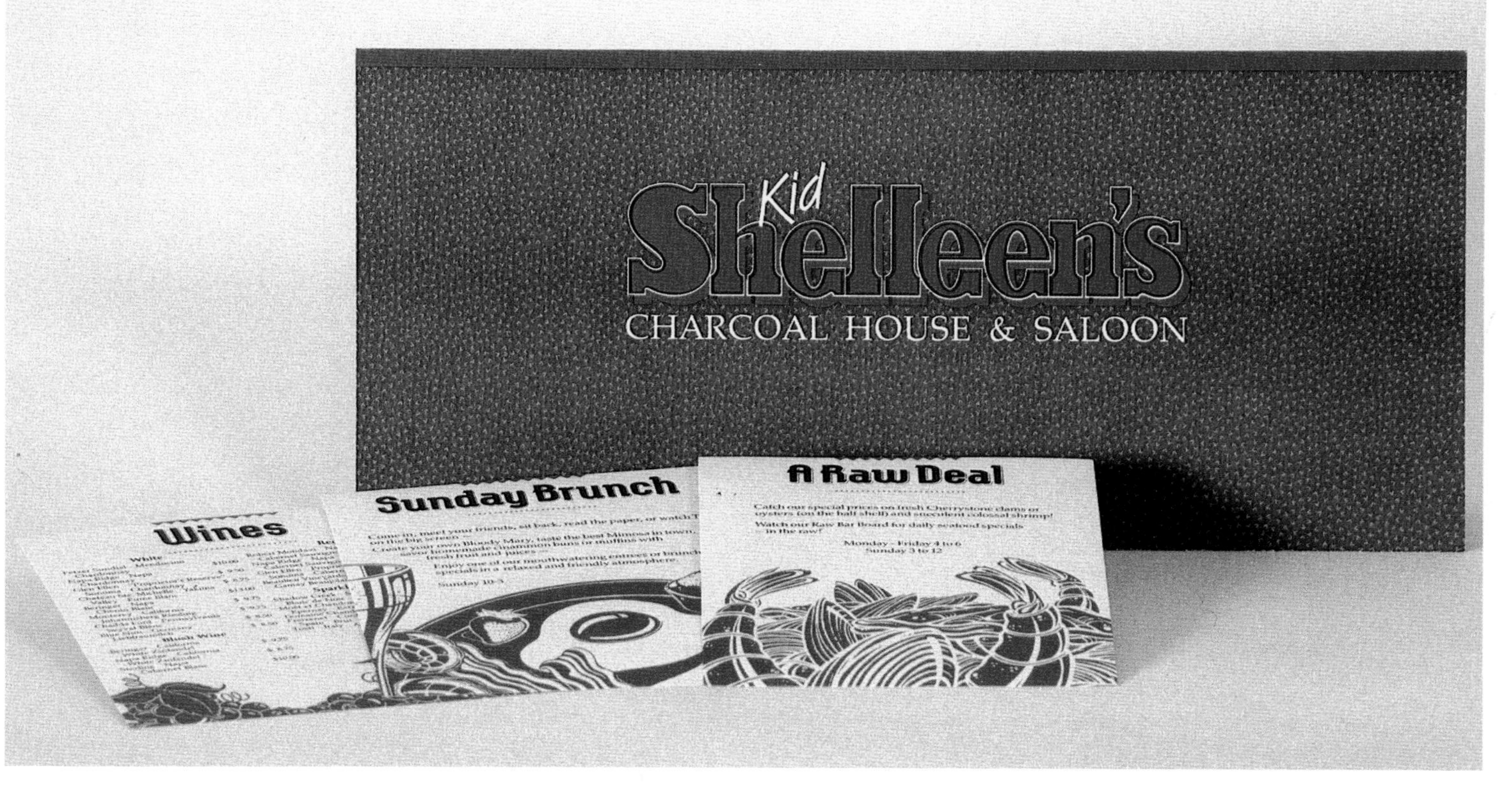

IMPORTED WINES
Squash Blossom
WINE LIST
A More Extensive Wine List is Available Upon Request.

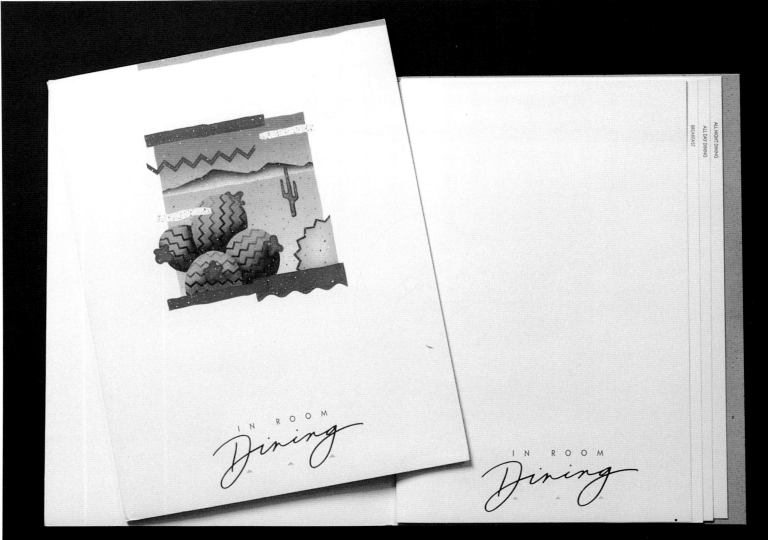

**Designer:** *Donna Milord*
*Associates Printing Service, Inc.*

**Restaurant:** *The Squash Blossom and In-Room Dining*
*Hyatt Regency Scottsdale*
*Scottsdale, AZ*

The vibrant colors of the desert splash cheerfully across the menus for this resort hotel. Palm trees, cacti and the distant mountains tie the illustrations to their geographical location.

The mountains are further suggested by the rick-rack edging which holds the changing insert cards in place in the wine list. Inside the dinner menu, the mountains reappear at bottom, along with a die-cut cactus, while the vivid red clouds of a Southwestern sunset hold the insert in place at the top.

The same colors and themes appear on each of the pieces in the program, including the children's menu, which appears elsewhere in this book. The effect is coordinated, without being trite.

# CHAPTER 6

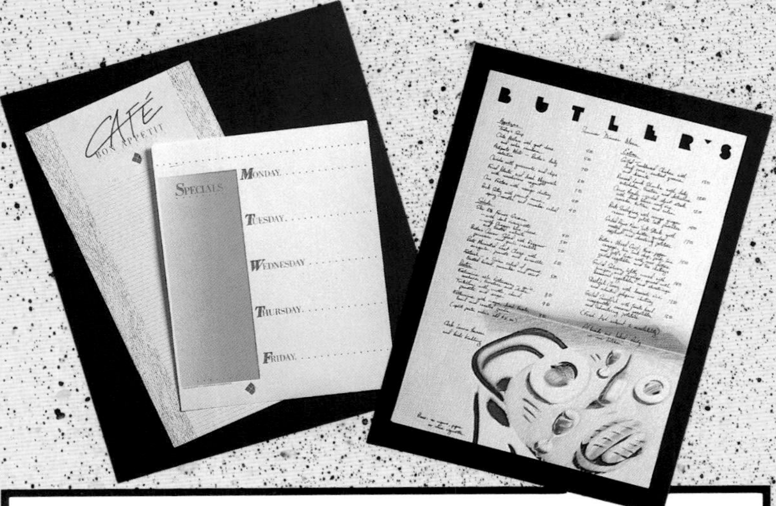


Growing public awareness of nutrition, together with the accompanying interest in fresh, rather than frozen foods, has made the adaptable menu an increasingly important segment of the field. Better communications between growers, fishermen and restaurateurs have made changing or "adaptable" menus more feasible, too. However, adaptable menus are a two-edged sword. Done properly, they permit a restaurant to feature the freshest items as they come into season. Done improperly, they can be a disaster.

One of the potential irritations with a daily menu is the flimsiness of the vehicle. Too thin a sheet, without a solid holder, can be difficult to read and is never satisfying to hold. In the America of the 1980's, going out to dinner involves a financial commitment. For the restaurant to expend less of a commitment is frustrating.

One of the changes we have observed in recent menus is the imaginative carriers currently being used for daily menus. Many restaurants still use letter-weight papers, but insert them in sturdy carriers to lend a solid feeling to the piece. Probably the most significant advance is the sheer volume of changing menus. There are so many that, for the first time, we are devoting a chapter to them.

# ADAPTABLE MENUS

Designer: *Niki Bonnett*
*Niki Bonnett Design*
Restaurant: *Brasserie*
*New York, NY*

The four-color shells for this menu are imprinted daily using in-house desk top publishing facilities. For greater legibility, the illustrations have been screened down. This technique also creates a softer note than might otherwise have been achieved. Daily specials are imprintined in the box at the top of the food side of the menu.

The selection of wines on the *"Cartes des Vins"* (menu of wines) is interesting, Where most wine lists in America feature French and Californian wines, this one also includes a small selection of Swiss vintages. This addition is appropriate for the generally informal, European menu selection.

NEW YORK'S
BRASSERIE
100 East 53rd Street · New York (212) 751-4840 · Open 24 hours.

Bieres
Biere de Paris 3.25 Kronenbourg de France 3.25 Heineken 3.25 Amstel Light 3.25
Hofbrau 3.25 Budweiser 2.95 Kronenbourg on Draught 2.75

Vins
Blanc de Blanc N.V. Glass 3.25 Half Carafe 6.75 Full Carafe 11.50 Wine Cooler 3.25

Eau Minerale
Perrier 2.50

Les Aperitifs
Kir Royale *Champagne and Cassis 3.50*
Kir *White Wine and Cassis 3.25*
Mimosa *Orange Juice and Champagne 3.50*
Campari *3.50*
Dubonnet *3.25*
Lillet *3.50*
Dry Sack *3.50*

Cartes Des Vins

French White

| | Half Bottle | Bottle |
|---|---|---|
| 001 Cuvée de la Brasserie N.V. *Blanc de Blanc* | | 10.95 |
| 002 Sylvaner 84 *Trimbach* | | 13.50 |
| 003 Macon-Lugny 85 *Les Charmes* | | 15.50 |
| 004 Riesling 84 *Trimback* | 8.50 | 14.50 |
| 005 Sancerre Le Chaillou 85 *Cordier* | | 16.75 |
| 006 Pouilly Fumé 86 *Domaine de St. Laurent* | | 17.50 |
| 007 Meursault 85 *Noirot Carrière* | | 29.50 |
| 008 Muscadet-Sur-Lie 85 *Domaine de la Batardière* | 7.00 | 13.00 |

Swiss White

| | Half Bottle | Bottle |
|---|---|---|
| 009 Johannisberg 82 *Cave Movenpick* | | 16.50 |
| 010 Epesses 83 *Cave Movenpick* | | 14.50 |

American White Chardonnay

| | Half Bottle | Bottle |
|---|---|---|
| 011 Kendall Jackson 85 | 9.75 | 19.00 |
| 031 Chateau St. Michelle 85 | | 17.00 |
| 012 Rutherford Hill 84 | 14.00 | 27.00 |
| 030 Sterling 84 | | 21.00 |
| 013 Monterey Vineyard *Chenin Blanc 85* | | 14.00 |
| 014 Sterling Vineyard *Sauvignon Blanc 85* | | 17.50 |

Blush

| | Half Bottle | Bottle |
|---|---|---|
| 015 Sutter Home White Zinfandel 85 | | 15.00 |

French Red

| | Half Bottle | Bottle |
|---|---|---|
| 017 Brouilly Chateau de la Chaize 85 *Marquise de Roussy de Sales* | 8.75 | 16.75 |
| 018 St. Emilion 85 *Cordier* | | 15.00 |
| 019 Chateau-Neuf-du-Pape 83 *Domaine de la Roquette* | 9.75 | 17.75 |
| 020 Beaujolais Village 85 *Louis Latour* | 8.95 | 14.95 |

Swiss Red

| | Half Bottle | Bottle |
|---|---|---|
| 021 Dole 83 *Cave Movenpick* | | 16.50 |

American Red

| | Half Bottle | Bottle |
|---|---|---|
| 022 Simi Cabernet Sauvignon 82 | | 21.00 |
| 023 BV Rutherford 83 *Cabernet Sauvignon* | | 11.50 |

French Champagne

| | Half Bottle | Bottle |
|---|---|---|
| 024 Perrier Jouet Brut N.V. | 19.00 | 39.00 |
| 025 Moet & Chandon N.V. | 18.00 | 37.00 |
| 026 Dom Perignon 1980 | | 79.00 |
| 027 Gratien Meyer | Split | 5.75 |

American Sparkling Wine

| | Half Bottle | Bottle |
|---|---|---|
| 028 Domaine Chandon Brut | | 28.00 |
| 032 Blanc de Noir | | 28.00 |
| 029 Schramsberg Blanc de Blanc 84 | | 38.00 |

BRASSERIE

Hors d'Oeuvres ou Potages
Banc de c'Ecailler *Raw Bar - Clams, Oysters, Spicy Shrimp Priced Accordingly*
Soupe a l'Oignon Gratinée *Large 4.95 Small 3.95*
Pâte de Canard au Calvados *Duck Pate with Apple Brandy 4.95*
La Salade de la Brasserie, Fromage de Chèvre *Farmer's Market Salad with Goat Cheese 4.50*
Clovisses au Four *Baked Clams 5.75*
Gazpacho Andalouse *3.50*
Escargots de Bourgogne *Marinated Snails, Herb Butter 5.75*
Melon et Prosciutto *4.95*
Tomates, Mozzarella avec Basilic *Tomatoes & Fresh Mozzarella with Basil 4.95*

Entrées
Fettuccine Noir Maison *Black Fettuccine with Shrimp, Scallops, Tomato & Basil 14.95*
Quiche Lorraine et Salade *10.95*
Penne aux Champignons Sauvage *Penne Pasta with Wild Mushrooms 13.75*
Barbecue Du Pêcheur *Seafood Mixed Grill 15.75*
Paillard de Poulet Grillé *Grilled Paillard of Chicken Breast 12.50*
Crêpe aux Fruits de Mer *Seafood Crepe 12.50*
Filet Mignon Grillé et Salade *18.95*
Choucroute à l'Alsacienne *Smoked Meats, Wine Sauerkraut & Potato 11.95*
Espadon Grillé aux Agrumes *Grilled Swordfish, Lemon-Lime Butter 15.95*
Poulet Roti St. Tropez *Half Roast Chicken with Fresh Herbs 12.75*
Entrecôte Parisienne, Frites et Salade *Grilled Angus Steak, Herb Butter, French Fries, Salad 18.95*
Escalopes de Veau Printanier *Medallions of Veal with Summer Vegetables 14.95*
Hamburger Provençale ou Fromage *Ratatouille & French Fries, Served on French Garlic Bread 8.95*
Petit Entrecôte Sur Toast *Steak Sandwich on Toast, French Fries 14.95*

Oeufs & Omelettes A Notre Façon
Oeufs Benedictine *Poached Eggs on English Muffin, Canadian Bacon, Hollandaise Sauce 9.75*
Omelette Lorraine *Bacon, Cheese, Chives 8.95*
Oeufs Florentine *Poached Eggs on Spinach, Mornay Sauce 9.75*
Omelette Igor *Golden Caviar & Sour Cream 8.95*

Buffet Froid
Saumon Fumé *Hickory Smoked Salmon Served with Flat Bread, Onion & Capers 12.75*
Poitrine de Poulet Poivrée, Salade d'Epinard *Peppered Breast of Chicken, Baby Spinach Leaf 9.75*
Salade du Chef *9.75*
Salade de César *Caesar Salade 9.75*
Saumon Froid Garni *Cold Poached Salmon Steak Garnished with Tomato & Cucumber Salad 14.50*
Steak Tartare, Frites *11.95*
Salade Niçoise *Tuna, Potato, String Beans & Tomato 9.75*
Brasserie Club Sandwich *9.75*

Desserts et Patisserie 3.95
Poire Belle Helene *Poached Pear with Vanilla Ice Cream & Chocolate Sauce*
Gâteau au Fromage de New York *New York Cheese Cake*
Tarte aux Pommes *French Apple Tart*
Pâtisserie Française *French Pastries*
Crêpe aux Pommes *Apple Crepe with Cinnamon & Raisins*
Gâteau de la Forêt Noire *Black Forest Cake*
Gâteau au Chocolat Suisse *Swiss Chocolate Cake*
Salade de Fruits *Fruit Salad*
Glâces et Sorbets *Ice Creams & Sherbets*
Fraises Fraiches Chocolat Blanc et Noir *Strawberries with Two Chocolates*
Creme Caramel

Boissons
Cafe 1.50 Décaféiné 1.50 Pot de The 1.50 Espresso 1.95 Cappuccino 2.25

Designer: *Lawrence E. Green*
*The Green Company*
Restaurant: *Washington Square Bar & Grill*
*San Francisco, CA*

This restaurant is the favored hang-out for the local literary crowd. While the owners wanted a menu they could change daily, a note of sophistication was needed to accommodate their audience. The solution was to create a series of graphic plays upon the ampersand in the restaurant's name.

Playful, yet elegant, the ampersand cartoons underline the raison d'être of the place — a meeting place and respite for the literatti. The straightforward color scheme and typeface provide a suitable backdrop for the mental pyrotechnics.

LUNCH -- Tuesday, December 22, 1987 – "MERRY CHRISTMAS FROM IDA"

**Appetizers**
Garlic Bread 1.95
Sauteed Mushrooms 3.95
Avocado Cocktail with Fresh Salsa 3.95
Herb and Garlic Marinated Goat Cheese with Red Peppers 4.95
Prosciutto & Melon 5.95
Carpaccio allo Cernobbio 5.95
Toasted Meat Ravioli 4.95
Truffle Pate & Orange Duck Pate, Garni 4.95
Artichoke Stuffed with Shrimp 6.95
Smoked Oregon Trout, Cucumber Salad and Horseradish Cream 5.95
Calamari & Scallops Vinaigrette 5.95

**Today's Soup**
Barley & Smoked Ham
Cup 1.95 Bowl 3.50

**Pasta**
Spaghettini, Meat or Tomato Sauce 7.95
Fettuccine Alfredo 8.25
Fettuccine Bardelli: Mushrooms, Tomato, Cream 8.50
Tortellini alla Panna: Cream 8.50
Penne Arrabbiata: Spicy Tomato 7.95
Spaghettini Pescatore: Spicy Calamari 8.95
Beef Ravioli, Tomato or Meat Sauce 8.25
(Small order any pasta above: 5.25)

**Salads & Vegetables**
Small Luncheon Salad 2.95
Salad with Star Route Farms Lettuce 4.25
with Roquefort or Goat Cheese 5.25
with Anchovies 5.25
Winter Tomatoes, Basil Dressing 5.25
with Anchovies 5.95
Side Order of Vegetables 2.50
French Fried Potatoes 1.95
Fishermen's Salad of Calamari & Scallops Vinaigrette, Entree Size 10.50
Salade Nicoise 10.50
Salad of Bay Shrimp, Egg, Red Pepper, Field Greens, Basil Dressing 10.95
Shrimp Louis 10.95

**Veal & Chicken**
Chicken Parmigiana 9.50
Grilled Chicken Breast 9.50
Veal Scaloppine, Piccata or Marsala 10.95
Eastern Veal Cutlet, Milanese 11.95
Eastern Veal Rib Chop 16.95

**Grill**
The WSB&G Hamburger Sandwich 6.50
The WSB&G Hamburger, Melted Cheese 6.95
Italian Sausage, Sweet Pepper, Onion & Cheese Sandwich 7.50
New York Strip Steak Sandwich 12.95
New York Strip Steak (dry–aged) with Maitre 'd Butter 16.95

All Menu Items Available for Takeout

Single portion for 2 persons $1.00 extra
Safflower Margarine, Low Calorie Dressing, Low Sodium Seasonings Available
Six & one half percent sales tax added to all items served at tables

**Today's Special**
Handmade Tortellini, Stuffed with Blue Cheese, served with Avocado Chive Sauce 9.95
Grilled Pacific Sea Bass, served with Tomato Vinaigrette 12.95

**Fish**
Calamari Fritti 9.95
Monterey Calamari Saute Arrabbiata 9.95
Monterey Calamari Saute with Mushrooms, alla Marsala 9.95
Petrale Dore, Lemon Velvet Sauce with Capers 13.95
Grilled Boned Rex Sole, Lemon Butter Sauce 9.95
Grilled Scandinavian Salmon, Basil Beurre Blanc 14.95
Fresh Scallops Sauteed, with Sauce Dill Beurre Blanc or Lemon Butter Sauce 13.95
Prawns della Casa, Aldo: Sauteed, Brandy Butter 13.95

**Eggs**
North Beach Omelette (Pesto, Ricotta Cheese & Ham) 7.95
Joe's Special (Chopped Beef, Egg, Spinach) 6.95
Joe's Special with Mushrooms 7.50
Vegetarian Joe with Mushrooms 7.50

**Beverages**
Graffeo's Coffee, Regular or Decaf; Milk; Irish Breakfast Tea; Fruit Tea 1.25

**Desserts**
Chocolate Mousse Cake with Raspberry Puree & Creme Anglaise 4.95
Coeur a la Creme, Raspberry Puree 3.95
Cheese Cake 3.95
Cheese Cake, Raspberry Puree 4.95
Ice Cream; choice of flavors 2.95
with Hot Chocolate Sauce 3.50
Housemade Sherbet 2.95

**Cheese & Fresh Fruit**
Fresh Fruit Sampler 3.95
Asiago Cheese & Fruit 4.95
Cambazola (Germany's Cream Bleu) Cheese & Fruit 4.95

"The Flavor of North Beach," The Insider's Guide to San Francisco's Historic Italian District, with 40 recipes, On sale here $2.95c

**Washington Square Bar & Grill**

1707 POWELL STREET SAN FRANCISCO, CALIFORNIA 94133 TELEPHONE (415) 982-8123

Service Non Compris ▪ Positively No Checks Cashed ▪ Minimum Charge For Table Service $6.00 Per Person

| | |
|---|---|
| Designer: | *Nancy Hunt-Weber* |
| | *Hunt-Weber Clark Design* |
| Restaurant: | *Corona Bar & Grill* |
| | *San Francisco, CA* |

This menu is an example of what can be achieved when the menu and restaurant are designed concurrently. The owners were looking for a sense of excitement and exploration, with a decidedly Mexican cast. The designer's decision to use a canvas-imprinted background and the colors of dawn, blue tropical skies and a copper highlight works well with the antiqued walls and woods used in the restaurant interior.

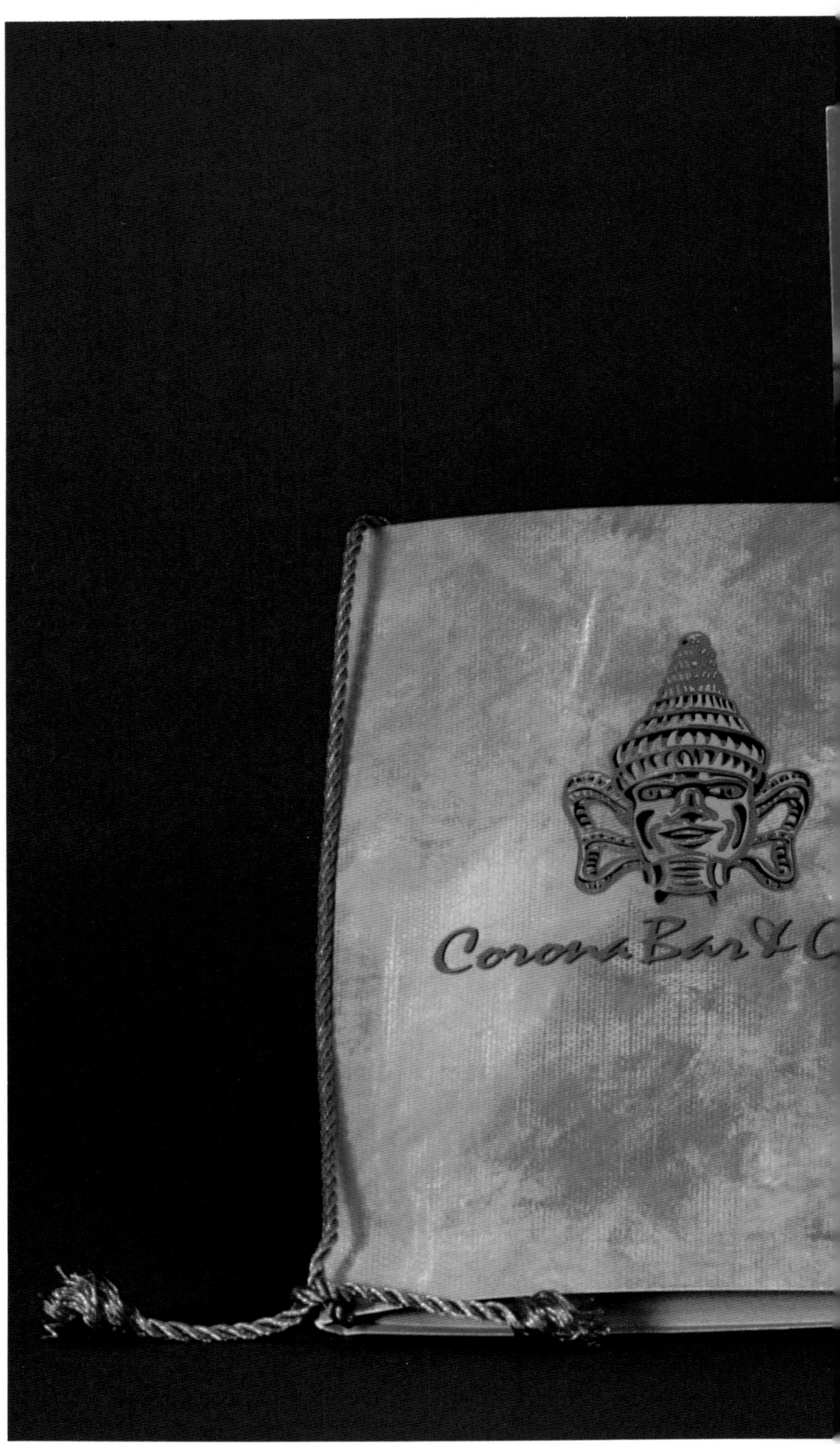

Cerveza Mexicana
Sol
Pacifico
Tecate
Chihuahua
Negro Modelo
Dos XX
Bohemia
Superior
2.50
Gringo Beer
Miller Lite
Amstel Light, Heineken
2.00
2.50
Margaritas
3.50
3.25
3.50
3.75
3.75
Especiale (with Gran Marnier float)
our version of a South of the Border
Punch!
Agua
1.50
1.75
(Grapefruit, Lemon, Sangria and plain)
Bar Appetizers
Fried Shoestring Onions
Pico de Gallo and Chips
Rillettes and Chips
Guacamole and Chips
Fresh Oyster Shooter with peppered Cuervo 1800
Mariscos Cocktail
Black Bean Cake with Grilled Prawns
Quesadillas
Duck, poblano chiles and jack cheese
Shitakes mushrooms, roquefort and onions
2.95
1.50
2.50
2.95
1.50
6.50
7.25
5.25
5.50
Corona
Bar & Grill

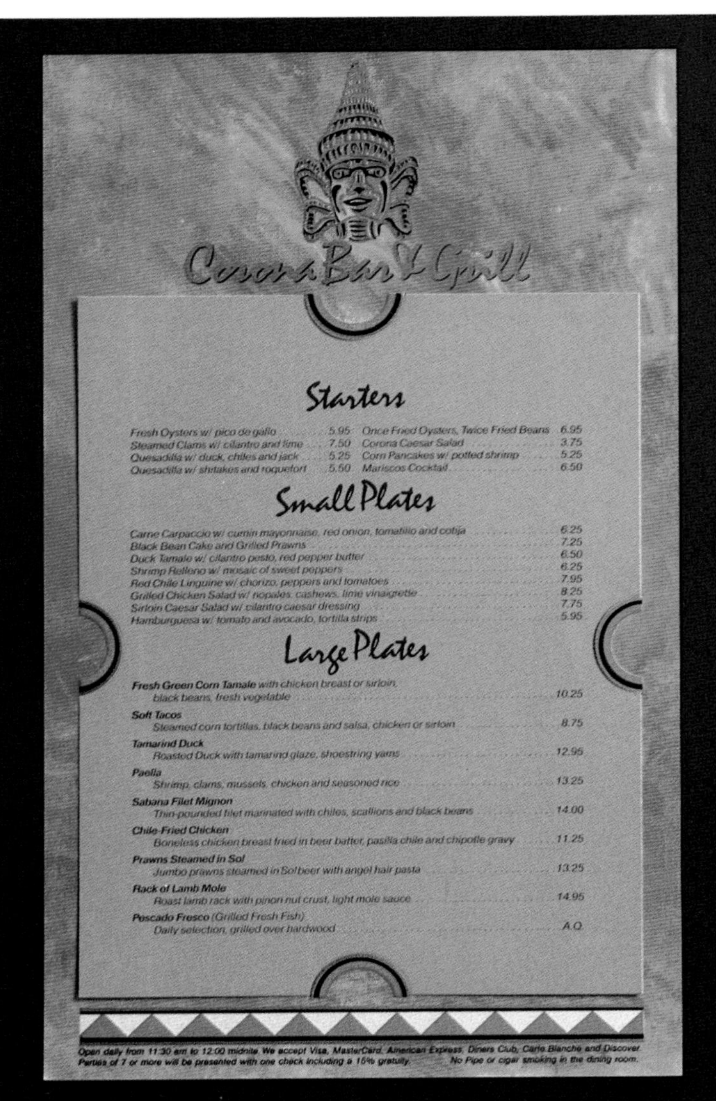

Corona Bar & Grill
Starters
Fresh Oysters w/ pico de gallo 5.95
Steamed Clams w/ cilantro and lime 7.50
Quesadilla w/ duck, chiles and jack 5.25
Quesadilla w/ shitakes and roquefort 5.50
Once Fried Oysters, Twice Fried Beans 6.95
Corona Caesar Salad 3.75
Corn Pancakes w/ potted shrimp 5.25
Mariscos Cocktail 6.50
Small Plates
Carne Carpaccio w/ cumin mayonnaise, red onion, tomatillo and cotija 6.25
Black Bean Cake and Grilled Prawns 7.25
Duck Tamale w/ cilantro pesto, red pepper butter 6.50
Shrimp Relleno w/ mosaic of sweet peppers 6.25
Red Chile Linguine w/ chorizo, peppers and tomatoes 7.95
Grilled Chicken Salad w/ nopales, cashews, lime vinaigrette 8.25
Sirloin Caesar Salad w/ cilantro caesar dressing 7.75
Hamburguesa w/ tomato and avocado, tortilla strips 5.95
Large Plates
Fresh Green Corn Tamale with chicken breast or sirloin, black beans, fresh vegetable 10.25
Soft Tacos
Steamed corn tortillas, black beans and salsa, chicken or sirloin 8.75
Tamarind Duck
Roasted Duck with tamarind glaze, shoestring yams 12.95
Paella
Shrimp, clams, mussels, chicken and seasoned rice 13.25
Sabana Filet Mignon
Thin-pounded filet marinated with chiles, scallions and black beans 14.00
Chile-Fried Chicken
Boneless chicken breast fried in beer batter, pasilla chile and chipotle gravy 11.25
Prawns Steamed in Sol
Jumbo prawns steamed in Sol beer with angel hair pasta 13.25
Rack of Lamb Mole
Roast lamb rack with pinon nut crust, light mole sauce 14.95
Poscado Fresco (Grilled Fresh Fish)
Daily selection, grilled over hardwood A.Q.
Open daily from 11:30 am to 12:00 midnite. We accept Visa, MasterCard, American Express, Diners Club, Carte Blanche and Discover.
Parties of 7 or more will be presented with one check including a 15% gratuity. No Pipe or cigar smoking in the dining room.


Rounded die-cuts hold the menu inserts firmly in place. The resulting menu can only be fully appreciated after viewing the initial sketches. The signature colors changed several times before the restaurant was opened. The designer gamely changed as the concept changed.

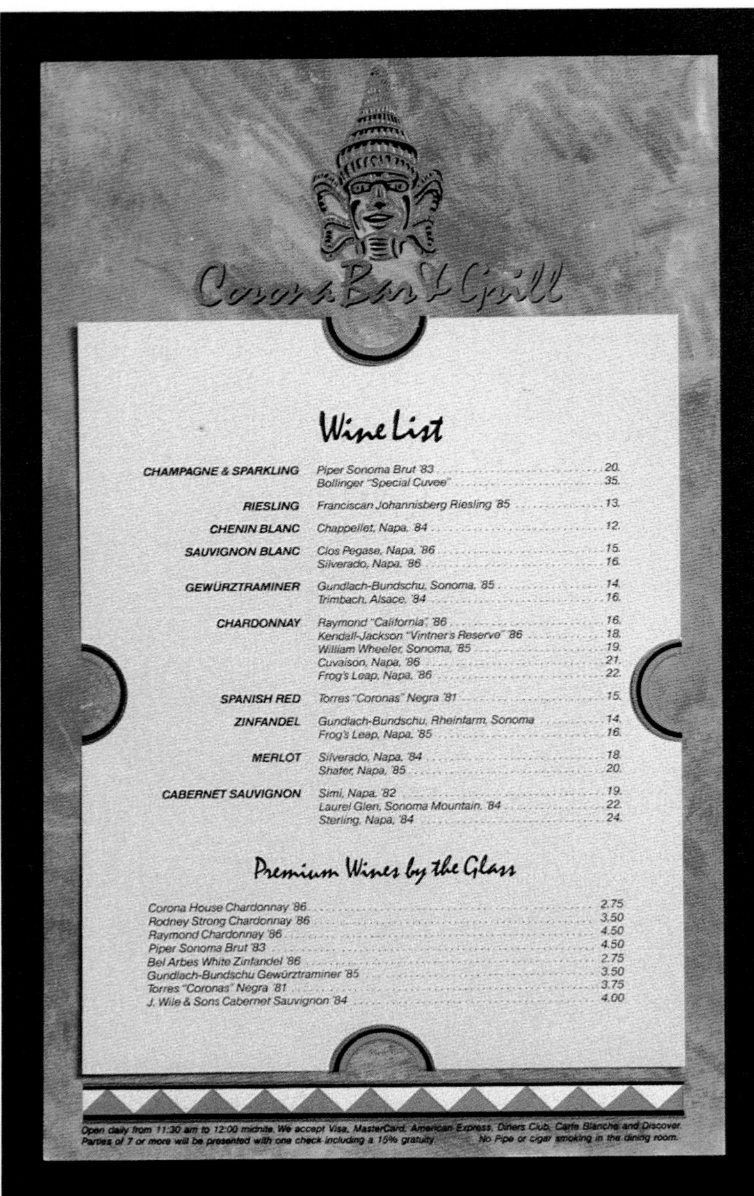

Corona Bar & Grill
Wine List
CHAMPAGNE & SPARKLING
Piper Sonoma Brut '83 20.
Bollinger "Special Cuvee" 35.
RIESLING
Franciscan Johannisberg Riesling '85 13.
CHENIN BLANC
Chappellet, Napa, '84 12.
SAUVIGNON BLANC
Clos Pegase, Napa, '86 15.
Silverado, Napa, '86 16.
GEWÜRZTRAMINER
Gundlach-Bundschu, Sonoma, '85 14.
Trimbach, Alsace, '84 16.
CHARDONNAY
Raymond "California", '86 16.
Kendall-Jackson "Vintner's Reserve" '86 18.
William Wheeler, Sonoma, '85 19.
Cuvaison, Napa, '86 21.
Frog's Leap, Napa, '86 22.
SPANISH RED
Torres "Coronas" Negra '81 15.
ZINFANDEL
Gundlach-Bundschu, Rheinfarm, Sonoma 14.
Frog's Leap, Napa, '85 16.
MERLOT
Silverado, Napa, '84 18.
Shafer, Napa, '85 20.
CABERNET SAUVIGNON
Simi, Napa, '82 19.
Laurel Glen, Sonoma Mountain, '84 22.
Sterling, Napa, '84 24.
Premium Wines by the Glass
Corona House Chardonnay '86 2.75
Rodney Strong Chardonnay '86 3.50
Raymond Chardonnay '86 4.50
Piper Sonoma Brut '83 4.50
Bel Arbes White Zinfandel '86 2.75
Gundlach-Bundschu Gewürztraminer '85 3.50
Torres "Coronas" Negra '81 3.75
J. Wile & Sons Cabernet Sauvignon '84 4.00
Open daily from 11:30 am to 12:00 midnite. We accept Visa, MasterCard, American Express, Diners Club, Carte Blanche and Discover.
Parties of 7 or more will be presented with one check including a 15% gratuity. No Pipe or cigar smoking in the dining room.

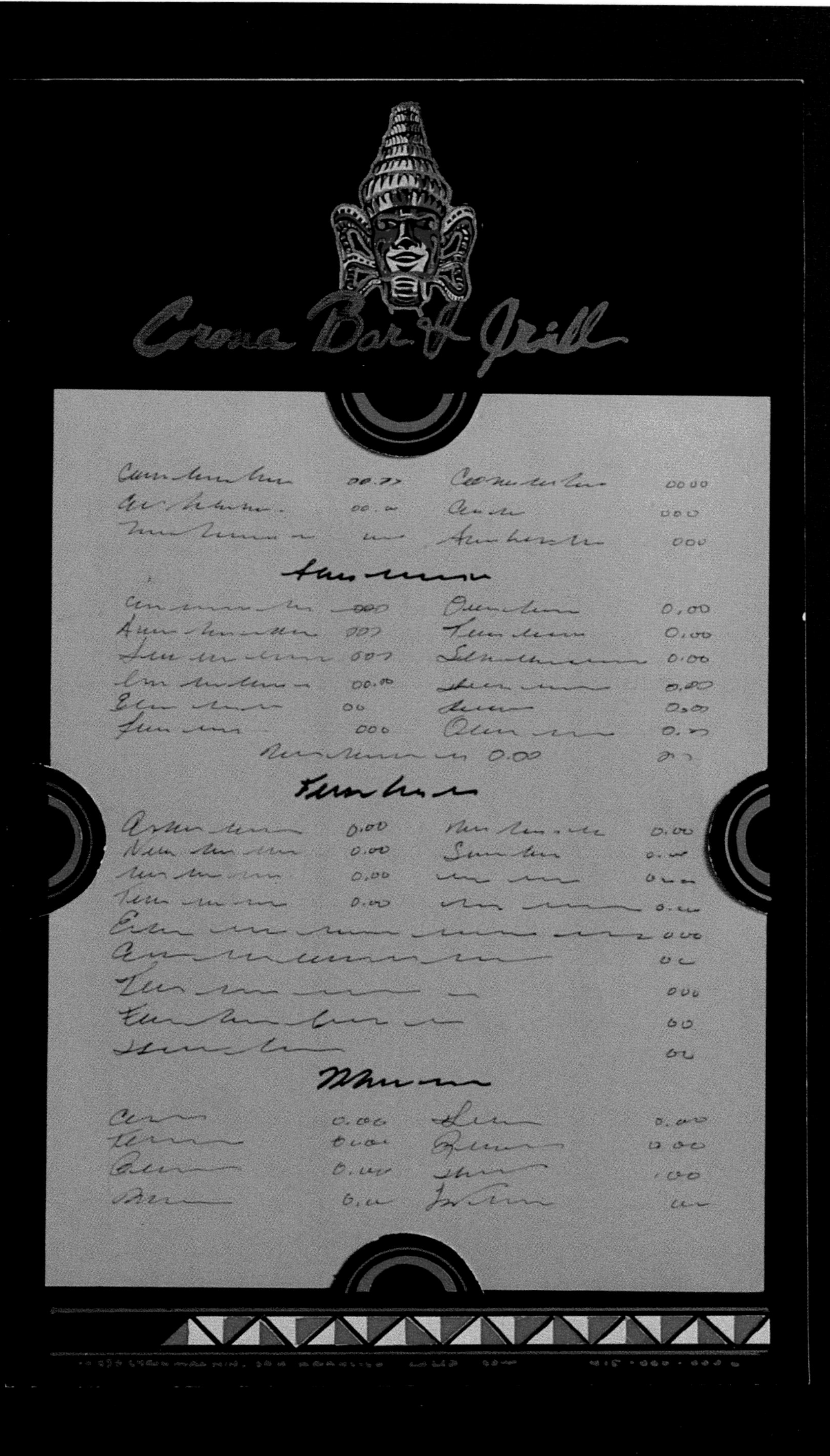


The final choices for menu (and restaurant) colors reflect the strong Mexican influence. Turquoise and copper are both found widely in Mexico. The pinks and golds of the background reflect both dawn and sunset in tropical climes. The final touch is supplied by the copper cord used to hold the wine list inserts into their cover.

Designer: *Lawrence E. Green*
*The Green Company*
Restaurant: *Butler's*
*Mill Valley, CA*

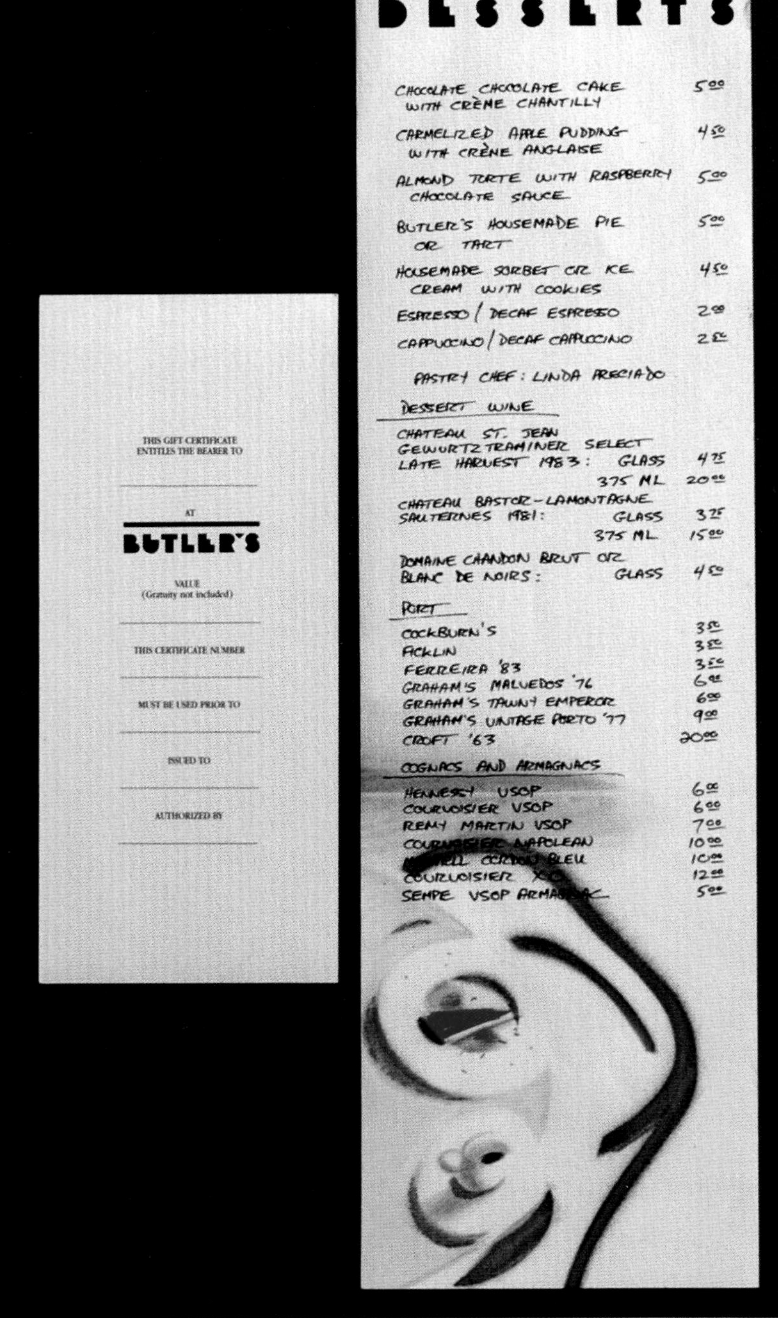


One water color illustration has been carefully cropped so that the portion on the dessert menu completes that on the main menu, just as dessert completes a meal. A different cropping appears on the gift certificate.

"Baby Teeth" is the typeface used for the restaurant name on the main menu and for the head on the dessert one. It is die-cut on the main one, set in black on the dessert menu. The handwriting used for the menu listings is that of Perry Butler, the owner. The menu has been designed so that the changing features can be imprinted in one color, black, for inexpensive updates. The management has chosen to list dessert wines on the dessert menu, rather than as part of the wine list. This makes good merchandising sense, as most diners would not think of asking for a second look at the wine list, after ordering a bottle to accompany the main part of the meal.

Designer: *Bruce Yelaska*
*Bruce Yelaska Design*

Restaurant: *Little City*
*San Francisco, CA*

The two-color menu shells are imprinted daily. The appropriate red dot is punched out for the corresponding date. The tiny red dot over the "double T" on the menu coordinates with the red dots in the calendar section. The back of the menu features the same design, but as a mirror image, to ensure the menu is presented properly to the diner. The associated matches include one match head which is colored red by hand whenever the servers have time to spare for the task.

The overall effect of the menu is immediate and exciting. Any menu that actually feels new every day (you can feel the raised type when you hold the menu in your hands) automatically makes the diner feel more special, more appreciated. The restaurant is situated in the heart of North Beach, San Francisco's cradle of Bohemian and artistic thought. This menu is perfect for the area's style.

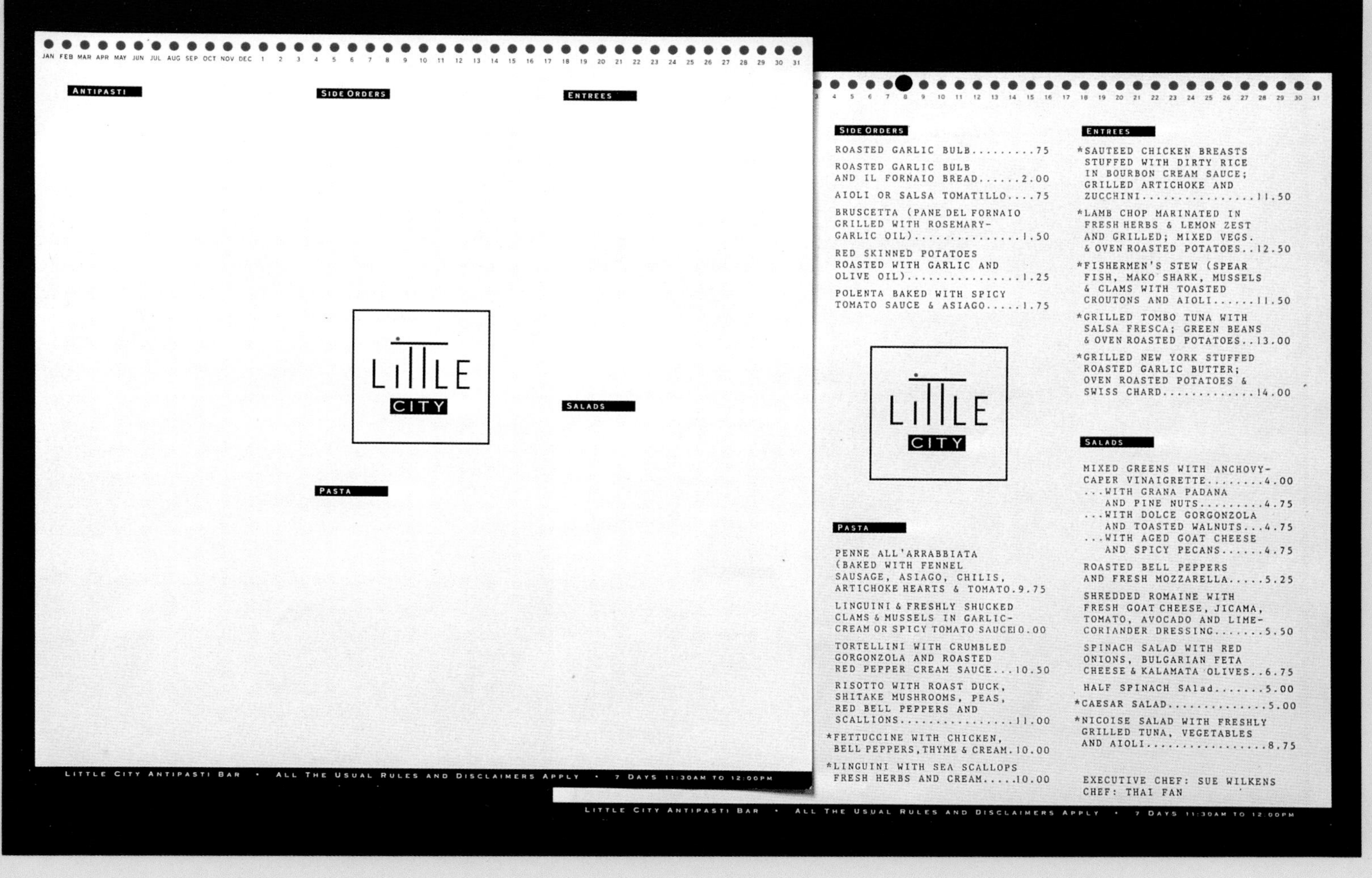

JAN FEB MAR APR MAY JUN JUL AUG SEP OCT NOV DEC 1 2 3 4 5 6 7 8 9 10 11 12 13 14 15 16 17 18 19 20 21 22 23 24 25 26 27 28 29 30 31
Antipasti
Side Orders
Entrees
LITTLE CITY
Salads
Pasta
Little City Antipasti Bar • All The Usual Rules and Disclaimers Apply • 7 Days 11:30am to 12:00pm
Side Orders
ROASTED GARLIC BULB.........75
ROASTED GARLIC BULB AND IL FORNAIO BREAD......2.00
AIOLI OR SALSA TOMATILLO....75
BRUSCETTA (PANE DEL FORNAIO GRILLED WITH ROSEMARY-GARLIC OIL)..............1.50
RED SKINNED POTATOES ROASTED WITH GARLIC AND OLIVE OIL)...............1.25
POLENTA BAKED WITH SPICY TOMATO SAUCE & ASIAGO.....1.75
Entrees
*SAUTEED CHICKEN BREASTS STUFFED WITH DIRTY RICE IN BOURBON CREAM SAUCE; GRILLED ARTICHOKE AND ZUCCHINI...............11.50
*LAMB CHOP MARINATED IN FRESH HERBS & LEMON ZEST AND GRILLED; MIXED VEGS. & OVEN ROASTED POTATOES..12.50
*FISHERMEN'S STEW (SPEAR FISH, MAKO SHARK, MUSSELS & CLAMS WITH TOASTED CROUTONS AND AIOLI......11.50
*GRILLED TOMBO TUNA WITH SALSA FRESCA; GREEN BEANS & OVEN ROASTED POTATOES..13.00
*GRILLED NEW YORK STUFFED ROASTED GARLIC BUTTER; OVEN ROASTED POTATOES & SWISS CHARD............14.00
LITTLE CITY
Salads
MIXED GREENS WITH ANCHOVY-CAPER VINAIGRETTE........4.00
...WITH GRANA PADANA AND PINE NUTS.........4.75
...WITH DOLCE GORGONZOLA AND TOASTED WALNUTS...4.75
...WITH AGED GOAT CHEESE AND SPICY PECANS......4.75
ROASTED BELL PEPPERS AND FRESH MOZZARELLA.....5.25
SHREDDED ROMAINE WITH FRESH GOAT CHEESE, JICAMA, TOMATO, AVOCADO AND LIME-CORIANDER DRESSING.......5.50
SPINACH SALAD WITH RED ONIONS, BULGARIAN FETA CHEESE & KALAMATA OLIVES..6.75
HALF SPINACH SAlad.......5.00
*CAESAR SALAD.............5.00
*NICOISE SALAD WITH FRESHLY GRILLED TUNA, VEGETABLES AND AIOLI................8.75
Pasta
PENNE ALL'ARRABBIATA (BAKED WITH FENNEL SAUSAGE, ASIAGO, CHILIS, ARTICHOKE HEARTS & TOMATO.9.75
LINGUINI & FRESHLY SHUCKED CLAMS & MUSSELS IN GARLIC-CREAM OR SPICY TOMATO SAUCE10.00
TORTELLINI WITH CRUMBLED GORGONZOLA AND ROASTED RED PEPPER CREAM SAUCE...10.50
RISOTTO WITH ROAST DUCK, SHITAKE MUSHROOMS, PEAS, RED BELL PEPPERS AND SCALLIONS...............11.00
*FETTUCCINE WITH CHICKEN, BELL PEPPERS,THYME & CREAM.10.00
*LINGUINI WITH SEA SCALLOPS FRESH HERBS AND CREAM.....10.00
EXECUTIVE CHEF: SUE WILKENS
CHEF: THAI FAN
Little City Antipasti Bar • All The Usual Rules and Disclaimers Apply • 7 Days 11:30am to 12:00pm

Designer: *Allen Eisbrenner*
*Associates Printing Service, Inc.*
Restaurant: *Squash Blossom*
*Hyatt Regency Scottsdale*
*Scottsdale, AZ*

A die-cut bleed frame holds the menu insert. While the cover is imprinted in multiple colors, the inserts feature two colors; one color is used for the menu headings, the second, for the items and prices. This solution permits not only the covers to be imprinted in advance, but also the insert masters.

The brilliant colors used for the menu identify this as the lunch menu, rather than that used for dinner. The designer, by evoking desert images and colors, conveys a strong sense of place.

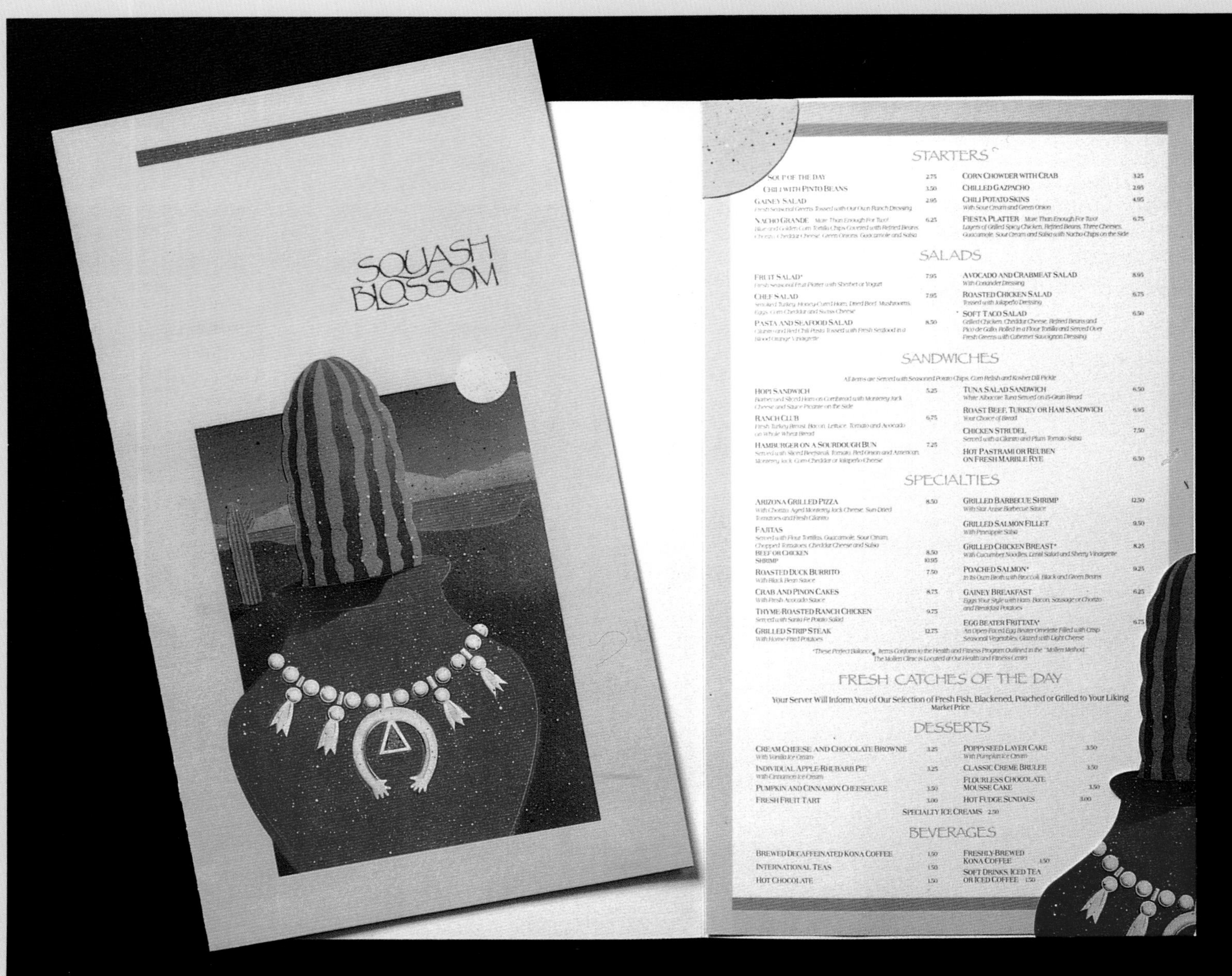

**Designer:** *Debra Tenuta*
*Associates Printing Service, Inc.*
**Restaurant:** *Andrea's*
*Glenview, IL*

The best solution for a daily menu is either a heavy cardstock or a holder that will not fall apart in the diner's hands. This menu uses the latter technique. The two-color insert sheet lends a note of refinement to the menu.

Designer: *Sara Love*
*Sara Love-Graphic Design*
Restaurant: *Fletcher's American Grill & Cafe*
*Indianapolis, IN*

Airiness was the key theme desired by the restaurateur, along with a commitment to America's heartland. The menu covers for Fletcher's are silkscreened on the inside of the plexiglass to protect the design from scratches. Hand-plaited cords hold the inserts in place.

The menu is designed with pockets to accommodate a menu which changes daily. Menu inserts are in colors drawn from the cover; these are, in turn, drawn from the restaurant's decor. Plexiglass was chosen for the menu covers because plexiglass panels are used in each booth for privacy.

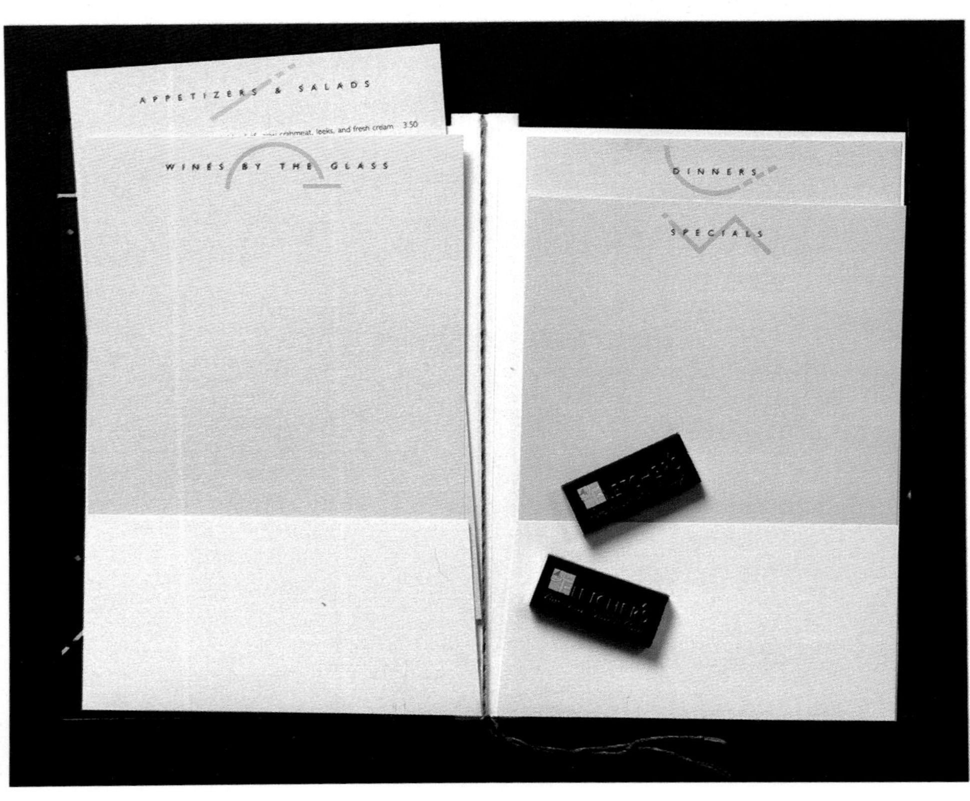

Designer: *Rick Tharp and Kim Tomlinson*
*Tharp Did It*
Restaurant: *Café Bon Appétit*
*San Francisco Bay Area, CA*

These two-color menu sheets were the first element in a design scheme which eventually was expanded to include banners, signage and architectural enhancements. The corporate logo, which appears on both the wine list and the daily menu sheet, is executed in grey on high-quality grey paper for the corporate peripherals. On the menu card, the soft aqua appears in a graduated screen, which lends the otherwise sophisticated treatment a certain softness.

The whole program is carefully planned to present a consistent and coherent image.

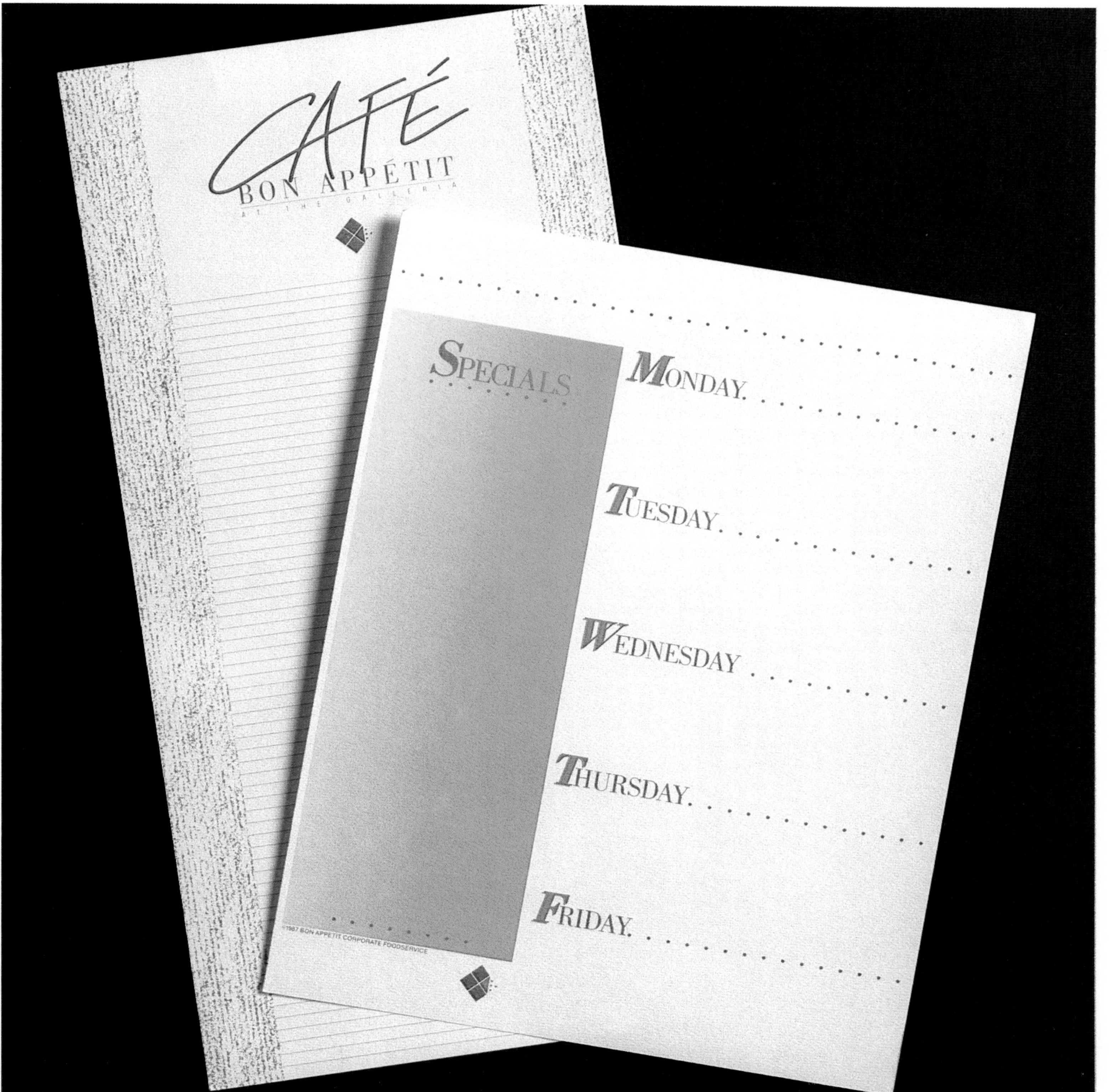

| | |
|---|---|
| Designer: | *Cynthia Lehman* |
| | *Associates Printing Service, Inc.* |
| Restaurant: | *Mrs. O'Leary's* |
| | *Hyatt Regency Chicago* |
| | *Chicago, IL* |

These simple, three-columned menu masters are imprinted with a daily menu listing via laser printer. The graphics used on the masters lend a note of greater formality to the menus than would be achieved by using typed inserts with a more permanent cover.

The menu design is made informal and fairly light-hearted by the use of "hand-written" heads for each section.

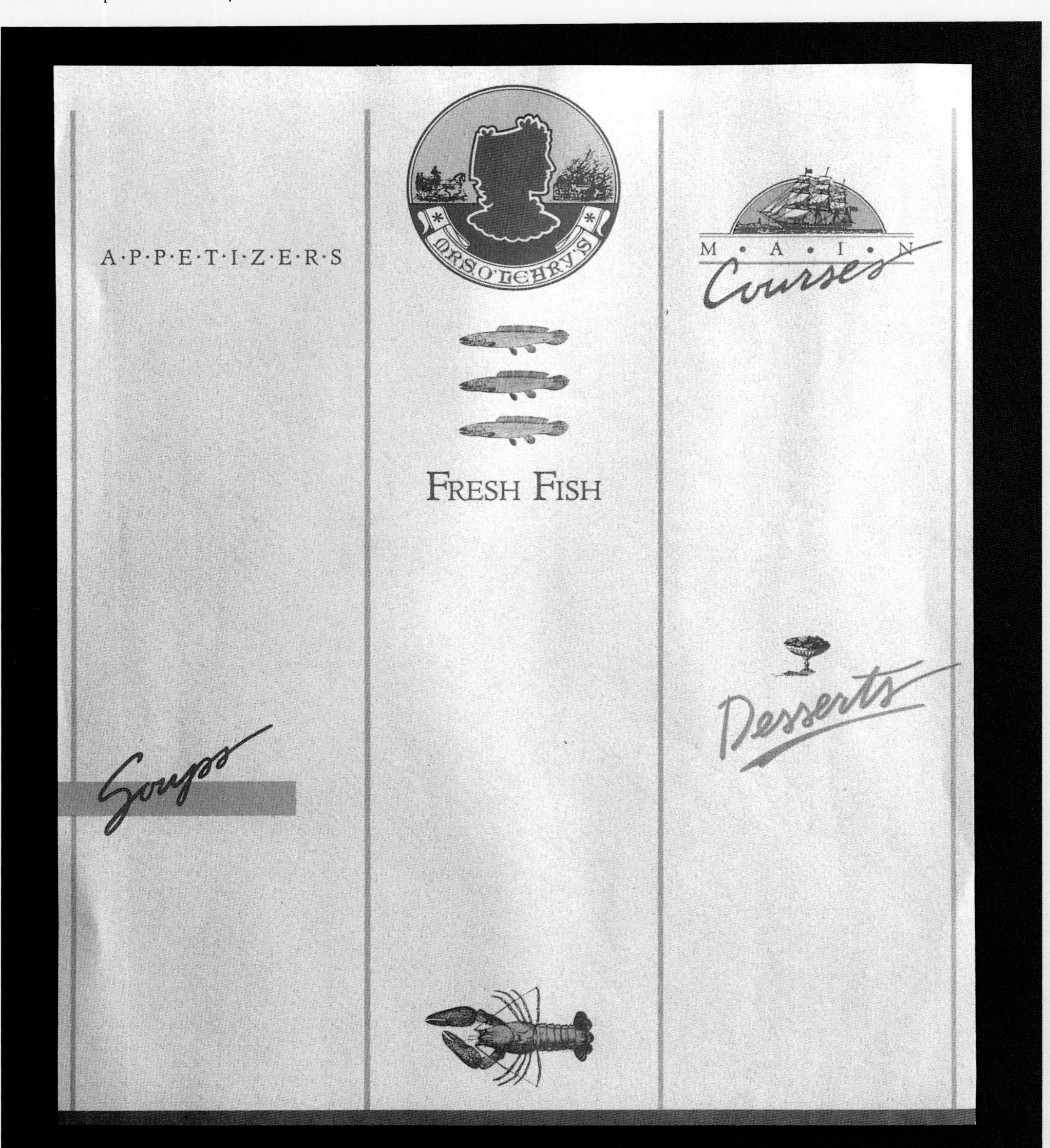

| | |
|---|---|
| **Designer:** | *Niki Bonnett* |
| | *Niki Bonnett Design* |
| **Restaurant:** | *Westchester Country Club* |
| | *Rye, NY* |

This country club restaurant, which caters to about 100 live-in guests as well as the general membership, wanted a menu with enough flexibility to permit daily specials. It was important, too, to pay tribute to the baroque feeling of the surroundings.

The solution was a menu imprinted in one color, burgundy, which could be screened down for the artwork. A special pocket was designed for the right-hand page. This permits production of a specials sheet which will not fall out during handling by the diners or serving staff.

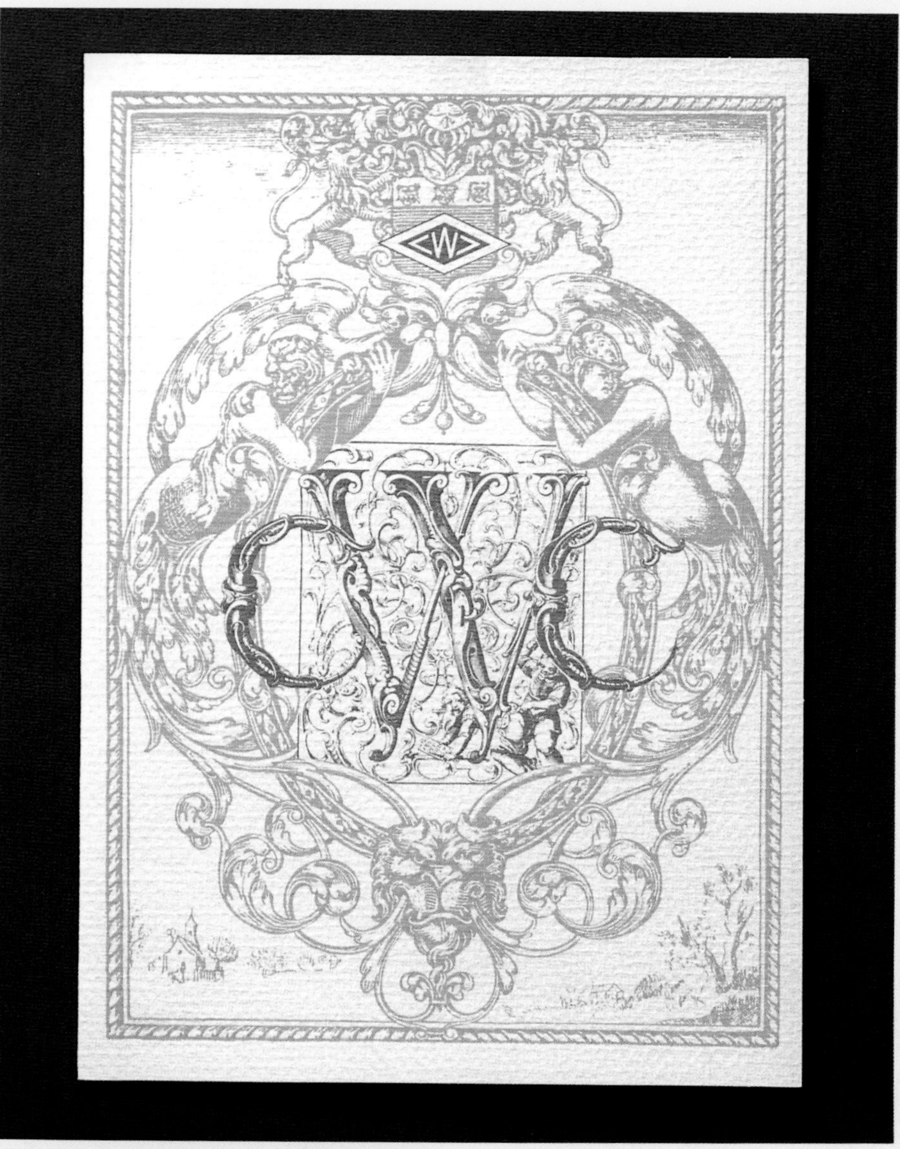

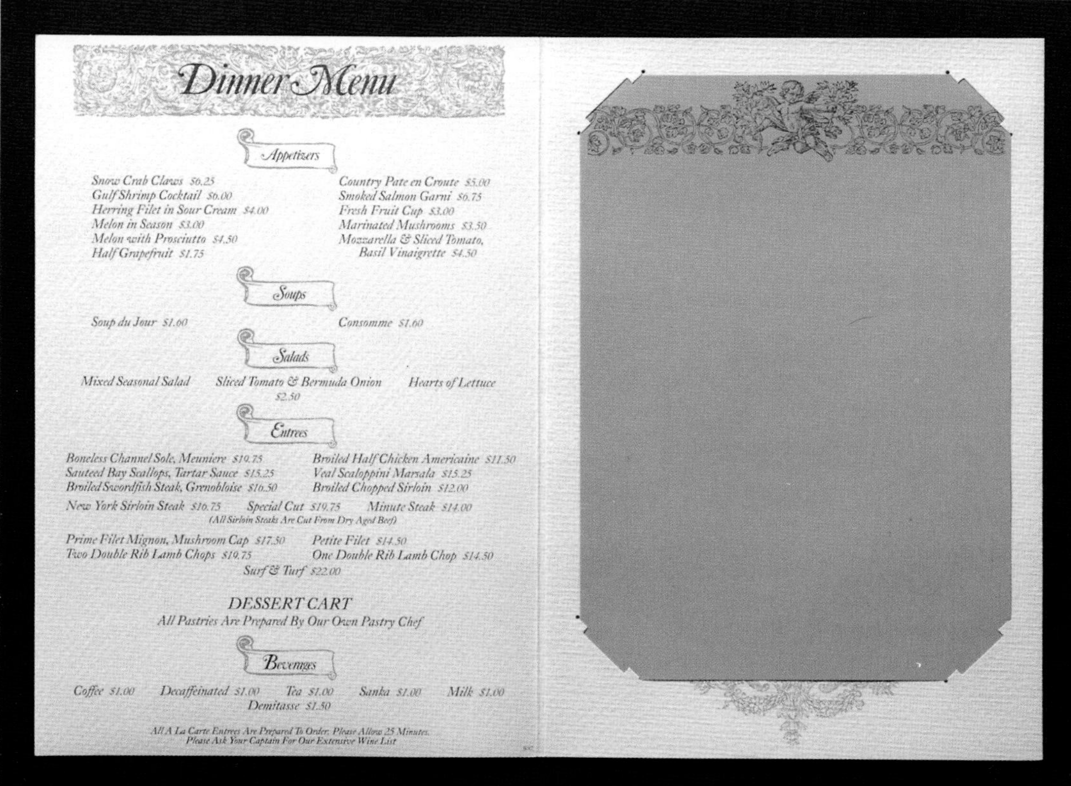

Dinner Menu
Appetizers
Snow Crab Claws $6.25
Gulf Shrimp Cocktail $6.00
Herring Filet in Sour Cream $4.00
Melon in Season $3.00
Melon with Prosciutto $4.50
Half Grapefruit $1.75
Country Pate en Croute $5.00
Smoked Salmon Garni $6.75
Fresh Fruit Cup $3.00
Marinated Mushrooms $3.50
Mozzarella & Sliced Tomato, Basil Vinaigrette $4.50
Soups
Soup du Jour $1.60
Consomme $1.60
Salads
Mixed Seasonal Salad
Sliced Tomato & Bermuda Onion
Hearts of Lettuce
$2.50
Entrees
Boneless Channel Sole, Meuniere $19.75
Sauteed Bay Scallops, Tartar Sauce $15.25
Broiled Swordfish Steak, Grenobloise $16.50
Broiled Half Chicken Americaine $11.50
Veal Scaloppini Marsala $15.25
Broiled Chopped Sirloin $12.00
New York Sirloin Steak $16.75
Special Cut $19.75
Minute Steak $14.00
(All Sirloin Steaks Are Cut From Dry Aged Beef)
Prime Filet Mignon, Mushroom Cap $17.50
Two Double Rib Lamb Chops $19.75
Petite Filet $14.50
One Double Rib Lamb Chop $14.50
Surf & Turf $22.00
DESSERT CART
All Pastries Are Prepared By Our Own Pastry Chef
Beverages
Coffee $1.00
Decaffeinated $1.00
Tea $1.00
Sanka $1.00
Milk $1.00
Demitasse $1.50
All A La Carte Entrees Are Prepared To Order. Please Allow 25 Minutes.
Please Ask Your Captain For Our Extensive Wine List


Each day's specials are typed by hand and mimeographed onto the special matched letterhead for inclusion into the shell. Because the letterhead sheet is relatively flimsy, the pocket for it is a double thickness of the shell stock.

# CHAPTER 7

Menus designed for catering and, especially, those for use at special events,present a real challenge to the designer. The menus must be both elegant, festive or amusing and yet fairly inexpensive to produce.

Catering menus must present a uniform image but always include a variety of elements. Even though room layouts, menu selections, prices and peripheral services must be discussed, they must all work together to create a cohesive image. One of the most effective ways to achieve this is to use coordinated, stepped inserts in a colorful folder. Using similar papers in harmonizing colors and typefaces is one effective technique in this application.

One decision faced by the restaurant itself is how many special events for which to produce unique menus. Such factors as profitability, public relations value and the specific audience of a given facility must be carefully considered.

In this chapter we will see menus for everything from the major holidays to a limited edition catering collection to a once-in-a-lifetime dinner. In each case, the designer has found a practical yet creative treatment.

# CATERING AND SPECIAL EVENTS

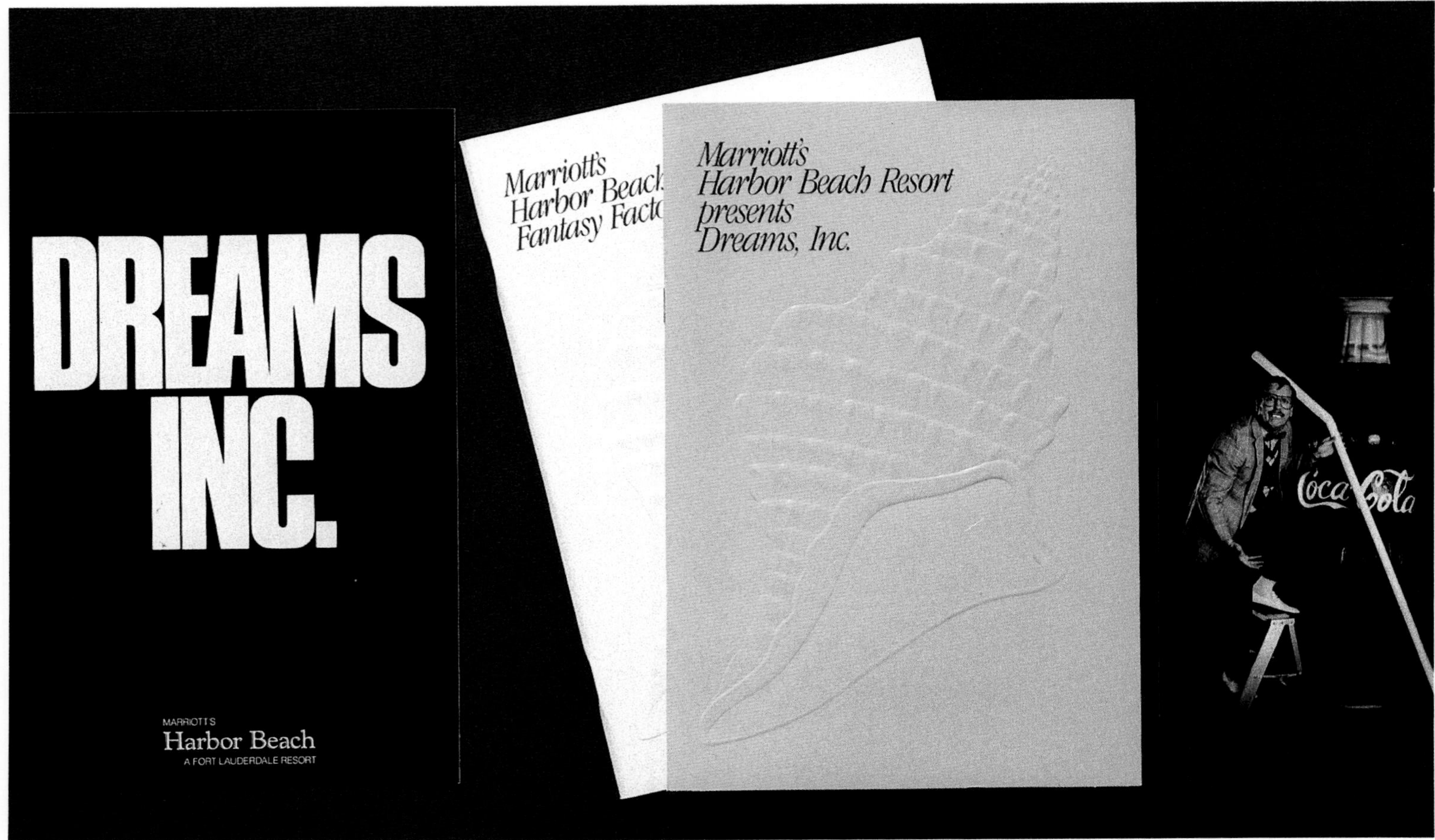


Designer: *G. Eugene Wigger*
Restaurant: *Marriott's Harbor Beach Resort*
*Fort Lauderdale, FL*

**1987 N.R.A. GREAT MENUS CONTEST WINNER: SECOND PLACE, BANQUET/CATERING**

The blind-embossed seashell set against a soft orange and turquoise background on the cover of this menu folder says 'Florida' to anyone who's ever been there. The beach is subtly implied by the horizontal lines, which grow closer together as they rise higher on the cover. The effect is of a horizon, giving a two-dimensional piece a three-dimensional feeling.

Inside, stepped inserts allow the potential host or hostess to choose from among a broad variety of carefully-orchestrated fantasies without confusion. A realistic seashell die cut limns one side of the inner flaps. Beautiful paper stock underlines the theme ... Dreams, Inc.

MARRIOTT'S
Harbor Beach
RESORT

AVOID BANQUET BOREDOM
Group meals can have many purposes—fun, a stage for announcements, relaxation, a gearing up for the evening ahead or plain nourishment. Determine yours, then plan carefully to achieve your objective.
Creative catering has become something of a hackneyed expression in the meetings business. Its goal, to inject excitement into a group meal experience, is certainly valid, but often takes the form of empty razzmatazz that is jazzing up what amounts to plain old mashed potatoes.
As with the meetings business itself, creative "show biz" catering is really effective only when it is grounded in tangible practices, each with an explainable raison d'etre.
MEETINGS
G. Eugene Wigger
Director of Catering
MARRIOTT'S
Harbor Beach
A FORT LAUDERDALE RESORT
3030 Holiday Drive
Fort Lauderdale, Florida 33316
305/766-6129
305/525-4000

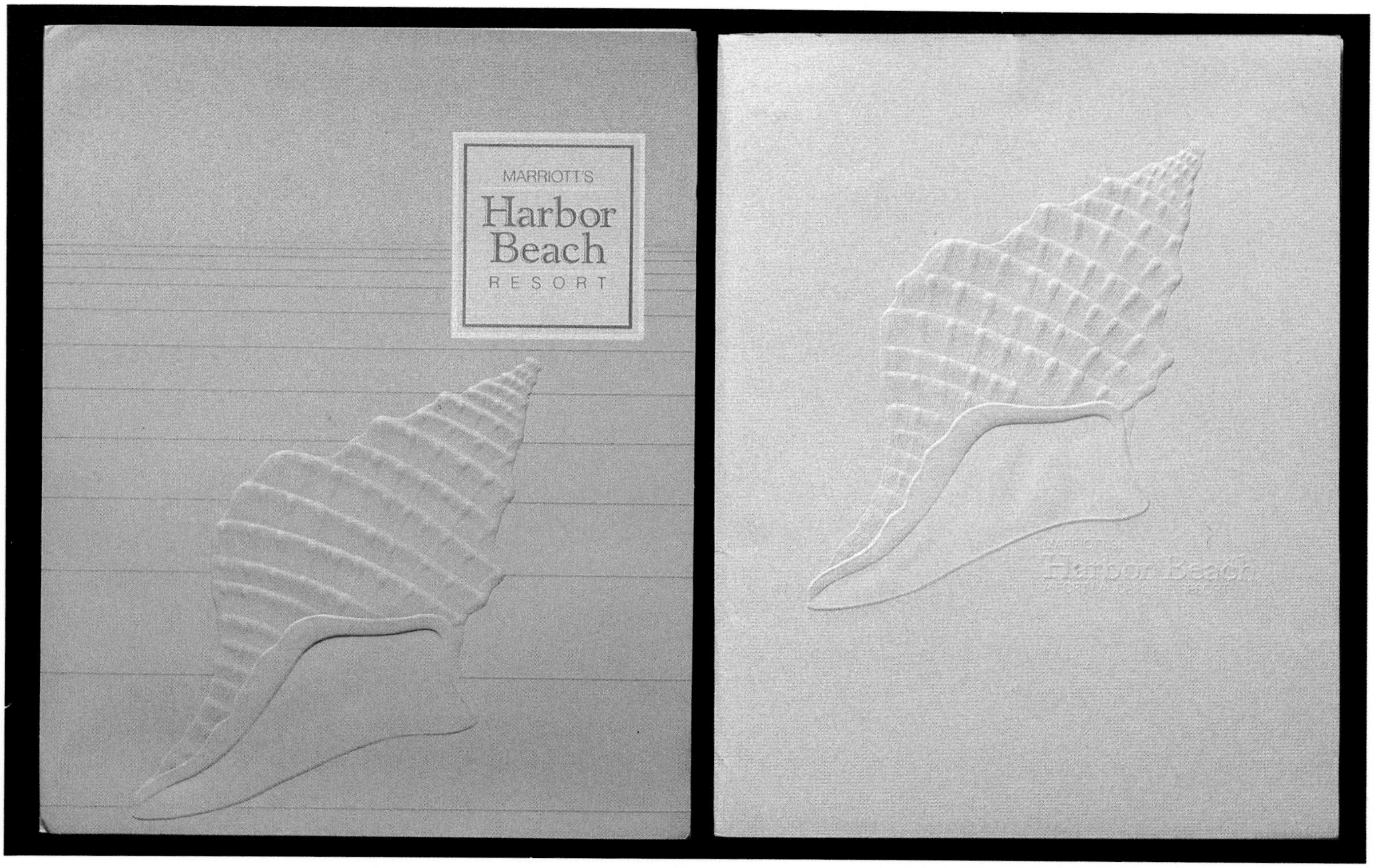

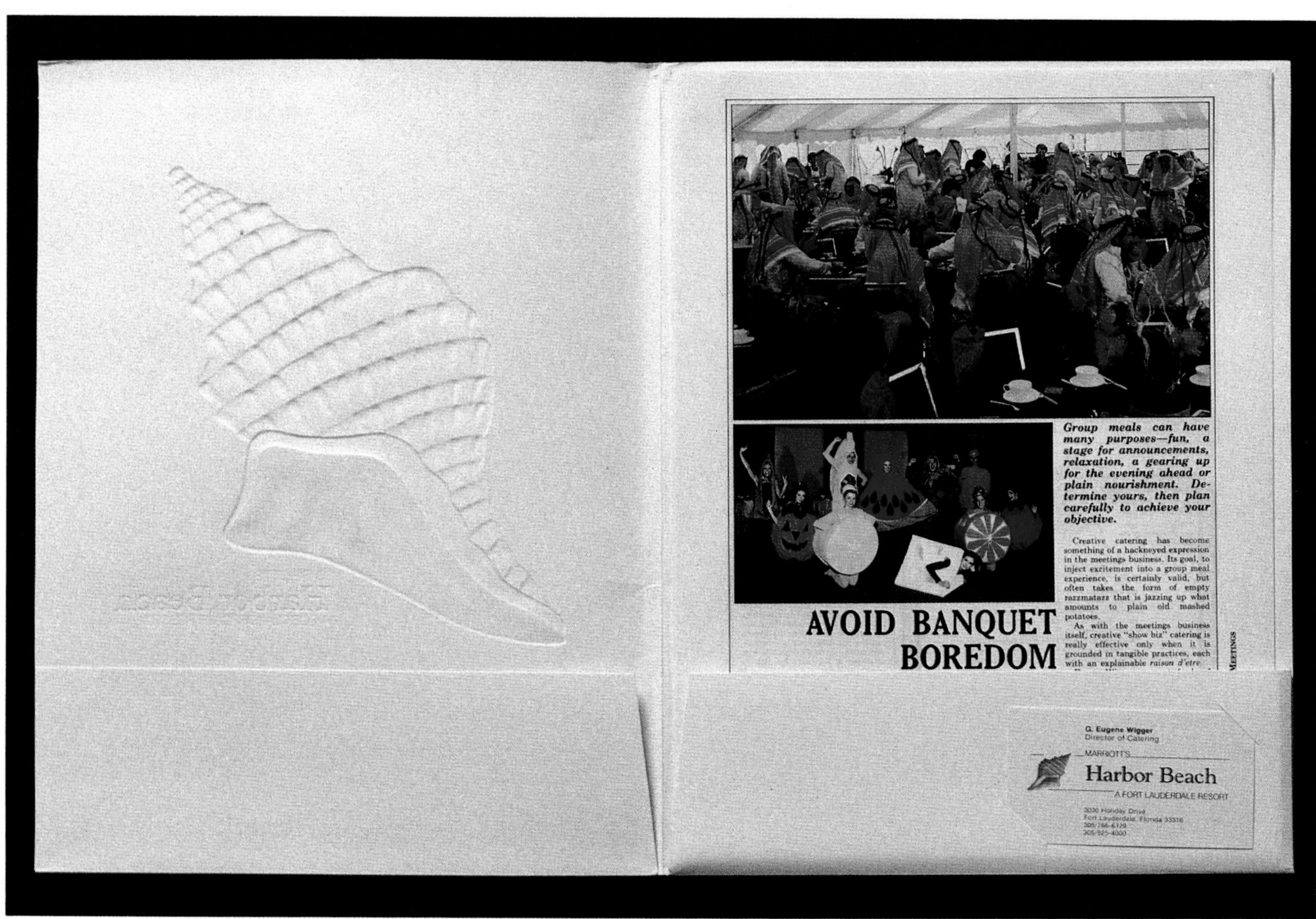

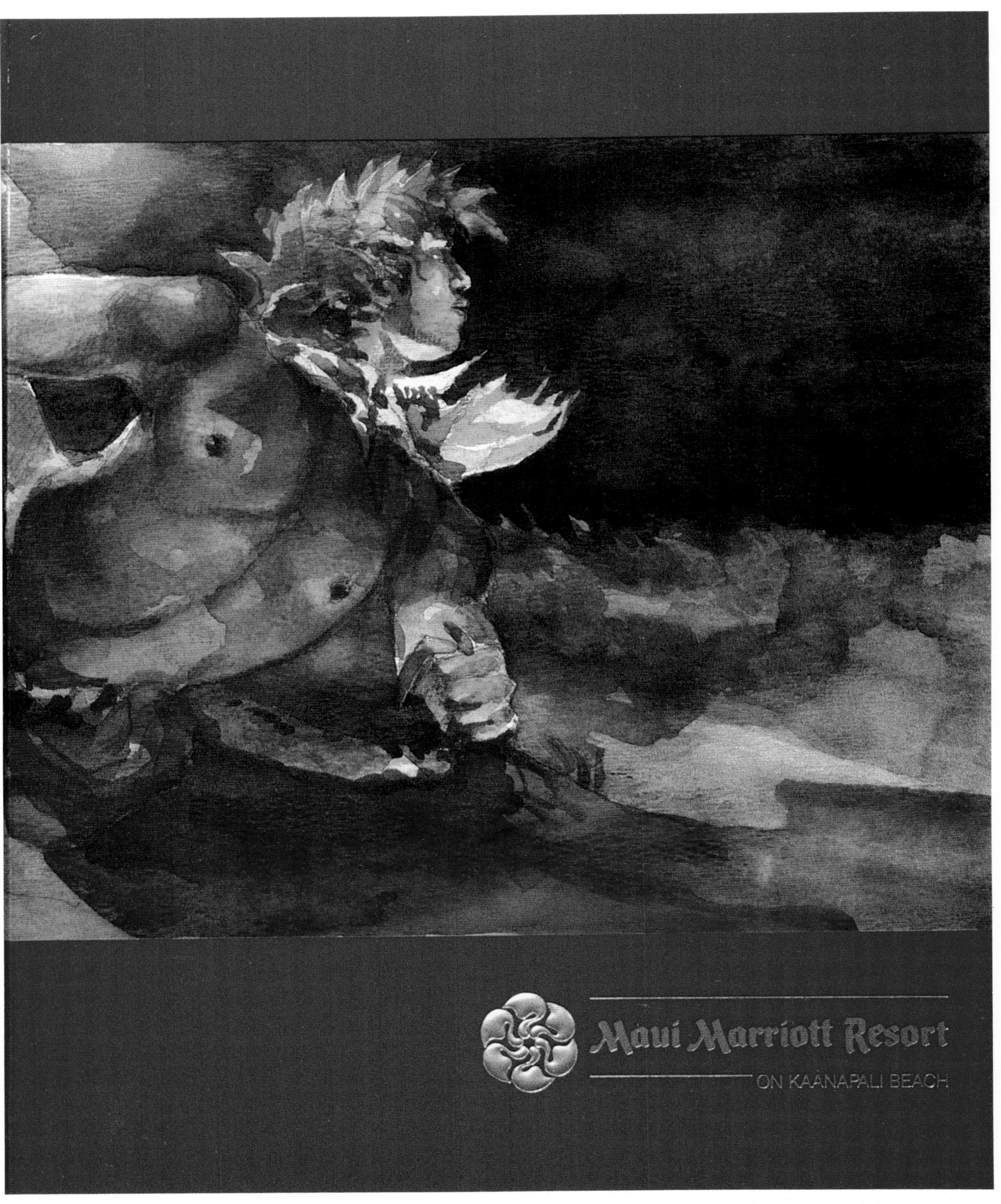
Maui Marriott Resort
ON KAANAPALI BEACH

Designer: *Al Lagunero*
*Prints Pacific*
Restaurant: *Maui Marriott Resort*
*Lahaina, Maui, Hawaii*

**1987 N.R.A. GREAT MENUS CONTEST WINNER: FIRST PLACE, BANQUET/CATERING**

This exquisite catering portfolio features watercolor paintings of Maui by a local artist, Al Kahekiliuila Lagunero, and was produced in a limited edition of 1500. The cover features a wraparound reproduction of a watercolor. Each insert is created in a different color of the same cover stock; interior pages are coordinated in a lighter weight stock of contrasting color.

There are six paintings laid into the various booklets. Each has been reproduced in full color, is perforated for removal and, if the customer so desires, framing. Each menu listing is also perforated for easy removal and submission to the catering department.

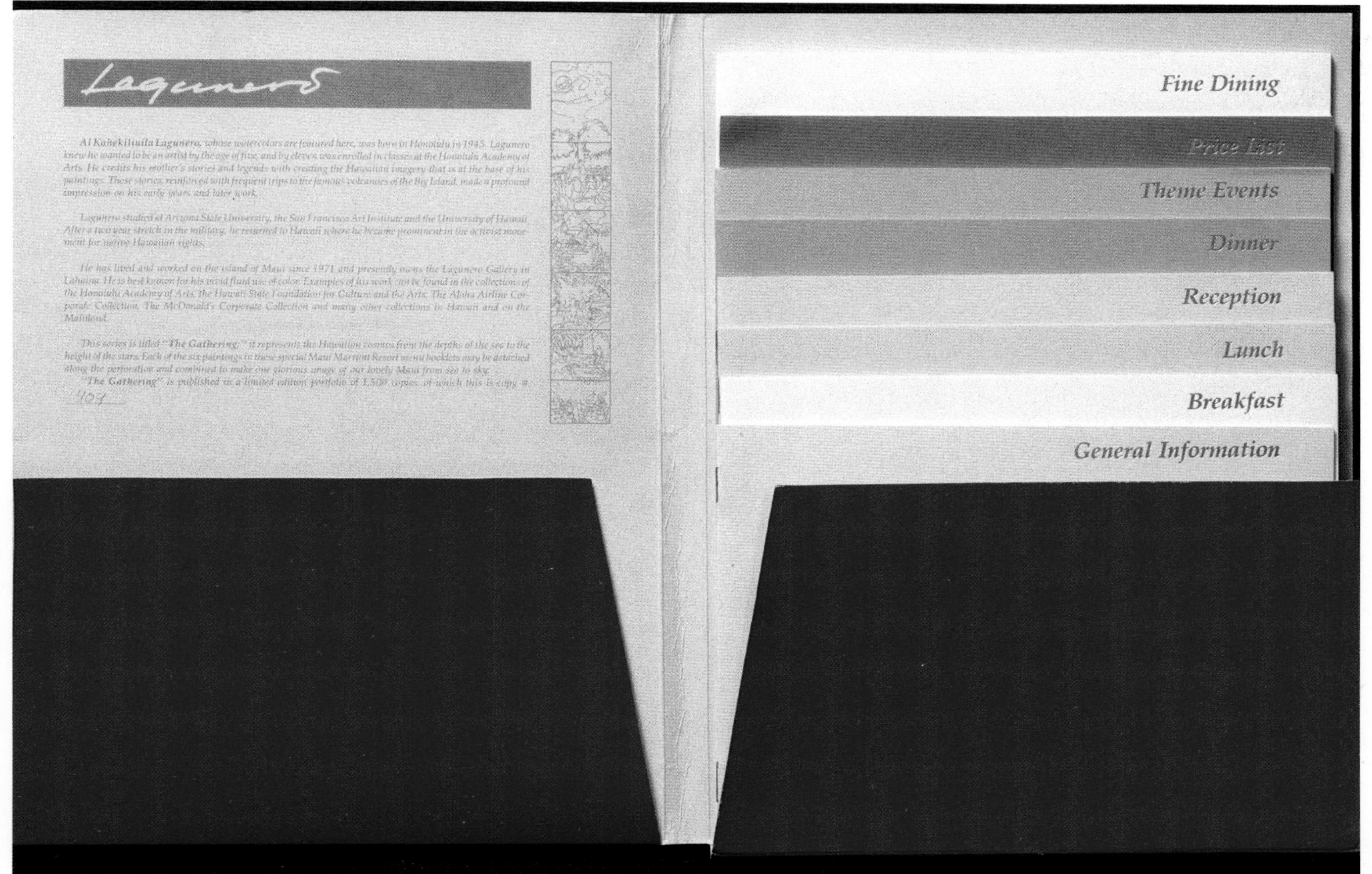

PICTURE YOUR BUSINESS MEETING IN THE
HYATT REGENCY O'HARE'S GARDEN OF DELIGHTS.
HYATT REGENCY O'HARE
9300 WEST BRYN MAWR AVENUE · ROSEMONT, ILLINOIS 60018 · 312/696-1234

HYATT REGENCY O'HARE
Imagine your wedding at the Hyatt Regency O'Hare . . . Elegant. Festive. In an enchanting setting of lush green foliage, with singing birds and bright flowers.

**Designer:** *Associates Printing Service, Inc.*
**Restaurant:** *Catering Menus*
*Hyatt Regency O'Hare*
*Rosemont, IL*

The basic design of these menus owes much to Henri Rousseau's *Jungle Scenery with Setting Sun.* A fanciful jungle scene provides the backdrop for whatever central figure is appropriate to the occasion for which the menu will be used. A chef, a wedding cake or a group of business people are all possibilities.

The underlying theme is that a catered event, whether for business or to celebrate one of life's own special events, is, in a sense, the embodiment of a fantasy. The illustration employs vivid colors but a softened outline to underscore this point. The copywriting, heavy on adjectives, completes the image of competence and imagination.

**Designer:** *Ann Werner*
*Associates Printing Service, Inc.*
**Restaurant:** *New Year's Eve Wine List*
*Regency Ballroom*
*Hyatt Regency Chicago*
*Chicago, IL*

Spatters of ink in lavender and turquoise suggest the confetti traditional for New Year's Eve on this festive wine list. Its sturdy coated stock should hold up well for one evening, even though spills are inevitable.

While the traditional sparklers are featured — both French Champagnes and American sparkling wines, there are also both red and white wines. This choice may, in fact, indicate that Americans are becoming more sophisticated about wines, choosing them not just for the occasion but to suit the foods they will accompany. What appears on a menu or wine list is often an indicator of a larger social trend.

CHAMPAGNE

TAITTINGER, BLANC DE BLANC $95.00

MOËT & CHANDON, BRUT $40.00

SCHRAMSBERG, BLANC DE BLANC $30.00

DOMAINE CHANDON, HYATT CUVEE $21.00

WHITE WINES

POUILLY-FUISSE, LOUIS JADOT 1985 $30.00

CHARDONNAY, BERINGER 1985 $21.00

CHARDONNAY, CHATEAU STE. MICHELLE 1985 $21.00

J. LOHR WHITE, N.V. $15.00

RED WINES

CABERNET SAUVIGNON, ROBERT MONDAVI 1985 $30.00

BORDEAUX, CHATEAU LA TOUR CARNET 1981 $30.00

BEAUJOLAIS-VILLAGES, LOUIS JADOT 1985 $18.00

J. LOHR N.V. $15.00

PRICES DO NOT INCLUDE TAX.

HYATT REGENCY CHICAGO

Designer: *Allen Eisbrener*
*Associates Printing Service, Inc.*
Restaurant: *Asparagus Festival*
*Hyatt Regency Chicago*
*Chicago, IL*

Designer: *Cynthia Lehman*
*Associates Printing Service, Inc.*
Restaurant: *Mushroom Festival*
*Hyatt Regency Chicago*
*Chicago, IL*

# M·U·S·H·R·O·O·M·S

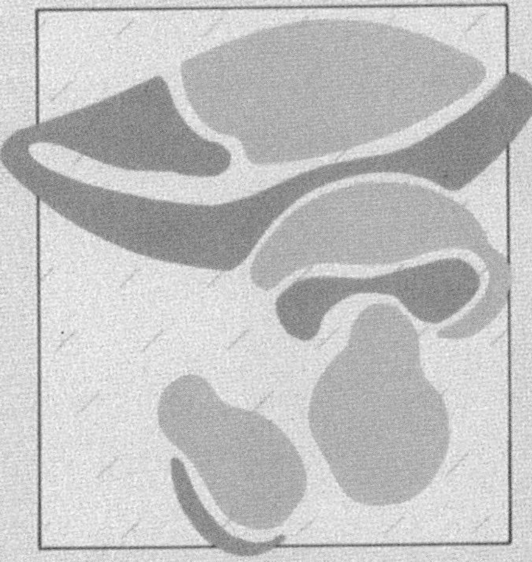

## A P P E T I Z E R S

*Tartar of Cèpes, Romaine and Chanterelle Mushrooms with a Tenderloin Carpaccio.*
5.95

*Quail Eggs Scrambled with Morel, Chanterelle and Lemon Tree Oyster Mushrooms. Apple Rösti and Quail Jus.*
5.50

*Essence of Shiitake and Truffles En Croûte.*
3.50

## DINNER ENTREES

BUFFALO, NEW YORK
*Grilled with Shiitake, Oyster and Portobello Mushrooms. Potato-Apple Pancakes and Rose Hip Sauce.*
22.95

TENDERLOIN OF VEAL
*With Duxelles of Crimini, Shiitake and Champignon Mushrooms rolled in Cole. Potato-Apple Pancakes and White Truffle Sauce.*
21.50

VENISON MEDALLIONS
*Sautéed and Served with a Treasure Chest of Maine Lobster Nuggets, Morel, Angel Trumpet, Chanterelle and Lobster Mushrooms. Venison Demi-Glace.*
22.50

SQUAB BREAST AND FRESH FOIE GRAS
*Sautéed Romaine, Portobello and Angel Trumpet Mushrooms. Potato-Apple Pancakes and Squab Jus.*
22.50

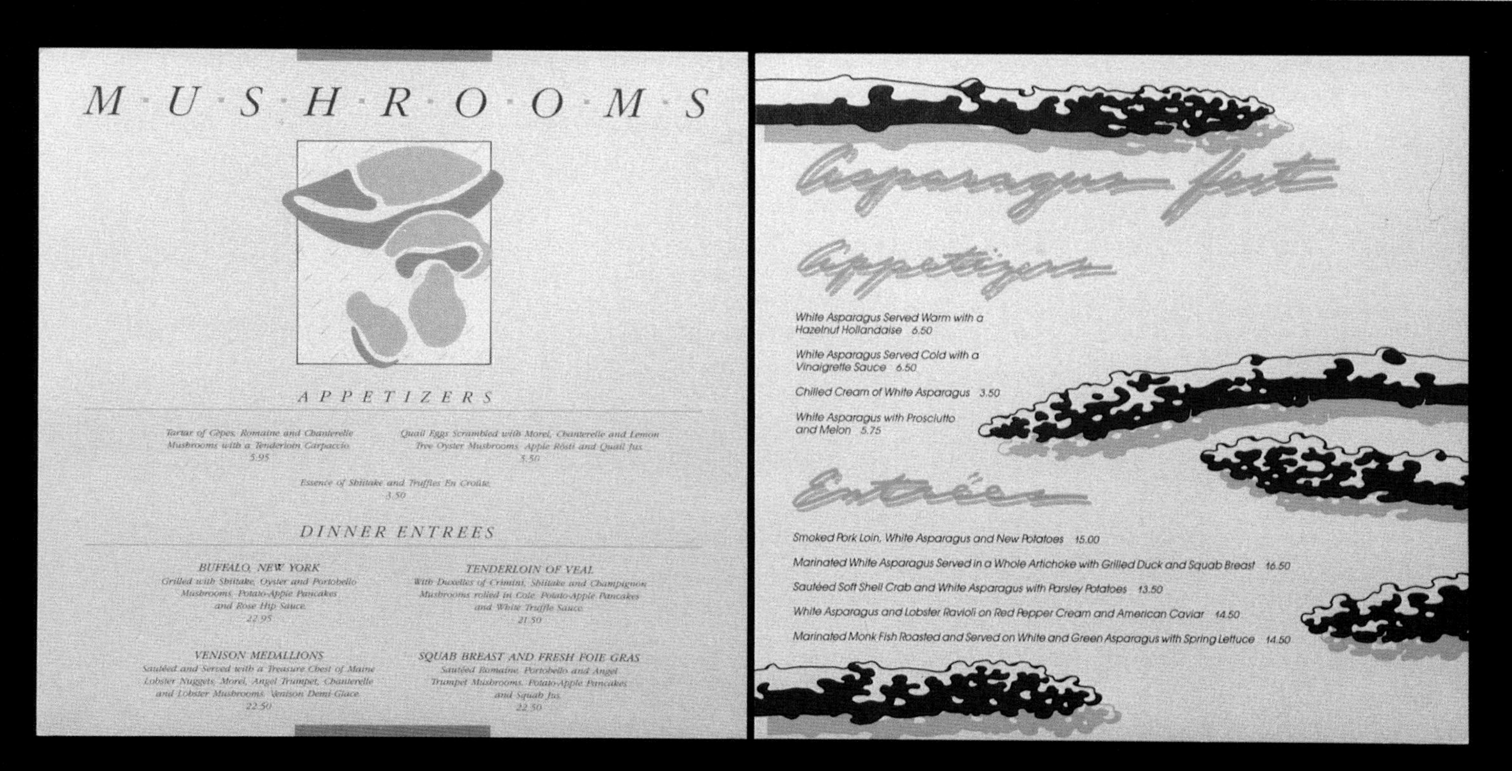


Both of these special event menus feature unusual foods which would be too daring for a regular menu. While asparagus is relatively well-known, many Americans have never eaten any but canned white asparagus. The growing method required — burying the stalks so that they never turn green — requires too much hand labor to be practical on a large scale in the United States. The mushrooms featured on the companion menu range from cepes and chanterelles to the more unusual angel trumpet and lobster mushrooms.

Each menu uses only two colors but drop shadows and screens, plus a stylized graphic, lend the asparagus piece a sophistication which amply supports the elegant food. The magenta and salmon on the mushroom menu actually appear to be three or more colors by virtue of the way the menu was shot. The holding line around the white box, for example, appears more vivid than does the lettering, simply because it is next to a white field. The mushroom shapes are sufficiently exotic to convince the viewer that these are not grocery store mushrooms but not so botanically exact as to lock the restaurant into providing only one type.

Both menus work well because they make the most of two colors and are printed only on one side. The asparagus menu, in particular, has a poster-like quality. This is an attractive and inexpensive solution to the limited use menu.

Designer: *Niki Bonnett*
*Niki Bonnett Design*
Restaurant: *Westchester Country Club*
*Rye, NY*

These holiday menus are an innovative design solution to the problem of producing festive menus in limited quantities. The full-color shells are mass produced and held for use as needed. The right-hand portion of the page is produced via desk-top publishing. The menus are stored on disk so any minor changes in the menu items can be made on-line and then printed out. The left-hand inside cover features changing clip art and thematic material appropriate to the season, which varies from year to year.

The Christmas menu cover is particularly apt. It features all of the gifts from "The Twelve Days of Christmas," arranged so as to form a visual image of a Christmas tree.

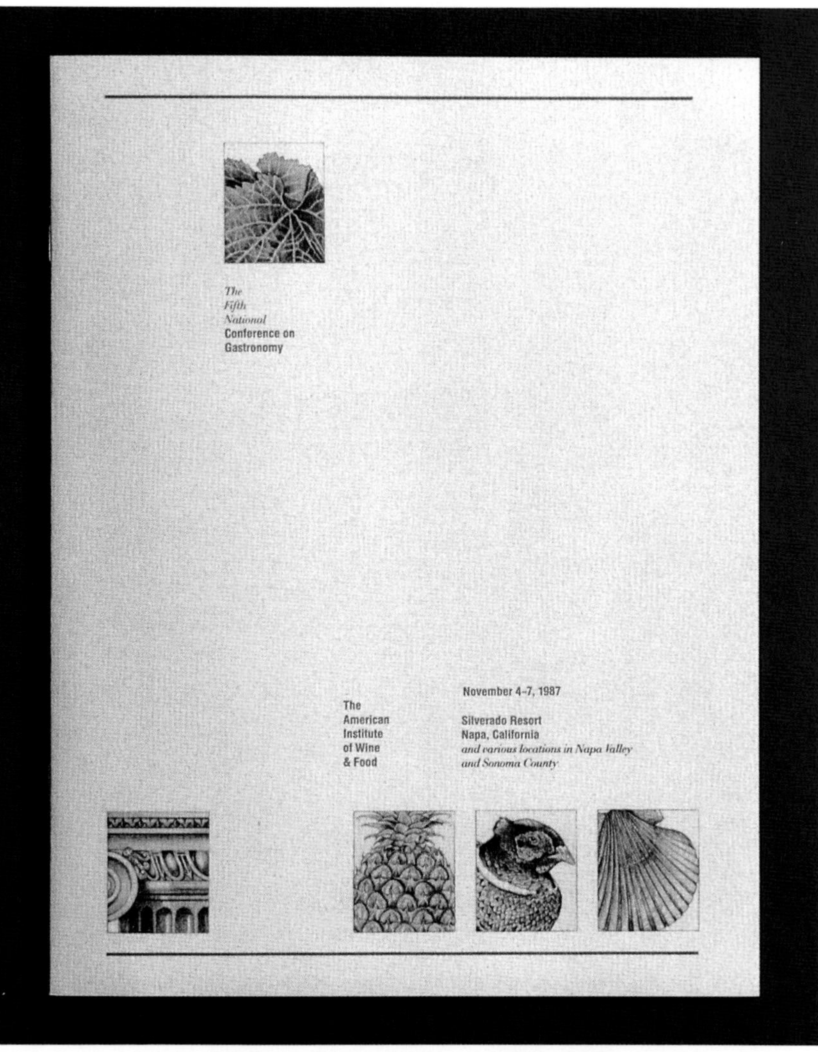


**Designer:** *Carol Dennison*
*Dennison Design Associates*

**Restaurant:** *Fifth Conference on Gastronomy*
*American Institute of Wine and Food*
*San Francisco, CA*

The American Institute of Wine and Food needed menus and collateral pieces with both dignity and legibility. This is, after all, one of the most prestigious organizations in the American food industry.

For its fifth conference, held at the Silverado Resort in Napa, California, the designer chose to use five illustrations, all related to the Institute's concerns. Food groups, a grape leaf to emphasize the location of the conference — amid the vineyards of the Napa Valley — and a column plinth to reflect the Institute's status as a teaching academy, were selected.

All five illustrations appear on the main program cover. Each was then used individually in a mortise against an enlarged screen of itself. The lovely Gainsborough stock lends a note of richness to the simple two-color pieces.

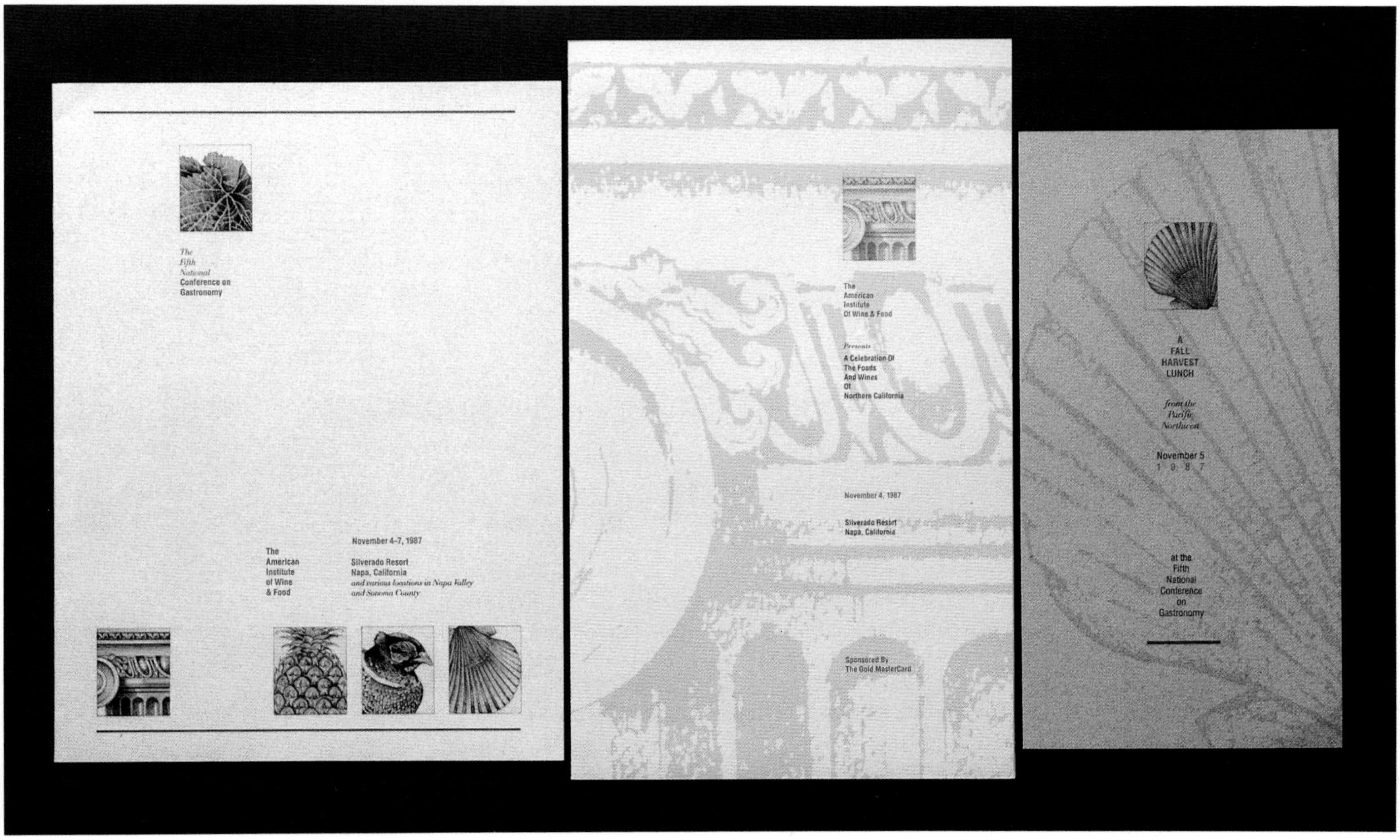

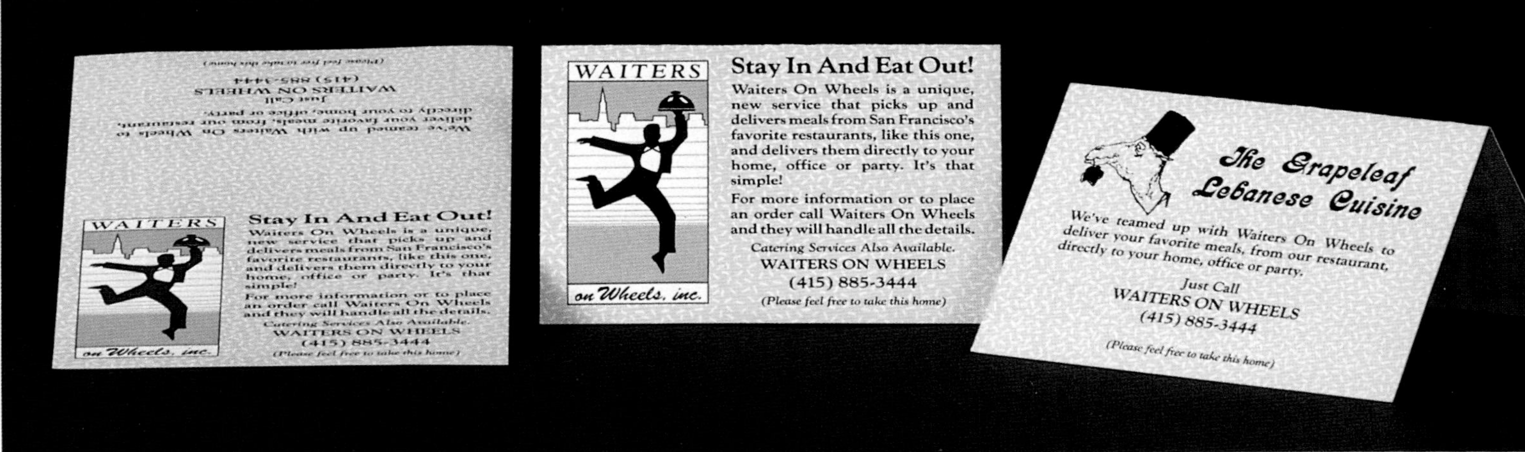


Designer: *Sargina A. Tamimi*
Restaurant: *Waiter's on Wheels, Inc.*
*San Francisco, CA*

Table tents are not exactly menus ... but Waiters on Wheels is not exactly a caterer, either. Rather, it is a computerized delivery service which provides home delivery of meals drawn from the regular menus of its member restaurants. Since the restaurants represented run the gamut from Lebanese to Chinese to Italian, the table tents had to be homogenous enough to fit in any decor, yet suggest speed.

The designer has used the company logo and a brief message about the service on one side of the card. The other features the name of the individual restaurant thermographed in black. The single-color piece is effective, yet inexpensive. Potential customers may also phone W.O.W. to receive its monthly newsletter, which includes reduced copies of each member restaurant's menu.

W.O.W. is a new service which began operations in winter of 1987-88. Although San Francisco rarely has weather any other part of the country would describe as "bad," during the winter months, it can get rainy and a bit chilly. Choosing to open this delivery service during months when people may not wish to go out anyway was a sound marketing strategy.

Designer: *Lisa Edson*
*Royal Viking Line*
Restaurant: *Australian Bicentennial*
*Royal Viking Star*
*berthed at Sydney,*
*New South Wales, Australia*

Designed to commemorate the Australian Bicentennial at a gala luncheon, the menu cover includes a takeoff on the port entry stamp. Rather than 'Bureau of Immigration,' it refers to the 'Bureau of Celebration.'

Faced with an extremely tight deadline, the designer was forced to forego even thumbnail sketches. Instead, she verbally explained the design and moved straight to finished art. The highly-textured paper stock was chosen to give a rough-hewn, frontier feeling to the piece. The eccentric fold and two-color "stamp" were designed to resemble a passport stamp.

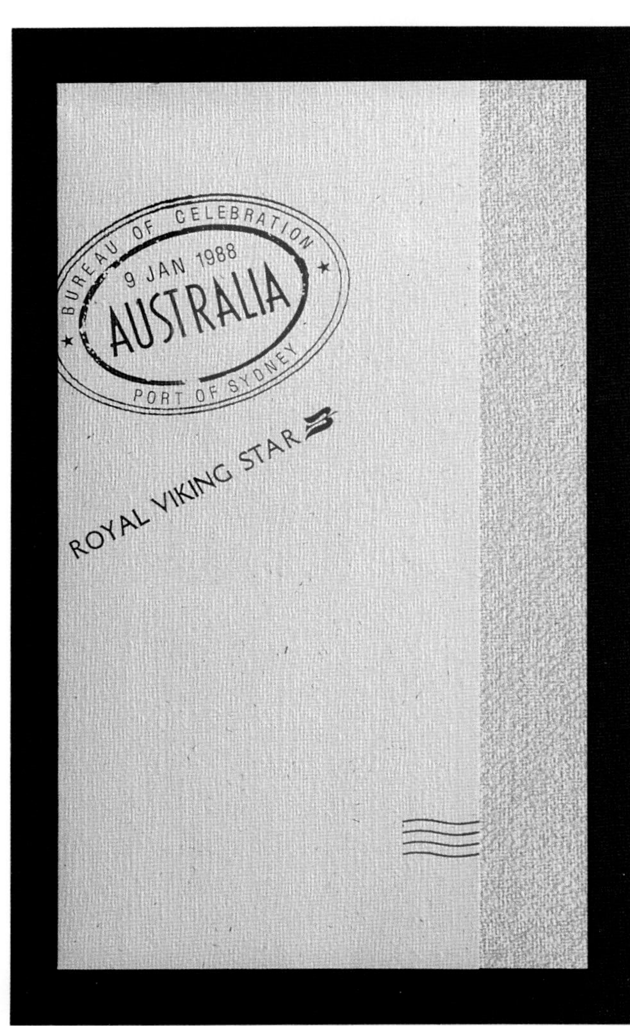

| | |
|---|---|
| Designer: | *Jerry Takagawa*<br>*Takagawa Design* |
| Restaurant: | *Wine Maker Dinner*<br>*Pacific's Edge Restaurant*<br>*Highlands Inn*<br>*Carmel, CA* |

This poster-like menu uses a pre-printed master which incorporates, via a modernistic collage, the physical elements typical of the area. Sand, sea, flowers, food and wine are all set against a brilliant orange background suggestive of sunset over the Pacific.

Long a favorite honeymoon destination on the West Coast, the Highlands Inn is located in the hills above Carmel-by-the-Sea. This dinner, featuring the wines of Duckhorn Vineyard, was carefully planned to compliment the wines. The general manager has signed the menu, and full credit is given to each of the professionals involved in its planning.

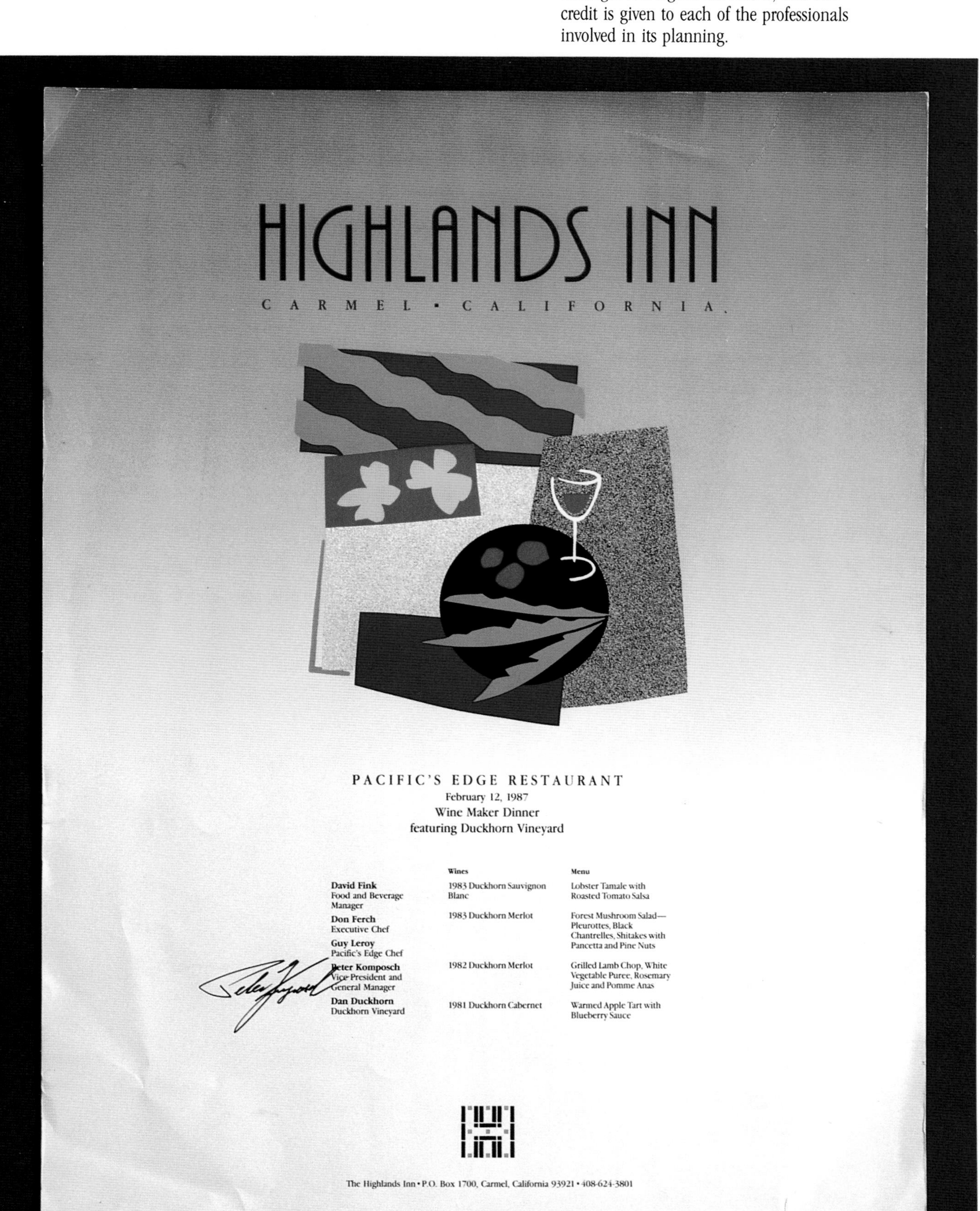

HIGHLANDS INN

CARMEL • CALIFORNIA

PACIFIC'S EDGE RESTAURANT
February 12, 1987
Wine Maker Dinner
featuring Duckhorn Vineyard

| | Wines | Menu |
|---|---|---|
| **David Fink**<br>Food and Beverage Manager | 1983 Duckhorn Sauvignon Blanc | Lobster Tamale with Roasted Tomato Salsa |
| **Don Ferch**<br>Executive Chef | 1983 Duckhorn Merlot | Forest Mushroom Salad—Pleurottes, Black Chantrelles, Shitakes with Pancetta and Pine Nuts |
| **Guy Leroy**<br>Pacific's Edge Chef | | |
| **Peter Komposch**<br>Vice President and General Manager | 1982 Duckhorn Merlot | Grilled Lamb Chop, White Vegetable Puree, Rosemary Juice and Pomme Anas |
| **Dan Duckhorn**<br>Duckhorn Vineyard | 1981 Duckhorn Cabernet | Warmed Apple Tart with Blueberry Sauce |

The Highlands Inn • P.O. Box 1700, Carmel, California 93921 • 408-624-3801

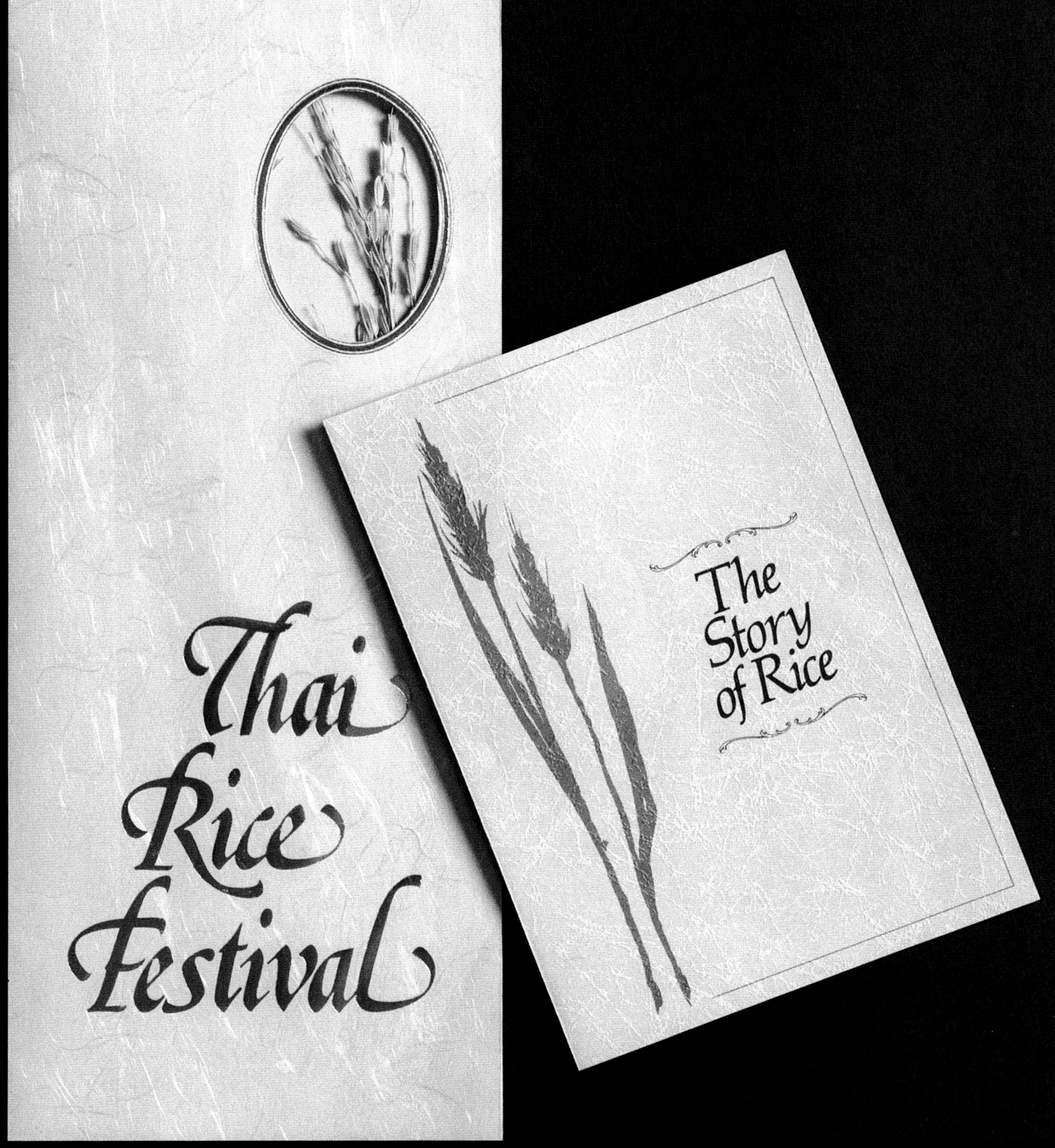
Thai
Rice
Festival
The
Story
of Rice

Thai
Rice
Festival

Designer: *Patrick Gauvain*
*Shrimp Studios, Ltd.*

Restaurant: *Thai Rice Festival*
*Suan Saranrom Garden Restaurant*
*Hilton International Bangkok*
*Bangkok, Thailand*

**1987 N.R.A. GREAT MENUS CONTEST WINNER: FIRST PLACE, IMAGINATION**

Designed for a special rice festival, this elegant menu is imprinted on paper into which silk threads have been incorporated. The silk strands impart the "feeling" of rice and the gold foil stamping makes the menu more distinctive.

The theme of the festival is supported by the hand-affixed stalks of rice which are silhouetted in the gold-foil-framed die-cut on the cover. This exquisite treatment, while too fragile for extended usage, amply supports the theme of the festival.

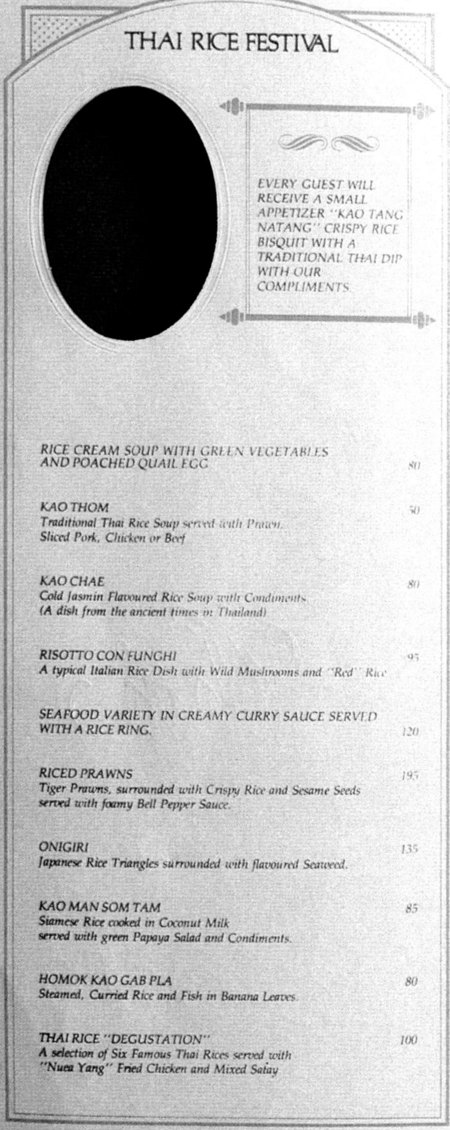

THAI RICE FESTIVAL

*EVERY GUEST WILL RECEIVE A SMALL APPETIZER "KAO TANG NATANG" CRISPY RICE BISQUIT WITH A TRADITIONAL THAI DIP WITH OUR COMPLIMENTS.*

RICE CREAM SOUP WITH GREEN VEGETABLES AND POACHED QUAIL EGG — 80

KAO THOM — 50
*Traditional Thai Rice Soup served with Prawn, Sliced Pork, Chicken or Beef*

KAO CHAE — 80
*Cold Jasmin Flavoured Rice Soup with Condiments (A dish from the ancient times in Thailand)*

RISOTTO CON FUNGHI — 95
*A typical Italian Rice Dish with Wild Mushrooms and "Red" Rice*

SEAFOOD VARIETY IN CREAMY CURRY SAUCE SERVED WITH A RICE RING. — 120

RICED PRAWNS — 195
*Tiger Prawns, surrounded with Crispy Rice and Sesame Seeds served with foamy Bell Pepper Sauce.*

ONIGIRI — 135
*Japanese Rice Triangles surrounded with flavoured Seaweed.*

KAO MAN SOM TAM — 85
*Siamese Rice cooked in Coconut Milk served with green Papaya Salad and Condiments.*

HOMOK KAO GAB PLA — 80
*Steamed, Curried Rice and Fish in Banana Leaves.*

THAI RICE "DEGUSTATION" — 100
*A selection of Six Famous Thai Rices served with "Nuea Yang" Fried Chicken and Mixed Satay*

THAI RICE FESTIVAL

THE CRYSTAL RICE PEAR — 70
*Poached William Pear in Vanilla Syrup on Sweetened Rice Soubise*

APPLE RICE TART — 60
*on Fluffy Chocolate Foam*

RICE SOUFFLE WITH STEWED RHUBARB — 60

KAO NEOW SANG KHAYA — 60
*Thai Coconut Custard with flavoured Sticky Rice.*

KAO LAM — 60
*Sweetened Sticky Rice in Bamboo Cane.*

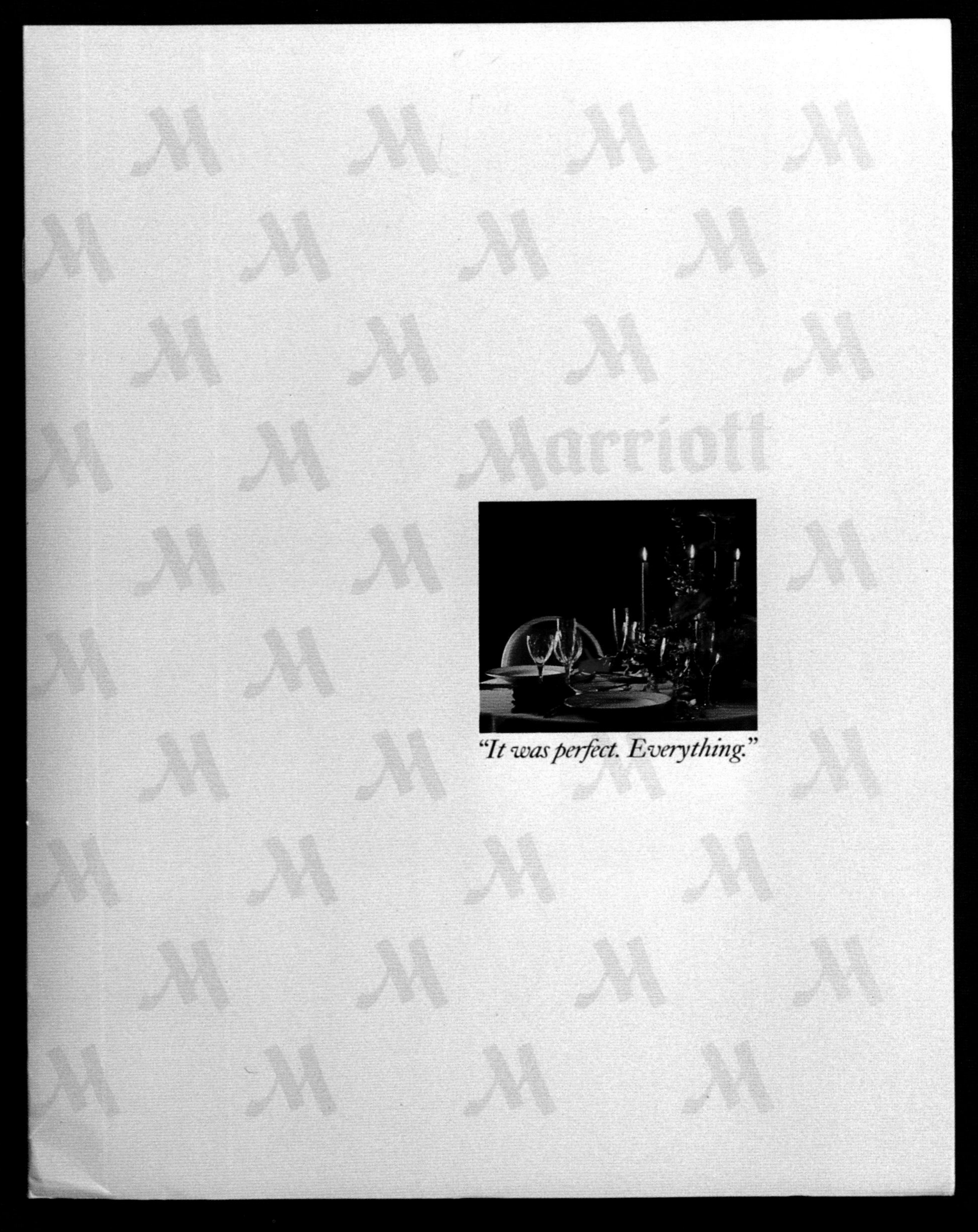
Marriott
"It was perfect. Everything."

| | |
|---|---|
| Designer: | *Cleveland Menu* |
| Restaurant: | *Marriott Cypress Creek*<br>*Interstate Hotel Corporation*<br>*Fort Lauderdale, FL* |

**1987 N.R.A. GREAT MENUS CONTEST WINNER: THIRD PLACE, BANQUET/CATERING**

Beautiful full-color photography of appetizing food and elegant appointments characterizes this catering brochure and menu list. The copywriting is designed to evoke an image of a perfectly orchestrated event in the customer's mind.

The stepped menu lists must be completely unfolded in order for the menus to be read. This device forces the reader to look at the whole menu, ensuring his or her total attention.

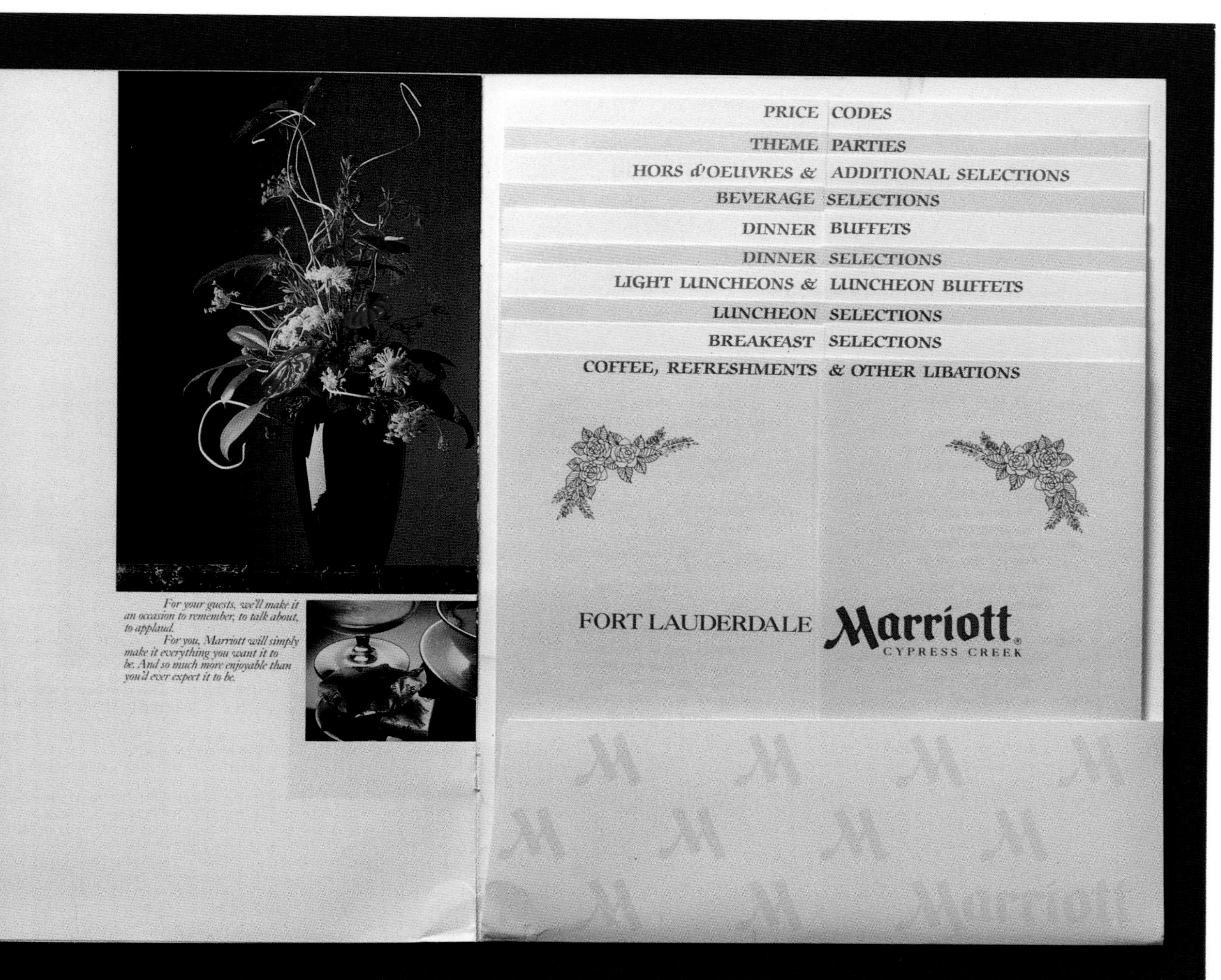

For your guests, we'll make it an occasion to remember, to talk about, to applaud.
For you, Marriott will simply make it everything you want it to be. And so much more enjoyable than you'd ever expect it to be.
PRICE CODES
THEME PARTIES
HORS d'OEUVRES & ADDITIONAL SELECTIONS
BEVERAGE SELECTIONS
DINNER BUFFETS
DINNER SELECTIONS
LIGHT LUNCHEONS & LUNCHEON BUFFETS
LUNCHEON SELECTIONS
BREAKFAST SELECTIONS
COFFEE, REFRESHMENTS & OTHER LIBATIONS
FORT LAUDERDALE
Marriott
CYPRESS CREEK

F E S T I V A L E

*Caribé*

SOPAS

SOUPS

SOPA DE TORTILLA ........ 2.75
Tortilla soup.

CALDO DE PESCADO ........ 3.00
Fish soup.

APERITIVOS Y ENSALADAS

APPETIZERS AND SALADS

ESCABECHE DE PESCADO ........ 5.50
Marinated seafood salad.

ALMEJAS AL CABALLO ........ 5.50
Clams brochette.

ENSALADA DE NOPALES ........ 3.50
Cactus leaves salad.

ENSALADA DE PALMITOS ........ 3.50
Fresh heart of palm salad.

LA ENTRADA

THE MAIN COURSE

CAMARONES SIERRA NEVADA ........ 15.50
Grated shrimp served with rice and poblano chile.

FILETE DE HUACHINANGO A LA CRIOLLA ........ 15.75
Fillet of red snapper with peppers, onions, tomatoes and rice.

CARNE ASADA TAPATIO ........ 16.50
Beef tenderloin with tamales, a chicken taco, rice and guacamole.

POLLO ACHIOTE ........ 11.50
A half-chicken marinated in Achiote, served with rice and tamales.

PIERNA DE CERDO ASADA ........ 12.75
Roasted pork leg with fried bananas and rice.

PASTELON DE CARNE ........ 11.00
Caribbean meat pie.

EL POSTRE

DESSERT

FLAN, TROPICAL FRUIT COCKTAIL, RICE PUDDING, PINEAPPLE TORTE, SORBETS ........ 3.00

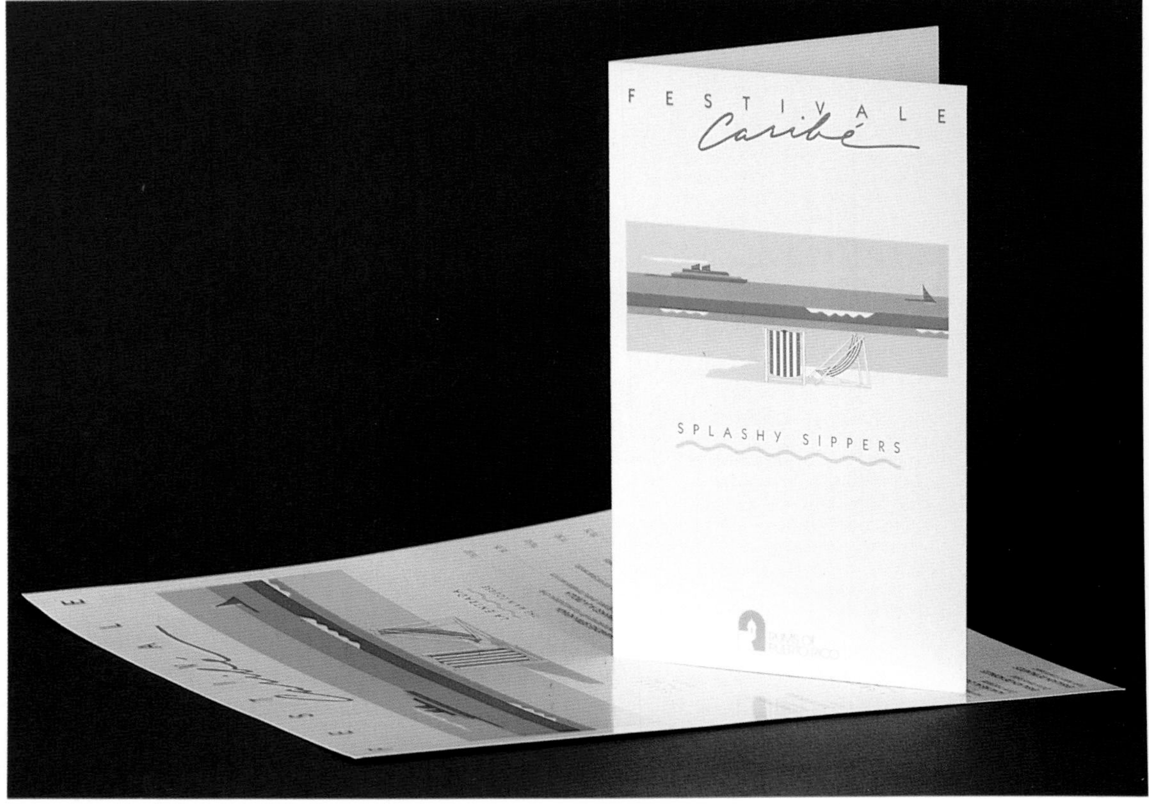

**Designer:** *Donna Milord*
*Associates Printing Service, Inc.*
**Restaurant:** *Festivale Caribé*
*Hyatt Regency Chicago*
*Chicago, IL*

This cheery three-color menu on coated stock uses beach chairs and a cruise ship to suggest the Caribbean on this special event menu. A wavy line in the sand color under each menu category suggests wave lines on the beach.

It is interesting to note that the associated drink menu specifies Barcardi rum in the tropical drinks. This co-op undoubtedly contributed greatly to the Hotel's ability to run the festival in the first place.

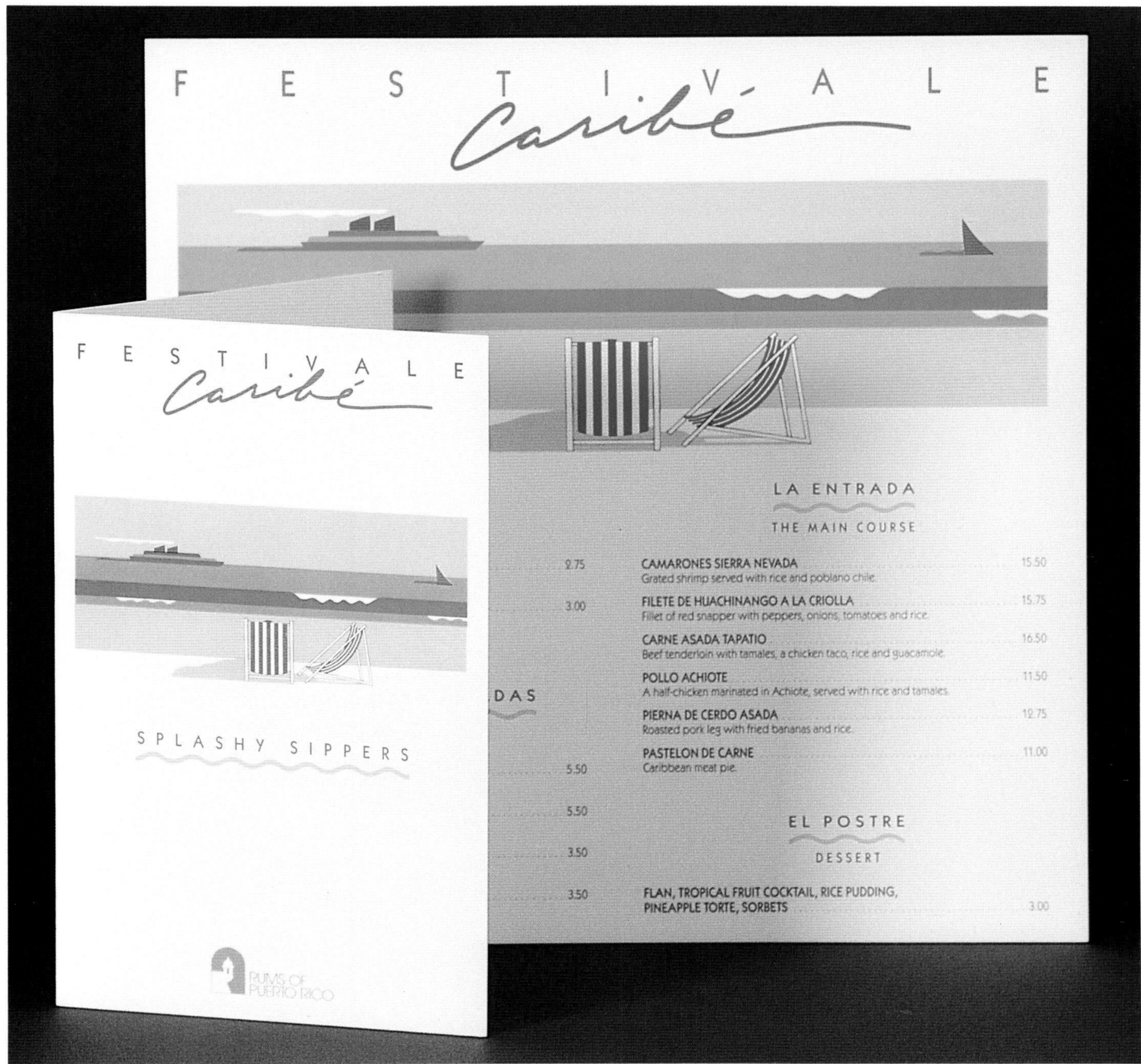

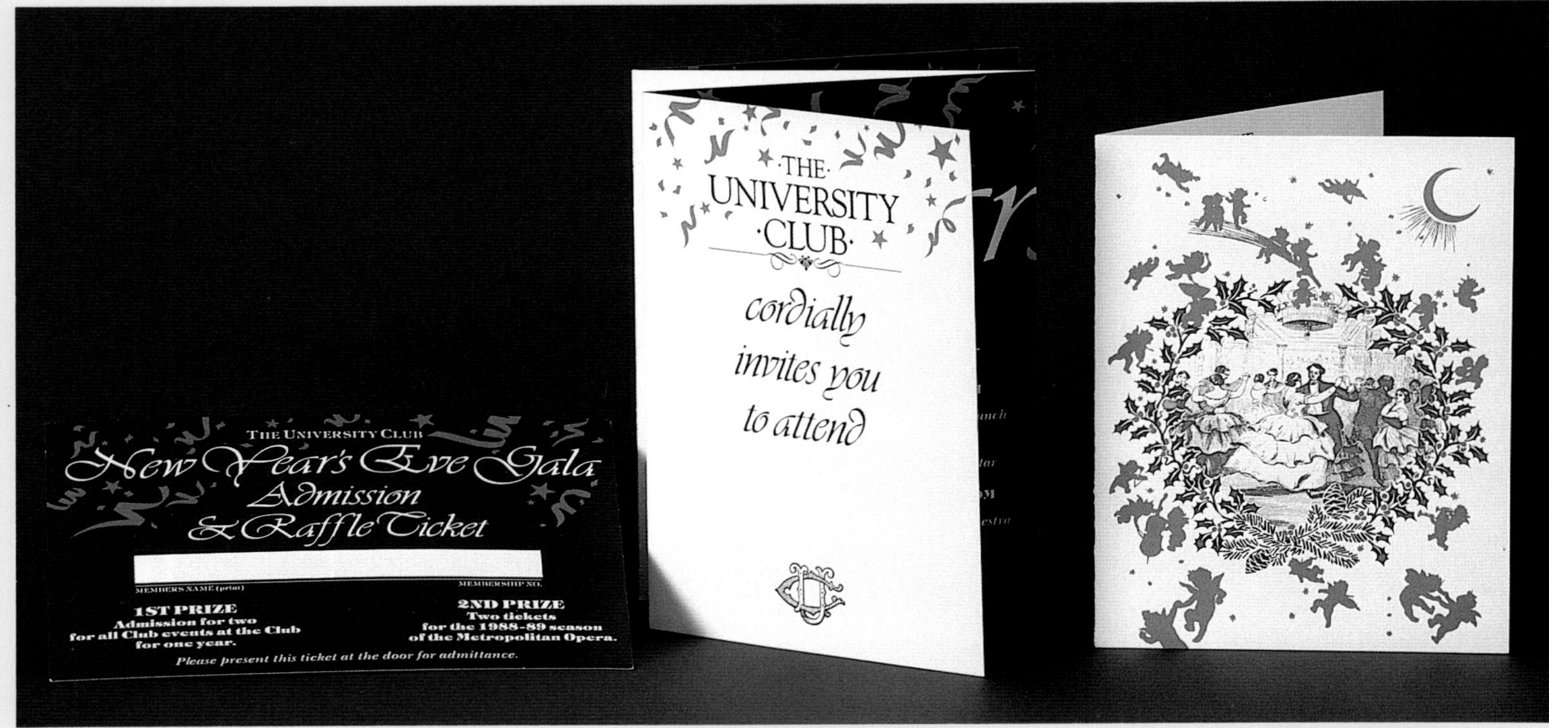


Designer: *Niki Bonnett*
*Niki Bonnett Design*
Restaurant: *Annual Dinner Dance Invitation*
*The University Club, Inc.*
*New York, NY*

Situated in a beautiful building modeled on an Italian Palazzo, the University Club caters to a membership composed of graduates of accredited universities. Accordingly, all invitations and other periphera must be both beautiful and sophisticated.

These invitations, for the annual dinner dances, pay homage to the nineteenth century origins of the building, while conveying a festive mood. The two-color invitations, executed in green and metallic gold ink on cream-colored stock, came with two separate reply cards, one in gold ink and one in green.

The idea was to return one card for the first of two available dates, the other, for the second. Since the reply cards were ganged with the invitations, printing each as a distinctly different piece (by virtue of the color difference) cost no more. The differentiation was a boon both to club members and the staff.

The illustration chosen for the front of the invitation was typical of nineteenth century woodcuts. Perhaps Scarlett O'Hara or one of the "Little Women" might have attended such a ball as is pictured.

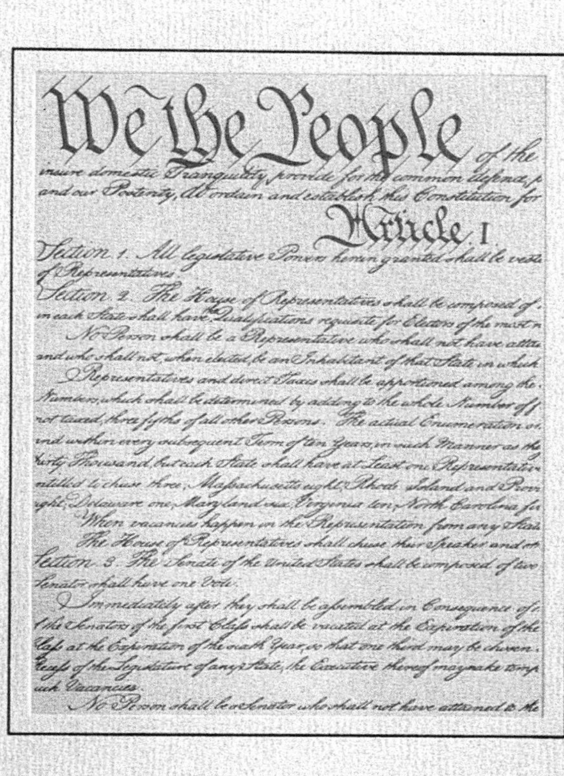


Designer: *Lisa Edson*
*Royal Viking Line*
Restaurant: *Constitution Day Celebration*
*Royal Viking Sky*
*berthed at Philadelphia, PA*

A screen of a portion of the handwritten Constitution, framed in red foil stamping, is debossed on the cover. The inside front cover contains a welcoming message framed in the embossed section created by the cover treatment. The copywriting reflects the same care as the balance of the festivities.

For this very special event — a "Thanksgiving" luncheon for 375 guests, including much of the Washington, D.C. diplomatic corps — a special and formal menu was needed. Held September 17, 1987, the two hundredth anniversary of the signing of the United States Constitution, the meal featured selections based on American foodstuffs available at the time the document was signed. The Line's culinary staff spent over two weeks in research before the menu was finalized; the same attention was given to the graphic design of the menu itself.

In an interesting twist, the designer has chosen the red foil again to depict the menu items. The accompanying wines are listed in a deep gray ink and set in italic type. The beautiful Gainsborough paper provides an elegant backdrop for the very formal menu presentation.

Designer: *Rafi Finke*
Restaurant: *Grand Premier Dinner*
*Tel Aviv Hilton*
*Tel Aviv, Israel*

This menu is silk-screened in white on a mirror. Presented in a blue velvet bag, as is the Torah, it is printed in French as well as Hebrew. This is an elaborate and unusual presentation for a very special event. Note also that Israel's national colors are blue and white.

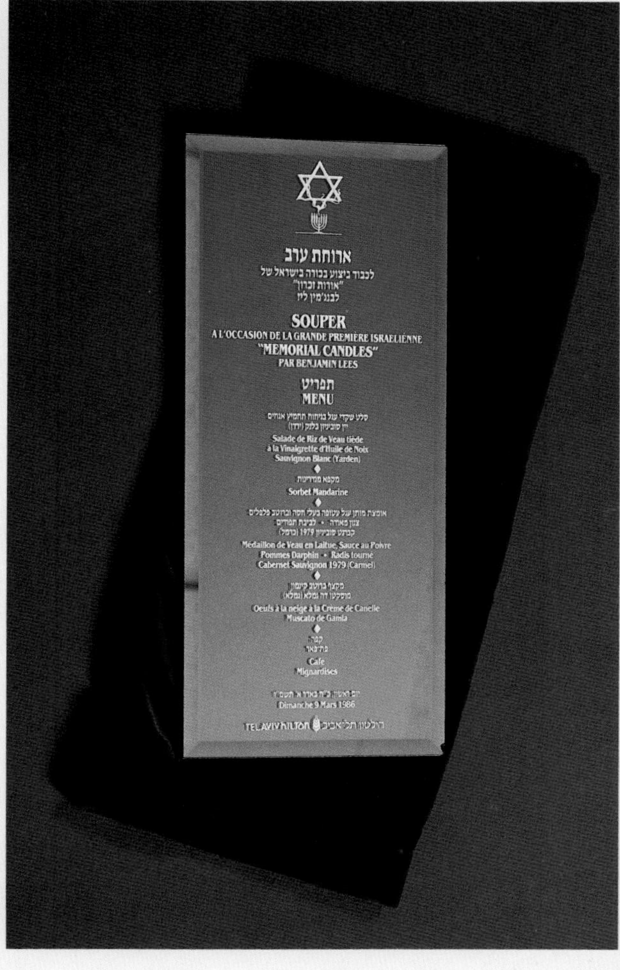

# CHAPTER 8

Who's the "other half"? That depends on who *you* are. If you're a vegetarian, it's meat eaters . . . if you love punk rock, it's Benny Goodman fans. Everything depends on your point of view.

This chapter features menus which run the gamut from truck stops to elegant dining houses. The one element which ties all of these menus together is imagination. Each of the menus featured appeal to some quality it found in its audience — a sense of fun, an appreciation of beauty, or even solid respectability — all are represented here.

**Designer:** *Rick Tharp*
*Tharp Did It*
**Restaurant:** *O'Henry's*
*Northern California*

O'Henry's was a doughnut shop chain seeking a fresh approach. The designer decided upon a 50's theme, to be embodied by the image of a fresh-faced young woman in a vaguely nautical cap and the slogan "every bite's a S-C-R-E-AM-I-N-G delight!"

The aqua and black of the tiles on the wall is also picked upon the business cards. A doughnut shop needs only a very limited menu. This one was executed on a "billboard" in the restaurant. The result is clean, readable and, especially for the milieu, very polished. The theme was further developed through the creation of peripherals such as caps, cups and the like.

O'HENRY'S
Fresh Donuts
EVERY BITE'S A S-C-R-E-A-M-I-N-G DELIGHT!
BAKER'S DOZEN $3.95
RAISED 45¢
OLD-FASHIONED 45¢
CAKE plain 40¢
decorated 45¢
BARS plain 55¢
custard 65¢
TWISTS 55¢
JELLY DONUTS 55¢
BUTTERMILK BARS 55¢
CINNAMON ROLLS 65¢
BUTTERFLIES 65¢
TURNOVERS 65¢
cherry, blueberry, lemon
APPLE FRITTERS 65¢
APPLE BEARCLAWS 65¢
Try Our Fresh Roast!
COFFEE or TEA 45¢
MILK 65¢
CHOC. MILK 65¢
SODA POP 75¢
ORANGE JUICE 95¢
FRUIT JUICES 95¢

HENRY'S

Designer: *Tony Donna*
*International Design Associates*

Restaurant: *Dynasty Restaurant*
*Osaka Hilton International*
*Osaka, Japan*

**1987 N.R.A. GREAT MENUS CONTEST WINNER: SECOND PLACE, OVER $15**

The restaurant's name is imprinted in glossy gold foil on the cover of this substantial menu. Beautiful die-cuts, reminiscent of "snowflakes" lend a delicate distinction to each of the interior pages. Menu copy is very simple throughout, but the astonishing die cuts lend the entire piece an air of elegant dignity.

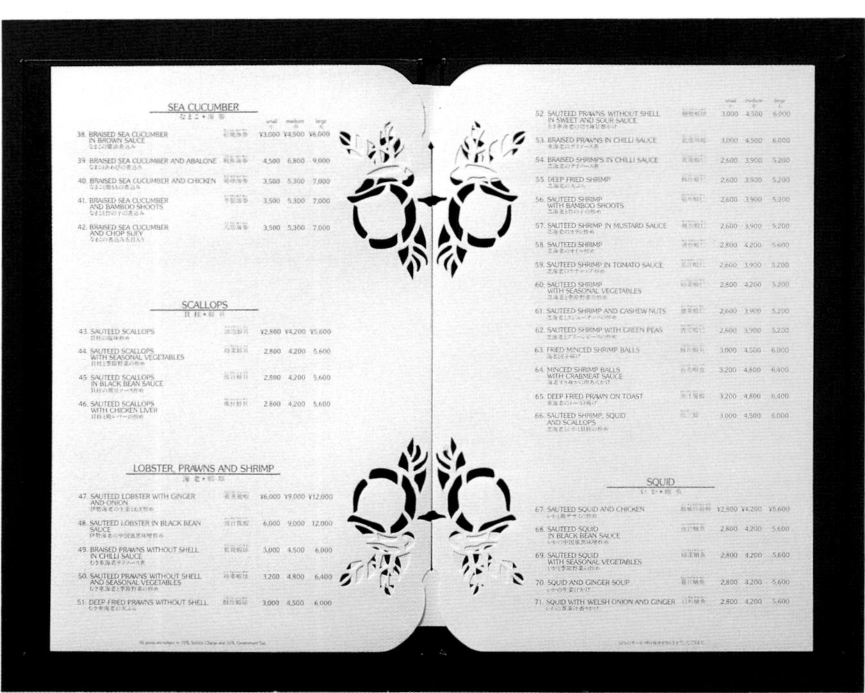

Designer: *Roberta Warehan*
*Associates Printing Service, Inc.*
Restaurant: *Hamilton's Chop House*
*Grand Hyatt Washington*
*Washington, DC*

A simulated wax seal and foil-stamped logo lend the cover of this menu its appeal. Alexander Hamilton's portrait, also on the cover, provides the theme for this decidedly American chop house. Copywriting on the back cover establishes the quality of the foodstuffs used.

Inside, changeable inserts are held in place via corner pockets, ensuring that half the menu won't fall in the diner's lap while he's making his selection. The "seal" from the front cover provides a note of continuity at the bottom of each insert sheet.

| | |
|---|---|
| Designer: | *Chuck Hart and Brian Barclay* |
| | *Bartels & Carstons, Inc.* |
| Restaurant: | *Crystal Terrace* |
| | *S.S. Admiral* |
| | *berthed at St. Louis, MO* |

This restaurant, located on the only known existing Art Deco riverboat, is on the bank at the Gateway Arch. The cover illustration is based on an earlier version of the logo, which used a silhouette only; on the menu, the designer has "brought her to life" via the Silver Screen.

Executed in four-color process and metallic ink, plus foil stamping, the cover uses a delicate screen of the curved lines characteristic of the style to further the Deco mood.

The insert sheets use an attractive typeface in one color, held in with a matching elastic cord. A "Fresh Sheet" is handwritten and affixed on a daily basis and the children's menu is listed on the back of the insert. There is also a coordinated wine list.

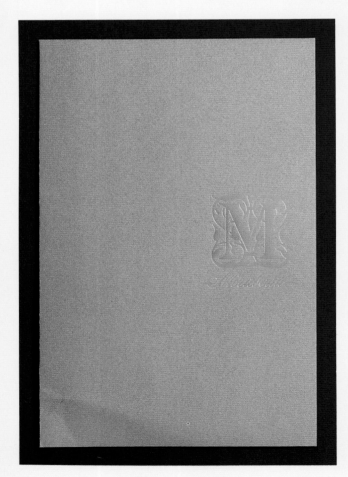

| | |
|---|---|
| Designer: | *Mike Wagner* |
| | *The Menu Workshop* |
| Restaurant: | *Mirabeau Restaurant* |
| | *Seattle, WA* |

Designed as a temporary menu during an ownership transfer, the menu is nonetheless very elegant. The logo is foil-embossed on the cover and the first page of the insert. It is repeated in gold ink in the interior.

**Designer:** *Roberta Warehan*
*Associates Printing Service, Inc.*
**Restaurant:** *Les Celebrites*
*Hotel Nikko*
*Chicago, IL*

The cover illustration is a multi-level embossed portrait of a lady of the late nineteenth century. She might well be taking tea at a cricket match; certainly, that is the milieu suggested by the background. Executed on a glossy stock, the embossing is then affixed to a linen stock cover which is protected with a Marcoat™ finish. The name of the restaurant is embossed in pink directly on the cover stock.

The inserts for the menu are held in place by folds turned up at bottom and down at the top.

**Designer:** *Ron Bergner*
*Howlett-Bergner & Associates*

**Restaurant:** *The Boat House*
*Continental Restaurant Systems*
*San Diego, CA*

The designer's imagination — both as to design and to choice of paper stock — is what raises this menu above the ordinary. The stock is exceptionally thick and substantial; it provides a beautiful medium for the multi-level embossings of sea shells, sand dollars and fish which are the main design motifs for the menu.

The menu for this upscale seafood house is imprinted in two colors on one side only. While red meats and chicken are also included among the offerings, seafood and fish are the stars of the show. Since this particular outlet is located on the West Coast, Pacific Ocean fish are the main attraction.

This menu is an unusual solution to the problem of showcasing seafood. Too often, humorous plays on "Davey Jones' Locker" are the only ideas brought forth. This designer has chosen, instead, to play up the bleached look of driftwood, shells and the sand itself. This way, the menu captures the feeling of being by the sea very effectively.

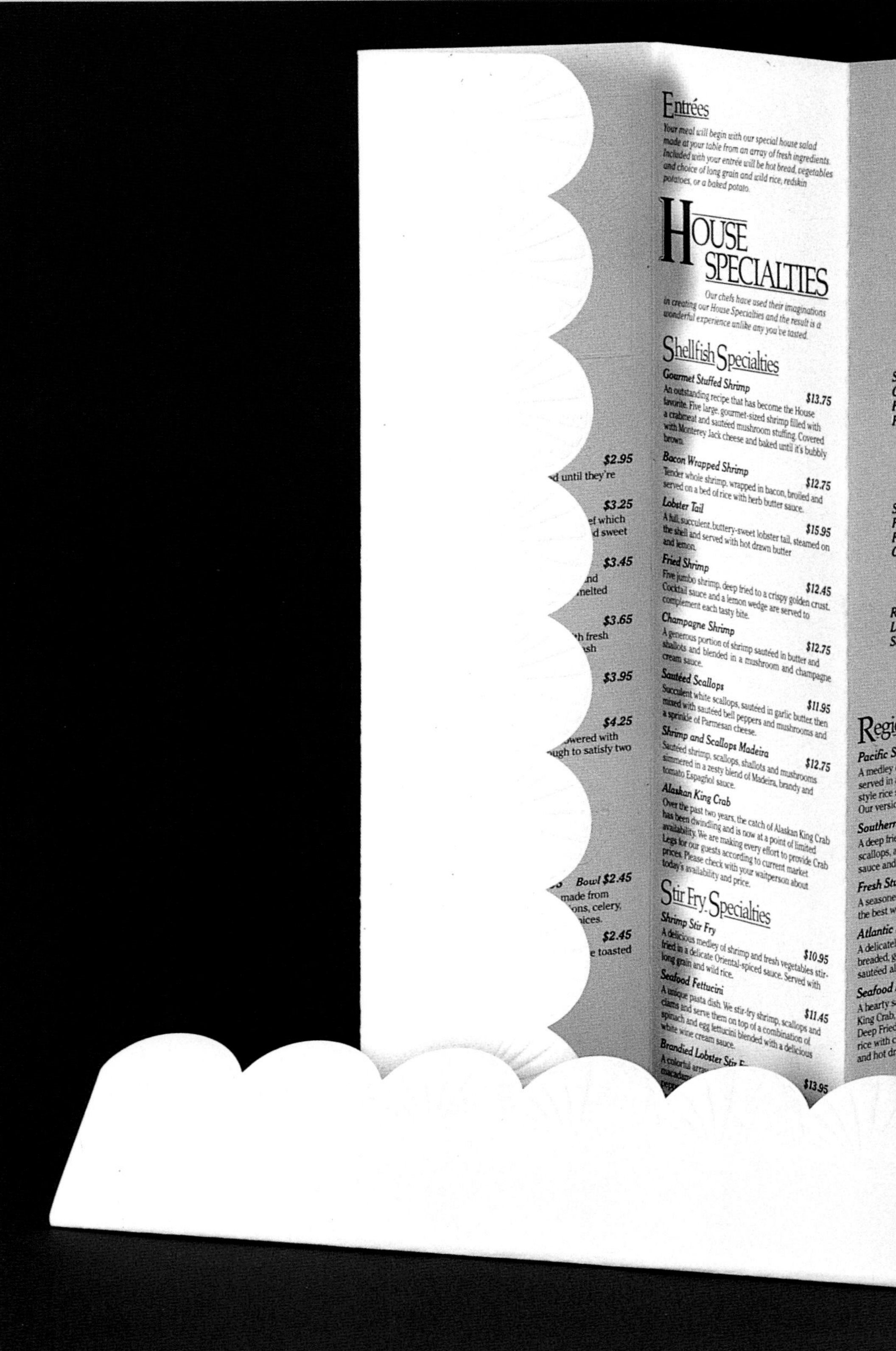

FRESH FISH

*We stake our reputation on the quality and freshness*
*afood and go to great lengths to provide a popular variety of*
*ly fresh items.*

*es are carefully designed so that the full flavor of each*
*rticularly enhanced for your enjoyment.*

*low are just some of the varieties of fresh seafood*
*ttempt to bring in throughout the year. For*
*atch and recipes, your waitperson will*
*complete list at your table.*

ic Ocean

*Yellowtail*
*Thresher Shark*
*Sockeye Salmon*
*King Salmon*
*Mahi Mahi*

*English Sole*
*Abalone*
*Grouper*
*Soupfin Shark*
*Yellowfin Tuna*

*White Seabass*
*Petrale Sole*
*Silver Salmon*
*Albacore*
*Sculpin*

tic Ocean

*Haddock*
*Boston Blue Fish*
*King Mackerel*

*Pollack*
*Monkfish*
*Swordfish*

*Rockfish*
*Sea Trout*
*Tilefish*

water Lakes & Streams

*Pickerel*
*Catfish*
*Northern Pike*

*Walleye Pike*
*Whitefish*
*Sturgeon*

*Lake Trout*
*Yellow Perch*
*Calico Bass*

alties

**$13.95**
ms, scallops and chicken
erranean-
age and herbs.
lla.

**Platter** **$12.75**
e delicious items: shrimp,
tartar

**$10.95**
this trout recipe one of

**$9.95**
h fillet served lightly
opped with crunchy

***$14.95 per person***
our favorites. Alaskan
d Sole Almondine and
a bed of freshly steamed
r sauce

COMBINATION SEAFOOD & BEEF

*If choosing between our famous savory seafood and our beef entrées is too difficult, don't. Choose both in a delicious combination of* ***Top Sirloin*** *or* ***Prime Rib*** *and ...*

***Lobster Tail*** **$17.95**
Rich, buttery-sweet lobster, steamed on the shell and served with hot drawn butter and lemon.

***Fried Shrimp*** **$14.25**
Plump, jumbo shrimp, deep fried to a golden brown in our special seafood batter. Crispy on the outside, tender and tasty on the inside.

***Scallops*** **$13.45**
A generous serving of tender sweet scallops, sautéed in garlic butter and mixed with sautéed bell peppers and mushrooms, then sprinkled with Parmesan cheese.

***Alaskan King Crab***
Over the past two years, the catch of Alaskan King Crab has been dwindling and is now at the point of limited availability. We are making every effort to provide Crab Legs for our guests according to current market prices. Please check with your waitperson about today's availability and price.

***Marinated Chicken*** **$12.95**
A broiled bon...
uce, sh... nd of soy

PRIME RIB & STEAK MARKET

*Our prime rib is expertly seasoned to enhance the flavor, then slowly roasted to perfection.*

***Prime Rib***
Petite Cut **$9.95**
Standard Cut **$12.95**

***Stuffed Filet Mignon*** **$13.95**
The favorite of the House. A tender cut of filet mignon stuffed with savory seasoned mushrooms, wrapped in bacon, broiled to order and served smothered with mushrooms in Chablis wine-butter.

***Filet Mignon*** **$12.95**
The tender gourmet cut, slowly broiled until it's ready to melt in your mouth. The steak for those who appreciate the ultimate in distinguished flavor.

***Rib Eye Steak*** **$11.95**
Also known as a Delmonico steak. A favorite choice for robust beef flavor.

***Top Sirloin*** **$9.45**
A juicy cut for smaller appetites, specially selected for those who enjoy the flavor of fine beef.

CHICKEN

***Marinated Chicken*** **$9.95**
Each bite sizzles with the flavor of the chef's own specially blended teriyaki marinade.

***Champagne Chicken*** **$9.95**
A boneless chicken breast lightly browned then covered with sautéed mushrooms and a champagne cream sauce.

BEVERAGES

Coffee, Tea,
Iced Tea, Milk, Sanka ***$ .80***

Sales tax will be added to all items served in the dining room.
© Continental Restaurant Systems 1983

SSN83

Designer: *Richard Higgs and Jim Sullivan*

Restaurant: *Hamburger Mary's*
*San Francisco, CA*

The 30's-style menu cover is exactly right for the restaurant. Unfortunately, it's impossible to say why, unless it's that the 30's had a style all their own. Because that is the essence of Hamburger Mary's; if you haven't been there, you don't know. In a city barely 200 years old, this is as close as you get to an underground tradition. Sooner or later, everybody with any sense of adventure in his soul turns up there.

The menu lives up to this grand tradition. Five different typefaces, clip art and a decidedly eclectic menu manage to peacefully co-exist on this menu. This is as it should be, since the wildly varied clientele manages to do likewise. The menu cover is plastic-coated in case of spills.

Restaurant: *Genji*
*Japan*

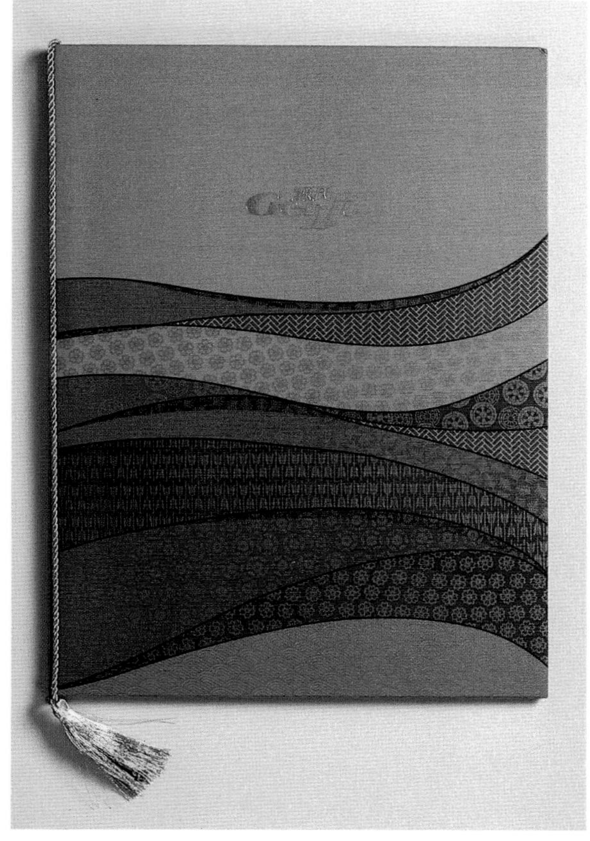

**1987 N.R.A. GREAT MENUS CONTEST WINNER: FIRST PLACE, OVER $15**

Billowing waves of traditional Japanese cloth patterns decorate the cover of this lovely menu. The restaurant's name is stamped in gold foil. The inside of the book-like covers is lined with a paper which feels and looks like silk. Menu items on the insert, executed in tranquil colors on the same paper as the "endpapers," are listed in both English and Japanese. The inserts are held in place with a thick gold fabric cord.

While the menu is created of luxurious fabrics, the simplicity of the design is very Japanese, as is the restaurant's name. The Tale of Genji is a romantic novel written by a lady of the court during the height of the power of the Shoguns.

Designer: *Jane Crowder*
*Playne Jane Design, Inc.*
Restaurant: *Cortland's*
*Houston, TX*

The hospitality of the South is legendary in the United States; no other region of the country can be as gracious and as charming. This restaurant attempts to blend that charm and grace with the cooking styles associated with the various sub-regions in its purview.

A potted plant was selected by the designer as the unifying element. It appears in gold foil on the cover, as a soft screen on the vellum sheet encasing the insert and at the top of each side of the insert of the menu proper.

A gold fabric cord holds the insert in place. The cover is distinguished by a blind-embossed treatment of the restaurant's name and an embellishment, which also appears at the bottom of each insert page.

The "flower" pattern appears on the restaurant's china. The color is drawn from that used in the interior design.

Fall 1986

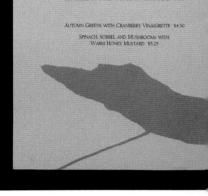

Bay Scallops, Green Pepper Pasta and Mustard Seeds $7.75

Grilled Cajun Pate $7.50

Pumpkin Ravioli with Wild Mushrooms and Sorrel Butter Sauce $6.75

Duck, Lobster, Chorizo Sausages with Southwestern Bean Relish $8.50

Baby Coho Salmon with Leek Couli and Fresh Sage $9.25

Mini Crab Cakes, Chiffonade of Cabbages and Tarragon Mustard Mayonnaise $10.25

Sweet Corn Chowder with Lobster $5.25

Consomme of Duck with Black Mushrooms $4.00

Autumn Greens with Cranberry Vinaigrette $4.50

Spinach, Sorrel and Mushrooms with Warm Honey Mustard $5.25

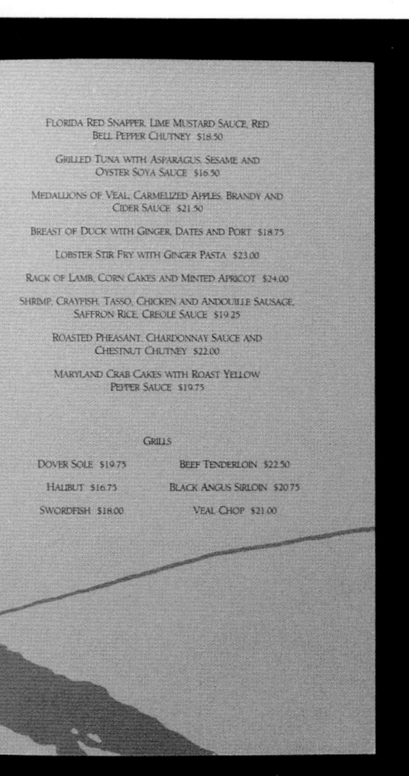

FLORIDA RED SNAPPER, LIME MUSTARD SAUCE, RED BELL PEPPER CHUTNEY $18.50

GRILLED TUNA WITH ASPARAGUS, SESAME AND OYSTER SOYA SAUCE $16.50

MEDALLIONS OF VEAL, CARMELIZED APPLES, BRANDY AND CIDER SAUCE $21.50

BREAST OF DUCK WITH GINGER, DATES AND PORT $18.75

LOBSTER STIR FRY WITH GINGER PASTA $23.00

RACK OF LAMB, CORN CAKES AND MINTED APRICOT $24.00

SHRIMP, CRAYFISH, TASSO, CHICKEN AND ANDOUILLE SAUSAGE, SAFFRON RICE, CREOLE SAUCE $19.25

ROASTED PHEASANT, CHARDONNAY SAUCE AND CHESTNUT CHUTNEY $22.00

MARYLAND CRAB CAKES WITH ROAST YELLOW PEPPER SAUCE $19.75

GRILLS

DOVER SOLE $19.75 BEEF TENDERLOIN $22.50

HALIBUT $16.75 BLACK ANGUS SIRLOIN $20.75

SWORDFISH $18.00 VEAL CHOP $21.00

Designer: *Bob Petz*
*Meliker Communications*
Restaurant: *Chardonnay*
*Park Terrace Hotel*
*Washington, DC*

**1987 N.R.A. GREAT MENUS CONTEST WINNER: FIRST PLACE, MERCHANDISING POWER**

The graphic treatment used on this menu insert is an exploded version of the logo; the treatment is continued on the interior of the insert.

Chardonnay features a changing, seasonal menu. The one shown here, for Fall 1986, is depicted in a very large, readable typeface. Since this is an upscale restaurant, the romanticism of candlelight is more appropriate, which makes the type choice practical as well as beautiful.

Designer: *Alan Colvin*
*Pirtle Design*
Restaurant: *Steak and Ale*
*Dallas, TX*

Not everybody who wants to eat out is a Rockefeller. But *everybody* wants to feel special sometimes. The audience for this solid, book-like menu doesn't want minced squab with three pieces of foreign mushroom on an otherwise naked plate when dining out; it wants a juicy steak or shrimp or chicken. What it *doesn't* want is to be surprised.

The two-color menu inserts are beautiful but subtle; they can be easily changed. The way they fit into the heavy carrier feels permanent. That's probably exactly what the clientele prefers. The insert on the inside front cover is set against a marbled paper pattern, but what it reinforces, via copywriting, is a dependable and comfortable dining experience.

Designer: *Charles Polonsky*
*Associates Printing Service, Inc.*
Restaurant: *La Tour*
*Park Hyatt Hotel*
*Chicago, IL*

A Rousseau-inspired illustration has been used in full color for the breakfast menu, and as a blind embossed addition on the dinner menu. Because the picture shows birds on the wing at early morning, the breakfast menu feels like the beginning of the day. On the dinner menu, the multi-level embossing makes the piece feel very luxurious under the fingers. The high-gloss finish and book-style opening chosen for the dinner menu, together with the fabric-covered elastic holding cord finished with a brass ball, make the evening piece much more formal. The dining room has a view of Water Tower Square, which makes the restaurant's name that much more appropriate. *La Tour* means 'the tower' in French.

## Buffet

Baked- CAJUN Fish Fillets
CATFISH Fillets
Fried Shrimp
Boiled Shrimp
BBQ Ribs
Hush puppies
French FRies
CAJUN FRies
CORN Nuggets
Fried OKRA
Grilled Chicken BREAST
Stuffed CRAB
Clam Strips
Gumbo

## Special orders
### Grill

STEAKS - 10oz Ribeye
7oz Chicken Breast

### Dessert Bar

cobblers
Ice Cream
Cinn. Rolls

Kenn

BBQ Beans
Cole Slaw
Corn on the Cob
Potato Salad
Tomato Relish
Onion Rings
Fried Biscuits
Baked Potatoes
Chicken Strips - Fried
Zesty Chicken Tenders

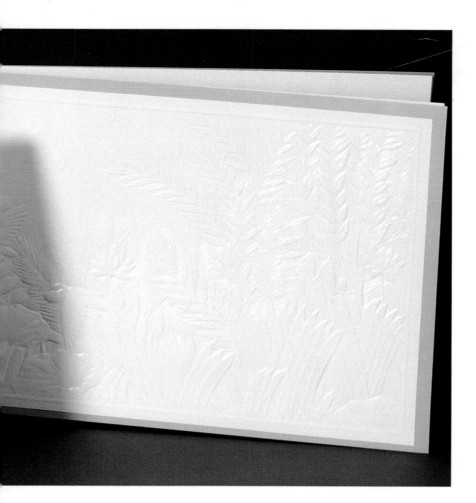

Designer: *Mike Ryan*
*Ryan Design*
Restaurant: *Tuba City Truck Stop*
*New York, NY*

**1987 N.R.A. GREAT MENUS CONTEST WINNER: SECOND PLACE, DESIGN**

From the tire tread across the front of the menu to the wrenches which replace the forks at the left side of the plate inside, this is a paean to the American love affair with the open road. Each menu section is headed by a variation on a road sign — "yield," "stop" and "dangerous curves" have all been appropriated.

The copywriting, particularly the names of the dishes offered, further supports the highway theme. But the final tribute to the speed of modern life lies in the fact that not a single price is listed . . . all are meant to be filled in by hand, as the market prices dictate.

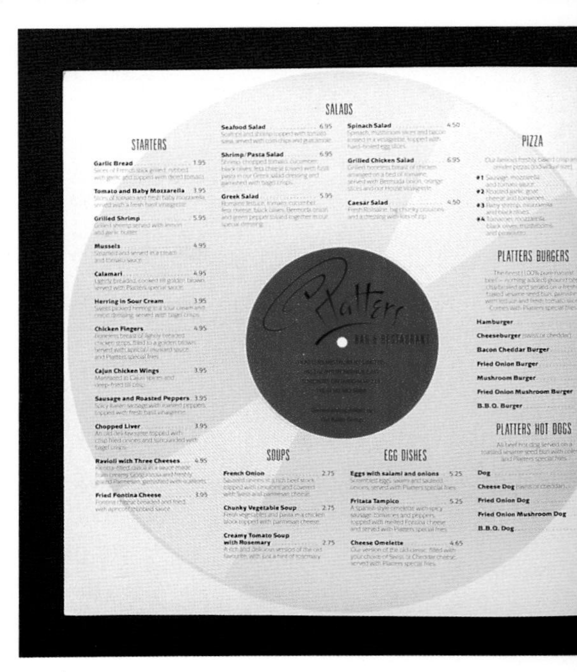

Platters
SALADS
Seafood Salad 6.95
Shrimp/Pasta Salad 6.95
Greek Salad 5.95
Spinach Salad 4.50
Grilled Chicken Salad 6.95
Caesar Salad 4.50
STARTERS
Garlic Bread 1.95
Tomato and Baby Mozzarella 3.95
Grilled Shrimp 5.95
Mussels 4.95
Calamari 4.95
Herring in Sour Cream 3.95
Chicken Fingers 4.95
Cajun Chicken Wings 3.95
Sausage and Roasted Peppers 3.95
Chopped Liver 3.95
Ravioli with Three Cheeses 4.95
Fried Fontina Cheese 3.95
PIZZA
PLATTERS BURGERS
Hamburger
Cheeseburger
Bacon Cheddar Burger
Fried Onion Burger
Mushroom Burger
Fried Onion Mushroom Burger
B.B.Q. Burger
PLATTERS HOT DOGS
Dog
Cheese Dog
Fried Onion Dog
Fried Onion Mushroom Dog
B.B.Q. Dog
SOUPS
French Onion 2.75
Chunky Vegetable Soup 2.75
Creamy Tomato Soup with Rosemary 2.75
EGG DISHES
Eggs with salami and onions 5.25
Fritata Tampico 5.25
Cheese Omelette 4.65

Designer: *Louis Fishauf*
*Reactor Art & Design*

Restaurant: *Platters*
*Toronto, Ontario*
*Canada*

The menu cover looks like a record album and, when the menu is opened, the items are imprinted atop a screen of the record itself. For variety's sake, there are three different covers. Juke box music and fifties-style diner food are the featured attractions. Of course, in a bow to the more sophisticated palate of the eighties, seafood stew, fritata and fried cheese seem to have crept in, too.

The menu design is playful and light. The covers have been printed in a variety of bright, cheerful color schemes. Interiors remain unchanged throughout. The playful theme is further enhanced by the associated book matches.

**LIQUOR & BEER**

**Cocktails 3.25**

Collins (gin/rum), Manhattan (scotch/rye)
Martini (gin/vodka), Rusty Nail
Black Russian, Harvey Wallbanger
Gimlet (gin/vodka), Sour (whiskey/gin)
Slings (gin/rum/vodka), Screwdriver
White Russian, Grasshopper

**Liquor**

Scotch, Vodka, Gin, Rum, Rye, Brandy, Tequila

House Selection 2.75
Premium Brands 2.95

**Aperitifs, Ports & Sherries 2.95**

Harvey Bristol Cream, Dry Sack, Lillet
Dubonnet
Sandeman Port, Tio Pepe, Campari

**Liqueurs 3.25**

Amaretto, Grand Marnier, Kahlua
Frangelico, Cointreau, Galliano
Southern Comfort, Blue Curacao, Pimms
Cherry Brandy, Strawberry Liqueur
Creme de Cacao, dark white, Peach Schnapps
Baileys, B & B, Tia Maria, Anisette
Drambuie, Sambucca, Ouzo, Triple Sec
Cassis, Melon Liqueur, Pernod
Creme de Menthe, green white

**Armagnac 3.75**

Marquis de Montesquiou

**Cognac 3.95**

Courvoisier, Remy Martin, Hennessy

**Domestic Beer 1.95**

Amstel, Amstel Light
Carlsberg, Carlsberg Light, Blue, Blue Light
Miller, Miller Lite, Export, Golden
Classic, Canadian, Schooner, Fosters

**Imported Beer 2.85**

Heineken, Grolsch, Becks, Harp, Michelob
Kronenbourg, Kirin, Tsingtao, Bass

**Imported House Special 2.50**

"Lone Star" (the national beer of texas)

**Draft Beer**

Regular & Lite
12 oz. 1.75 20 oz. 2.95

**PLATTERS SPECIALTY COCKTAILS 3.50**

**Pina Colada**
Island Rum, cream of coconut & pineapple juice – blended in ice

**Fresh Fruit Daiquiris**
Banana, Raspberry or Strawberry

**Blue Hawaii**
Island Rum, Blue Curacao, lemon juice & pineapple juice – Aloha!

**Platters Island Iced Tea**
Gin, Vodka & Rum with lemon juice. Special ingredients added for an iced tea flavour!

**Blue Margarita (house special)**
Tequila, Blue Curacao, Triple Sec, sweet & sour lemon juice – Ole!

**Strawberry Margarita**
Tequila, Triple Sec, sweet & sour lemon juice with fresh strawberries

**Mai Tai**
Island Light Rum, Dark Rum, Amaretto, orange juice, sweet & sour lemon juice – tie one on for size

**Platters Punch**
Island Dark Rum, Light Rum, pineapple juice & orange juice – what a kick (punch)

**Mimosa**
Tangy sensation of orange juice, bubbly Champagne & a hint of Cointreau

**Chocolate Island Monkey**
Banana Liqueur, thick chocolate syrup & fresh banana blended with select Island Rum – rock n' roll

**Strawberry Pina Colada**
Island Light Rum, cream of coconut, pineapple juice & fresh strawberries

**Cranberry Cocktail**
Bubbly Champagne, cranberry juice & a hint of Cointreau

**Platters Cooler**
Raspberry Liqueur, Rum, & fresh tropical juices

**Cranberry Cooler**
Amaretto, cranberry & orange juice

**Blue Suede Shoes**
Island Rum, Blue Curacao, sweet & sour lemon juice

**Platters Perfect Passion**
Island Rum, Curacao, half & half, fresh orange juice & chocolate

**Platters Bloody Mary/Bloody Caesar**
The best Volga Vodka with tangy tomato juice or climatic cocktail juice. Complete with celery stick

**Blue Moon**
Vodka, Blue Curacao, Casis, sweet & sour lemon juice

**WINE & WINE SPECIALTIES**

**Imported House Wine**
Dry Red, Dry White or Rose

Glass 3.45 ½ Litre 6.85 Litre 12.95
Kir, Spritzer, and Cooler 3.29
Sangria (pitcher) 7.49

**Estate Bottle Wines – White**

French

| | |
|---|---|
| La Gamine | $11. |
| Pichet D'Alsace | 14. |
| Savignon | 15. |
| Cuvee des Chavalliers | 12. |
| La Bordelaise | 14. |
| Vin de France | 15. |

German

| | |
|---|---|
| Deninmosselle | 12. |
| Hambacher Riesling | 17. |

Italian

| | |
|---|---|
| Galestro | 14. |
| Frascati Superiore | 14. |
| Orvieto | 13. |
| Soave | 13. |

Canadian

| | |
|---|---|
| Chateau des Charmes Chardonnay | 14. |
| Inniskillin Riesling | 13. |

**Estate Bottle Wines – Red**

French

| | |
|---|---|
| Chateau Martouret | 14. |
| Oliver de France | 15. |
| Chabanais Macon | 15. |
| Chateau Geniguet (1983) | 14. |
| Beaujolais | 17. |
| Le Piat d'Or | 12. |
| Corbieres | 12. |

Italian

| | |
|---|---|
| Bardolino | 12. |
| Rubesco | 14. |
| Chionti Classico Riserva | 16. |
| Pinot Nero | 12. |
| Barbera | 14. |

Canadian

| | |
|---|---|
| Chateau des Charmes Gamay Beaujolais | 16. |
| Inniskillin Millot – Chambourcin (1982) | 14. |

**Sparkling Wines**

| | |
|---|---|
| Henkell Trocken – Germany | 17. |
| Freixenet Carta Nevada – Spain | 14. |

**Champagnes**

| | |
|---|---|
| Dom Perignon (1976) – French | 75. |
| Mumm Extra Dry – French | 37. |
| Brights President Brut – Canadian | 18. |

(P.S.T. EXTRA)

# CHAPTER 9

When is a menu "picture perfect"? When it's a menu masquerading as something else, of course. The French call it *'trompe l'oeil'* — something which, literally, fools the eye. Each of the menus featured in this chapter is designed to look like something else. The portrayed object may be an article of clothing, a bottle or a seemingly unrelated item. All have in common, however, a strong sense of the identity of the restaurant itself.

Choosing when to be playful, or to poke gentle fun, is critical to the success of this type of design. Before embarking on a "picture perfect" menu design, the designer should have a clear notion of what mood the restaurant is trying to evoke.

The following menus present some success stories in the lighter vein of the menu design business. We strongly suspect that these were a delight to design. We hope you will find them delightful as well.

## PICTURE PERFECT

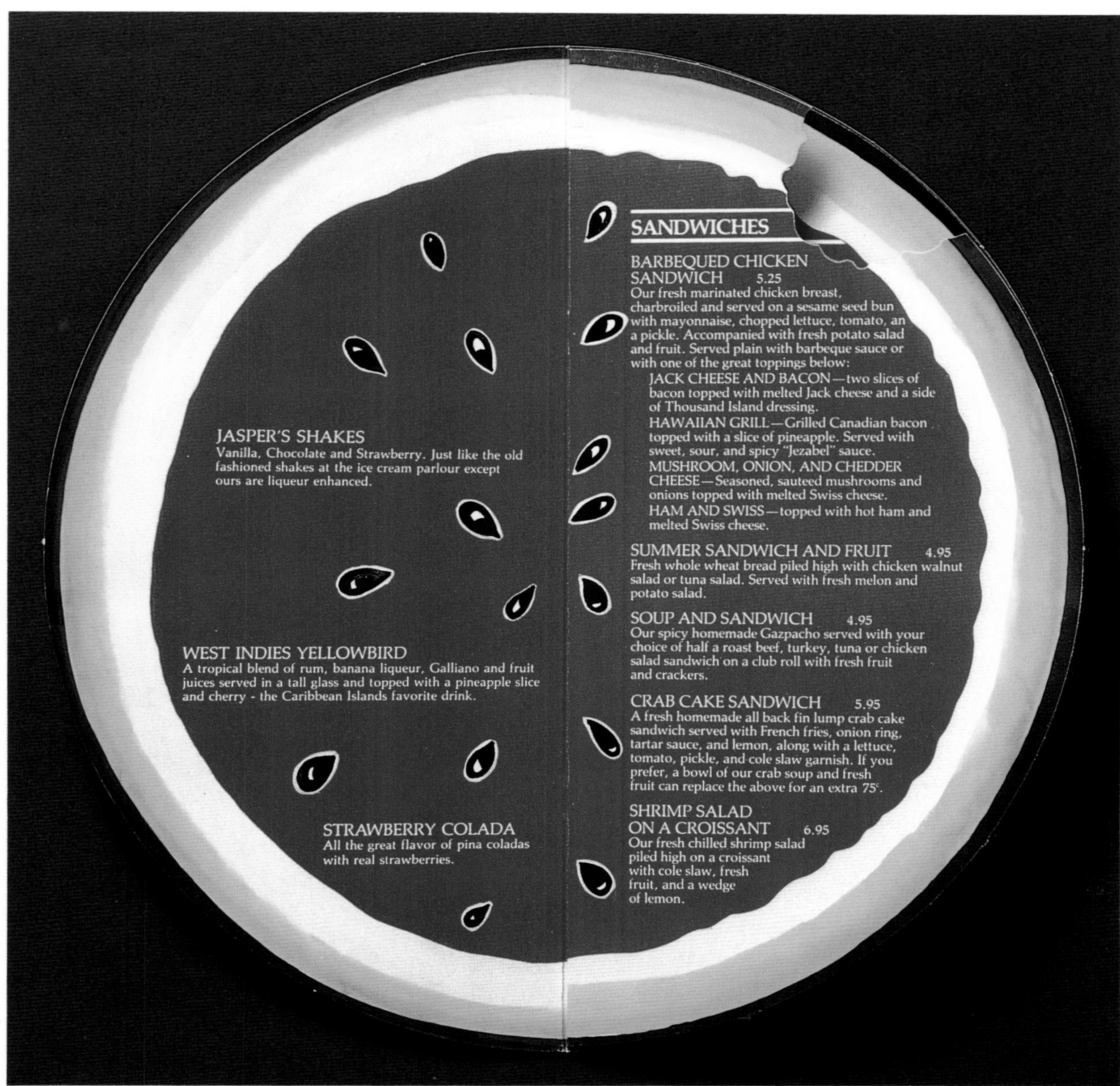

SANDWICHES
BARBEQUED CHICKEN SANDWICH 5.25
Our fresh marinated chicken breast, charbroiled and served on a sesame seed bun with mayonnaise, chopped lettuce, tomato, an a pickle. Accompanied with fresh potato salad and fruit. Served plain with barbeque sauce or with one of the great toppings below:
JACK CHEESE AND BACON—two slices of bacon topped with melted Jack cheese and a side of Thousand Island dressing.
HAWAIIAN GRILL—Grilled Canadian bacon topped with a slice of pineapple. Served with sweet, sour, and spicy "Jezabel" sauce.
MUSHROOM, ONION, AND CHEDDER CHEESE—Seasoned, sauteed mushrooms and onions topped with melted Swiss cheese.
HAM AND SWISS—topped with hot ham and melted Swiss cheese.
SUMMER SANDWICH AND FRUIT 4.95
Fresh whole wheat bread piled high with chicken walnut salad or tuna salad. Served with fresh melon and potato salad.
SOUP AND SANDWICH 4.95
Our spicy homemade Gazpacho served with your choice of half a roast beef, turkey, tuna or chicken salad sandwich on a club roll with fresh fruit and crackers.
CRAB CAKE SANDWICH 5.95
A fresh homemade all back fin lump crab cake sandwich served with French fries, onion ring, tartar sauce, and lemon, along with a lettuce, tomato, pickle, and cole slaw garnish. If you prefer, a bowl of our crab soup and fresh fruit can replace the above for an extra 75¢.
SHRIMP SALAD ON A CROISSANT 6.95
Our fresh chilled shrimp salad piled high on a croissant with cole slaw, fresh fruit, and a wedge of lemon.
JASPER'S SHAKES
Vanilla, Chocolate and Strawberry. Just like the old fashioned shakes at the ice cream parlour except ours are liqueur enhanced.
WEST INDIES YELLOWBIRD
A tropical blend of rum, banana liqueur, Galliano and fruit juices served in a tall glass and topped with a pineapple slice and cherry - the Caribbean Islands favorite drink.
STRAWBERRY COLADA
All the great flavor of pina coladas with real strawberries.


Designer: *A.B. Motley III*

Restaurant: *Jasper's Summertime Menu*
*Xanadu, Ltd.*
*Greenbelt, MD*

What better way to capture the essence of summer than with watermelon? Viewed in profile on the cover, the melon opens up into a full cross-section for the interior pages. A "bite" has been taken from the middle page to complete the illusion.

The full range of summer specialties is covered in the menu. Everything from alcoholic beverages to salads and desserts appears. Copywriting uses lots of adjectives to enhance the coolness of the menu's theme.

Designer: *A.B. Motley III*

Restaurant: *Jasper's Drink and Snack Menu*
*Xanadu, Ltd.*
*Greenbelt, MD*

Billing itself as "in the spirit of fun," Jasper's is exuberantly Mexican. Its menu reflects the scope of the North American heritage, as does this drink menu, designed to resemble a bottle of Kahlua.

The restaurant's theme is repeated at the top of succeeding pages of the extensive list. In addition to the usual fruit rum/ tequila concoctions, the restaurant has chosen to feature light alcohol and no-alcohol beverages as well. The slightly wacky illustrations of the main menu reappear here. The back cover sells both Sunday brunch and what is referred to as "Unwind Time," Jasper's version of 'happy hour.'

## ICE CREAM DRINKS

*STRAWBERRY SHORTCAKE*
Our delicious blend of Strawberries and Liqueurs. Close your eyes and you're in a French Pastry Shoppe.

*ICE CREAM SANDWICH*
Chocolate liqueur, blended with Oreo cookies and vanilla ice cream. You don't even have to take off the wrapper.

*CREAMSICLE*
A smooth blend of vanilla ice cream, orange sherbet, and our own special liqueurs. Just like the one you used to buy from the Good Humor Man.

*JASPER'S SHAKES*
Vanilla, Chocolate, and Strawberry. Just like the old-fashioned shakes at the ice-cream parlor . . . except ours are liqueur enhanced.

*KAHLUA BANANA*
A thick ice-creamy, banana drink with a sophisticated hint of Kahlua.

*PEACHY KEEN*
A salute to Georgia, the Peach State, with peach liqueur and peaches, blended with vanilla ice cream.

*BUTTER PECAN*
When served frozen, this blend of vanilla ice cream and Praline Liqueur tastes just like Butter Pecan ice cream.

*PEANUT BUTTER CUP*
Look out "Reese's"! One of Jasper's favorites.

*KREEMIES*
All our original ice cream drinks without the liquor. Ask for your favorite, and just add . . . "KREEMIE."

## JASPER EAZIES

We've captured the great flavor and taste of these drinks *without* the alcohol.

*VIRGIN DAIQUIRIS*
Pick your favorite: Strawberry, Raspberry, Peach and Tangerine.

*COOL AND FRUITY*
TROPICAL BREEZE . . . Grapefruit and pineapple juices.
OCEAN SPRAY . . . Grapefruit and Cranberry juices.
BACK BAY . . . Orange and Cranberry juices.

*NADA-COLADAS*
PINA-NADA-COLADA or STRAWBERRY-NADA-COLADA
Both have that great tropical juice taste . . . your choice.

*PEACH MELBA*
A WOW blend of vanilla ice cream, raspberries, and peaches.

*PINK PANTHER*
A tangy blend of grapefruit and apple juices, a dab of grenadine served up or over cracked ice.

*G-WIZZ*
Slightly sweetened grapefruit juice blended carefully with gingerale.

*ORANGE KONG*
Orange and pineapple juices blended with banana and rum flavors.

*SPARKLING CATAWBA*
Tastes like Asti-Spumante. Available by the glass or bottle.

*CRASSANE PEAR SODA*
A Yuppie dee-lite! Fresh and natural.

*MOUSSY BEER*
Beer lovers will never know this Danish Beer has no alcohol. The drink to choose when you choose not to drink.

*PERRIER*
An old favorite with a wedge of lime, and now new orange twist flavor.

Designer: *Ron Bergner*
*Howlett-Bergner and Associates*
Restaurant: *Carlos Murphy*
*San Diego, CA*

This chain of restaurants advertises its units as "a celebration." The atmosphere sought was fun and the food items offered are many. The designer felt that the best way to make sense of the menu and convey that atmosphere was to create a "game board." Creative copywriting on the first menu unfold explains the rules of the "game."

The wacky 'Mexican-Irish' theme of the place is supported by the use of Kelly green as the predominant color on the menu. Fanciful illustrations, including a winged burger, support the playful note desired.

Restaurant: *Rusty Scupper*
*Beer Selections*
*California*

This die-cut, plastic-coated menu is unusual for more than its clever design. Americans tend to associate beers with specific brands; Europeans refer to ales, pilseners and lagers. The copywriting on this menu is a compromise between the two views.

Upon opening the 'washtub,' one finds beer bottles peeping from a bed of ice. The specific characteristics of each beer are outlined against the icy background. The selection includes both the most popular beers from the United States and a variety of Canadian, Mexican and European imports. The historical background of each brewery and the various hop varieties are discussed in some detail.

This menu represents an unusual effort to market beers to Americans in the same way as wines are sold.

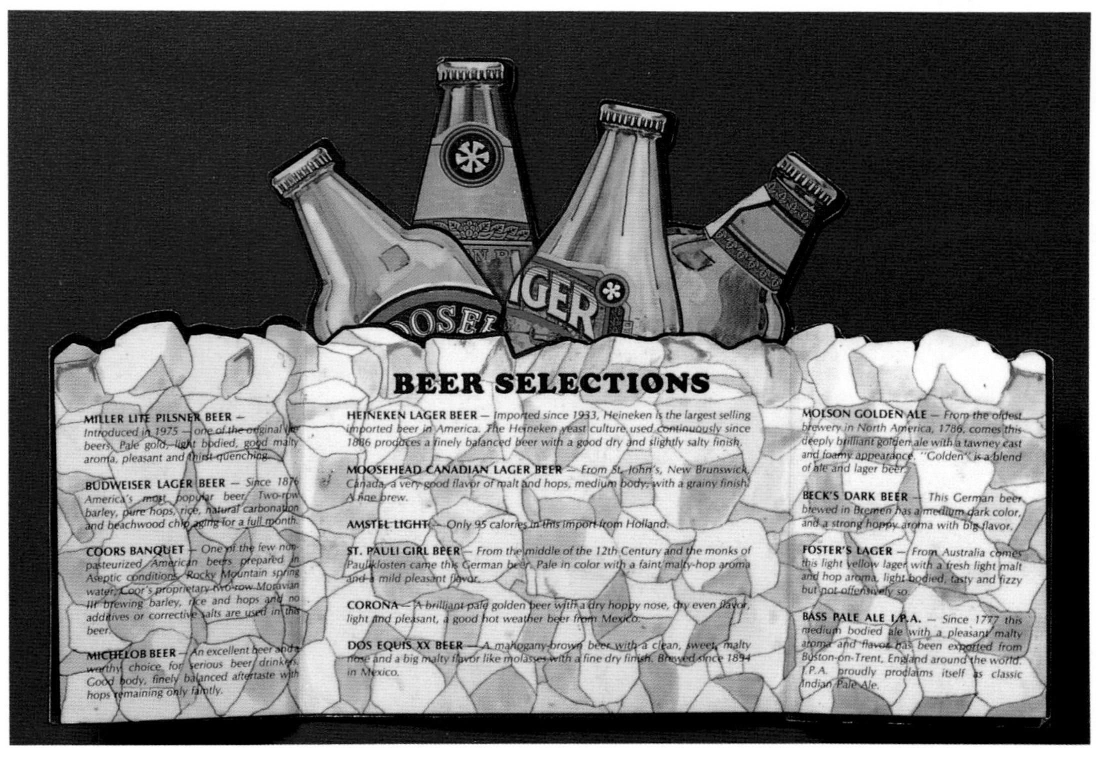

**BEER SELECTIONS**

**MILLER LITE PILSNER BEER** — *Introduced in 1975 — one of the original lite beers. Pale gold, light bodied, good malty aroma, pleasant and thirst quenching.*

**BUDWEISER LAGER BEER** — *Since 1876 America's most popular beer. Two-row barley, pure hops, rice, natural carbonation and beachwood chip aging for a full month.*

**COORS BANQUET** — *One of the few non-pasteurized American beers prepared in Aseptic conditions. Rocky Mountain spring water, Coor's proprietary two-row Moravian III brewing barley, rice and hops and no additives or corrective salts are used in this beer.*

**MICHELOB BEER** — *An excellent beer and a worthy choice for serious beer drinkers. Good body, finely balanced aftertaste with hops remaining only faintly.*

**HEINEKEN LAGER BEER** — *Imported since 1933, Heineken is the largest selling imported beer in America. The Heineken yeast culture used continuously since 1886 produces a finely balanced beer with a good dry and slightly salty finish.*

**MOOSEHEAD CANADIAN LAGER BEER** — *From St. John's, New Brunswick, Canada, a very good flavor of malt and hops, medium body, with a grainy finish. A fine brew.*

**AMSTEL LIGHT** — *Only 95 calories in this import from Holland.*

**ST. PAULI GIRL BEER** — *From the middle of the 12th Century and the monks of Paulklosten came this German beer. Pale in color with a faint malty-hop aroma and a mild pleasant flavor.*

**CORONA** — *A brilliant pale golden beer with a dry hoppy nose, dry even flavor, light and pleasant, a good hot weather beer from Mexico.*

**DOS EQUIS XX BEER** — *A mahogany-brown beer with a clean, sweet, malty nose and a big malty flavor like molasses with a fine dry finish. Brewed since 1894 in Mexico.*

**MOLSON GOLDEN ALE** — *From the oldest brewery in North America, 1786, comes this deeply brilliant golden ale with a tawney cast and foamy appearance. "Golden" is a blend of ale and lager beer.*

**BECK'S DARK BEER** — *This German beer brewed in Bremen has a medium dark color, and a strong hoppy aroma with big flavor.*

**FOSTER'S LAGER** — *From Australia comes this light yellow lager with a fresh light malt and hop aroma, light bodied, tasty and fizzy but not offensively so.*

**BASS PALE ALE I.P.A.** — *Since 1777 this medium bodied ale with a pleasant malty aroma and flavor has been exported from Burton-on-Trent, England around the world. I.P.A. proudly proclaims itself as classic Indian Pale Ale.*

Designer: *Ron Bergner*
*Howlett-Bergner & Associates*
Restaurant: *El Torito*
*Texas units*

This national chain wanted a special menu for its Texas units that would have more of a regional feeling. This three-color die-cut of a rough, tough Texan torso delivers.

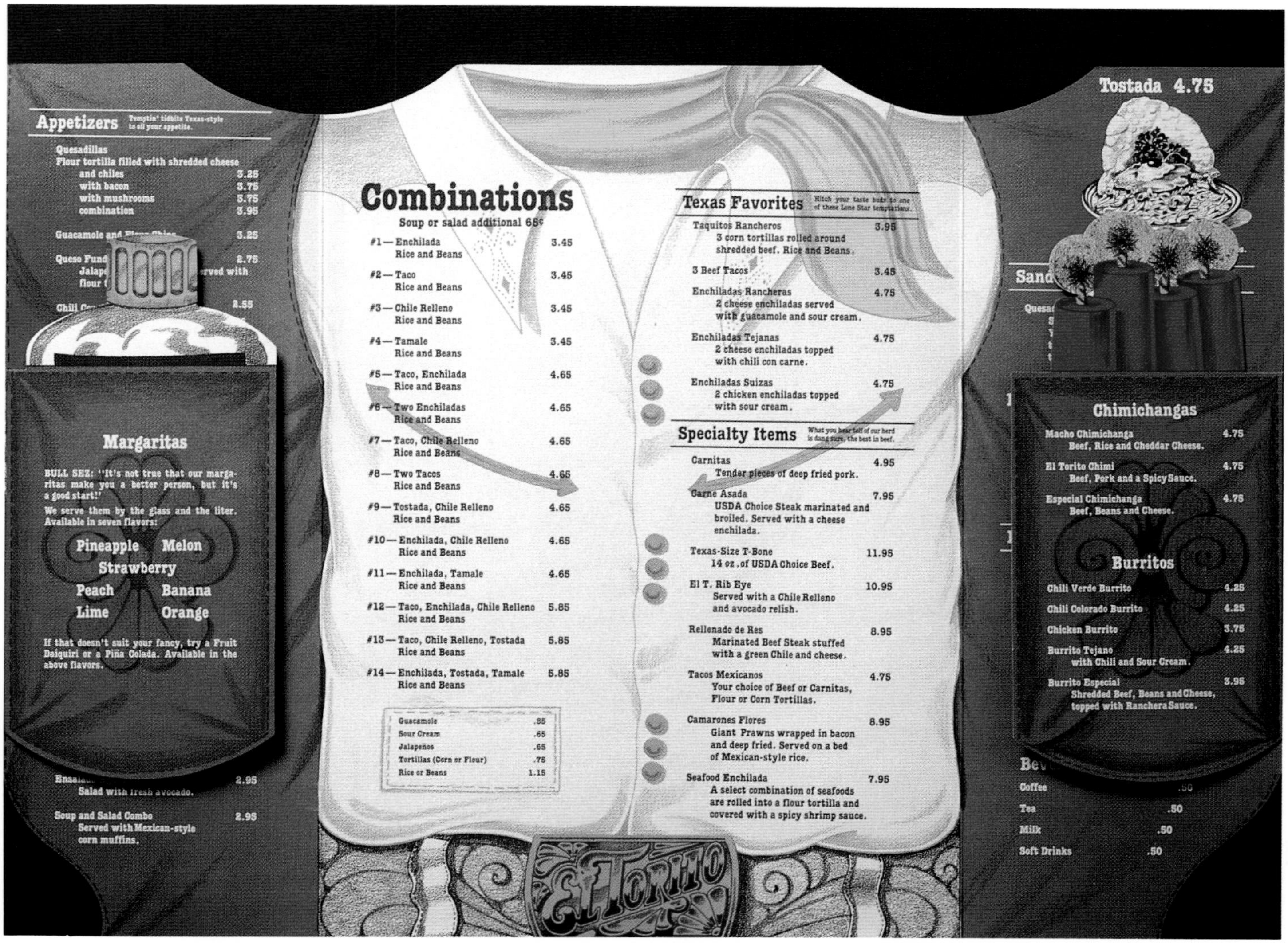

## Appetizers
Temptin' tidbits Texas-style to oil your appetite.

Quesadillas
Flour tortilla filled with shredded cheese
- and chiles 3.25
- with bacon 3.75
- with mushrooms 3.75
- combination 3.95

Guacamole and ... 3.25

Queso Fund... 2.75

Chili ... 2.55

## Margaritas

BULL SEZ: "It's not true that our margaritas make you a better person, but it's a good start!"
We serve them by the glass and the liter. Available in seven flavors:

Pineapple Melon
Strawberry
Peach Banana
Lime Orange

If that doesn't suit your fancy, try a Fruit Daiquiri or a Piña Colada. Available in the above flavors.

Ensalada ... 2.95
Salad with fresh avocado.

Soup and Salad Combo 2.95
Served with Mexican-style corn muffins.

## Combinations
Soup or salad additional 65¢

| | |
|---|---|
| #1—Enchilada, Rice and Beans | 3.45 |
| #2—Taco, Rice and Beans | 3.45 |
| #3—Chile Relleno, Rice and Beans | 3.45 |
| #4—Tamale, Rice and Beans | 3.45 |
| #5—Taco, Enchilada, Rice and Beans | 4.65 |
| #6—Two Enchiladas, Rice and Beans | 4.65 |
| #7—Taco, Chile Relleno, Rice and Beans | 4.65 |
| #8—Two Tacos, Rice and Beans | 4.65 |
| #9—Tostada, Chile Relleno, Rice and Beans | 4.65 |
| #10—Enchilada, Chile Relleno, Rice and Beans | 4.65 |
| #11—Enchilada, Tamale, Rice and Beans | 4.65 |
| #12—Taco, Enchilada, Chile Relleno, Rice and Beans | 5.85 |
| #13—Taco, Chile Relleno, Tostada, Rice and Beans | 5.85 |
| #14—Enchilada, Tostada, Tamale, Rice and Beans | 5.85 |

| | |
|---|---|
| Guacamole | .65 |
| Sour Cream | .65 |
| Jalapeños | .65 |
| Tortillas (Corn or Flour) | .75 |
| Rice or Beans | 1.15 |

## Texas Favorites
Hitch your taste buds to one of these Lone Star temptations.

Taquitos Rancheros 3.95
3 corn tortillas rolled around shredded beef. Rice and Beans.

3 Beef Tacos 3.45

Enchiladas Rancheras 4.75
2 cheese enchiladas served with guacamole and sour cream.

Enchiladas Tejanas 4.75
2 cheese enchiladas topped with chili con carne.

Enchiladas Suizas 4.75
2 chicken enchiladas topped with sour cream.

## Specialty Items
What you hear tell of our herd is dang sure, the best in beef.

Carnitas 4.95
Tender pieces of deep fried pork.

Carne Asada 7.95
USDA Choice Steak marinated and broiled. Served with a cheese enchilada.

Texas-Size T-Bone 11.95
14 oz. of USDA Choice Beef.

El T. Rib Eye 10.95
Served with a Chile Relleno and avocado relish.

Rellenado de Res 8.95
Marinated Beef Steak stuffed with a green Chile and cheese.

Tacos Mexicanos 4.75
Your choice of Beef or Carnitas, Flour or Corn Tortillas.

Camarones Flores 8.95
Giant Prawns wrapped in bacon and deep fried. Served on a bed of Mexican-style rice.

Seafood Enchilada 7.95
A select combination of seafoods are rolled into a flour tortilla and covered with a spicy shrimp sauce.

El Torito

Tostada 4.75

## Chimichangas

Macho Chimichanga 4.75
Beef, Rice and Cheddar Cheese.

El Torito Chimi 4.75
Beef, Pork and a Spicy Sauce.

Especial Chimichanga 4.75
Beef, Beans and Cheese.

## Burritos

Chili Verde Burrito 4.25
Chili Colorado Burrito 4.25
Chicken Burrito 3.75
Burrito Tejano 4.25
with Chili and Sour Cream.
Burrito Especial 3.95
Shredded Beef, Beans and Cheese, topped with Ranchera Sauce.

Bev...
Coffee .50
Tea .50
Milk .50
Soft Drinks .50

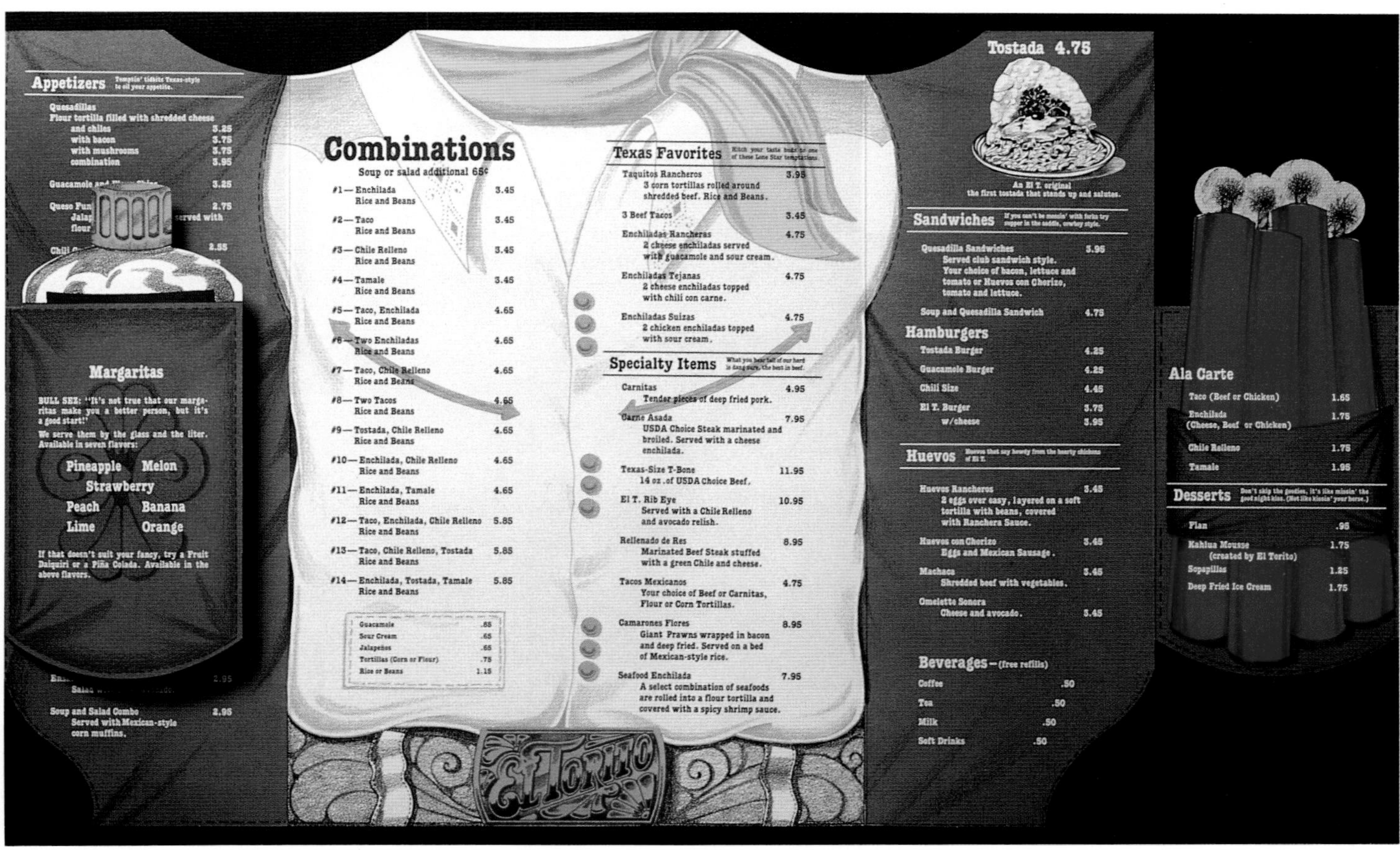

Appetizers
Margaritas
Combinations
Texas Favorites
Specialty Items
El Torito
Tostada 4.75
An El T. original the first tostada that stands up and salutes.
Sandwiches
Quesadilla Sandwiches 3.95
Served club sandwich style. Your choice of bacon, lettuce and tomato or Huevos con Chorizo, tomato and lettuce.
Soup and Quesadilla Sandwich 4.75
Hamburgers
Tostada Burger 4.25
Guacamole Burger 4.25
Chili Size 4.45
El T. Burger 3.75
w/cheese 3.95
Huevos
Huevos Rancheros 3.45
2 eggs over easy, layered on a soft tortilla with beans, covered with Ranchera Sauce.
Huevos con Chorizo 3.45
Eggs and Mexican Sausage.
Machaca 3.45
Shredded beef with vegetables.
Omelette Sonora 3.45
Cheese and avocado.
Beverages—(free refills)
Coffee .50
Tea .50
Milk .50
Soft Drinks .50
Ala Carte
Taco (Beef or Chicken) 1.65
Enchilada (Cheese, Beef or Chicken) 1.75
Chile Relleno 1.75
Tamale 1.95
Desserts
Flan .95
Kahlua Mousse (created by El Torito) 1.75
Sopapillas 1.25
Deep Fried Ice Cream 1.75

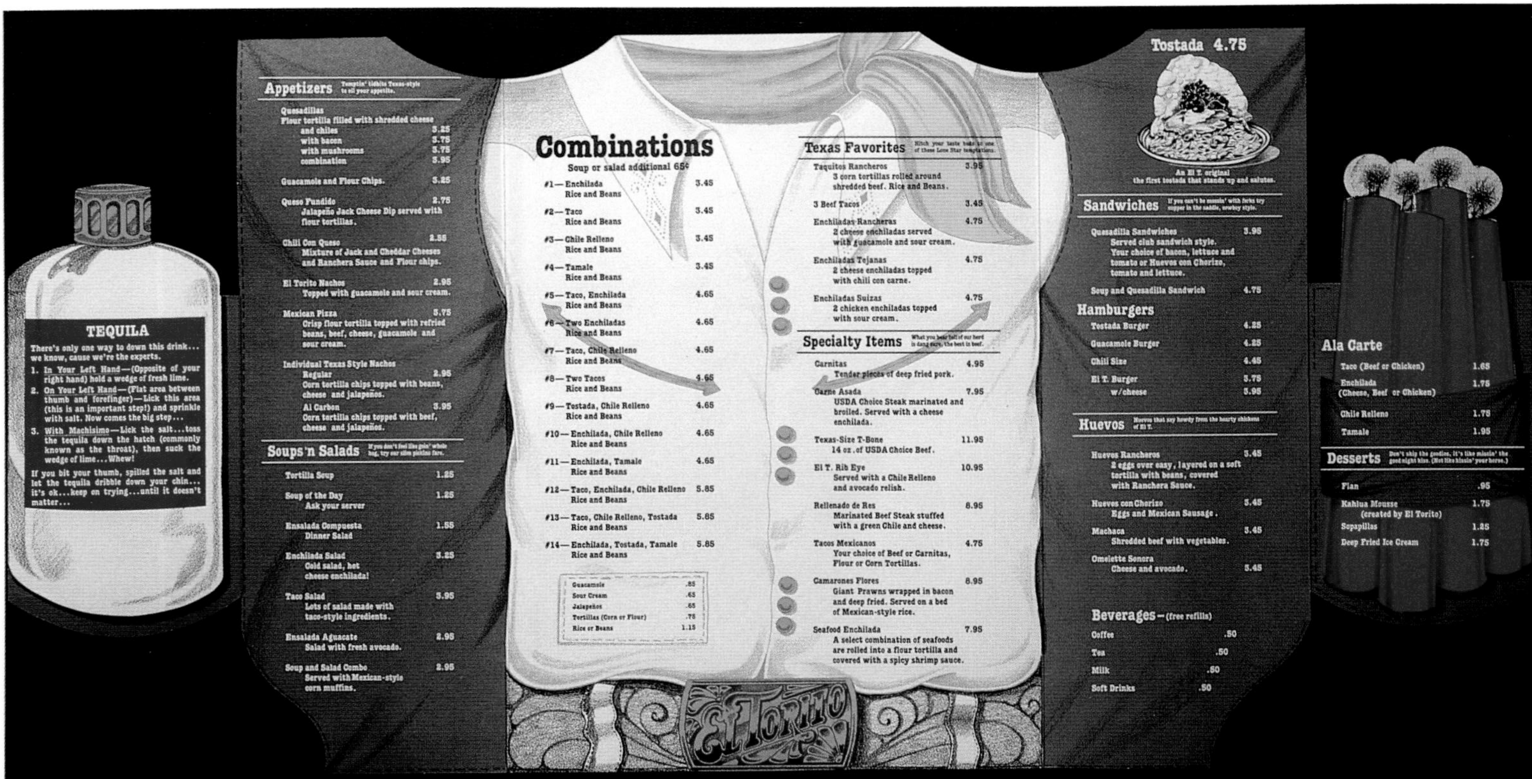
TEQUILA
There's only one way to down this drink... we know, cause we're the experts.
1. In Your Left Hand—(Opposite of your right hand) hold a wedge of fresh lime.
2. On Your Left Hand—(Flat area between thumb and forefinger)—Lick this area (this is an important step!) and sprinkle with salt. Now comes the big step...
3. With Machisimo—Lick the salt...toss the tequila down the hatch (commonly known as the throat), then suck the wedge of lime...Whew!
If you bit your thumb, spilled the salt and let the tequila dribble down your chin... it's ok...keep on trying...until it doesn't matter...
Appetizers
Temptin' tidbits Texas-style to oil your appetite.
Quesadillas
Flour tortilla filled with shredded cheese
and chiles 3.25
with bacon 3.75
with mushrooms 3.75
combination 3.95
Guacamole and Flour Chips. 3.25
Queso Fundido 2.75
Jalapeño Jack Cheese Dip served with flour tortillas.
Chili Con Queso 2.55
Mixture of Jack and Cheddar Cheeses and Ranchera Sauce and Flour chips.
El Torito Nachos 2.95
Topped with guacamole and sour cream.
Mexican Pizza 3.75
Crisp flour tortilla topped with refried beans, beef, cheese, guacamole and sour cream.
Individual Texas Style Nachos
Regular 2.95
Corn tortilla chips topped with beans, cheese and jalapeños.
Al Carbon 3.95
Corn tortilla chips topped with beef, cheese and jalapeños.
Soups'n Salads
Tortilla Soup 1.25
Soup of the Day 1.25
Ask your server
Ensalada Compuesta 1.55
Dinner Salad
Enchilada Salad 3.25
Cold salad, hot cheese enchilada!
Taco Salad 3.95
Lots of salad made with taco-style ingredients.
Ensalada Aguacate 2.95
Salad with fresh avocado.
Soup and Salad Combo 2.95
Served with Mexican-style corn muffins.
Combinations
Soup or salad additional 65¢
#1—Enchilada Rice and Beans 3.45
#2—Taco Rice and Beans 3.45
#3—Chile Relleno Rice and Beans 3.45
#4—Tamale Rice and Beans 3.45
#5—Taco, Enchilada Rice and Beans 4.65
#6—Two Enchiladas Rice and Beans 4.65
#7—Taco, Chile Relleno Rice and Beans 4.65
#8—Two Tacos Rice and Beans 4.65
#9—Tostada, Chile Relleno Rice and Beans 4.65
#10—Enchilada, Chile Relleno Rice and Beans 4.65
#11—Enchilada, Tamale Rice and Beans 4.65
#12—Taco, Enchilada, Chile Relleno Rice and Beans 5.85
#13—Taco, Chile Relleno, Tostada Rice and Beans 5.85
#14—Enchilada, Tostada, Tamale Rice and Beans 5.85
Guacamole .85
Sour Cream .65
Jalapeños .65
Tortillas (Corn or Flour) .75
Rice or Beans 1.15
Texas Favorites
Taquitos Rancheros 3.95
3 corn tortillas rolled around shredded beef. Rice and Beans.
3 Beef Tacos 3.45
Enchiladas Rancheras 4.75
2 cheese enchiladas served with guacamole and sour cream.
Enchiladas Tejanas 4.75
2 cheese enchiladas topped with chili con carne.
Enchiladas Suizas 4.75
2 chicken enchiladas topped with sour cream.
Specialty Items
Carnitas 4.95
Tender pieces of deep fried pork.
Carne Asada 7.95
USDA Choice Steak marinated and broiled. Served with a cheese enchilada.
Texas-Size T-Bone 11.95
14 oz. of USDA Choice Beef.
El T. Rib Eye 10.95
Served with a Chile Relleno and avocado relish.
Rellenado de Res 8.95
Marinated Beef Steak stuffed with a green Chile and cheese.
Tacos Mexicanos 4.75
Your choice of Beef or Carnitas, Flour or Corn Tortillas.
Camarones Flores 8.95
Giant Prawns wrapped in bacon and deep fried. Served on a bed of Mexican-style rice.
Seafood Enchilada 7.95
A select combination of seafoods are rolled into a flour tortilla and covered with a spicy shrimp sauce.
El Torito
Tostada 4.75
An El T. original
the first tostada that stands up and salutes.
Sandwiches
If you can't be messin' with forks try supper in the saddle, cowboy style.
Quesadilla Sandwiches 3.95
Served club sandwich style. Your choice of bacon, lettuce and tomato or Huevos con Chorizo, tomato and lettuce.
Soup and Quesadilla Sandwich 4.75
Hamburgers
Tostada Burger 4.25
Guacamole Burger 4.25
Chili Size 4.45
El T. Burger 3.75
w/cheese 3.95
Huevos
Huevos Rancheros 3.45
2 eggs over easy, layered on a soft tortilla with beans, covered with Ranchera Sauce.
Huevos con Chorizo 3.45
Eggs and Mexican Sausage.
Machaca 3.45
Shredded beef with vegetables.
Omelette Sonora 3.45
Cheese and avocado.
Beverages—(free refills)
Coffee .50
Tea .50
Milk .50
Soft Drinks .50
Ala Carte
Taco (Beef or Chicken) 1.65
Enchilada (Cheese, Beef or Chicken) 1.75
Chile Relleno 1.75
Tamale 1.95
Desserts
Don't skip the goodies, it's like missin' the goodnight kiss. (Not like kissin' your horse.)
Flan .95
Kahlua Mousse (created by El Torito) 1.75
Sopapillas 1.25
Deep Fried Ice Cream 1.75

Complete with tin star and long-horn ring, the cover depicts a cowboy, or perhaps a desperado. We don't know for sure until we open the menu to discover that this "cowboy" is toting lit sticks of dynamite and a flask in his inside vest pockets. Clever copywriting and distinctly Texas-style cuisine further support the regional theme. The restaurant modestly limits use of its name to the figure's belt buckle. The designer is credited on the menu's back cover.

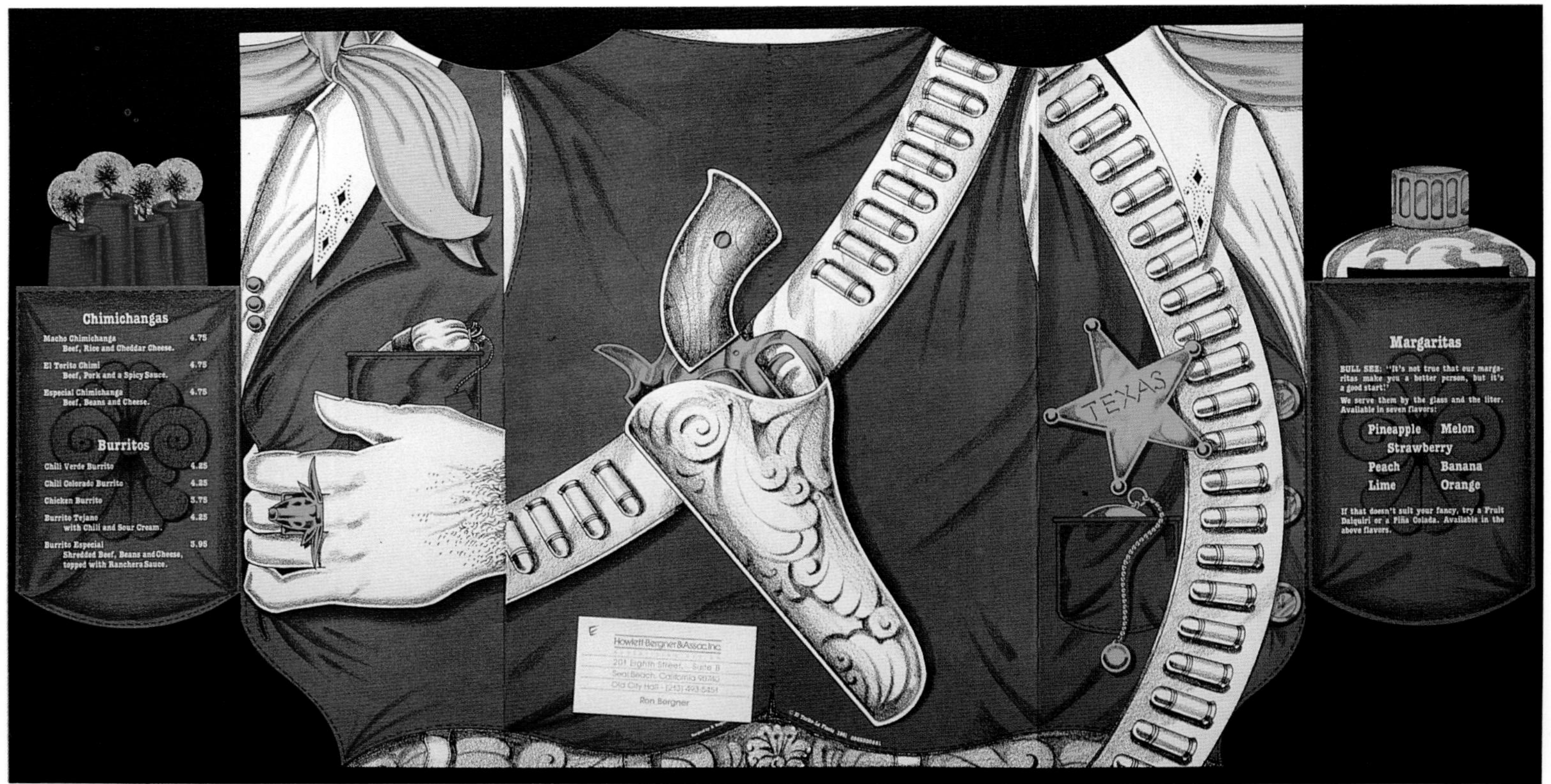
Chimichangas
Macho Chimichanga 4.75
Beef, Rice and Cheddar Cheese.
El Torito Chimi 4.75
Beef, Pork and a Spicy Sauce.
Especial Chimichanga 4.75
Beef, Beans and Cheese.
Burritos
Chili Verde Burrito 4.25
Chili Colorado Burrito 4.25
Chicken Burrito 3.75
Burrito Tejano 4.25
with Chili and Sour Cream.
Burrito Especial 3.95
Shredded Beef, Beans and Cheese, topped with Ranchera Sauce.
Howlett Bergner & Assoc. Inc.
Ron Bergner
TEXAS
Margaritas
BULL SEZ: "It's not true that our margaritas make you a better person, but it's a good start!"
We serve them by the glass and the liter. Available in seven flavors:
Pineapple Melon
Strawberry
Peach Banana
Lime Orange
If that doesn't suit your fancy, try a Fruit Daiquiri or a Piña Colada. Available in the above flavors.

| | |
|---|---|
| Designer: | *Ann Werner* |
| | *Associates Printing Service, Inc.* |
| Restaurant: | *Images* |
| | *John Hancock Center* |
| | *Chicago, IL* |

Designed as a book of matches, this drink and snack menu uses merchandising savvy to make its points. The restaurant, located atop the John Hancock Center, makes note of its spectacular view and, with the very first page, offers the diner a distinguished selection of champagnes and American sparkling wines to celebrate the achievement!

Succeeding sheets of "matches" offer liqueur-spiked coffees, specialty drinks and a variety of snacks to soak it all up. The quality of the beverages and foods offered is emphasized throughout. Liquor brands are called by name, cheeses featured include some of America's finest and the sparkling wines offered feature California's finest at the "low" end.

The designer has achieved a festive and easy-to-read design with the use of only two colors, a light screen to suggest the match sticks and a coated cover.

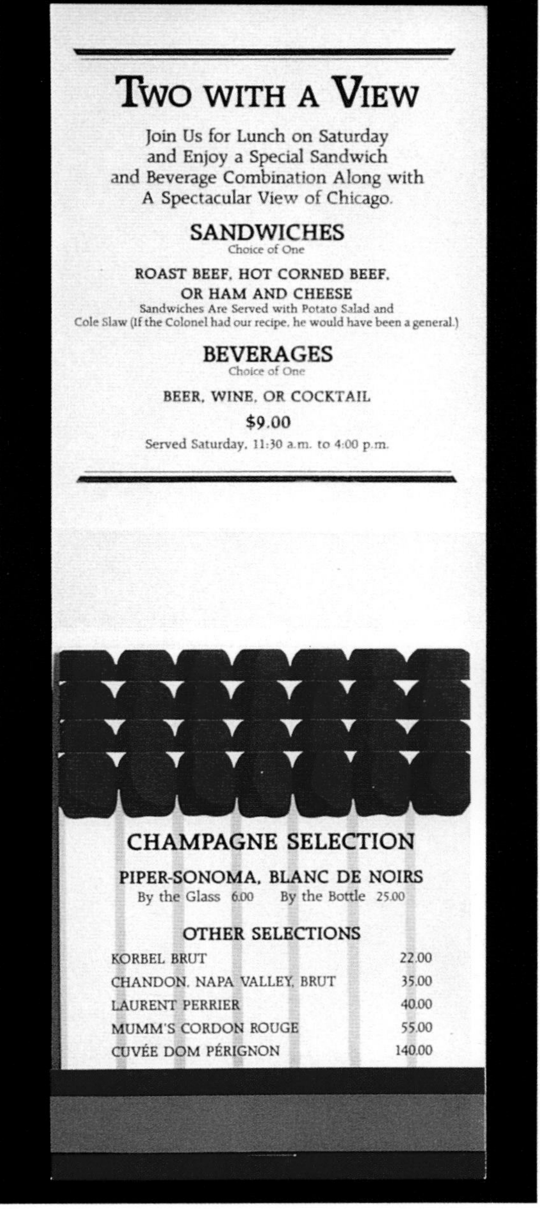

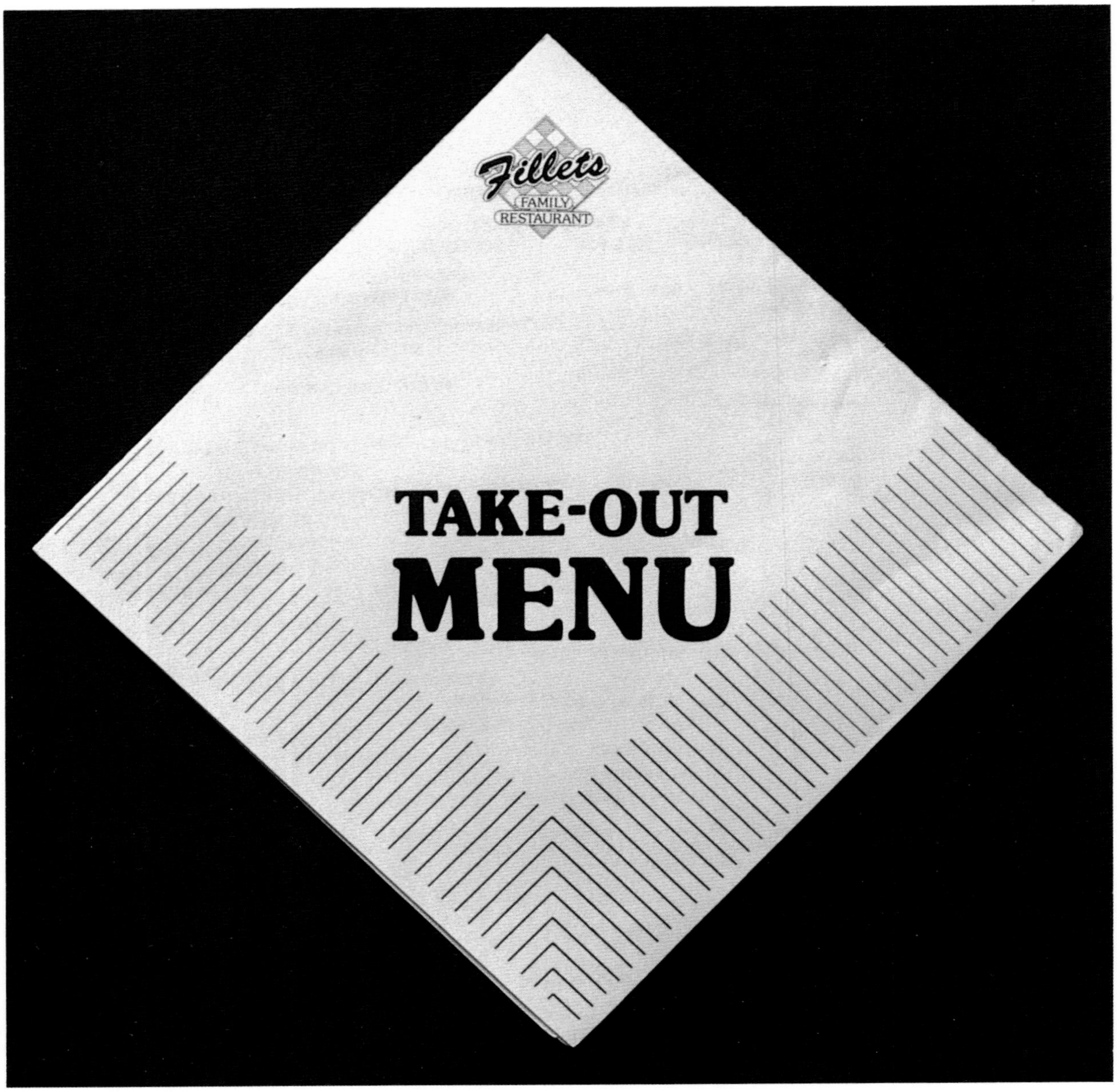

Fillets
FAMILY
RESTAURANT

TAKE-OUT
MENU

Designer: *Mike Weston*
Restaurant: *Fillets, Inc.*
*Pascagoula, MS*

**1987 N.R.A. GREAT MENUS CONTEST WINNER: THIRD PLACE, IMAGINATION**

This simple two-color menu, designed to resemble a cocktail napkin, unfolds to reveal a family-style menu. The first unfold, however, reveals catering details and the restaurant's hours of operation. Type on the interior is set at a slant, with each day's specials featured in the right-hand quadrant, children's specials at bottom and the main part of the menu at top and to the left. The placement has been well thought out as the most important items are featured where the diner's eyes will travel first.

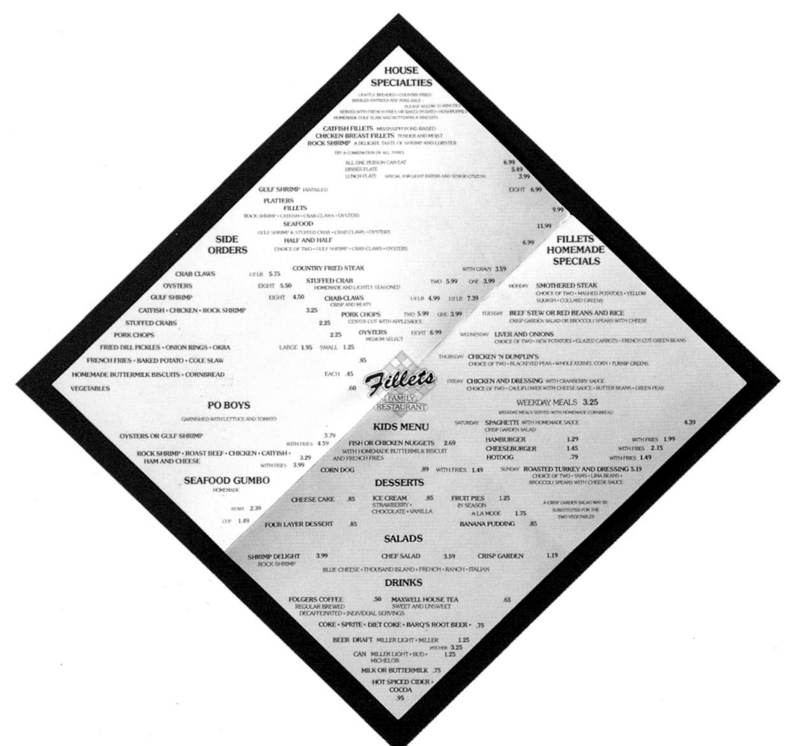

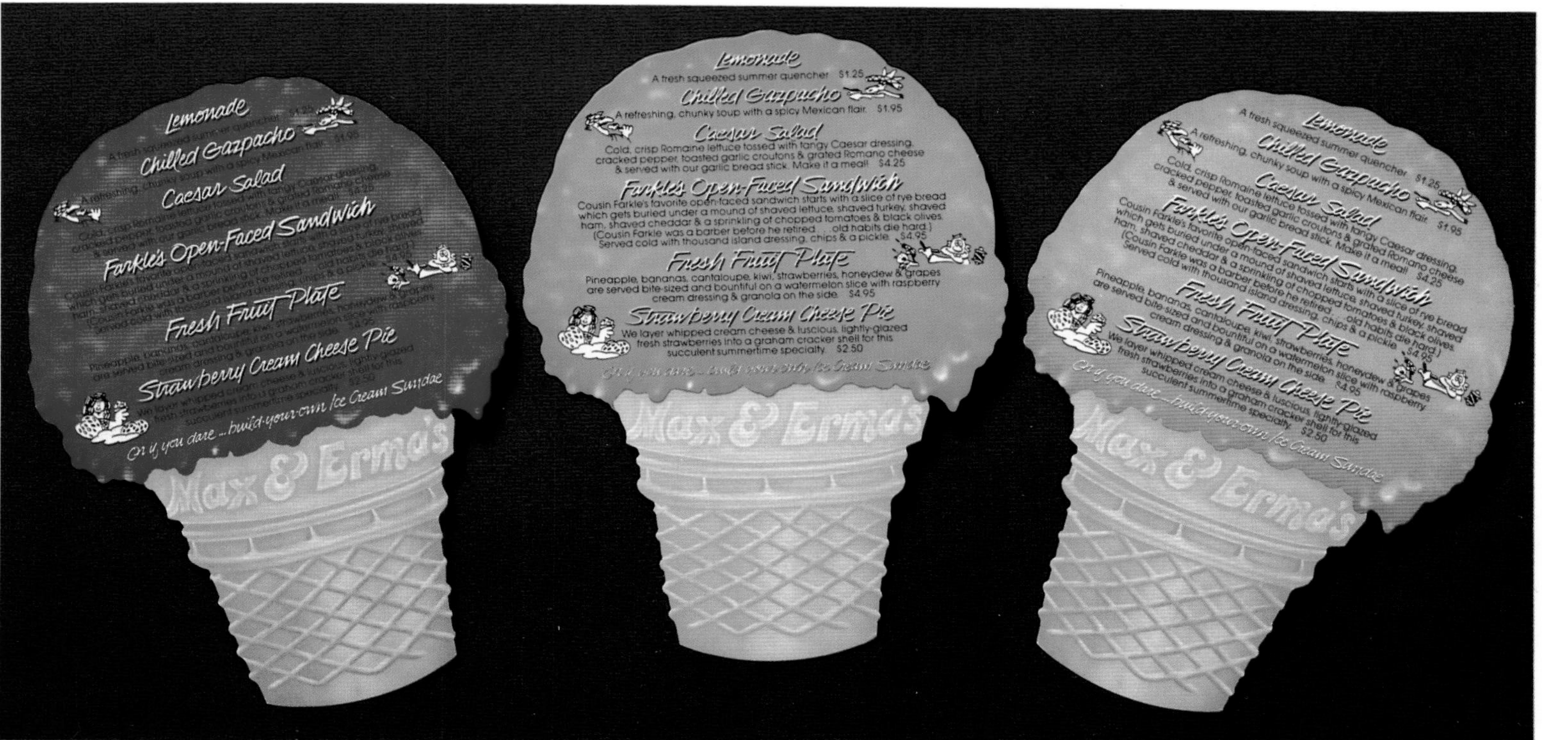


Designer: *David Browning*
*Browning Design*
Restaurant: *Max and Erma's*
*Columbus, OH*

It gets hot in Ohio during the summer months. The summer menus designed for this restaurant attempt to counteract that humid heat by using ice cream cones to depict the lighter choices offered during the season.

Actually, raspberry, lime and orange sherbets are depicted as the background for the menu, each pictured atop a realistic cone. The design challenge was to use no more than two match colors per side, yet achieve a spark of color, while retaining readability.

The menus were designed to sit in the menu caddies at each table, with the colors displayed varying from one table to the next. The menus are short enough so as not to interfere with the customer's conversation. A side benefit was that the menus contributed a burst of fresh, seasonal colors for the restaurant decor.

Restaurant: *The Great Lost Bear*
*Portland, ME*

The menu cover for this informal restaurant is a gentle spoof of the picture post cards common in the late 1940's and early 1950's. "Eatings from the Great Lost Bear Maine" is a pun on such post card copy as "Greetings from the Great Lost Bear Mine."

The vivid sunset hues of the background and picture disassembled into letters are quite typical of the genre. Interior copywriting further supports the tongue-in-cheek theme of the restaurant.

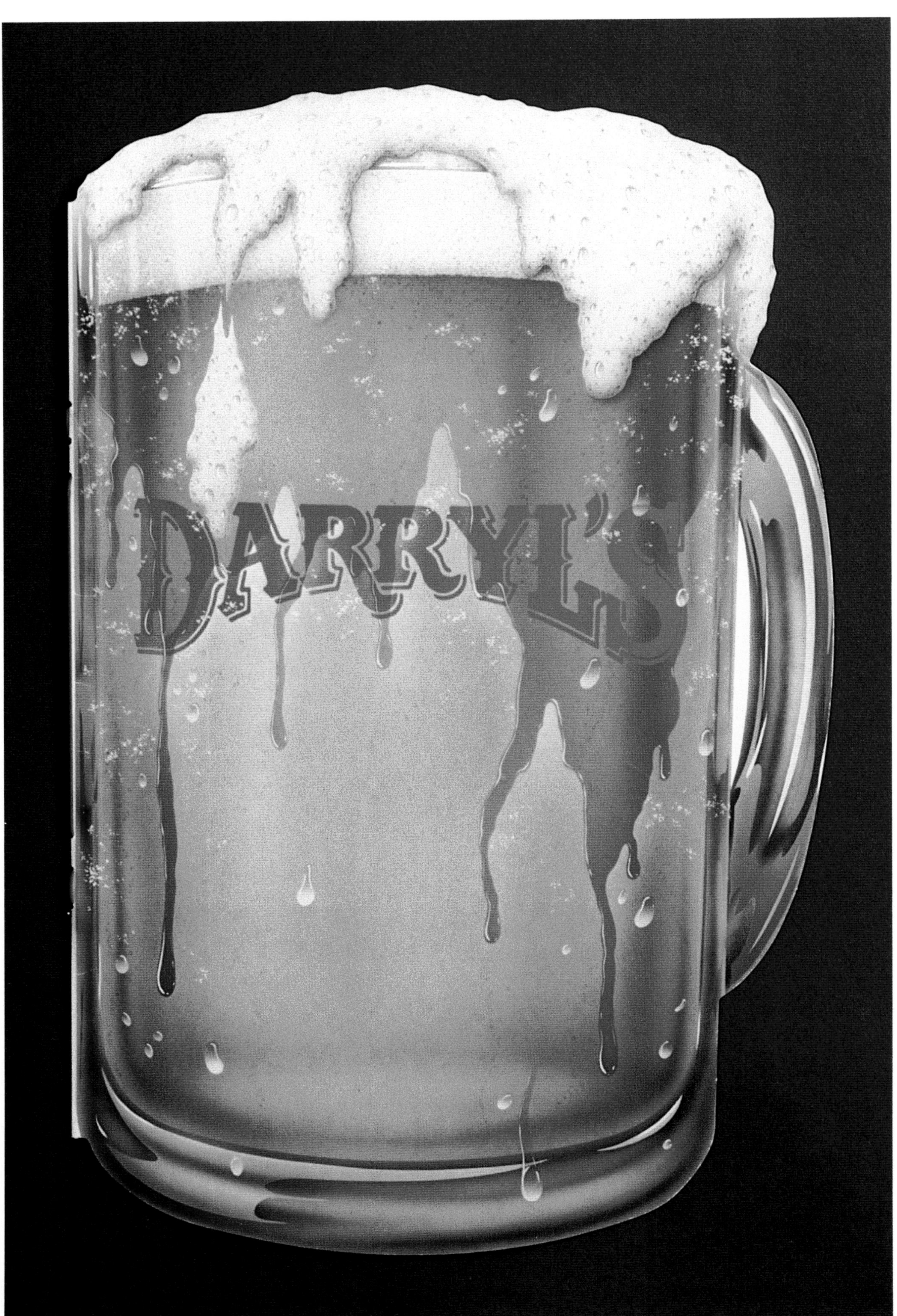
DARRYL'S

Designer: *Studio 100*
Restaurant: *Darryl's*
*Kansas City, MO*

**1987 N.R.A. GREAT MENUS CONTEST WINNER: THIRD PLACE, $5-$15 CHECK AVERAGE**

The frosty beer mug on the cover invites the hungry diner to explore the informal menu within. Menu items are listed in one color for easy updates and are executed in a clear type.

Copywriting is used to whet the appetite for the selection of traditional American foods, spiced with a little Tex-Mex and, of course, the barbecued meats for which Kansas City is so justly famous.

Gourmet Burgers

All Hamburgers are made with fresh ground beef, char-grilled to order and served on a toasted egg bun with lettuce, tomato, red onion and a side order of Darryl's specially seasoned french fries.

BACON & CHEESE BURGER With Crisp Bacon Strips and melted Old English Cheese ........ 5.25

CHEESEBURGER With your choice of Melted Swiss, Old English, Colby, Provolone or Jack Cheese ........ 4.95

ULTIMATE CHEESEBURGER Topped with ¼ pound of your favorite cheese ........ 5.25

BLACKENED CAJUN BURGER Coated in our special Cajun-Spice blend and blackened on the open broiler. Topped with Peppers, Onions and melted Provolone Cheese ........ 5.25

JUST PLAIN DELICIOUS BURGER Seasoned and cooked to your liking ........ 4.45

Sandwiches

CHICKEN-WALNUT CROISSANT Large tender chunks of Roasted Chicken mixed with Walnuts, Mayonnaise, and special seasonings mounded over Lettuce and Tomato Slices in a flaky, extra-large Croissant. Served with French Fries and Fresh Fruit Garnish ........ 5.95

B.L.T. & E CROISSANT Crisp Bacon Strips, Fresh Lettuce, Mayonnaise, and Sliced Tomatoes topped with two Fried Eggs. Served with French Fries and Fresh Fruit Garnish ........ 4.65

CAJUN FRIED CHICKEN SANDWICH PLATTER Boneless Breast coated in our special Cajun-Spice Blend then fried crisp and golden brown. Topped with Sauteed Peppers and Onions and melted Provolone Cheese. With Cole Slaw, French Fries and Cajun Sauce. ........ 5.95

FRENCH DIP Tender, Hot Roast Beef, sliced extra thin, piled on a Hoogie Bun and topped with melted Provolone Cheese. Served with French Fries and Au Jus ........ 4.95

STEAK & CHEESE DARRYL'S STYLE Tender Sliced Beef with Sauteed Onions, Green Peppers and Mushrooms. Topped with melted Provolone Cheese. French Fries and Pickle ........ 5.25

GRILLED REUBEN Swiss Cheese melted into layers of thinly sliced Corned Beef, topped with Sauerkraut and Thousand Island Dressing. Served on grilled Marble Rye Bread with Fries and Pickle ........ 4.95

CHAR-BROILED CHICKEN & CHEESE A tender Boneless Breast lightly marinated and char-broiled to order. Topped with melted Old English Cheese. Served on a toasted Egg Bun with Lettuce, Tomato, Red Onion, and French Fries ........ 5.25
WITH CRISP BACON STRIPS ........ 5.50

CLUB SANDWICH Three toasted Whole Wheat Slices stacked with Lettuce, Tomato, Bacon, Turkey, Ham and Old English Cheese. French Fries and Pickle ........ 4.95

HOT SICILIAN GRILL Thinly sliced, grilled Ham and Pepperoni piled high on a Hoagie Roll with Crisp Bacon, Lettuce, and Tomato. Topped with melted Provolone Cheese and Italian Dressing. A classic! French Fries and Pickle ........ 4.95

QUESADILLAS A jumbo Flour Tortilla filled with Monterey Jack and Old English Cheese, Sauteed Bell Peppers, Red Onion, Green Chiles, and your choice of Beef or Chicken. Served with Guacamole and Sour Cream.
BEEF ........ 5.95 CHICKEN ........ 5.65

4

Ribs & Rib Combinations

All Ribs and Rib Combos served with a Baked Potato (French Fries before 5 p.m.), Cole Slaw, and Parmesan Cheese Toast.

BAR-B-Q BEEF RIBS Jumbo Beef Ribs, baked with Darryl's Bar-B-Q Sauce and cooked to tender perfection
EVE'S (4 ribs) ........ 8.95 ADAM'S (6 ribs) ........ 9.95

STEAK & RIBS A smaller cut of our New York Strip Steak char-broiled to order and served with your choice of two Bar-B-Q Beef Ribs or a Half Slab of Honey-Glazed Pork Back Ribs ........ 9.95

BAR-B-Q PORK BACK RIBS A slab of char-broiled Pork Back Ribs, basted with a glaze of 100% Pure Honey and Darryl's Bar-B-Q Sauce ........ 9.75
For the hearty rib eater, an additional Half Slab for only ........ 3.65

CHICKEN & RIBS A Boneless Chicken Breast, marinated and char-broiled, served with your choice of two Bar-B-Q Beef Ribs or a Half Slab of Honey-Glazed Pork Back Ribs ........ 8.95

RIBS & RIBS A rib eater's fancy, two Bar-B-Q Beef Ribs and a half slab of Honey-Glazed Bar-B-Q Pork Back Ribs ........ 9.45

Sizzling Fajitas (fah-hee-tahs)

A mingling of Southwestern flavors comes together in this tantalizing presentation. We provide you with warm flour tortillas to fill with your own select combination of ingredients. Mix char-grilled beef or chicken with sauteed fresh bell peppers and red onion, iceberg lettuce, pico de gallo, guacamole, grated cheese, sour cream, and mild salsa. Served on a sizzling hot skillet.

CHICKEN ........ 7.95 BEEF ........ 8.95 COMBINATION ........ 8.45

Steak & Steak Combos

The finest USDA Choice grain-fed Beef, aged for tenderness & flavor. Served with Baked Potato (French Fries before 5 p.m.) & Parmesan Cheese Toast.

NEW YORK STRIP Known as the King of Steaks ........ 10.95

RIBEYE STEAK 8 ounces of Choice Beef cut from the heart of the rib. Char-broiled to order ........ 9.95

CAJUN BLACKENED RIBEYE 8 ounces of Choice Ribeye Steak coated in Cajun Seasonings and blackened on the grill. With Cajun Sauce ........ 9.95

PRIME RIB Choice aged beef for the real Beef Lover (available Friday & Saturday after 5 p.m.)
REGULAR CUT ........ 9.95 DARRYL'S CUT ........ 12.95

FILET 9 ounces of Choice Beef Tenderloin char-grilled to order ........ 11.45

STEAK & SHRIMP A smaller cut of our New York Strip cooked to order. Served with Cajun Fried Shrimp ........ 10.95

STEAK & CHICKEN A smaller cut of our New York Strip with a boneless, marinated and char-broiled Chicken Breast ........ 8.95

STEAK & RIBS A smaller cut of our New York Strip Steak char-broiled to order and served with your choice of two Bar-B-Q Beef Ribs or a half slab of Honey-Glazed Pork Back Ribs ........ 9.95

5

| | |
|---|---|
| Designer: | *Lanny Sommese* |
| | *Lanny Sommese Design* |
| Restaurant: | *The Deli* |
| | *Dante's Restaurants, Inc.* |
| | *State College, PA* |

From the front cover through each unfold, the dignified vest, shirt and tie dissolve into clouds of steam generated first by the entree and then by the coffee which will finish the meal.

Menu copy is very simple. This is designed as a drinks and dessert menu. It probably supplements daily specials listed on a chalk board in the restaurant. Aimed at a college and young urban crowd, the menu connotes a playful note into the serious business of eating.

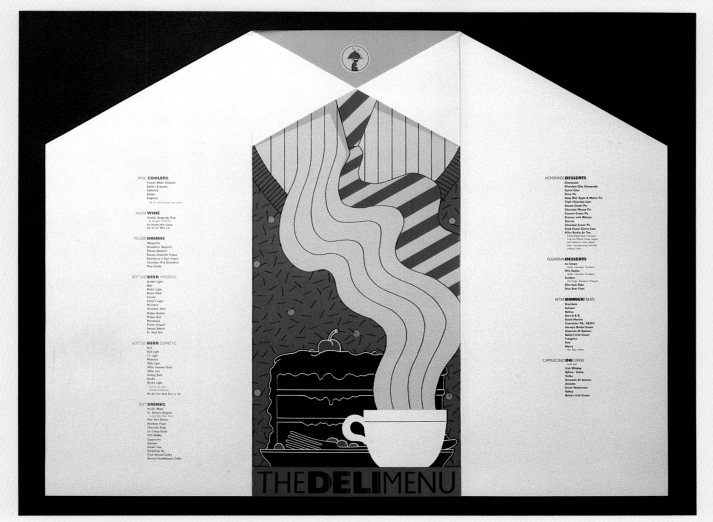

Designer: *Peter Pavenayotin*
Restaurant: *Phirasak's Thai Kitchen*
*Los Angeles, CA*

What more appropriate vehicle is there for an Asian restaurant than a menu which is also a fan? This one, executed in red on a pale green paper, is designed for use as a take-out menu as well as for use in the restaurant.

To save space, the various meat possibilities for each dish are abbreviated, but a key to the abbreviations appears at bottom. The restaurant offers house wines by the glass or carafe but also offers the option of bringing one's own for a modest corkage fee. If storage space is limited, this is a very practical solution to the problem of "what about accompanying wines?"

This fan is an excellent example of how any restaurant can creatively improve on the simple 8½″ x 11″ sheet. Just because a restaurant is not part of a major chain doesn't mean its menu must be boring.

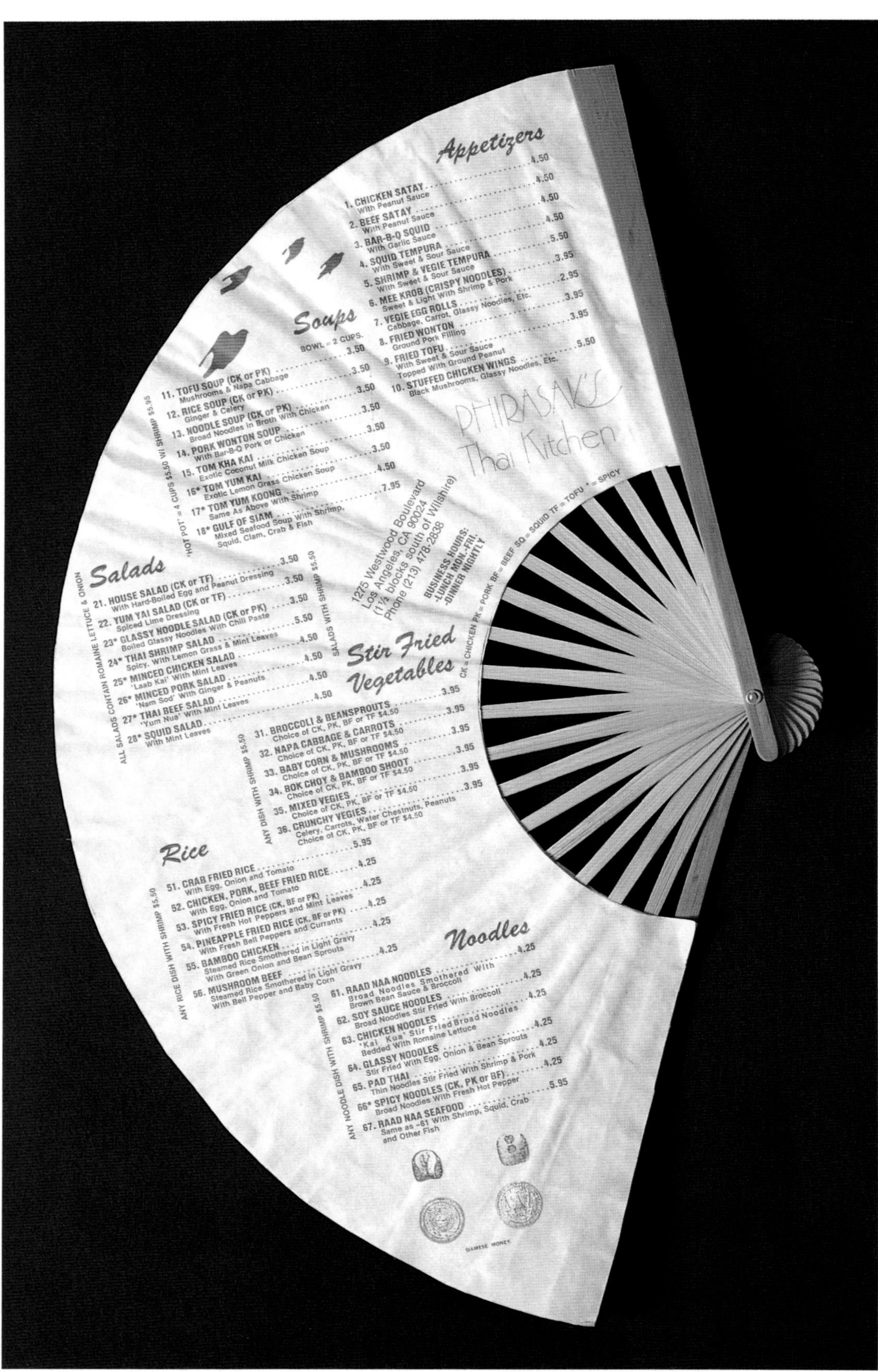

Designer: *John Patterson*
*Larry McAdams Design*
Restaurant: *Elephant Bar and Restaurant*
*Santa Barbara, CA*

The theme of the restaurant for which these tables tents were designed is exploration — of new tastes, new places, new ideas. A "safari" is the unifying element. These little trunks, with their colorful labels, provide merchandising support, not only for the underlying idea, but also for the gift certificates and private parties available.

The menu offered is wildly varied — everything from Mexican/Southwestern appetizers through pasta, wines by the glass and ice cream-based desserts.

Out of kindness to the servers, the designer specified that instructions for assembly be included on those parts of the table tent which would not be seen by patrons.

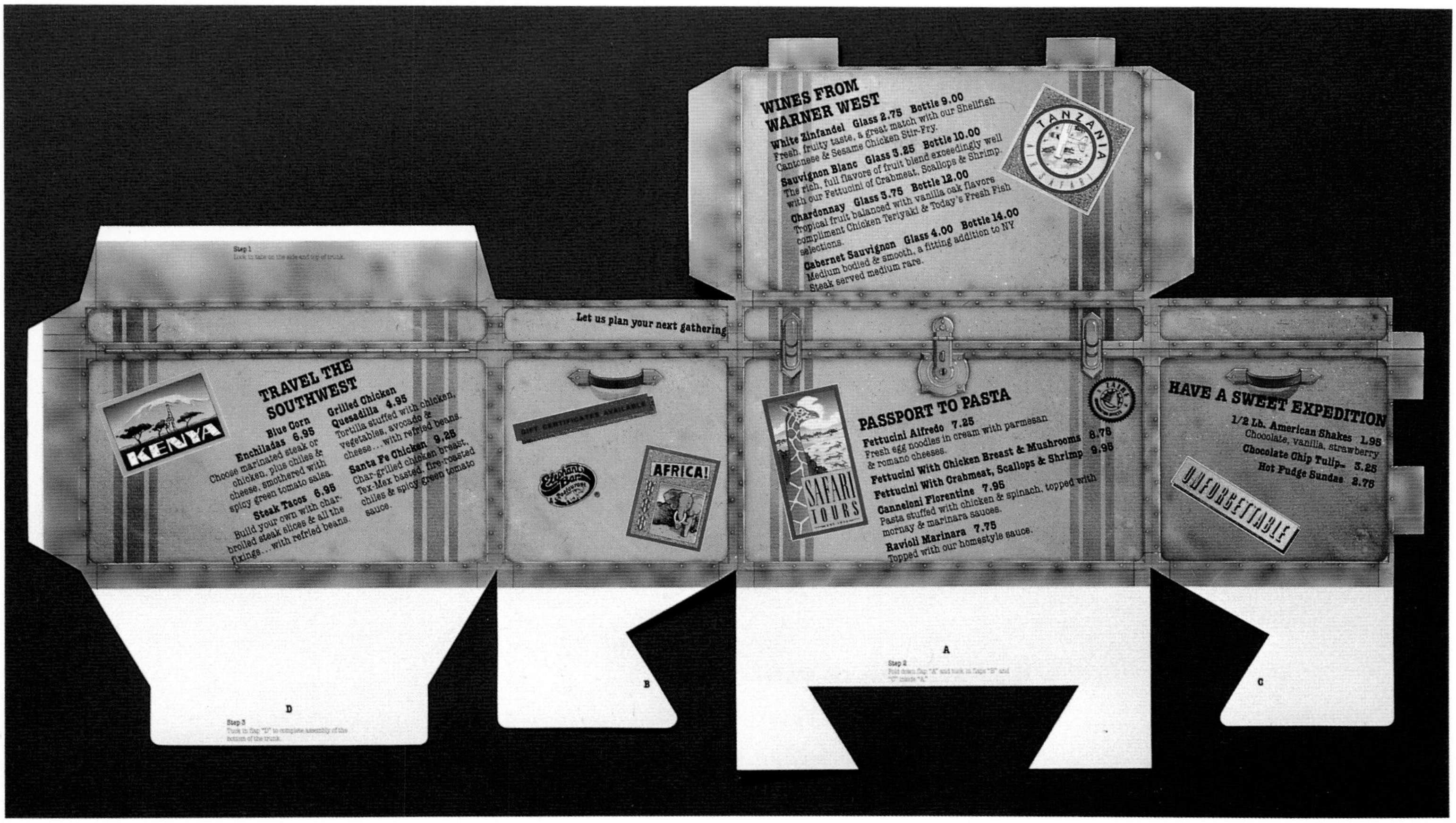

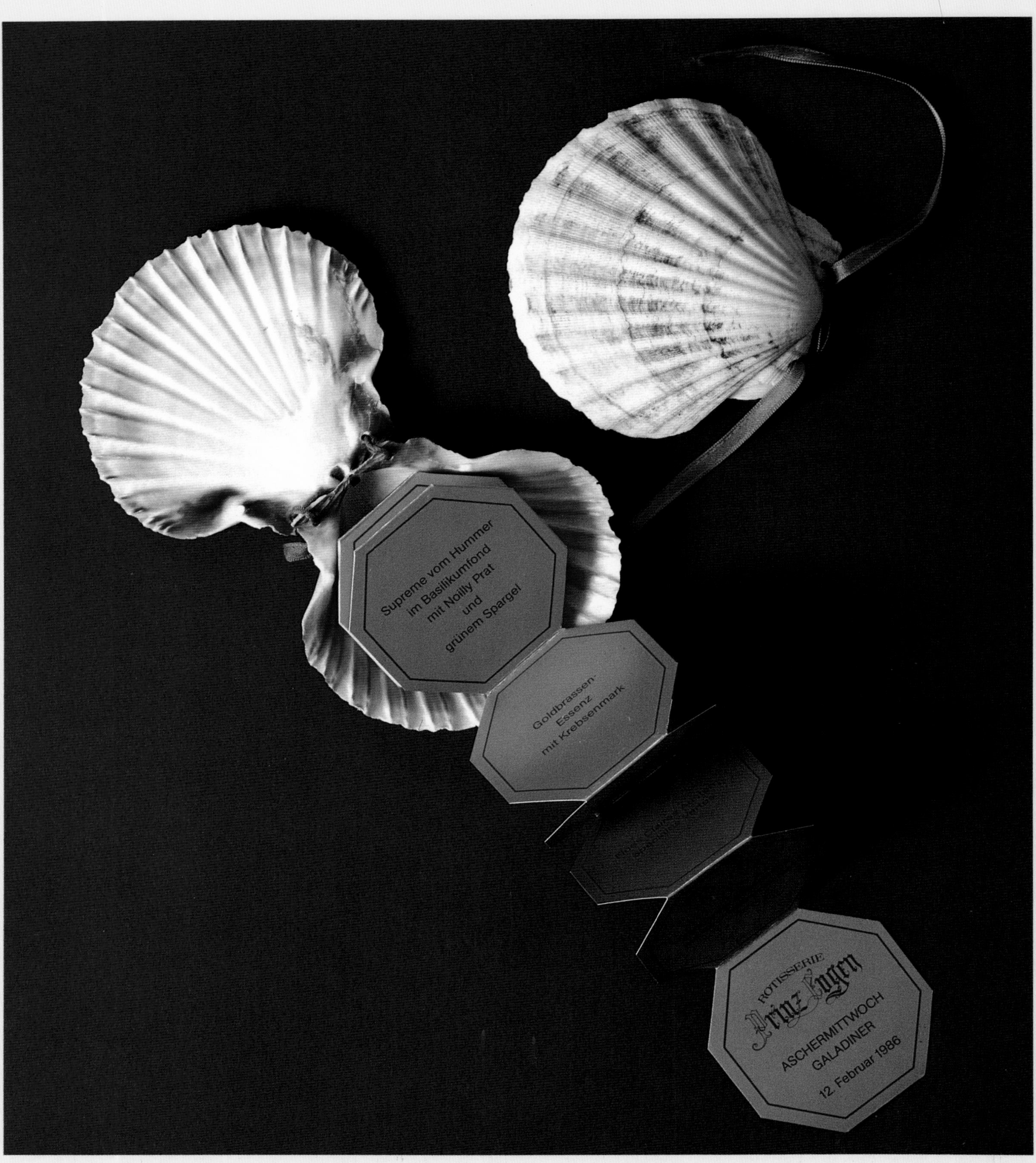
Supreme vom Hummer
im Basilikumfond
mit Noilly Prat
und
grünem Spargel
Goldbrassen-
Essenz
mit Krebsenmark
ROTISSERIE
Prinz Eugen
ASCHERMITTWOCH
GALADINER
12. Februar 1986

Designer: *Hilton International*
Restaurant: *Rotisserie Prinz Eugen*
*Hilton International Wien*
*Late Night Fasching Menu*
*Vienna, Austria*

**1987 N.R.A. GREAT MENUS CONTEST WINNER: SECOND PLACE, IMAGINATION**

Fasching is the German equivalent of Shrove Tuesday and is celebrated with all the gusto the French devote to their equivalent, Mardi Gras. This menu, imaginatively packaged in scallop shells, is designed to be the last sumptuous meal before Lent. Featuring such delicacies as steak served with a sauce of black truffles, passionfruit sorbet and accompanied by the finest wines, this late-night, last minute feast should be memorable.

The menu itself has been printed accordion fashion in a simple blue ink on a silver background. The shells, joined with a pretty blue silk ribbon, lend further distinction to the presentation.

Designer: *King Menus*
Restaurant: *El Sombrero*
*San Francisco, CA*

The restaurant is called El Sombrero and that's what the menu is ... a die-cut sombrero. The menu is reproduced in three colors on the cover, two inside. The simple menu includes favorite Mexican dishes.

In a bow to California's familiarity with the cuisine, many items are simply listed in Spanish without further explanation.

Though this is a small, neighborhood place, by coating the menus in plastic for durability, the restauranteur has found a way to use creative design at a price he can afford.

Restaurant: *Skihütte Carmenna*
*Arosa, Switzerland*

This black and white photo of a ski parka opens to reveal the menu of drinks and snacks. Hot drinks offered range from spirit and coffee concoctions to the homey Ovaltine. A broad selection of cold beers, wines and other spirits is also featured.

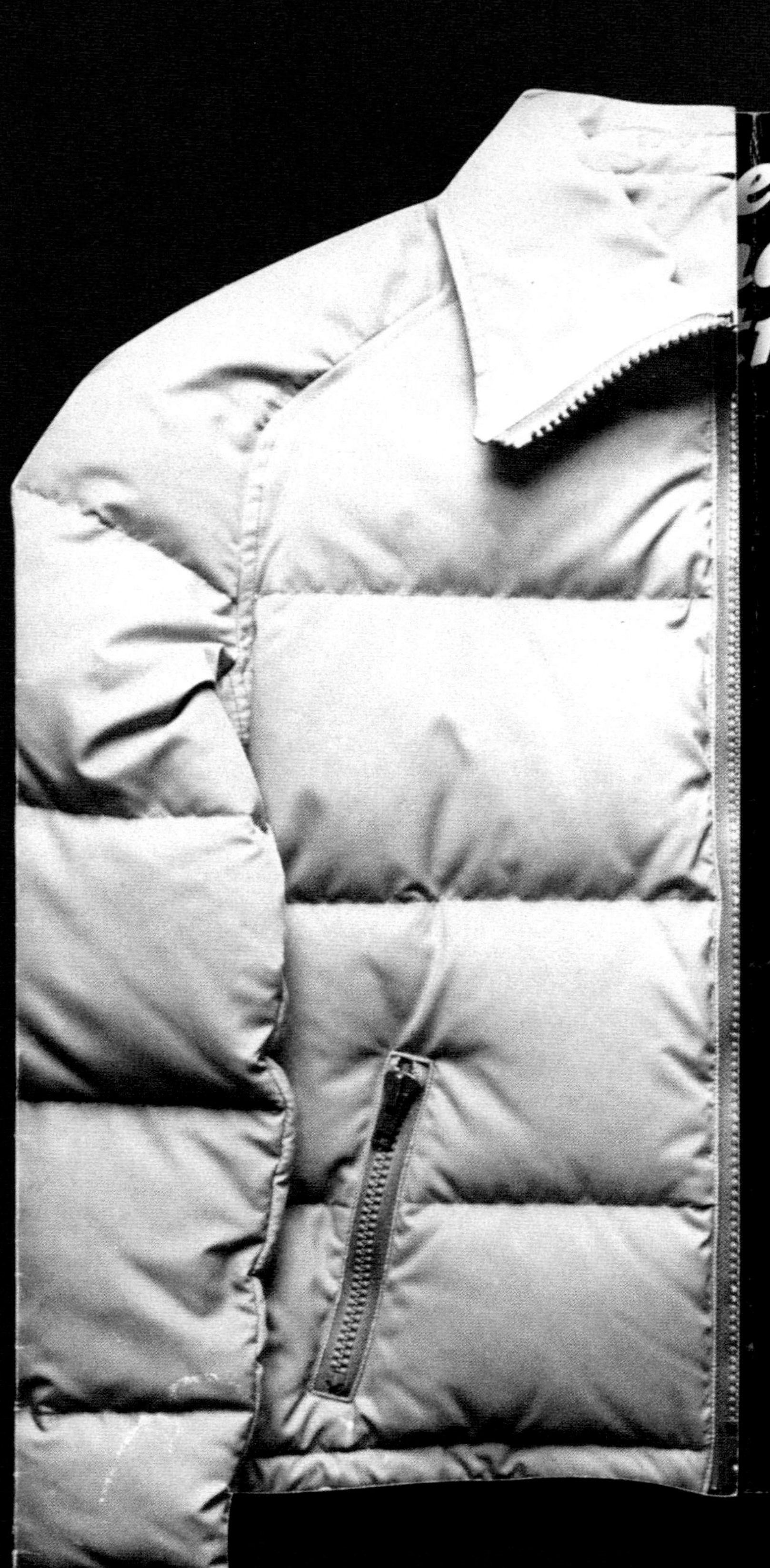
en
d
ränke
Sekt und Champagner
Henkell Piccolo 2 dl
Henkell Trocken oder Brut 7,5 dl
Cupli, Champagner Brut 10 cl
Cupli, Champagner Rosé 10 cl
Champagner Brut 7,5 dl
Champagner Rosé 7,5 dl
Champagner de Luxe 7,5 dl
Warme Speisen
Tagessuppe 3 dl
Gulaschsuppe 3 dl
Bouillon mit Ei
Bouillon nature
1 Paar Wienerli
1 Paar Aroserli
1 Engadiner vom Grill
1 Bratwurst vom Grill
1 Servelat kalt oder vom Grill
Fleischkäse kalt oder vom Grill
Fleischkäse mit 2 Eiern
Carmenna-Toast
Käseschnitte
Käseschnitte mit 2 Eiern
Spiegeleier nature (2 Eier)
Spiegeleier mit Schinken
Spiegeleier mit Speck
Spiegeleier mit Rösti
Rippli mit Kraut
Käserösti
Speckrösti
Rösti, Kartoffelsalat oder Sauerkraut als Beilage
Rösti, Kartoffelsalat oder Sauerkraut als Portion

Spezialitäten Fr.
Kotelett vom Grill 12.50
Entrecôte vom Grill 19.–
‹Spatz aus dem Gamellendeckel› Portion 9.50
Käsefondue (2 Pers.) 30.–
Apfelkuchen 3.50
Apfelkuchen mit Rahm 4.50
Kalte Speisen
Bündnerfleisch 100 g 17.–
Bündner Rohschinken 100 g 17.–
‹Buura-Speck› am Stck. 100 g 9.–
Salami Nostrano 100 g 9.–
Bündner Teller (Bündnerfleisch,
Speck und Salami gem.) 13.–
Original Bündner Salsiz am Stück 6.–
Appenzeller Käse 120 g 7.50
Aroser Alpkäse 120 g 7.50
Forellenfilet geräuchert 7.50
Schinkenbrot 5.–
Salamibrot 5.–
Bündnerfleischbrot 7.–
Brot extra –.50
Buttermödeli 20 g –.50
Liegestühle
½ Tag 5.–
ganzer Tag 8.–


Both hot and cold "cuts" or plates are available. These range from a variety of wursts and roasts to salami and two Swiss specialties — bundnerfleisch and cheese fondue. The former is paper thin slices of beef which are specially air-dried with spices.

The menu interior is further enhanced by a black and white photo of the surrounding ski slopes. The name of the resort appears in a brilliant yellow against the cover. It is placed about where an insignia would appear on the jacket, which enhances the illusion.

Restaurant: *Children's Menu*
*Hilton International*
*Brisbane, Queensland, Australia*

If you can face a menu which is a pineapple whose "face" is composed of sunnyside up egg eyes, tomato nose and banana mouth, you are undoubtedly a child. Children are, of course, the audience for this menu.

The bright colors are reinforced by the interior design, which resembles a child's first scrawled letters, enhanced by an adult sense of fun. The fun is manifested in the use of a carrot in place of an "i", an apple to replace an "o".

To ease the waiting period for the food, a black on white paper insert offers a variety of puzzles for the child to complete. The menu itself is on a sturdy coated stock for durability.

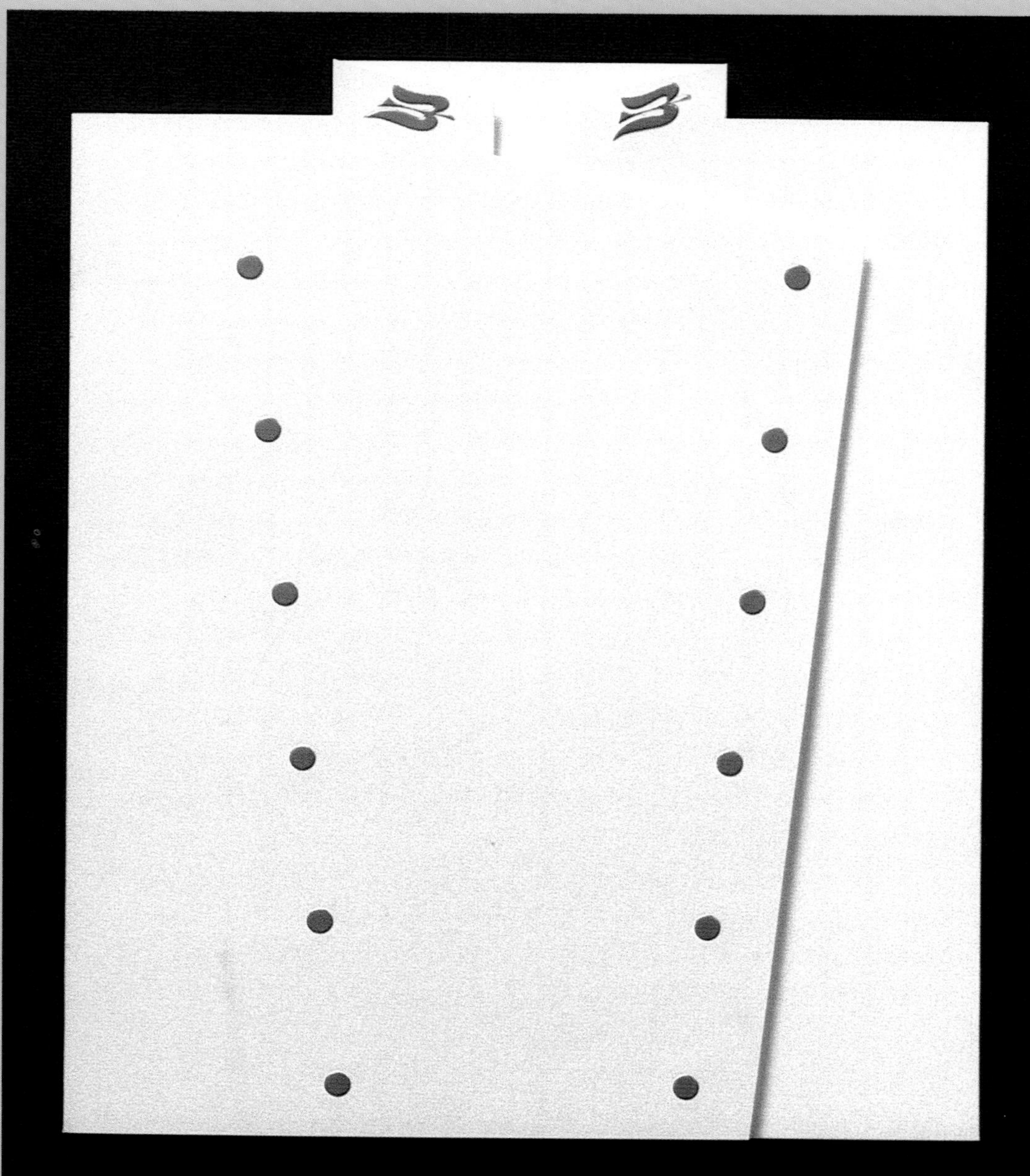

**Designer:** *Daniel Durand*
*Royal Viking Line*

**Restaurant:** *Royal Viking Sky*
*at San Francisco, CA*
*August 30, 1987*

*Epicurean Rendezvous,* a noted restaurant guide to Northern California, hosted this luncheon honoring the premier chefs and restaurateurs of the region aboard a cruise ship also noted for the excellence of its cuisine.

The menu, designed as a keepsake for those in attendance, was actually conceived by the Line's culinary advisor. It is a graphic rendering of the jackets worn by the chefs on all of Royal Viking Line's ships. The gold buttons and Line insignia on the collar are rendered in foil embossing for an elegant note. The use of the jacket as the menu makes it suitably informal for a mid-day luncheon.

The menu items in the interior, likewise chosen by Durand, are also rendered in foil embossing. Since no printing other than the embossing is included on the menu, printing costs were much less than one might suppose. Foil embossing, when *not* combined with another imprinting technique, is very cost-effective in small quantities.

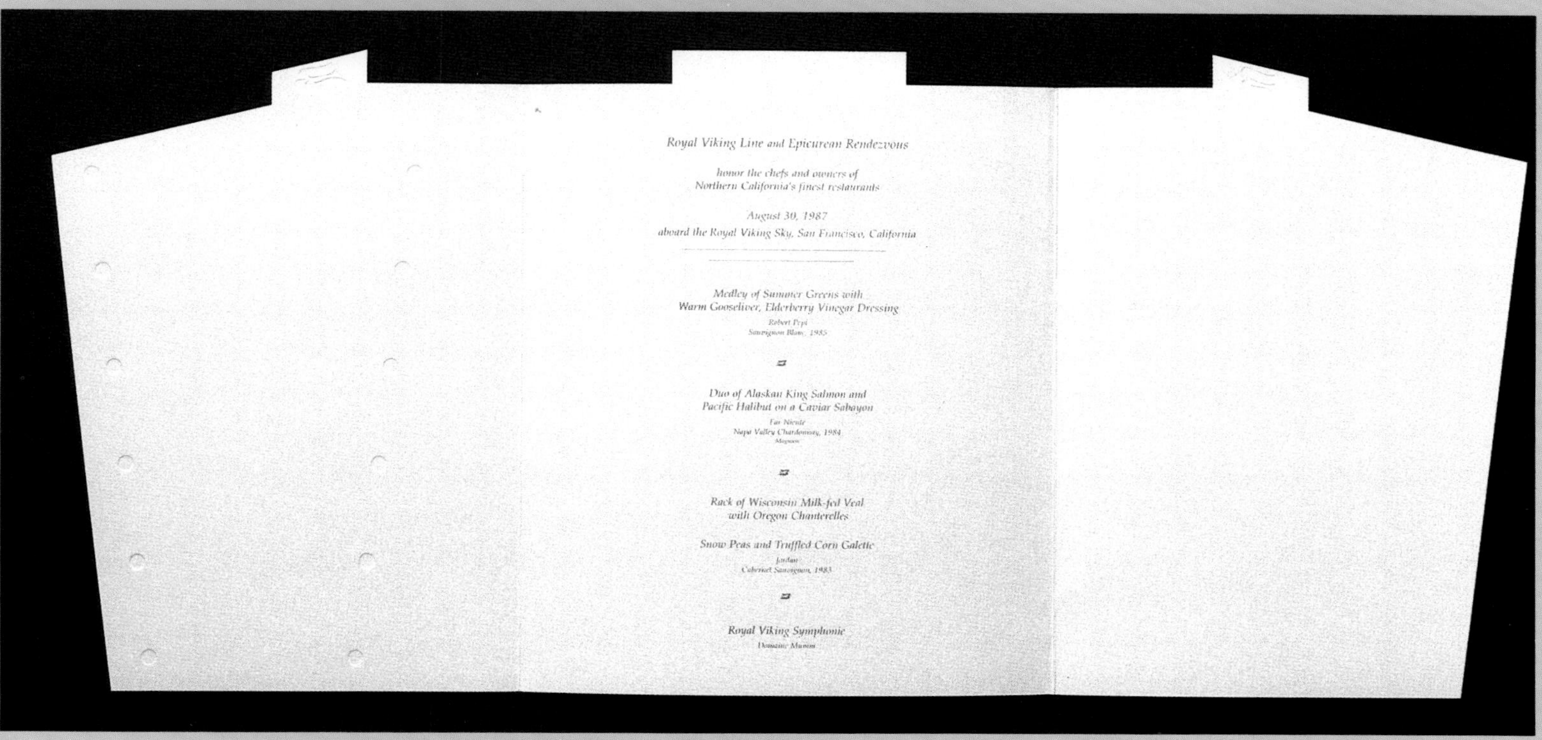

*Royal Viking Line and Epicurean Rendezvous*

*honor the chefs and owners of*
*Northern California's finest restaurants*

*August 30, 1987*
*aboard the Royal Viking Sky, San Francisco, California*

*Medley of Summer Greens with*
*Warm Gooseliver, Elderberry Vinegar Dressing*
*Robert Pepi*
*Sauvignon Blanc, 1985*

*Duo of Alaskan King Salmon and*
*Pacific Halibut on a Caviar Sabayon*
*Far Niente*
*Napa Valley Chardonnay, 1984*
*Magnum*

*Rack of Wisconsin Milk-fed Veal*
*with Oregon Chanterelles*

*Snow Peas and Truffled Corn Galette*
*Jordan*
*Cabernet Sauvignon, 1983*

*Royal Viking Symphonie*
*Domaine Mumm*

# CHAPTER 10

Institutional menus are not only from hospitals. They are, in fact, menus from any organization whose primary business is not purveying food. In this chapter, you will find room service menus from hotels, train and plane menus and a menu from a university's student union.

Like any other artifact that is aimed at a mass market, menus can provide a key to the state of society. Nowhere is this more true than in the area of institutional menus. Where hospitals once provided simple lists of foods available or simply put whatever a physician had recommended in front of a patient, without permitting any choice, now, hospital menus are produced in multiple colors and market other services available as well as providing lists of food. Of course, the increased competition among health care providers is only one side of the coin. Psychological studies have demonstrated that the healing process is aided when a patient feels he retains some control over his life ... even if only in choosing what to eat.

Other social trends which become apparent from perusing this chapter include the return of train travel as a chic means of getting from point A to point B. In a society where lots of people have more disposable income, the new status symbol is free time.

# INSTITUTIONAL MENUS

Designer: *Vaughn/Wedeen Creative, Inc.*
Restaurant: *House Calls*
*Presbyterian Healthcare Services*
*Albuquerque, NM*

This doctor's bag was created as a direct mail marketing piece for a catering service whose primary audience is doctors. The festive colors (even confetti strewn across the front of the bag) and sprightly copy are quite a departure from the marketing usually seen by physicians.

The top of the die-cut bag folds down to reveal a lavender on silver illustration of party food. The logo features the mid-section of a formally attired butler with a stethoscope. It is repeated on the business card. The business card is also lavender and the envelope in which the "bag" was mailed is a soft lilac. Using a decidedly non-medical color scheme ensured that the piece would be given more attention than a plain white envelope would.

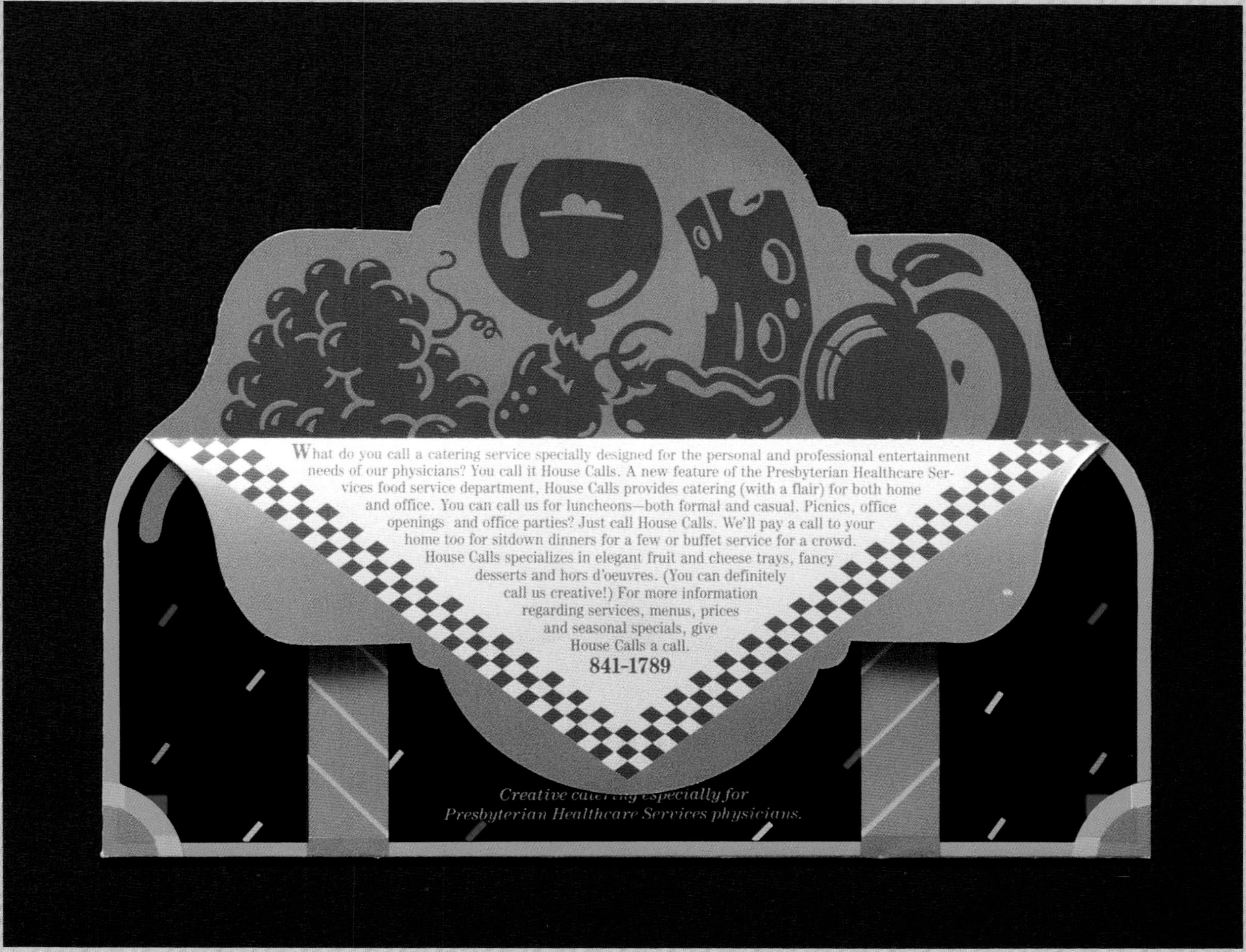

What do you call a catering service specially designed for the personal and professional entertainment needs of our physicians? You call it House Calls. A new feature of the Presbyterian Healthcare Services food service department, House Calls provides catering (with a flair) for both home and office. You can call us for luncheons—both formal and casual. Picnics, office openings and office parties? Just call House Calls. We'll pay a call to your home too for sitdown dinners for a few or buffet service for a crowd. House Calls specializes in elegant fruit and cheese trays, fancy desserts and hors d'oeuvres. (You can definitely call us creative!) For more information regarding services, menus, prices and seasonal specials, give House Calls a call.

**841-1789**

*Creative catering especially for*
*Presbyterian Healthcare Services physicians.*

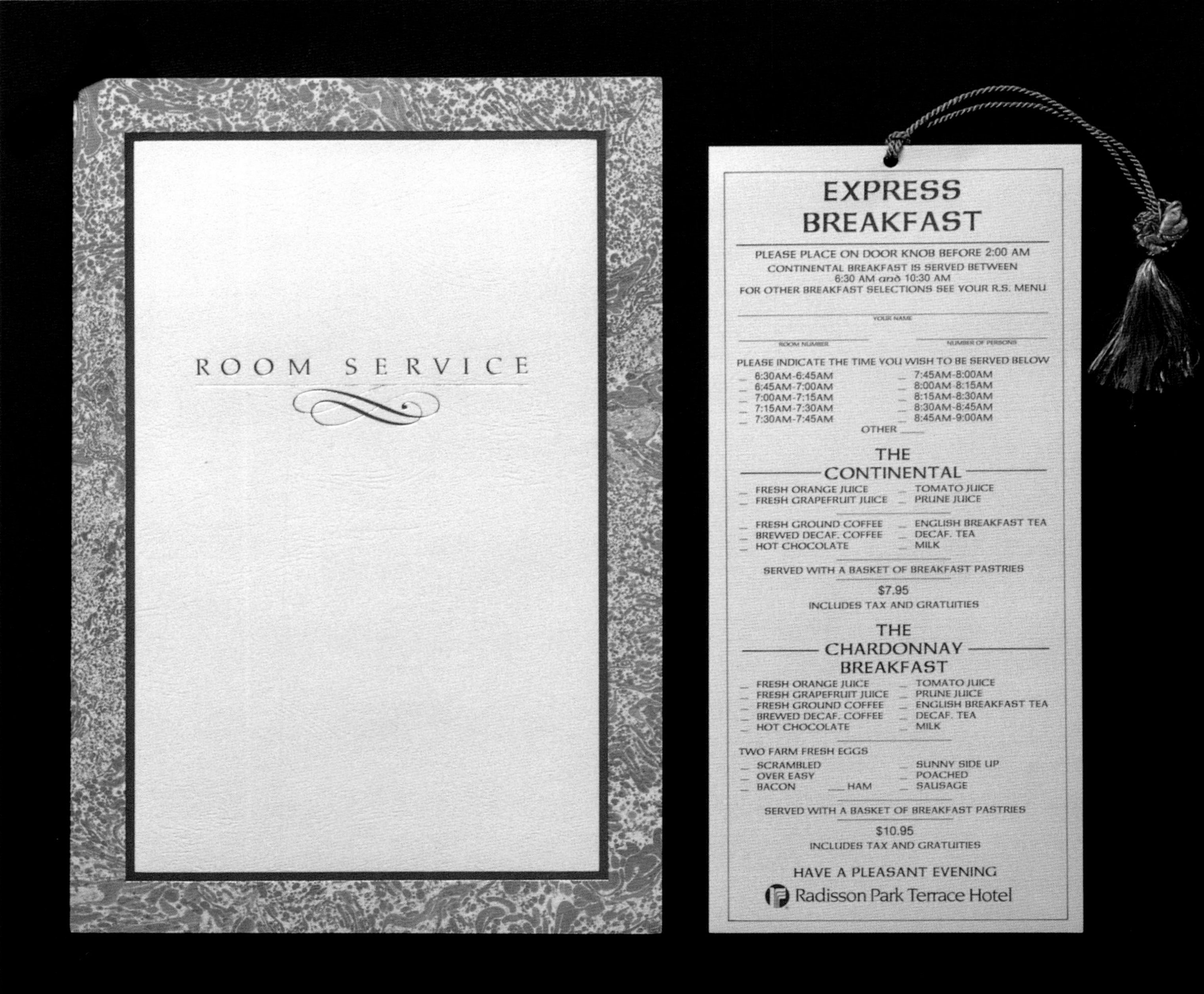

ROOM SERVICE
EXPRESS BREAKFAST
PLEASE PLACE ON DOOR KNOB BEFORE 2:00 AM
CONTINENTAL BREAKFAST IS SERVED BETWEEN
6:30 AM and 10:30 AM
FOR OTHER BREAKFAST SELECTIONS SEE YOUR R.S. MENU
PLEASE INDICATE THE TIME YOU WISH TO BE SERVED BELOW
6:30AM-6:45AM
6:45AM-7:00AM
7:00AM-7:15AM
7:15AM-7:30AM
7:30AM-7:45AM
7:45AM-8:00AM
8:00AM-8:15AM
8:15AM-8:30AM
8:30AM-8:45AM
8:45AM-9:00AM
OTHER
THE CONTINENTAL
FRESH ORANGE JUICE
FRESH GRAPEFRUIT JUICE
TOMATO JUICE
PRUNE JUICE
FRESH GROUND COFFEE
BREWED DECAF. COFFEE
HOT CHOCOLATE
ENGLISH BREAKFAST TEA
DECAF. TEA
MILK
SERVED WITH A BASKET OF BREAKFAST PASTRIES
$7.95
INCLUDES TAX AND GRATUITIES
THE CHARDONNAY BREAKFAST
FRESH ORANGE JUICE
FRESH GRAPEFRUIT JUICE
FRESH GROUND COFFEE
BREWED DECAF. COFFEE
HOT CHOCOLATE
TOMATO JUICE
PRUNE JUICE
ENGLISH BREAKFAST TEA
DECAF. TEA
MILK
TWO FARM FRESH EGGS
SCRAMBLED
OVER EASY
BACON
HAM
SUNNY SIDE UP
POACHED
SAUSAGE
SERVED WITH A BASKET OF BREAKFAST PASTRIES
$10.95
INCLUDES TAX AND GRATUITIES
HAVE A PLEASANT EVENING
Radisson Park Terrace Hotel


**Designer:** *Bob Petz*
*Meliker Communications*

**Restaurant:** *Room Service/Express Breakfast*
*Radisson Park Terrace Hotel*
*Washington, DC*

Executed in coordinating shades of turquoise, these two menus work well together. The main room service menu features rich gold foil stamping on a leather-like paper. The border of *faux* marble paper lends it distinction.

The Express Breakfast menu, with its tassel of blue fabric cord, is much more straightforward. The rushed executive can choose what to have the night before by checking items off, specify a time for delivery and not have to worry about it in the morning.

The main room service menu uses single-color inserts in the rich covers. These can be inexpensively replaced as needed.

**Designer:** *Ann Werner*
*Associates Printing Service, Inc.*
**Restaurant:** *In-Room Dining Door Knob Menu*
*Mariner Corp.*
*Houston, TX*

Tranquil colors and a slightly impressionistic watercolor illustration make this menu softly appealing. Process printing was used throughout and the use of varying screens permitted a rich effect with a limited number of colors.

This piece is unusual in that, rather than uses a round opening with tabs, a die-cut square has been chosen for the part of the menu that slips over the door knob. Careful planning was required to ensure the success of the piece.

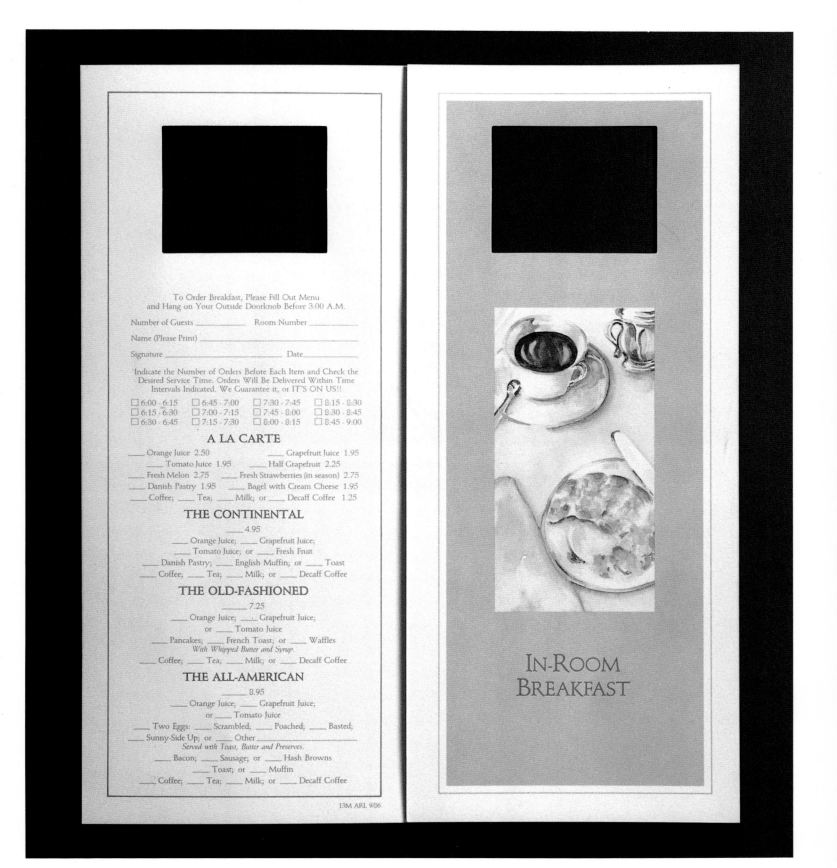

To Order Breakfast, Please Fill Out Menu
and Hang on Your Outside Doorknob Before 3:00 A.M.

Number of Guests ________ Room Number ________

Name (Please Print) ________________

Signature ________________ Date________

Indicate the Number of Orders Before Each Item and Check the Desired Service Time. Orders Will Be Delivered Within Time Intervals Indicated. We Guarantee it, or IT'S ON US!!

☐ 6:00 - 6:15 ☐ 6:45 - 7:00 ☐ 7:30 - 7:45 ☐ 8:15 - 8:30
☐ 6:15 - 6:30 ☐ 7:00 - 7:15 ☐ 7:45 - 8:00 ☐ 8:30 - 8:45
☐ 6:30 - 6:45 ☐ 7:15 - 7:30 ☐ 8:00 - 8:15 ☐ 8:45 - 9:00

## A LA CARTE

____ Orange Juice 2.50 ____ Grapefruit Juice 1.95
____ Tomato Juice 1.95 ____ Half Grapefruit 2.25
____ Fresh Melon 2.75 ____ Fresh Strawberries (in season) 2.75
____ Danish Pastry 1.95 ____ Bagel with Cream Cheese 1.95
____ Coffee; ____ Tea; ____ Milk; or ____ Decaff Coffee 1.25

## THE CONTINENTAL

____ 4.95
____ Orange Juice; ____ Grapefruit Juice;
____ Tomato Juice; or ____ Fresh Fruit
____ Danish Pastry; ____ English Muffin; or ____ Toast
____ Coffee; ____ Tea; ____ Milk; or ____ Decaff Coffee

## THE OLD-FASHIONED

____ 7.25
____ Orange Juice; ____ Grapefruit Juice;
or ____ Tomato Juice
____ Pancakes; ____ French Toast; or ____ Waffles
*With Whipped Butter and Syrup.*
____ Coffee; ____ Tea; ____ Milk; or ____ Decaff Coffee

## THE ALL-AMERICAN

____ 8.95
____ Orange Juice; ____ Grapefruit Juice;
or ____ Tomato Juice
____ Two Eggs: ____ Scrambled; ____ Poached; ____ Basted;
____ Sunny-Side Up; or ____ Other ________________
*Served with Toast, Butter and Preserves.*
____ Bacon; ____ Sausage; or ____ Hash Browns
____ Toast; or ____ Muffin
____ Coffee; ____ Tea; ____ Milk; or ____ Decaff Coffee

13M ARL 9/86

IN-ROOM
BREAKFAST

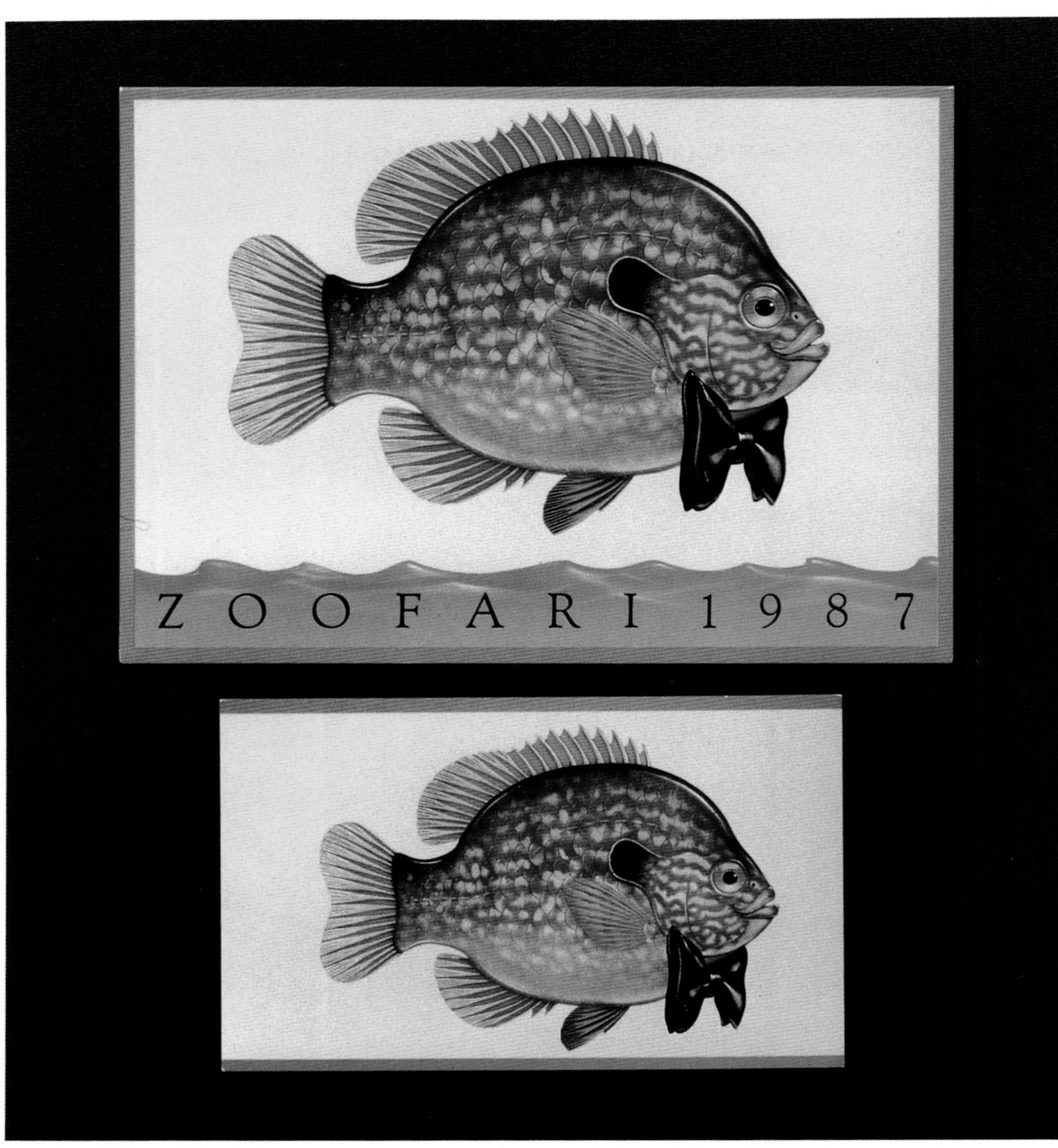


Designer: *Keith Anderson*
*Bartels & Carstens, Inc.*
Restaurant: *Zoofari 1987*
*Saint Louis Zoo Friends Association*
*Saint Louis, MO*

The fish in a bow tie is appropriate for the special event for which this invitation/menu and reply card were designed. The specific exhibit the event benefited is the "Living Stream," a 60-foot model of a typical Missouri Ozarks stream.

The image is playful but effective. It's nice that the designer specified the same design for the reply card, ensuring that it would not be lost among other mail.

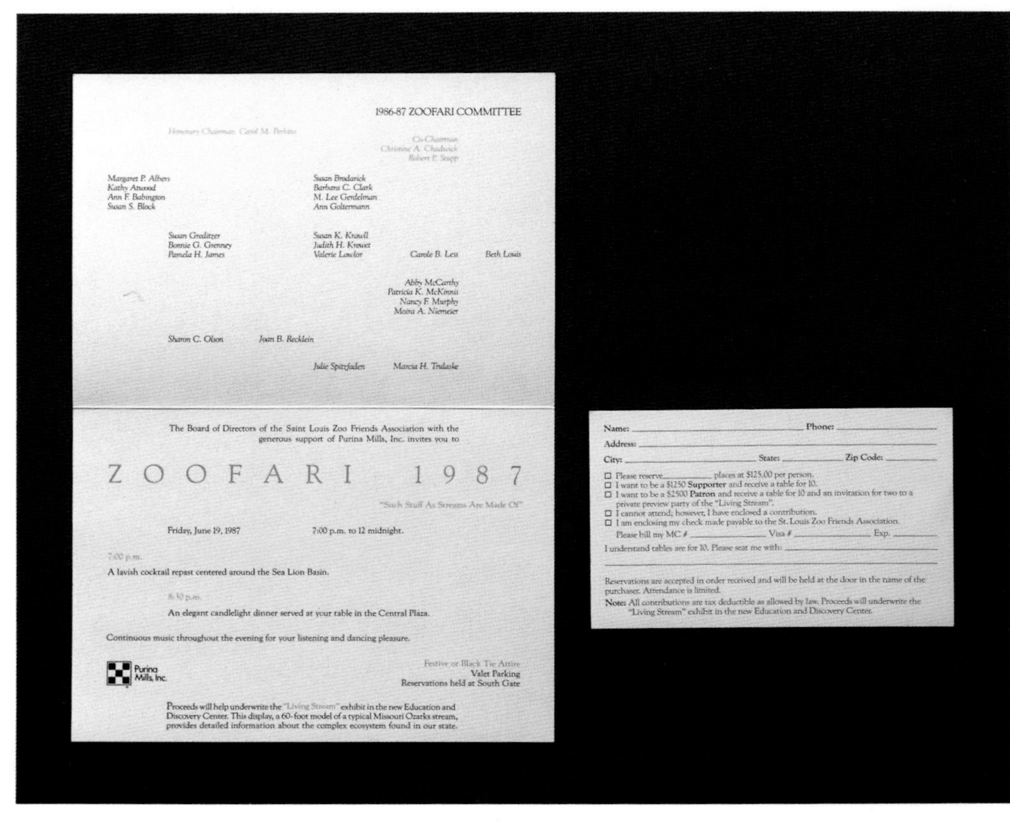

1986-87 ZOOFARI COMMITTEE

Honorary Chairman Carol M. Perkins

Co-Chairman
Christine A. Chadwick
Robert P. Stupp

Margaret P. Albers
Kathy Atwood
Ann F. Babington
Susan S. Block

Susan Brodarick
Barbara C. Clark
M. Lee Gendelman
Ann Goltermann

Susan Greditzer
Bonnie G. Grenney
Pamela H. James

Susan K. Kraull
Judith H. Krewet
Valerie Lawlor

Carole B. Less
Beth Louis

Abby McCarthy
Patricia K. McKinnis
Nancy F. Murphy
Moira A. Niemeier

Sharon C. Olson
Joan B. Recklein

Julie Spitzfaden
Marcia H. Trulaske

The Board of Directors of the Saint Louis Zoo Friends Association with the generous support of Purina Mills, Inc. invites you to

ZOOFARI 1987

"Such Stuff As Streams Are Made Of"

Friday, June 19, 1987 7:00 p.m. to 12 midnight.

7:00 p.m.
A lavish cocktail repast centered around the Sea Lion Basin.

8:30 p.m.
An elegant candlelight dinner served at your table in the Central Plaza.

Continuous music throughout the evening for your listening and dancing pleasure.

Purina Mills, Inc.

Festive or Black Tie Attire
Valet Parking
Reservations held at South Gate

Proceeds will help underwrite the "Living Stream" exhibit in the new Education and Discovery Center. This display, a 60-foot model of a typical Missouri Ozarks stream, provides detailed information about the complex ecosystem found in our state.

Name: ______ Phone: ______
Address: ______
City: ______ State: ______ Zip Code: ______

☐ Please reserve______ places at $125.00 per person.
☐ I want to be a $1250 **Supporter** and receive a table for 10.
☐ I want to be a $2500 **Patron** and receive a table for 10 and an invitation for two to a private preview party of the "Living Stream".
☐ I cannot attend; however, I have enclosed a contribution.
☐ I am enclosing my check made payable to the St. Louis Zoo Friends Association.
Please bill my MC # ______ Visa # ______ Exp. ______

I understand tables are for 10. Please seat me with: ______

Reservations are accepted in order received and will be held at the door in the name of the purchaser. Attendance is limited.

**Note:** All contributions are tax deductible as allowed by law. Proceeds will underwrite the "Living Stream" exhibit in the new Education and Discovery Center.

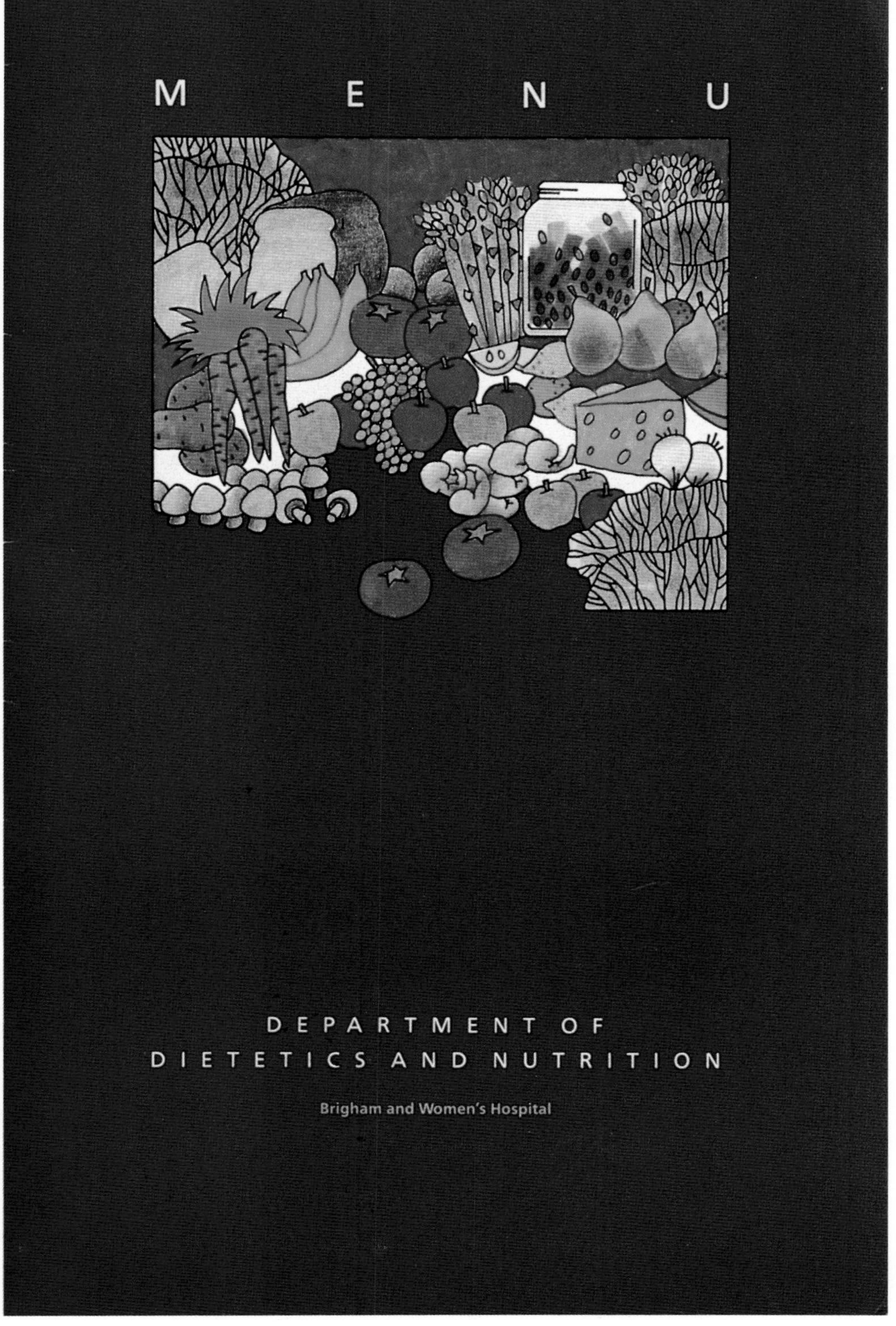


Designer: *Heidi Price*
Establishment: *Brigham and Women's Hospital*
*Boston, MA*

**1987 N.R.A. GREAT MENUS CONTEST WINNER: SECOND PLACE, INSTITUTIONAL**

A colorful illustration of raw food items brightens the cover of this hospital menu. Sections of the illustration, executed as line drawings, provide graphic heads for each division of the menu. Use of raw foods as a menu theme promotes the idea of healthy eating habits, an important point in a hospital setting. Menu item descriptions include serving size and the number of calories in each. The back page provides general guidelines for a healthy diet.

Designer: *Suzanne Vorlicek & Veronica Hyde*
*Baptist Memorial Hospital*
Restaurant: *Baptist Memorial Hospital*
*Memphis, TN*

A four-color menu cover shows all three of the Hospital's branches. The two-color interior pages allow the patient to make a number of choices. Complete instructions for filling out the menu are included.

It's interesting that the hospital is using its menus to make marketing points. Obviously, like any other business, hospitals now need to market services via advertising.

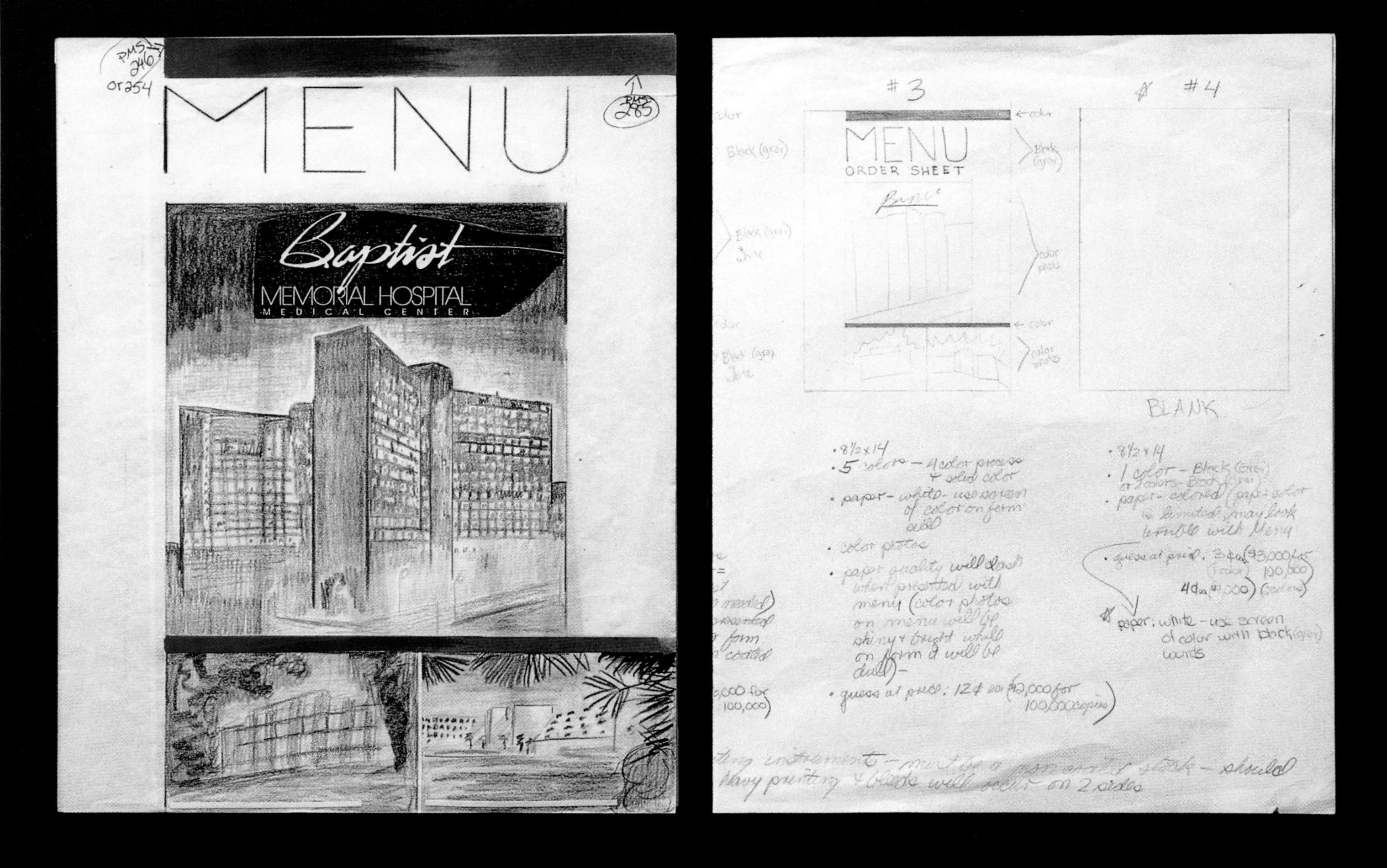

# MENU

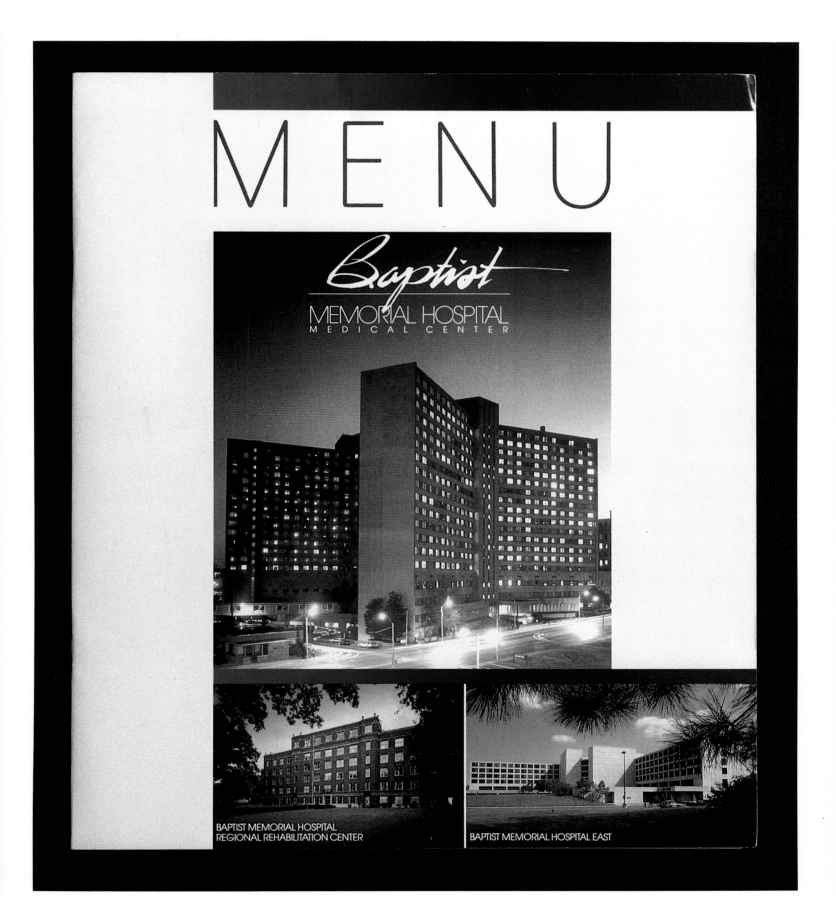

Baptist
MEMORIAL HOSPITAL
MEDICAL CENTER

BAPTIST MEMORIAL HOSPITAL
REGIONAL REHABILITATION CENTER

BAPTIST MEMORIAL HOSPITAL EAST

**Designer:** *Morris Graphics Ltd.*
**Restaurant:** *Air Canada*
*Montreal, Quebec, Canada*

To celebrate its 50th year of service, Air Canada chose to "salute the next generation of air travelers with the 'Child at Play' menu series." Apart from the enchanting photographs, the menus feature the airline's logo blind-embossed on the cover. The interior lists both the particular flight (e.g., London to Bombay) and the anticipated flying time in a soft gray screen. Menu items are in a clear, legible typeface and are repeated in German as well as the expected French and English. It is very unusual for an airline to attempt such an ambitious menu treatment. That Air Canada has not only tried, but succeeded in creating such a charming series is a triumph.

AIR CANADA

AIR CANADA

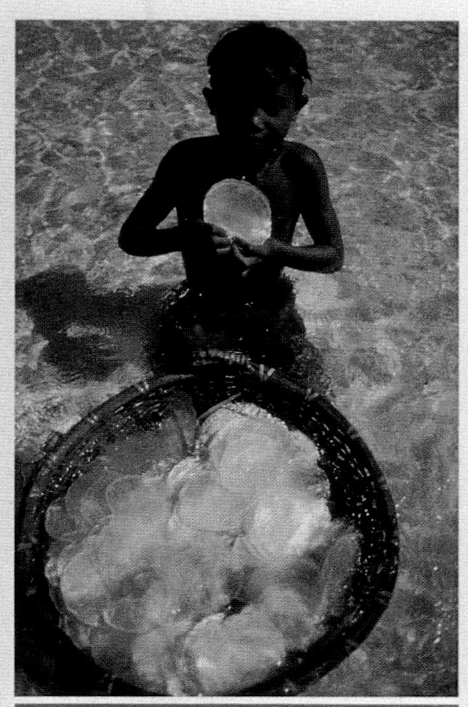

AIR CANADA

AIR CANADA

Designer: *John Breslin*
*St. Joseph's Hospital Centers*
Establishment: *St. Joseph's Hospital Centers*
*Mt. Clemens, MI*

**1987 N.R.A. GREAT MENUS CONTEST WINNER: FIRST PLACE, INSTITUTIONAL**

Embossed printing in a graduated screen repeats the name of the hospital on the cover of this maternity ward menu. A die-cut window reveals the first photograph of the new mother's own baby. The baby's vital statistics are entered by hand below the photo, which makes this personalized piece a souvenir as well as a menu.

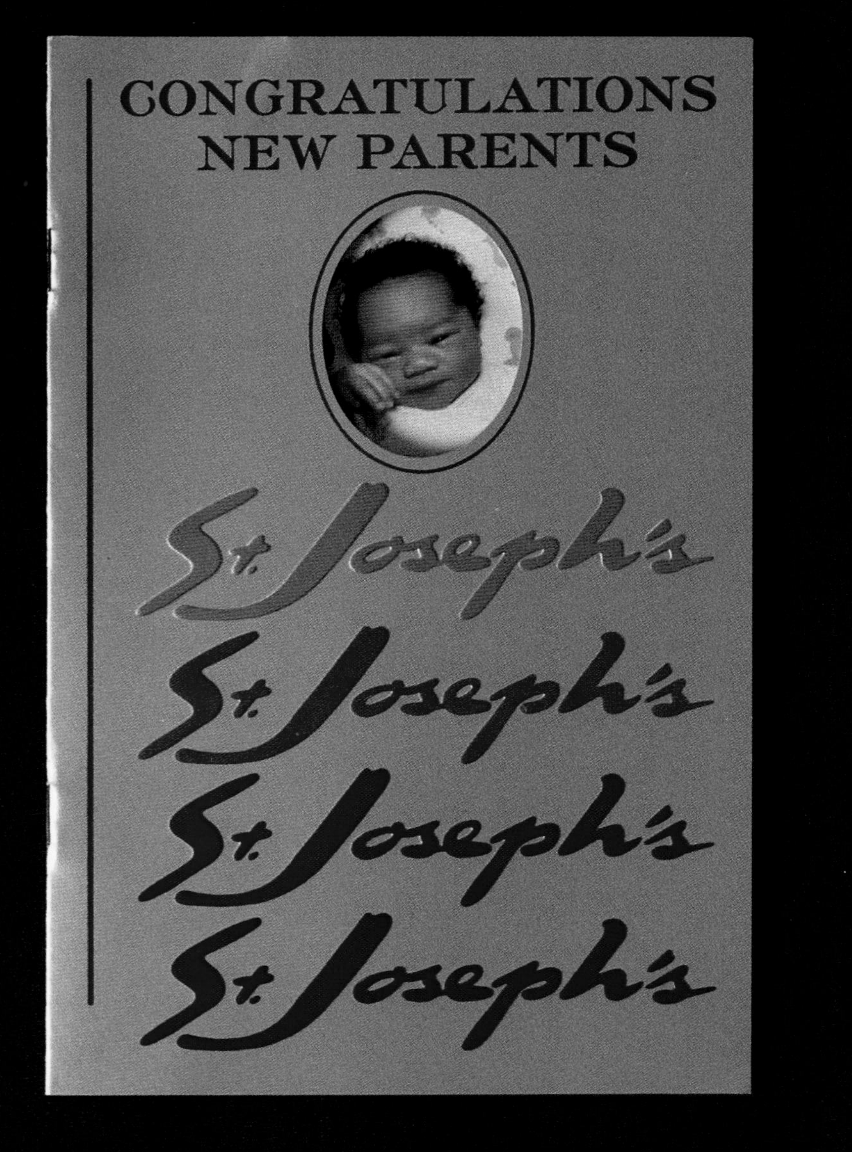


I am Your Baby
And I need you Badly

Please look at me carefully the next time you see me.
Please notice that I am so small and need so much.
Please listen to me carefully the next time you see me.
Please notice that I don't know much.
Like you I was born helpless. And growing up so I can take care of myself will take me a long time too.
I need food.
I need rest.
I need to be kept clean.
I need to be kept warm in winter and cool in summer.
I need to be taken in your arms or sat on your lap.
I need to feel your skin against my skin.
I need you to heal my hurts.
I need you to play with just so you and I can have some good times together.
I need you to teach me everything you can so I'll have a chance in this world when I grow up.

I need your patience. I know I'm not very orderly. I cry out for things like food and attention the second I need them. I can't help it, and I know that bothers you sometimes. All I can hope is that you will be patient with me until I can learn to be patient, too.

Above all, I need to know you love me so I can give a little love to my children and they can give a little to their children.
I need so much from you, yet I have only one thing I can give you in return.
That is my Love.
today and tomorrow and forever.

Homemade Soup of the Day
*piping hot cup of soup prepared just for you.*

"Mr. B." Salad — Our Specialty
*blend of mixed greenery, bleu cheese, bacon crumbles and croutons — highlighted by a secret formula creamy dressing.*

Land & Sea
*combination of succulent broiled Gulf Shrimp bursting from the shell and a tender choice cut Colorado Steak. In addition a piping hot baked Idaho Potato capped with a cheese topping.*

Garden Vegetable de Jour
*garden Fresh Vegetables, served with a savory butter sauce*

Oven Warm Dinner Roll

Dairy Fresh Butter

S.J.H. Black Forest Torte
*Layer of rich cake filled with whipped cream, cherries, walnuts and topped with drizzled chocolate*

To Complement Your Meal
*an iced bottle of sparkling Champagne.*

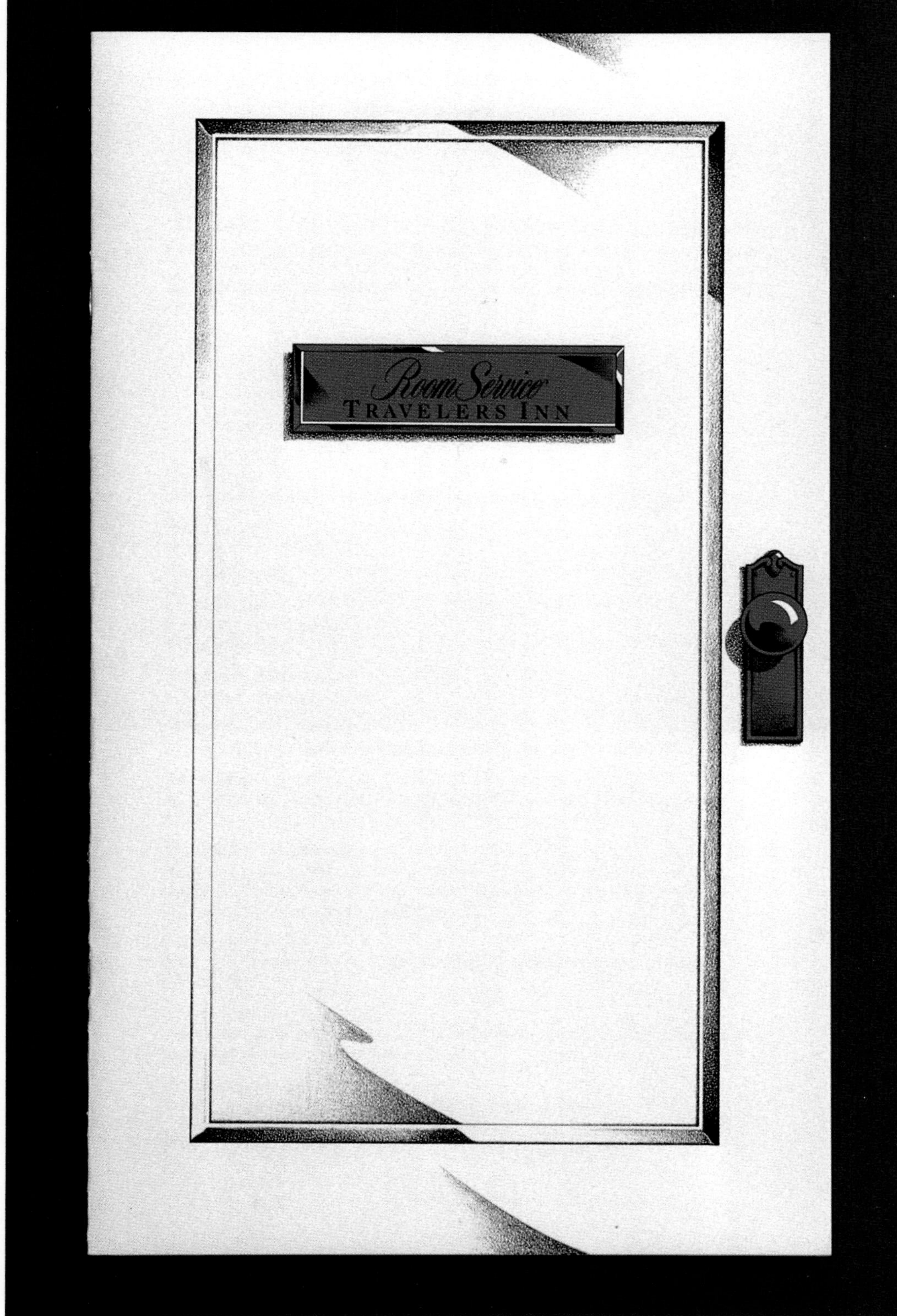


Designer: *Mike Wagner*
*The Menu Workshop*
Restaurant: *Room Service*
*Traveler's Inn*
*Seattle, WA*

The front of the menu invites the guest to open the door to a variety of foods available in-room; its back shows the door again, presumably closing behind the staff member who delivered the food. Using only two colors, black and gold, the menu is an imaginative way to convince the diner to look inside. Who can resist opening a closed door?

The back page of the menu interior lists other restaurants in the hotel. This type of cross-selling is fairly common in hotels but is only now beginning to crop up in other types of establishments.

Designer: *Carl Splitt*
*Art Department,*
*University of Arizona*
Restaurant: *The Union Club Restaurant*
*University of Arizona,*
*Student Union*
*Tucson, AZ*

The menu and theme for this restaurant changes each Fall, with the opening of a new school year. Part of the reason for this timing is that all of the menus are designed by the students themselves. This menu was designed for use with displays highlighting Arizona's copper mining industry.

The basic design of the menu is an extension of an earlier one, which was featured in *Menu Design II.* In the original version, torn paper was used to create a stylized portrait of the hills surrounding the school. In this treatment, the torn paper has been softened and the colors were selected to reflect the copper theme and the brilliant azure skies above Arizona.

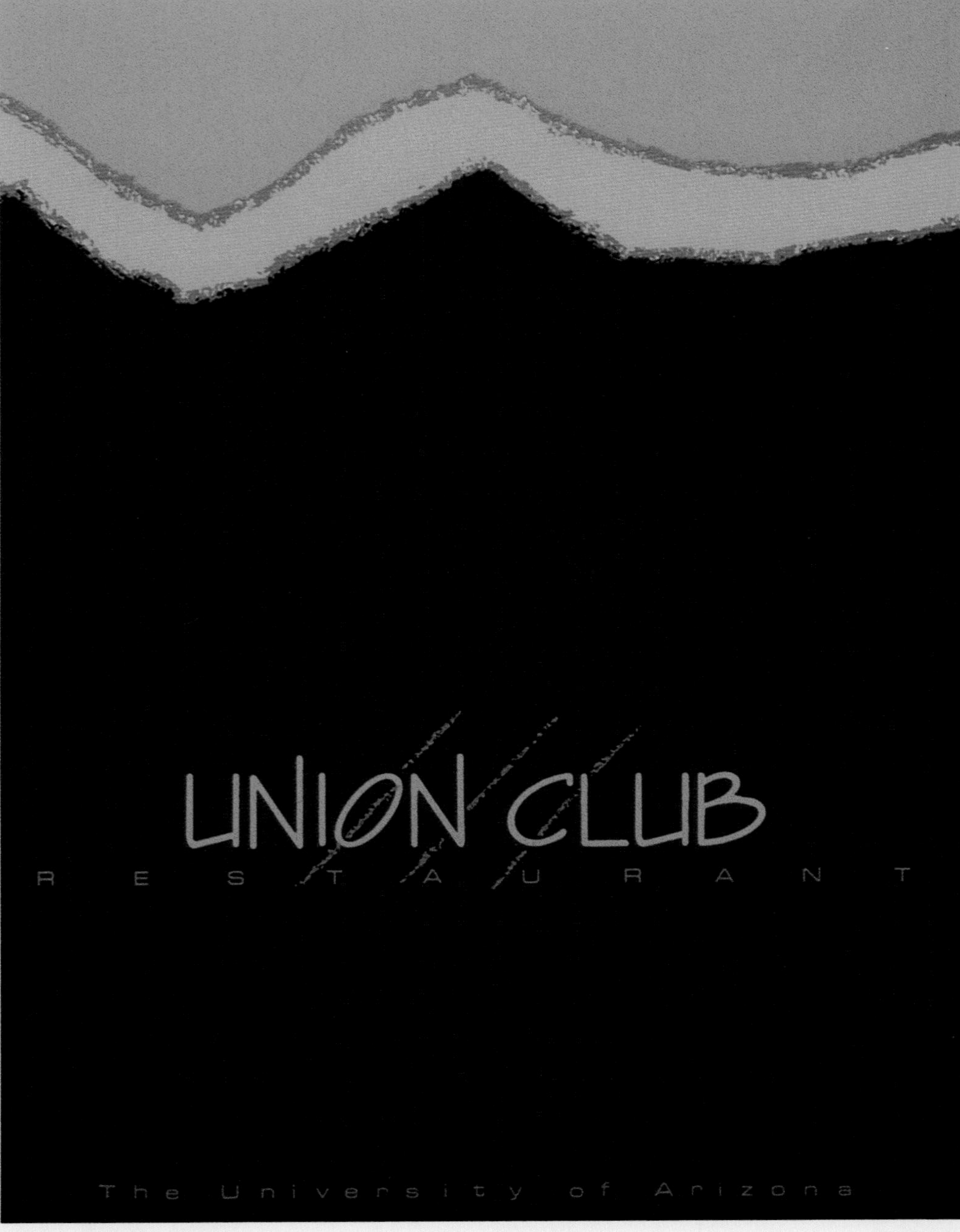

## GREAT TASTES OF MEXICO

**Chalupa Bar**
Start with a cup of cool Gazpacho soup, then fill your crispy fried corn tortilla "boat" with an assortment of toppings such as seasoned ground beef, lettuce, onion, cheese and salsa. $4.75

**Taquitos**
Three corn tortillas filled with spicy chicken chunks, rolled and deep fried. Served with salsa, guacamole and Spanish rice. $3.95

**Chimichanga**
Beef chunks simmered in a red chile sauce, folded in a flour tortilla and deep fried. Topped with shredded lettuce and grated cheddar cheese. $3.95

**Combinaciones Mexican**
Choice of CHICKEN or BEEF taco with green corn tamale, Spanish rice or beans. $4.25

## BEVERAGES

Fresh ground gourmet coffee .75
Iced tea, freshly brewed .75
Soft drinks .75
Lemonade .75
Milk .60
Perrier Water $1.00
Assorted sparkling waters $1.00
Hanson's Natural Apple Juice .75
Beer (non-alcoholic) $1.15
Wine (non-alcoholic)
St Regis split $1.75
bottle $5.50
glass $1.15

## DESSERT TRAY

An irresistable pleasure presented at your table.

## GELATO TRUFFLES

A gourmet Italian ice cream with assorted fillings. $2.25

Water served upon request.
Tax & gratuity not included.

## SUNDAY BRUNCH

Join us every Sunday for the best brunch buy in town! 11:00am–1:30pm.
$7.00 – tax included.
Lots of parking.

## GARDEN SPOT AND SOUP POT

Enjoy our fresh garden vegetables and chilled fruit bar with hearty homemade soups. $4.45

**Soup of the Day**

Monday – Chicken Noodle
Tuesday – Cream of Broccoli
Wednesday – Hearty Vegetable
Thursday – French Onion Au Gratin
Friday – Carl's Clam Chowder

Second Cup
Cup .80
Bowl $1.40
Tureen $3.50

– Chef's Choice
Clam Chowder
Cup .90
Bowl $1.50
Tureen $3.90

**Garden Spot Only** $3.95

Tossed green salad with choice of dressing. $1.10

## COLD SANDWICHES

**The Union "Club"**
Sliced turkey, bacon, tomato, sprouts, avocado and Monterey Jack cheese. $3.45

**Turkey & Swiss on a Bagel**
Thinly sliced gourmet turkey breast with imported Gruyere cheese on a freshly made bagel. $3.15

**Albacore Tuna Salad**
Mixed with celery, red onion, capers, mayonnaise. Choice of vita bread, pumpernickel, wheat or rye. $3.25

**Gourmet Chicken Salad**
Chunks of chicken breast, baked in our special blend of herbs and spices. Blended with sour cream, mayonnaise and scallions. Your choice of bread. $3.95

**Half Sandwich and Soup**
Choice of tuna or chicken salad sandwich with a cup of today's soup. $2.95

## MINER'S SPECIAL

Entree changes daily. Your server will explain.

## HOT SANDWICHES

**Barbeque Beef**
Tender slices of choice beef marinated in our special sauce, served on Kaiser or onion roll with a side dish of coleslaw. $3.95

**Monte Cristo**
Turkey, ham and Swiss cheese on French bread, lightly battered and fried. Served with a dish of fresh fruit $3.95

**Corned Beef Plus**
Hot corned beef stacked high on pumpernickel bread with sauerkraut and provolone cheese. $3.95

**Half Sandwich and Soup**
Choose from the above selections accompanied by a cup of today's soup. $3.25

## COPPER MINING IN ARIZONA

Copper has played a very important role in the development of Arizona. Mining camps like Bisbee, Jerome and Globe attracted people with money from the East. Railroads were built to link the camps with market centers and wherever the miners went, farmers, shopkeepers and modern civilization followed.

The amount of copper that has been mined in Arizona is phenomenal – in excess of 35 billion pounds. That is enough to form a solid copper cube whose sides are one and one third as long as a football field. By-products of the copper mining were other metals such as silver and gold. Bisbee alone produced almost 3 million ounces of gold and 100 million ounces of silver.

Although some of the copper mined is in the form of the native element, most of it is tied up in various minerals. Copper minerals are some of the most beautiful known. Characteristic colors are bright greens, blues and reds. Below is a list of some of the more common copper minerals:

### AZURITE
A bright blue copper carbonate. Bisbee produced the world's best specimens.

### MALACHITE
A green copper carbonate. It often forms in crusts which look like velvet.

### TURQUOISE
A copper phosphate which is commonly used in southwestern jewelry.

### CUPRITE
A bright red copper oxide. The fibrous form is known as chalcotrichite.

### CHALCOCITE
A black copper sulfide. Chalcocite is the primary ore mineral.

### CHRYSOCOLLA
A blue copper silicate. Solid masses larger than 50 feet on a side have been mined at Ray.

ROOM
SERVICE

# ALL DAY DINING

All food from the cold kitchen is served from noon to midnight. Hot meals from noon - 3. p. m. and 6. p. m. - 11. p. m.

## APPETIZERS

| | |
|---|---|
| Norwegian Shrimps Cocktail, Brandy Sauce | DM 16,00 |
| Fillets of Herring in a sour Cream with Apples, Cucumbers and Onions | DM 14,00 |
| Home marinated Salmon "Swedish Style", Dill-Mustard Sauce | DM 24,00 |
| Avocado-Grapefruit with Yoghourt-Sauce | DM 15,00 |

## SOUPS

| | |
|---|---|
| Soup of the Day | DM 6,50 |
| Beef Consommé | DM 6,50 |
| French Onion Soup gratinated with Parmesan Cheese | DM 7,00 |
| Tomato Soup with Gin | DM 7,00 |
| Hungarian Goulash-Soup | DM 7,00 |
| Cream of Chicken Soup | DM 7,00 |

## FISH

| | |
|---|---|
| Fillets of Plaice "Meunière" Parsley Potatoes, green Salad | DM 22,00 |
| Grilled Trout in brown Lemon Butter, Parsley Potatoes, mixed Salad | DM 25,00 |
| Medaillons of Salmon in a Champagne Sauce, Parsley Potatoes, mixed Salad | DM 32,00 |
| Shrimps Curry in a Timbale of Almond Rice, tropical Garnishes | DM 33,00 |

## MEATS AND POULTRY

| | |
|---|---|
| Escalope of Veal Viennoise, Fried Potatoes, mixed Salad | DM 26,00 |
| Two Fillets Mignon in a Pepper Sauce, Buttered Rice, mixed Salad | DM 34,00 |
| Fillet Steak, 180 gr., Sauce Bearnaise, Baked Potato with sour Cream, Iceberg Salad with Thousand Island Dressing | DM 36,00 |
| Rump Steak, with grilled Tomato, Grated Horse-Radish, French fried Potatoes and mixed Salad | DM 33,00 |
| Roast Baby-Chicken, grilled Tomato and French fried Potatoes | DM 28,00 |
| Spaghetti "Bolognaise", Parmesan Cheese, mixed Salad | DM 19,00 |
| Grilled Hamburger on a toasted Bun, sliced Onions Tomatoes, French fried Potatoes | DM 15,00 |
| Cheeseburger with Chester on a toasted Bun, French fried Potatoes | DM 17,00 |

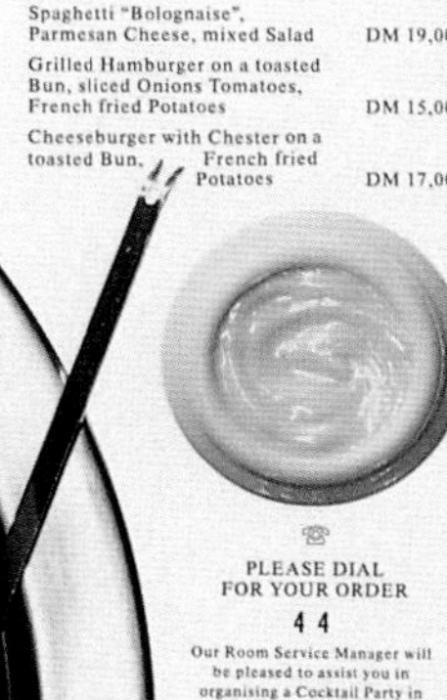

PLEASE DIAL FOR YOUR ORDER

44

Our Room Service Manager will be pleased to assist you in organising a Cocktail Party in your room.

The prices include 15% service and tax.

## MENU

Scandinavian Hors D'Œuvre Platter

★ ★ ★

T-Bone-Steak of Veal
Grilled Tomato, Baked Potato
Iceberg Salad with Thousand Island Dressing

★ ★ ★

Chocolate Mousse

DM 49,50

## DESSERTS

| | |
|---|---|
| Warm Apple Strudel with Vanilla Sauce | DM 7,50 |
| Selection of our Cake Specialities per piece | DM 6,00 |
| HILTON Ice Cream Cup | DM 7,50 |
| Strawberries with Vanilla Ice Cream | DM 15,00 |
| Crème Caramel | DM 6,00 |
| Chocolate Mousse | DM 8,50 |

## SANDWICHES / SALADS

| | |
|---|---|
| "Club Sandwich" The traditional Triple Decker Sandwich with Crisps | DM 15,00 |
| Chef's Salad Bowl Strips of Chicken Breast, Ham, Sausage and Cheese on a green Salad with Sauce Vinaigrette and Mayonnaise Dressing | DM 17,00 |
| Chicken Salad "Hawaii" | DM 16,00 |
| Salad of Tuna Fish "Niçoise" | DM 17,00 |
| Assorted Cheese Platter | DM 15,00 |
| Large mixed Salad Platter with Shrimps and Slices of Egg | DM 24,00 |

## ALL NIGHT DINING

From 11. p. m. - 6. a. m.

| | |
|---|---|
| Home marinated Salmon "Swedish Style", Dill-Mustard Sauce | DM 24,00 |
| Hungarian Goulash Soup | DM 7,00 |
| Selection of Sandwiches with Breast of Chicken, Ham, Roastbeef or Edam Cheese | DM 8,50 |

## HOT BEVERAGES

| | |
|---|---|
| Pot of Assam- or Darjeeling Tea | DM 5,50 |
| Pot of Coffee | DM 5,50 |
| Pot of decaffeinated Coffee | DM 5,50 |
| Pot of hot Chocolate | DM 5,50 |

# TAGESKARTE

Wir servieren Ihnen alle Speisen aus der kalten Küche durchgehend von 12.00 Uhr bis 24.00 Uhr. Warme Küche von 12.00 Uhr bis 15.00 Uhr und 18.00 Uhr bis 23.00 Uhr.

## VORSPEISEN

| | |
|---|---|
| Norwegischer Shrimps-Cocktail, Cognacsauce | DM 16,00 |
| Heringsfilet in saurer Sahne mit Äpfeln, Gurken und Zwiebeln | DM 14,00 |
| Hausgebeizter Lachs „Schwedische Art", Dill-Senf-Sauce | DM 24,00 |
| Avocado-Grapefruit mit Joghurtsauce | DM 15,00 |

## SUPPEN

| | |
|---|---|
| Tagessuppe | DM 6,50 |
| Doppelte Rinderkraftbrühe | DM 6,50 |
| Französische Zwiebelsuppe mit Parmesankäse überbacken | DM 7,00 |
| Tomatencreme mit Gin | DM 7,00 |
| Ungarische Gulaschsuppe | DM 7,00 |
| Geflügelcreme | DM 7,00 |

## FISCHGERICHTE

| | |
|---|---|
| Schollenfilets „Müllerin Art" Petersilienkartoffeln, Kopfsalat | DM 22,00 |
| Gebratene Forelle in Zitronen-butter, Petersilienkartoffeln, gemischter Salat | DM 25,00 |
| Lachsmedaillon in Champagner-sauce, Petersilienkartoffeln, gemischter Salat | DM 32,00 |
| Curry von Hummerkrabben-schwänzen im Mandelreisrand, tropische Beilagen | DM 33,00 |

## FLEISCHGERICHTE

| | |
|---|---|
| Wiener Schnitzel Bratkartoffeln, gemischter Salat | DM 26,00 |
| Zwei kleine Rinderfilets in Pfeffersauce, Butterreis, gemischter Salat | DM 34,00 |
| Filetsteak, 180 g, Sauce Bearnaise, in der Folie gebackene Kartoffel mit Schnittlauchcreme, Eisbergsalat mit Thousand Island Dressing | DM 36,00 |
| Rumpsteak mit Grilltomate geschabtem Meerrettich, Pommes Frites und gemischtem Salat | DM 33,00 |
| Ganzes Stubenküken gebraten, mit Grilltomate, Pommes Frites und gemischtem Salat | DM 28,00 |
| Spaghetti „Bolognaise" Parmesankäse, gemischter Salat | DM 19,00 |
| Gegrillter Hamburger auf getoastetem Brötchen, Zwiebelringe, Tomaten, Pommes Frites | DM 15,00 |
| Cheeseburger mit Chesterkäse überbacken, Pommes Frites | DM 17,00 |

## MENU

Nordischer Vorspeisenteller

★ ★ ★

Kalbs-T-Bone Steak
Grilltomate, gebackene Kartoffel
Eisbergsalat, Thousand Island Dressing

★ ★ ★

Schokoladen Mousse

DM 49,50

## DESSERTS

| | |
|---|---|
| Warmer Apfelstrudel mit Vanillesauce | DM 7,50 |
| Auswahl von Kuchenspezialitäten aus eigener Konditorei Stück | DM 6,00 |
| HILTON Eisbecher | DM 7,50 |
| Erdbeeren mit Vanilleeis | DM 15,00 |
| Karamel-Creme | DM 6,00 |
| Schokoladen Mousse | DM 8,50 |

## SANDWICHES / SALATE

| | |
|---|---|
| „Club Sandwich" das traditionelle Turmsandwich mit Kartoffelchips | DM 15,00 |
| Küchenchef's Salatschüssel Streifen von Geflügelbrust, Schinken, Fleischwurst und Käse auf grünem Salat mit Sauce Vinaigrette und Mayonnaise | DM 17,00 |
| Geflügelsalat „Hawaii" | DM 16,00 |
| Thunfischsalat „Nizzaer Art" | DM 17,00 |
| Gemischter Käseteller | DM 15,00 |
| Großer gemischter Salatteller mit Shrimps und Eischeiben | DM 24,00 |

## KLEINE NACHTKARTE

Von 23.00 Uhr bis 6.00 Uhr

| | |
|---|---|
| Hausgebeizter Lachs „Schwedische Art" Dill-Senf-Sauce | DM 24,00 |
| Ungarische Gulaschsuppe | DM 7,00 |
| Auswahl von Sandwiches mit Geflügelbrust, gekochtem Schinken, Roastbeef oder Edamer Käse | DM 8,50 |

## HEISSE GETRÄNKE

| | |
|---|---|
| Kännchen Assam- oder Darjeeling-Tee | DM 5,50 |
| Kännchen Kaffee | DM 5,50 |
| Kännchen Kaffee Hag | DM 5,50 |
| Kännchen Schokolade | DM 5,50 |

BITTE WÄHLEN SIE FÜR IHRE BESTELLUNG DIE NUMMER

44

Unser Etagenkellner ist Ihnen gerne bei der Organisation einer Veranstaltung auf Ihrem Zimmer behilflich.

Die Preise enthalten 15% Bedienungsgeld und die gesetzliche Mehrwertsteuer.

**Designer:** *Joop Groypink*

**Restaurant:** *Room Service*
*Hilton International Düsseldorf*
*Düsseldorf, West Germany*

This laminated menu features large bleed photos which have been cropped in unusual ways for a note of excitement. By showing only a portion of the food in each overhead shot, the menu is lent an air of mystery … what is on the rest of the plate? Will it be as tempting as what appears here? By arousing the diner's curiosity, the menu sells very effectively, but subtly. This is a great menu because it *hints,* rather than bludgeoning the diner with the obvious.

Boxes highlight special selections in both English and German.

**Designer:** *Sigurd Lynne*
*Sigurd Lynne Advertising*
**Establishment:** *Pediatric Menu*
*St. John's Regional*
*Medical Center*
*Oxnard, CA*

**1987 N.R.A. GREAT MENUS CONTEST WINNER: SECOND PLACE, GRAND PRIZE**

The crayoned drawing on the cover suggests the uses to which a child can put the menu interior. There are pictures to color, a "connect the dots" puzzle and a crossword puzzle. There's even a suggestion for making funny sentences out of the answers to the crossword puzzle.

The menu is designed so that, with a little assistance, even very young children can make their own food choices. The menu choices are to be circled and, to remind a child who doesn't yet read, the word "circle" is itself circled. The three-fold glossy finished menu is not too big for even very small hands. In view of the primary purpose of hospitals — healing — it's nice that somebody took the time to design a menu that will amuse some of the youngest patients, for whom hospitalization must be the hardest to bear.

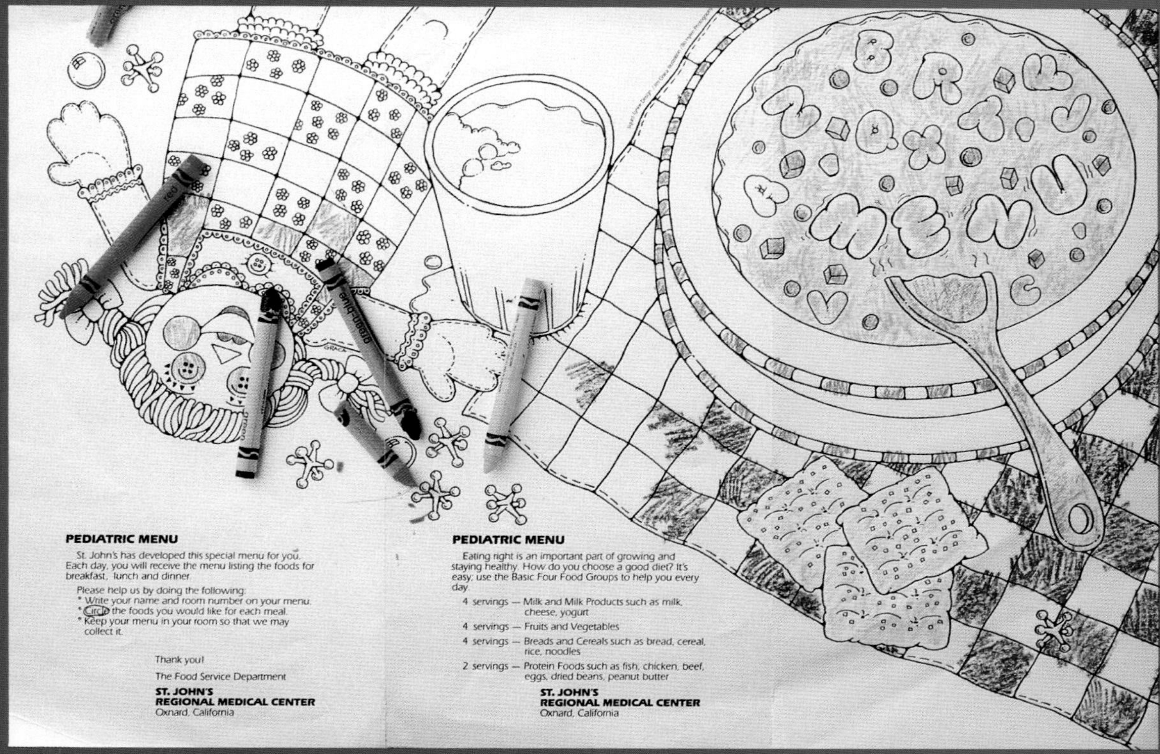

PEDIATRIC MENU

St. John's has developed this special menu for you. Each day, you will receive the menu listing the foods for breakfast, lunch and dinner.

Please help us by doing the following:
* Write your name and room number on your menu.
* Circle the foods you would like for each meal.
* Keep your menu in your room so that we may collect it.

Thank you!

The Food Service Department

ST. JOHN'S
REGIONAL MEDICAL CENTER
Oxnard, California

PEDIATRIC MENU

Eating right is an important part of growing and staying healthy. How do you choose a good diet? It's easy; use the Basic Four Food Groups to help you every day.

4 servings — Milk and Milk Products such as milk, cheese, yogurt

4 servings — Fruits and Vegetables

4 servings — Breads and Cereals such as bread, cereal, rice, noodles

2 servings — Protein Foods such as fish, chicken, beef, eggs, dried beans, peanut butter

ST. JOHN'S
REGIONAL MEDICAL CENTER
Oxnard, California

Draw a line starting on number 1 to get the whole picture, then color in.

# BREAKFAST

Please circle your selections:

**FRUITS AND JUICES**

| | | |
|---|---|---|
| Orange Juice | Pear Half | Fresh Banana |
| Apple Juice | Applesauce | Fresh Fruit in Season |

**HOT AND COLD CEREALS (served with milk)**

| | | |
|---|---|---|
| Oatmeal | Corn Flakes | Special K |
| Cream of Wheat | Rice Krispies | Cherrios |
| | Raisin Bran | Granola |

**BREAKFAST ENTREES**

| | | |
|---|---|---|
| Scrambled Egg | Bacon | Whole Wheat Pancakes |
| Poached Egg | Sausage | Golden Waffle |
| Soft Cooked Egg | | Pigs in a Blanket |

**BREADS AND SPREADS**

| | | |
|---|---|---|
| Bagel | Flour Tortilla | Butter |
| Biscuit | Doughnut | Margarine |
| Blueberry Muffin | Toasted English Muffin | Jelly |
| | | Cream Cheese |

**HOT AND COLD BEVERAGES**

| | | |
|---|---|---|
| Whole Milk | Nonfat Milk | Hot Cocoa |
| Lowfat Milk | Chocolate Milk | |

**SEASONINGS**

| | | |
|---|---|---|
| Sugar | Honey | Salt |
| Brown Sugar | Catsup | Pepper |

Name ______________________ Room # __________

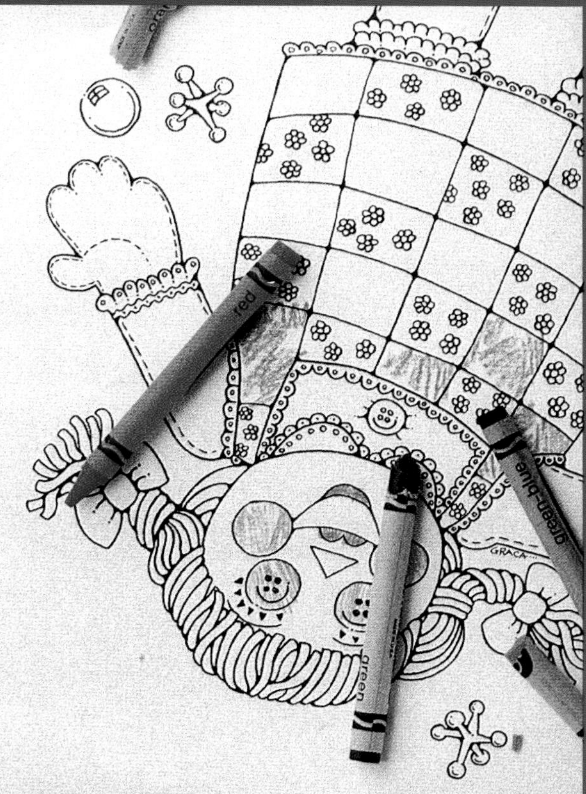



**PEDIATRIC MENU**

St. John's has developed this special menu for you. Each day, you will receive the menu listing the foods for breakfast, lunch and dinner.

Please help us by doing the following:
* Write your name and room number on your menu.
* Circle the foods you would like for each meal.
* Keep your menu in your room so that we may collect it.

Thank you!

The Food Service Department

**ST. JOHN'S**
**REGIONAL MEDICAL CENTER**
Oxnard, California

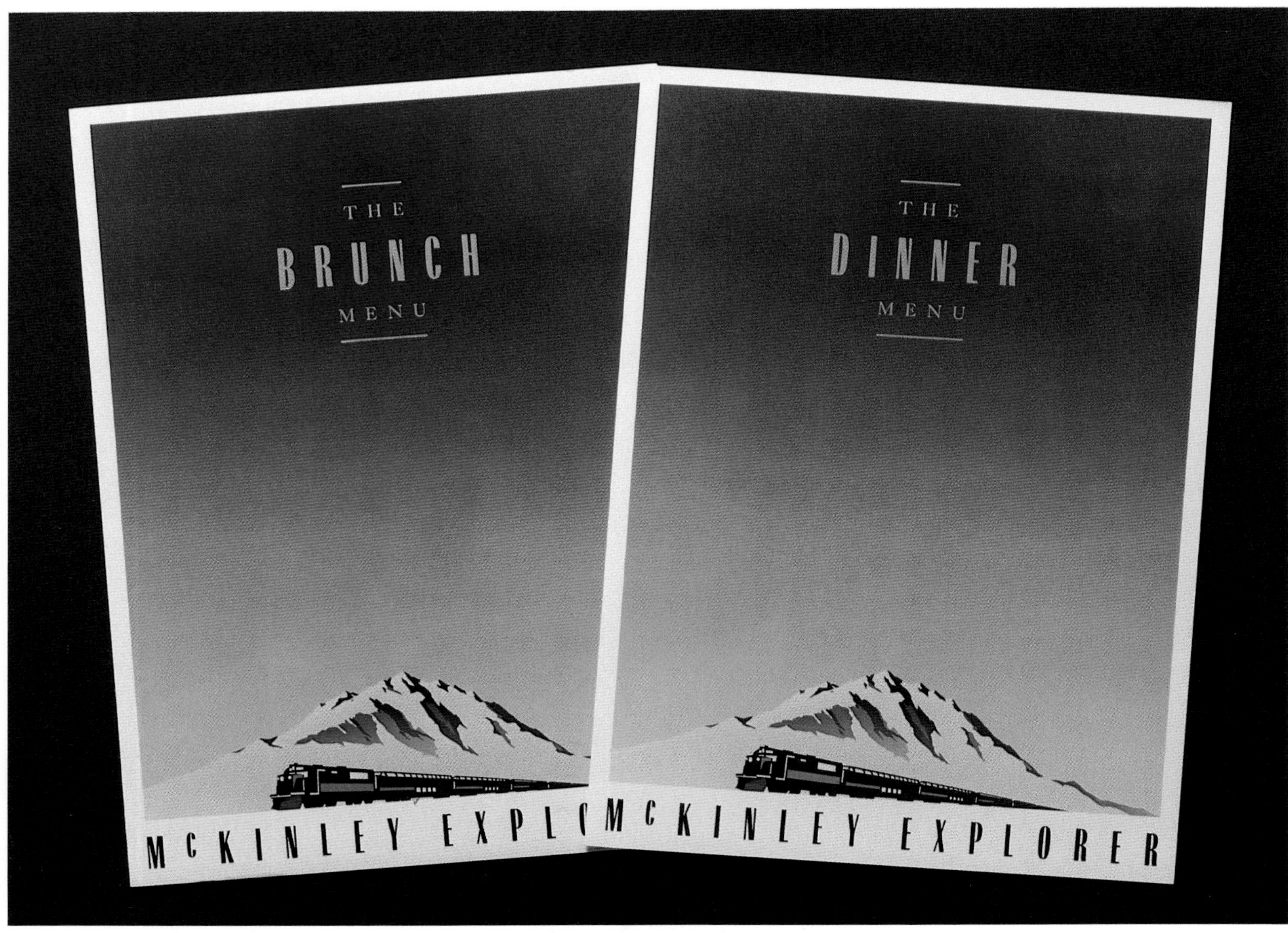


Designer: *Mike Wagner*
*The Menu Workshop*
Restaurant: *Brunch and Dinner Menus*
*The McKinley Explorer*
*Anchorage, AK*

For the past several years, travelers in Europe have been able to experience the luxury of 1930's style train travel on the Orient Express. The McKinley Explorer, while its cars do not include the fabulous hand-finished marquetry of its European counterpart, has far more exciting scenery to offer its passengers. It offers 30's-era graciousness in completely renovated cars and outside the windows of the train, the majestic beauty of Alaska.

The menus for use in its dining car depict a tiny train against a slightly higher snow-capped mountain which may be Mt. McKinley itself. Above all, the Aurora Borealis paints the northern sky. Because, in Alaska, nature seems to dwarf mere humans and their works, the scale is appropriate to the setting.

Silver foil stamping on the menu cover lends a final touch of distinction to the menus.

Designer: *Nancy Rosenbloom & K.G. Kleeberg Saint Francis Memorial Hospital*
Establishment: *Saint Francis Memorial Hospital San Francisco, CA*

**1987 N.R.A. GREAT MENUS CONTEST WINNER: THIRD PLACE, INSTITUTIONAL**

This looks more like the menu from a first-class restaurant than something to be shown to hospital patients. It takes advantage of the most famous landmark in its city for cover photography. The Golden Gate Bridge, shot on a (rare) perfectly clear day, appears with the city of San Francisco in the background. A cord of 'international orange,' the same color as the paint used on the Bridge, holds the menu inserts in place.

The inserts are printed on a beautiful paper in easy-to-read type. The interior of the menu cover is imprinted in a soft abstract design. In response to the ethnic mix of patients served, some menu items are Chinese and the descriptions are printed in both English and Chinese characters for the patient's convenience.

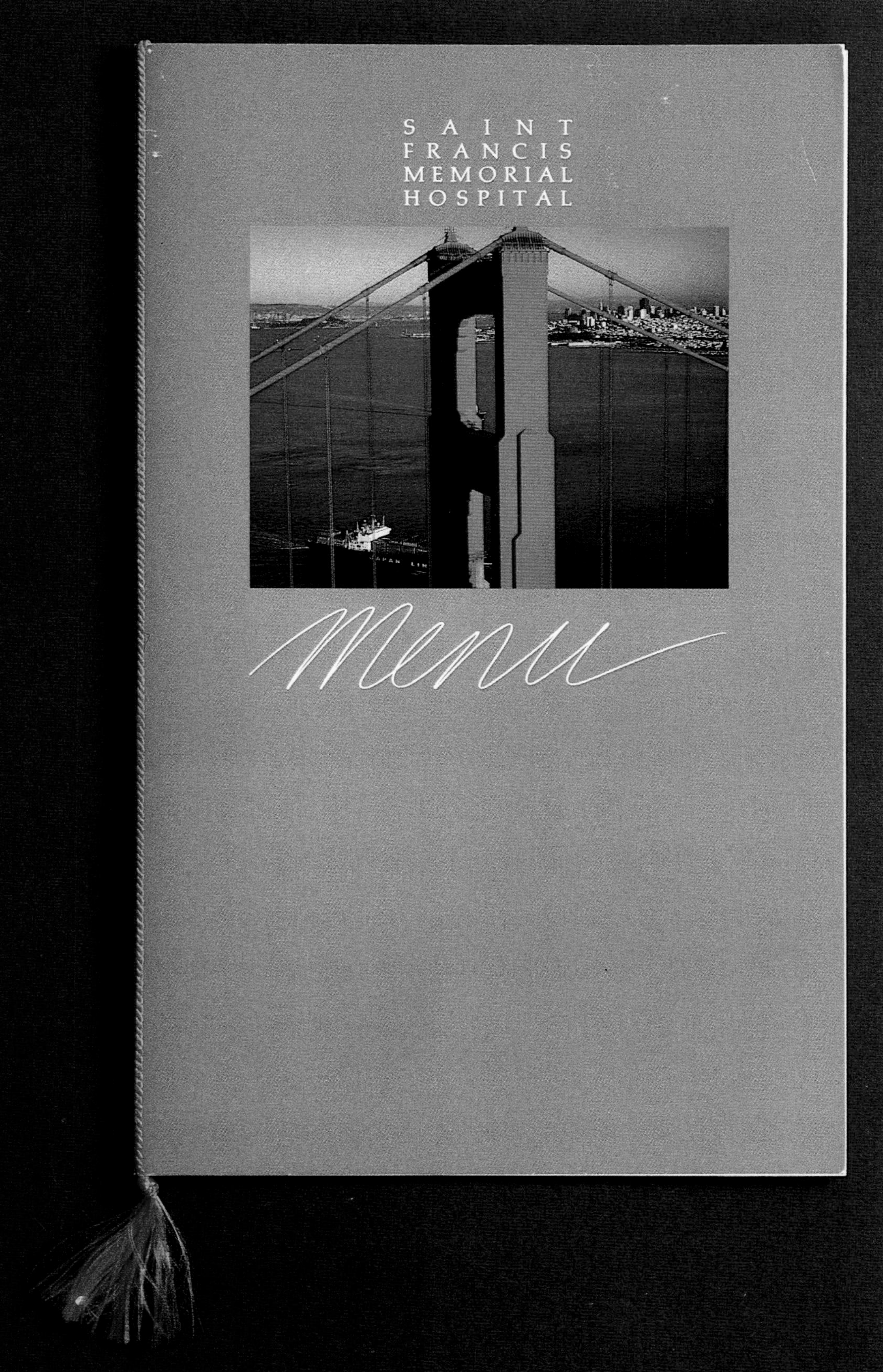

# CHAPTER 11

When restaurant graphics are planned, the star attraction is the main menu. Various restaurants and, most especially, hotels may choose to produce one or more special menus to accompany the major menu statement.

Most frequently, these "side shows" offer special drink/dessert selections, children's food or appetizers. In some instances, they are public relations/advertising pieces which promote a new branch of an old friend. Because the field is so broad, we have chosen to divide this chapter into three sub-sections; a brief comment on each sub-genre precedes each.

# SIDE SHOWS

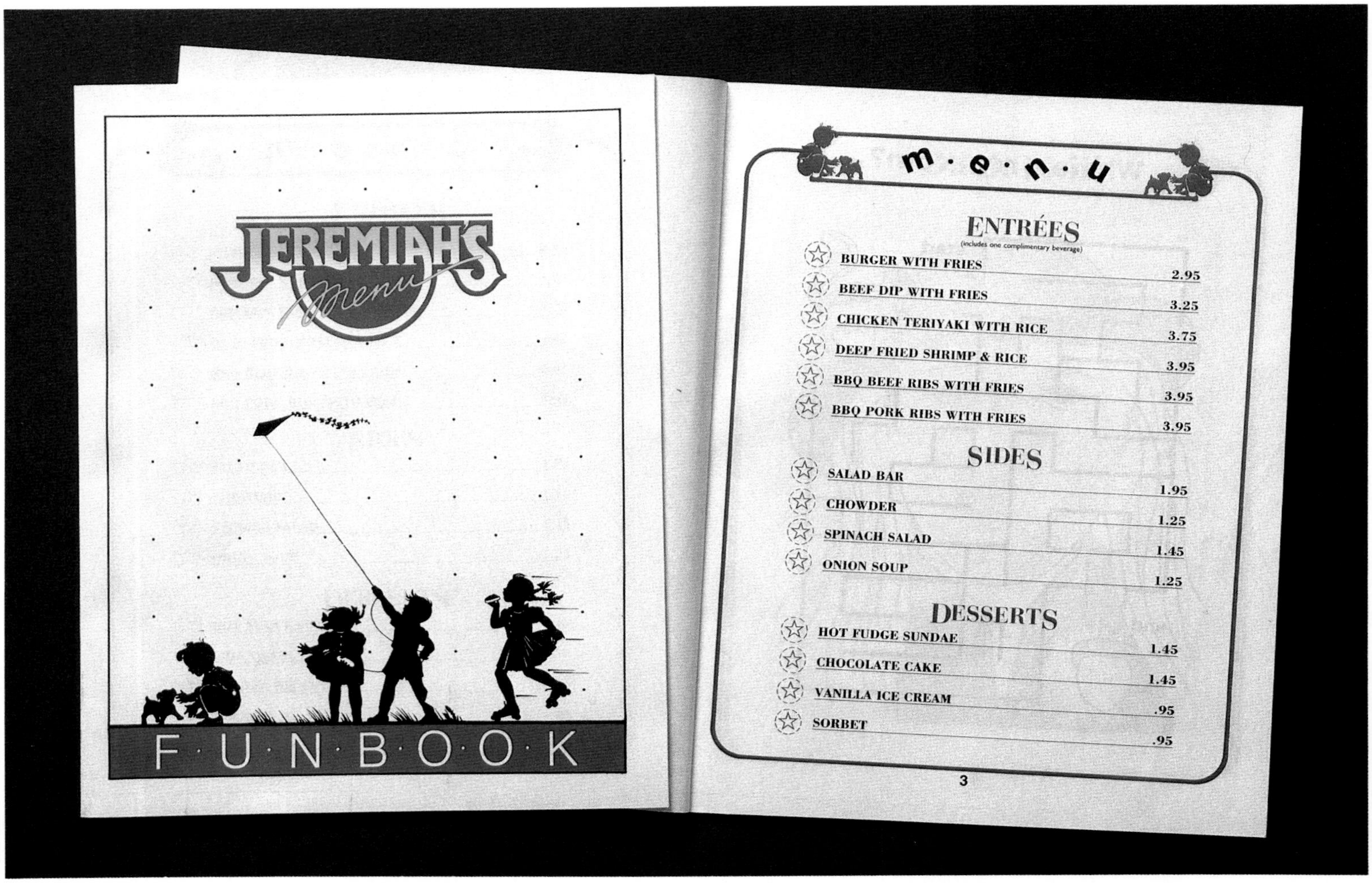

JEREMIAH'S
Menu
F·U·N·B·O·O·K
m·e·n·u
ENTRÉES
(includes one complimentary beverage)
BURGER WITH FRIES 2.95
BEEF DIP WITH FRIES 3.25
CHICKEN TERIYAKI WITH RICE 3.75
DEEP FRIED SHRIMP & RICE 3.95
BBQ BEEF RIBS WITH FRIES 3.95
BBQ PORK RIBS WITH FRIES 3.95
SIDES
SALAD BAR 1.95
CHOWDER 1.25
SPINACH SALAD 1.45
ONION SOUP 1.25
DESSERTS
HOT FUDGE SUNDAE 1.45
CHOCOLATE CAKE 1.45
VANILLA ICE CREAM .95
SORBET .95
3

Very Nice
Super Smart
Good Work
I'm hungry
I'm tired
I'm thirsty
JEREMIAHS
JEREMIAHS
JEREMIAH'S
Menu
F·U·N·B·O·O·K

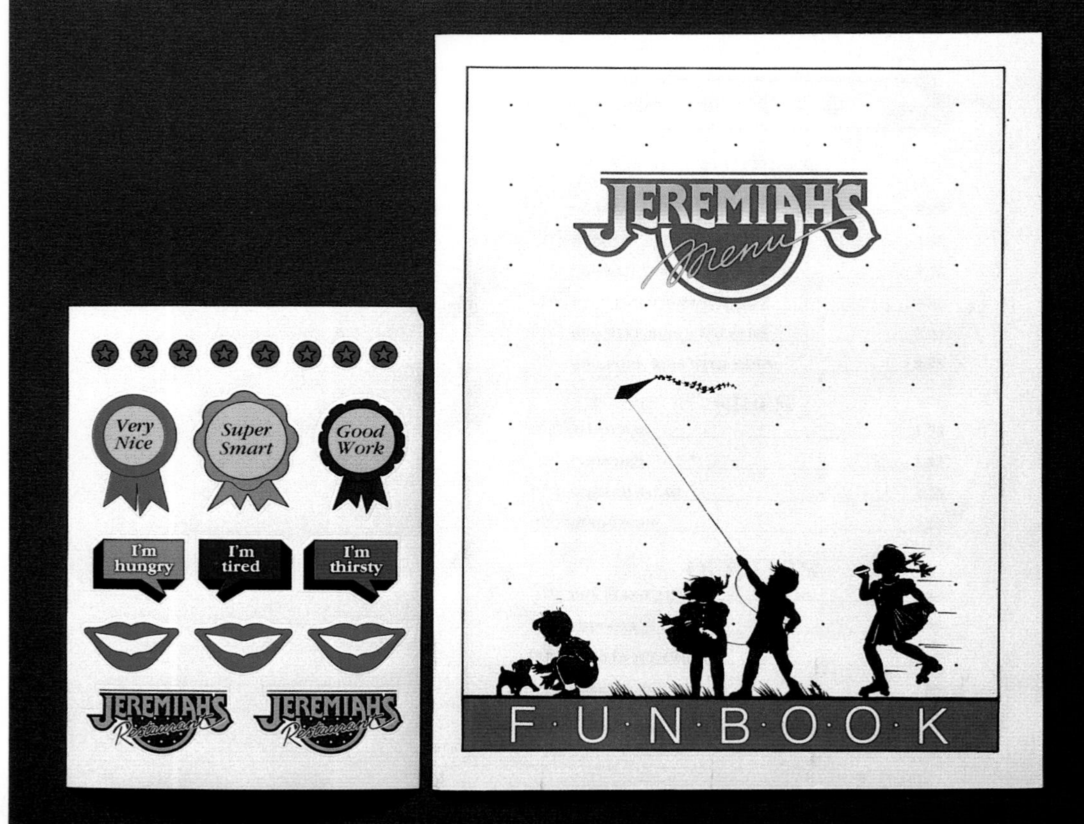

Designer: *Jack Biesek*
*Biesek Design*

Restaurant: *Jeremiah's Funbook*
*12 locations from Palm Springs to Houston*

This three-color menu on inexpensive paper both lists children's food items and provides entertainment. It includes a broad range of mazes, multiple choice picture puzzles and a "stick-on" picture for children to complete.

Some of the interior pictures can be colored and the back page is completely blank to provide further space for young artists.

The pressure sensitive stickers which accompany the menu are not only bright and cheerful, they also provide the child with a choice of which to use. Several would be appropriate for the picture they are designed to complete.

All in all, this menu is a practical and sensitive solution to dining out with small children.

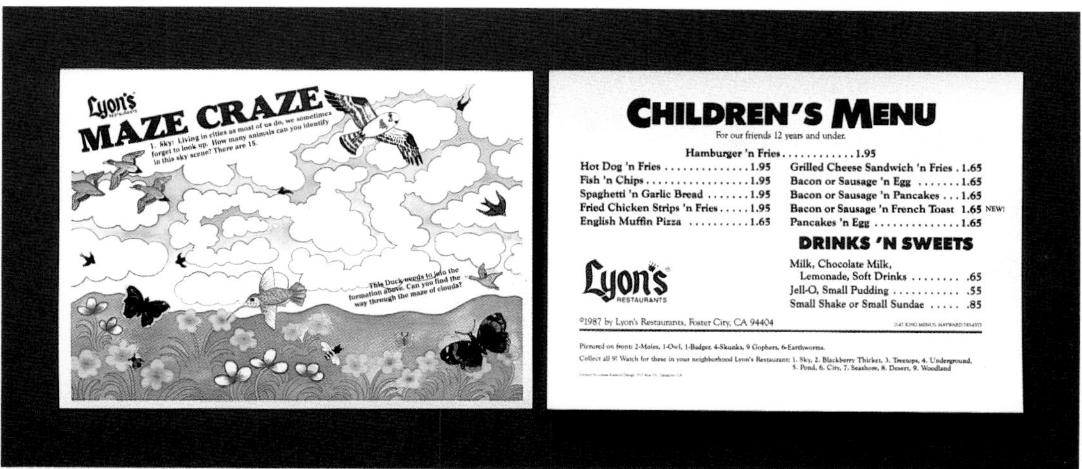


CHILDREN'S MENU

For our friends 12 years and under.

Hamburger 'n Fries . . . . . . . . . . . . 1.95

Hot Dog 'n Fries . . . . . . . . . . . . . . 1.95
Fish 'n Chips . . . . . . . . . . . . . . . . . . 1.95
Spaghetti 'n Garlic Bread . . . . . . . 1.95
Fried Chicken Strips 'n Fries . . . . . 1.95
English Muffin Pizza . . . . . . . . . . 1.65

Grilled Cheese Sandwich 'n Fries . 1.65
Bacon or Sausage 'n Egg . . . . . . . 1.65
Bacon or Sausage 'n Pancakes . . . 1.65
Bacon or Sausage 'n French Toast 1.65 NEW!
Pancakes 'n Egg . . . . . . . . . . . . . . 1.65

DRINKS 'N SWEETS

Milk, Chocolate Milk,
Lemonade, Soft Drinks . . . . . . . . .65
Jell-O, Small Pudding . . . . . . . . . . . .55
Small Shake or Small Sundae . . . . . .85

Lyon's RESTAURANTS

©1987 by Lyon's Restaurants, Foster City, CA 94404

Pictured on front: 2-Moles, 1-Owl, 1-Badger, 4-Skunks, 9 Gophers, 6-Earthworms.

Collect all 9! Watch for these in your neighborhood Lyon's Restaurant: 1. Sky, 2. Blackberry Thicket, 3. Treetops, 4. Underground, 5. Pond, 6. City, 7. Seashore, 8. Desert, 9. Woodland

Designer: *Louise Riswold Evans*

Restaurant: *Children's Menus*
*Lyon's Restaurant*
*Foster City, CA*

Each of the nine different "Maze Crazes" draws on an environment with which the child will be at least moderately familiar. Included are the sky, the forest, the desert and the city. Each works as two separate games — a maze puzzle and a challenge to find or name all of the animals pictured.

These menus are imprinted four-color on one side, simple black on uncoated white on the menu side. This permits gang printing of the maze side with inexpensive updates to the menu listings. In addition, copy at the bottom of the menu side identifies the other mazes in the series — subtle marketing to convince the child this would be a good restaurant for repeat visits.

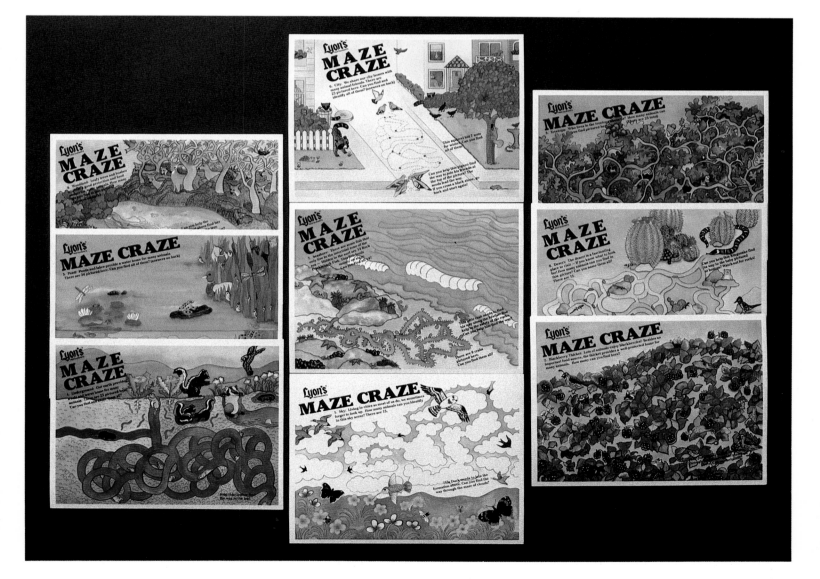

Designer: *Debra Tenuta*
*Associates Printing Service, Inc.*
Restaurant: *Children's Menu*
*Squash Blossom*
*Hyatt Regency Scottsdale*
*Scottsdale, AZ*

While playing off the main menu's color scheme and Southwestern scheme, this menu is uniquely designed for children on several different levels.

On one side, a Kachina doll waits to be colored and taken home for use as a cut-out, stand-up souvenir of the visit. On the other, the menu advises that, in addition to half portions of items on the main menu — available at half price, the special menu of children's favorites is available at all times.

What this means for the harassed parent traveling with a small child is that a child whose biological clock says it's time for dinner may have dinner items, even if the clock on the wall says it's time for breakfast. Copywriting and menu item names are geared to a child's vocabulary.

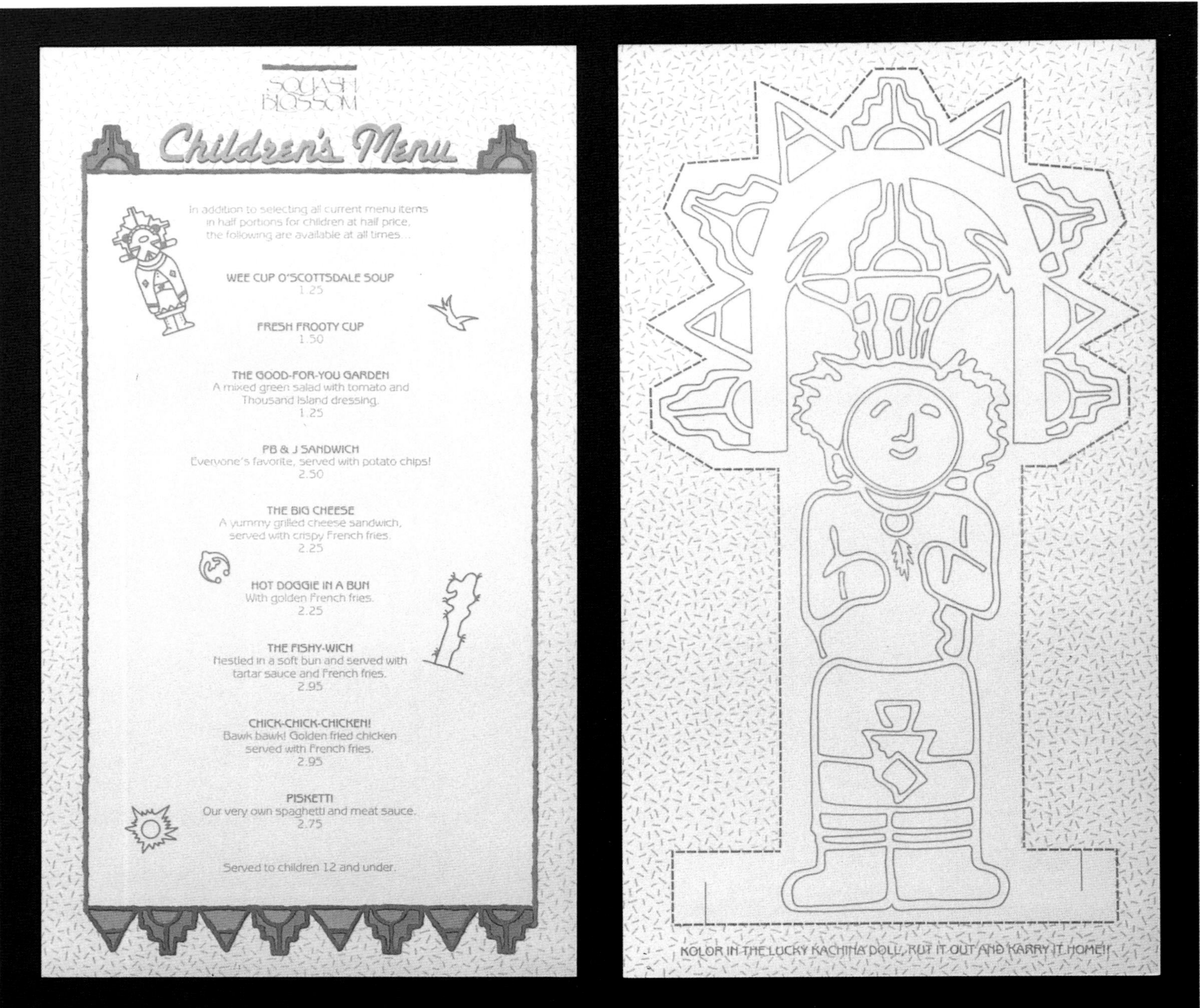

| | |
|---|---|
| Designer: | *Ron Bergner* |
| | *Howlett-Bergner and Associates* |
| Restaurant: | *Children's Menu* |
| | *Coco's* |
| | *Japan* |

This chain of simple, clean "family-style" restaurants in Japan wanted a children's menu that was American in feeling and would appeal to all children. The designer, after reviewing a broad range of Japanese children's menus, came up with this sturdy plastic-coated shell. On one side, the menu wheel spins through a scene with a doll. The price of each meal appears on one face of a die-cut alphabet block. The meal itself rotates through a die-cut plate in front of the doll.

The reverse of the shell features a space ship with a lovable alien. Here, the menu item appears in the center window of the ship, the price, as part of the control panel readouts.

For more sophisticated children, the menu also appears in written form on each side.

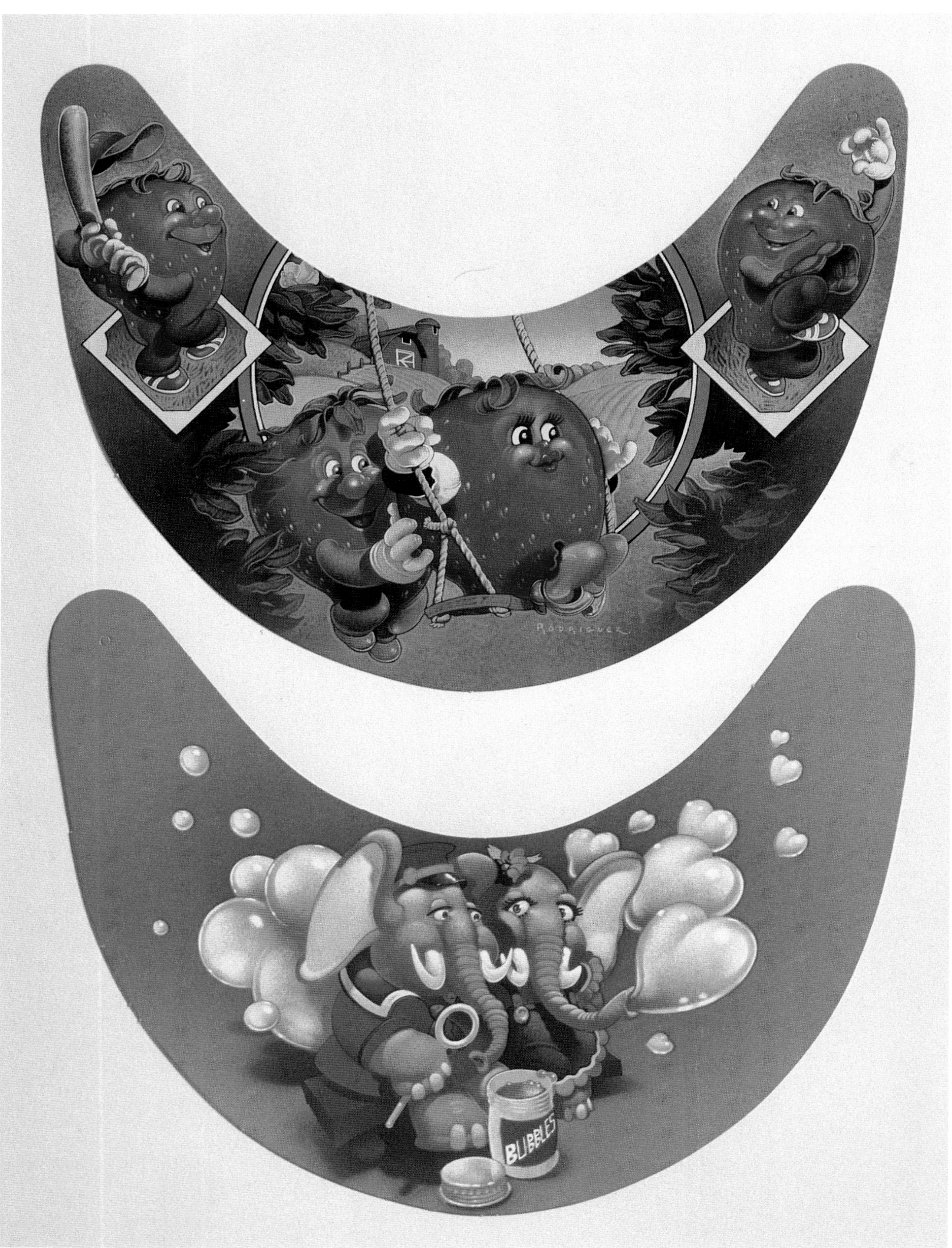
RODRIGUEZ
BUBBLES

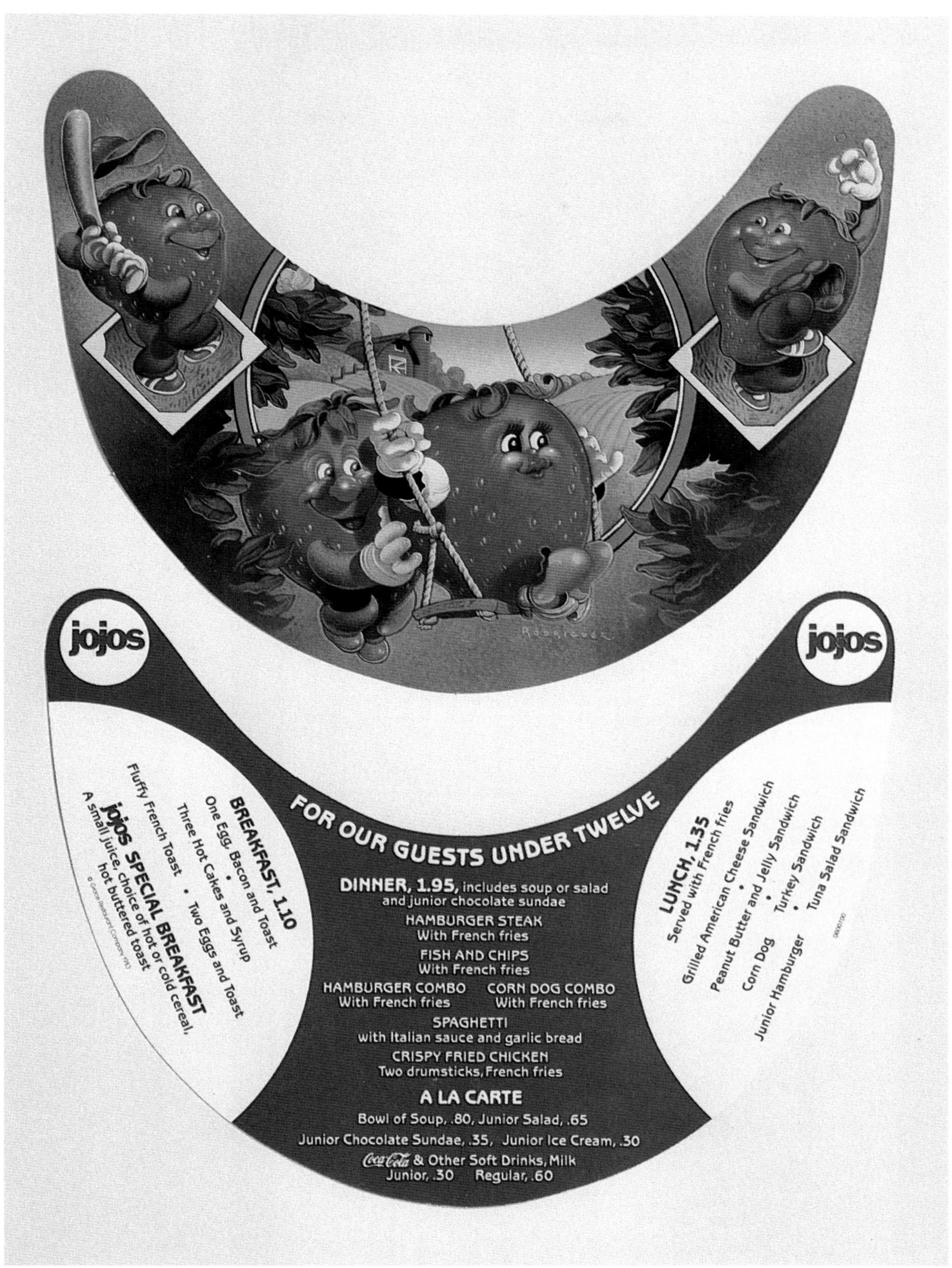


| | |
|---|---|
| Designer: | *Ron Bergner* |
| | *Howlett-Bergner and Associates* |
| Restaurant: | *Children's Menu* |
| | *Jojo's/Coco's* |
| | *Irvine, CA* |

Designed to be taken home, outfitted with string and used as a visor, these menus are periodically redesigned to prevent boredom.

Using playful and imaginative images, the menus are printed four-color on one side, one color with some types reversed on the other.

Designing the menus to be taken home provides the restaurant with a secondary marketing device. The hope is that the entertainment value of the piece will provide an impetus to return.

Ll eopard Lady
Chocolate chips, orange sherbet and vanilla ice cream for a roaring good time. $1.75
Tt ropical Island
Banana, coconut cream and fresh orange juice for a refreshing tangy delight. $1.75
Cc hocolate Coconut Caboose
Milk chocolate, coconut and almonds make a flavorful chocolatey drink. $1.75
Cc herry Chocolate Tree
Chocolate and cherry syrups and chocolate ice cream with bits of maraschino cherries. $1.75
Bb anana Kong
A colorful, fruity drink of strawberries, bananas, orange sherbet and vanilla ice cream. $1.75
Pp eppermint Panther
Tastes like a chocolate peppermint patty shake. $1.75


Designer: *Woody Pirtle*
*Pirtle Design*

Restaurant: *Children's Menu*
*T.G.I. Friday's*
*Addison, TX*

**1987 N.R.A. GREAT MENUS CONTEST WINNER: FIRST PLACE, SPECIALTY**

Using a combination of crayoned "children's" drawings and both capital and lower case letters of the alphabet, this menu provides a creative means of involving the child in choosing his or her own food.

Many of the illustrations are funny. The entire menu is produced on a series of plastic-coated cards held together with a binder ring, reminiscent of the "flash cards" used in school. This format is both durable and easily updated. The bright colors and imaginative drawings make it appealing.

Hh ot Dog Platter
A grilled hot dog on a toasted bun with fries and thin onion rings. $1.95
Aa round the World Burger
A smaller version of Friday's burgers on a toasted sesame bun with fries and thin onion rings. $2.75
Cc hicken Little
Breast of Chicken breaded and deep fried, on a toasted sesame bun with fries and thin onion rings. $2.60

Designer: *Kensington Falls*
*Family Communications, Inc.*
Restaurant: *Eat 'n Park Restaurants, Inc.*
*Pittsburgh, PA*

**1987 N.R.A. GREAT MENUS CONTEST WINNER: SECOND PLACE, SPECIALTY**

Menus that are also flip charts are one way to entertain a child waiting for his meal. The illustrations of the food items also permit even very young children to participate in choosing their own meals. The menus are colorful and, more to the point, small enough to be comfortably held in small hands.

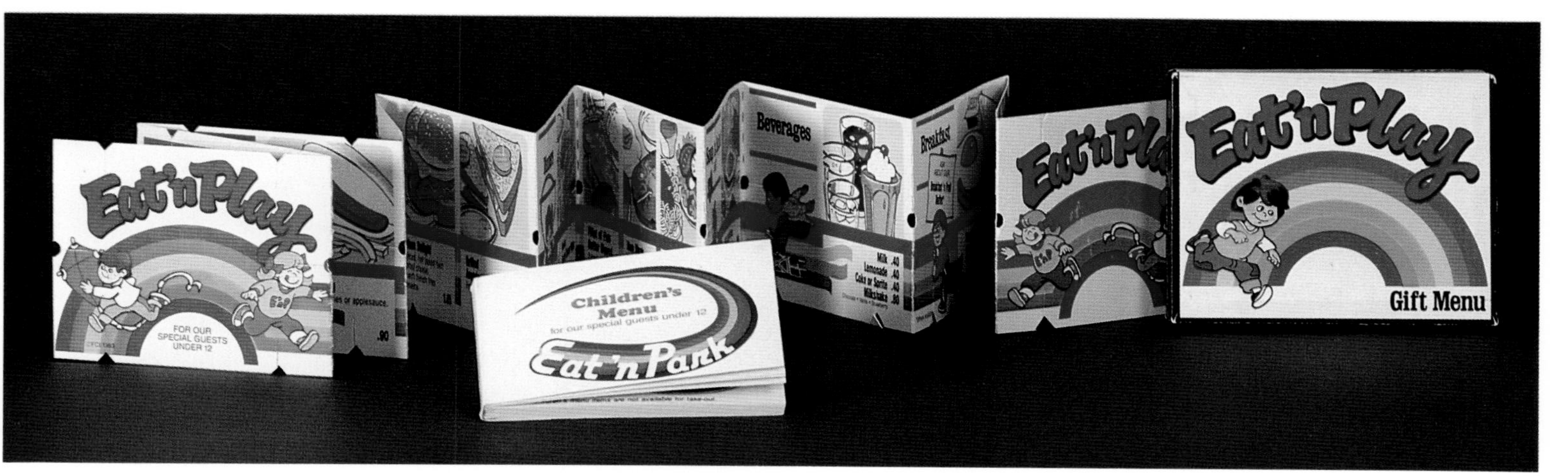
Eat'n Play
FOR OUR SPECIAL GUESTS UNDER 12
Children's Menu
for our special guests under 12
Eat'n Park
Beverages
Eat'n Play
Gift Menu

Pancake Special
Two pancakes with warm syrup, two strips of bacon or two sausage links.
1.20

Boneless Breaded Chicken Fillets
French fries, applesauce and roll.
1.95

## MUNCHIES

POTATO SKINS
Crisply Fried and Covered with Cheese, Bacon Bits, Chives and Sour Cream.
3.95

MACHO NACHOS
Crisp Tortilla Chips Mounded High and Covered with Jalapeño Cheese and Spicy Beef, Served with Guacamole and Salsa Sauce.
4.75

BUFFALO WINGS
Chicken Wings Crispy and Spicy Accompanied with Celery Sticks and Our Special Seasoned Sauce.
4.50

SHRIMP COCKTAIL
Six Huge Gulf Shrimp
Served with Our Tangy Cocktail Sauce.
7.95

OYSTERS
A Half-Dozen Freshly Shucked Oysters
Served with Oyster Crackers.
5.95

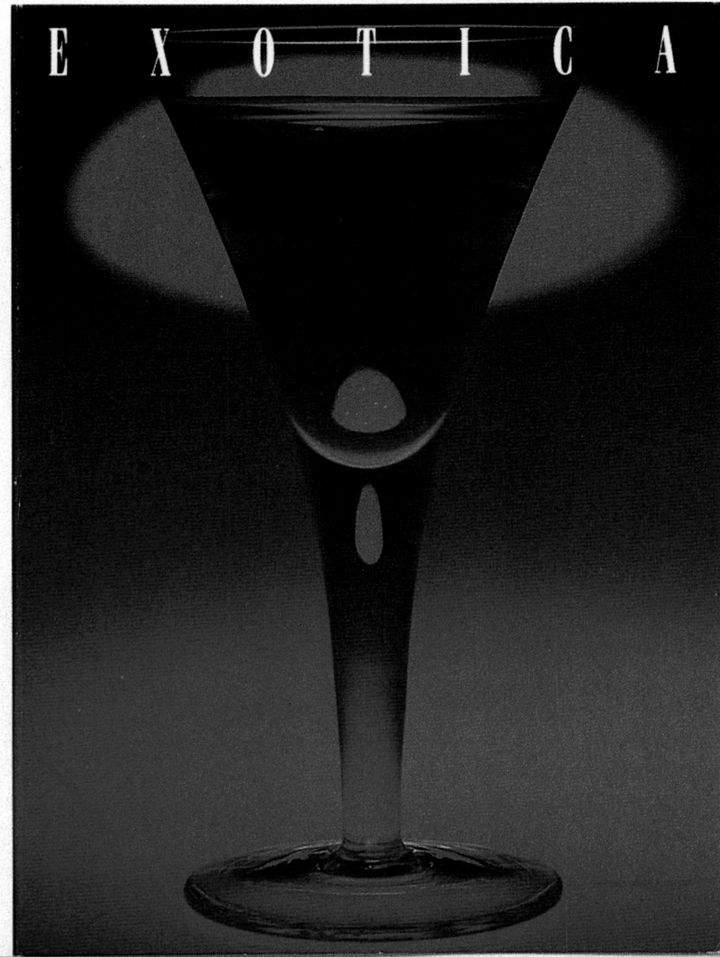


**Designer:** *Donna Milord*
*Associates Printing Service, Inc.*
**Restaurant:** *Table Tent*
*Hyatt Regency Chicago*
*Chicago, IL*

Exquisite photography and an unusual color combination let this menu sell ambience as much as the drinks and accompaniments it offers.

Interior design is simple. The second color is used only for holding lines, the main color, a deep blue, for the type. The type is set in a relatively large size for readability in dim light conditions.

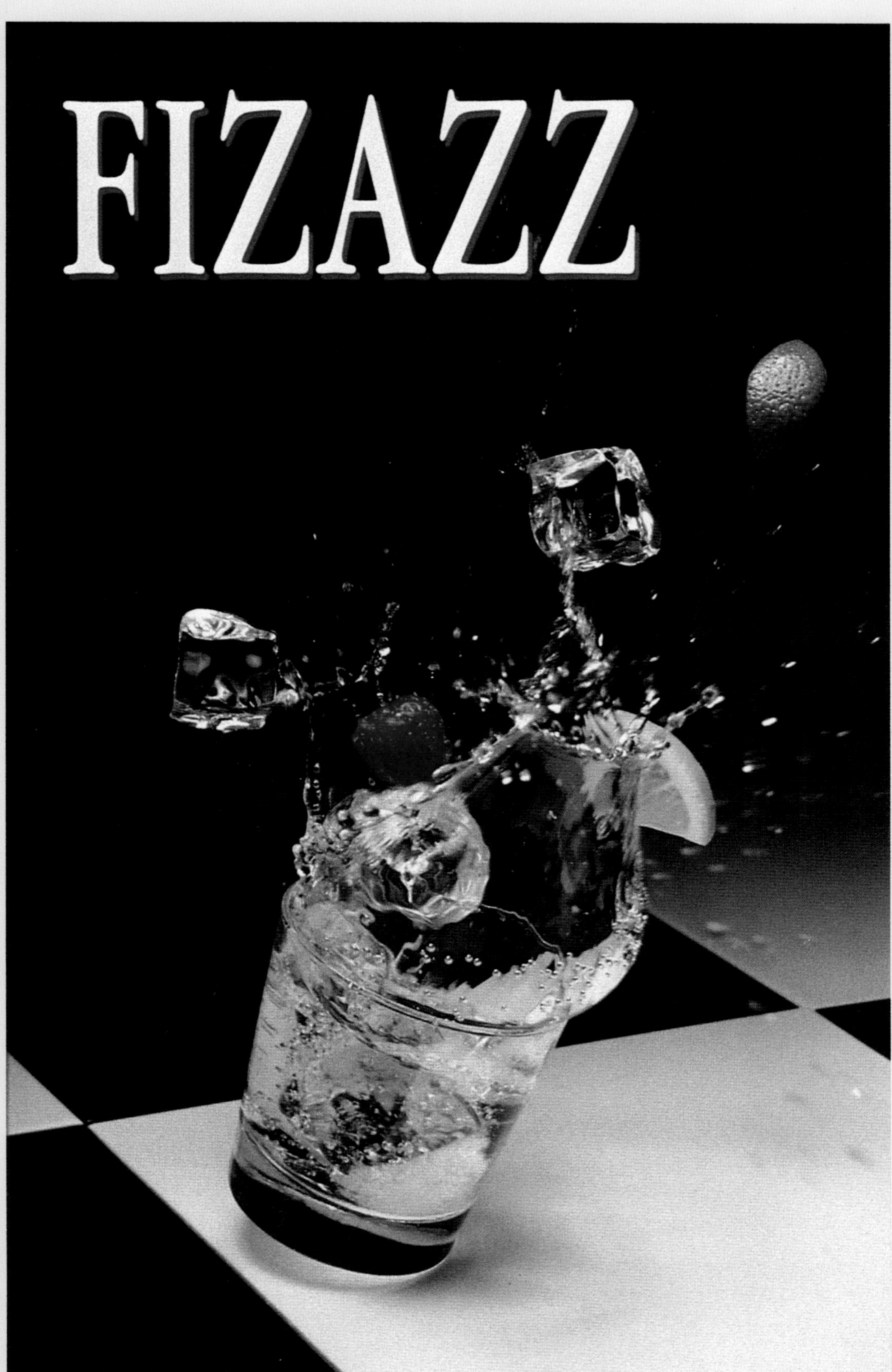


**Designer:** *Georgia Korzenowski*
*Associates Printing Service, Inc.*
**Restaurant:** *Corporate Drink Menu*
*Hyatt Hotels Corporation*
*Chicago, IL*

Vivid color photography sets the mood for this drink menu. The ice cubes, fruit and liquid flying through the air against the simple black and white background evoke excitement and daring in the consumer.

In keeping with current trends, a full selection of low-alcohol and non-alcoholic specialties is offered.

The two-color copy specifies the brands used in each drink to assure high quality. Among the sparkling wines offered is a special "Hyatt Cuvée" produced by one of America's premier sparkling wine specialists.

**BURNETTI**
1ST PRIZE
Created by Brendan Ryan
CAMPARI
CANADIAN CLUB
GRAND MARNIER
ORANGE JUICE
SODA WATER $7.50

**MISSISSIPPI AFFAIR**
2ND PRIZE
Created by Tony Lui
SOUTHERN COMFORT
TIA MARIA
COCONUT LIQUEUR
CREAM $7.50

**SLIGHTLY JADED**
3RD PRIZE
Created by Matthew Shakeshaft
GRAND MARNIER
MIDORI MELON LIQUEUR
BLUE CURACAO
PINEAPPLE JUICE
LEMON JUICE $7.50

**LE MIRAGE**
Created by Suzanne Albert
SMIRNOFF VODKA
MIDORI MELON LIQUEUR
CREME DE MENTHE
HONEY-DEW MELON $7.50

**PINK PASSION**
Created by Glyn Lewis
CAMPARI
GRAND MARNIER
MALIBU
PINEAPPLE JUICE
CREAM
FRESH STRAWBERRIES $7.50

**CARIBBEAN QUEEN**
Created by Robert Berg
SMIRNOFF VODKA
TIA MARIA
CREAM
CREME DE BANANE
FRESH BANANA $7.50

These original cocktails were created by the Bartenders of Hilton International Australia for the SWIFT & MOORE/HILTON Cocktail Competition.

Designer: *Simmon Wooller*
Restaurant: *Table Tents*
*Juliana's Supperclub*
*Hilton International Sydney*
*Sydney, Australia*

These drink menus feature entries for a drink competition. The first, second and third prize winners, created by the hotel's bartenders, are included.

The menus themselves feature a coated black stock with copy reversed in both bright colors and white. The Supperclub itself is an elegant discotheque/supperclub. The decor uses black marble table tops and a pink and grey color scheme to produce an elegant atmosphere. The pastel lines used in the images on the cover are repeated as section heads in the interior.

Designer: *Lanny Sommese*
*Lanny Sommese Design*
Restaurant: *Opening Announcement*
*Tussey Mountain Inn*
*State College, PA*

This matched-fold announcement was distributed at other restaurants owned by the same organization to announce the opening of this new restaurant at a local ski area.

The announcement uses creative illustrations with only one ink to make an interesting statement. The paper used has a beautiful ribbed finish.

The designer noted, somewhat ironically, that registration was important. Since the piece is designed to reveal one illustration when closed and another, based on half of the cover illustration, when open, registration was not merely important, but critical.

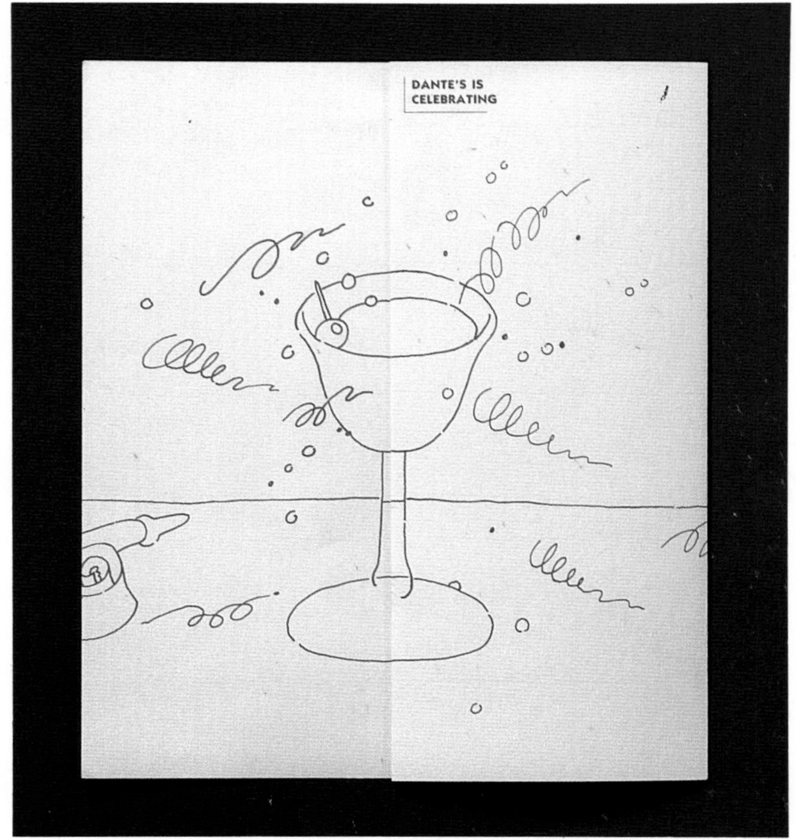

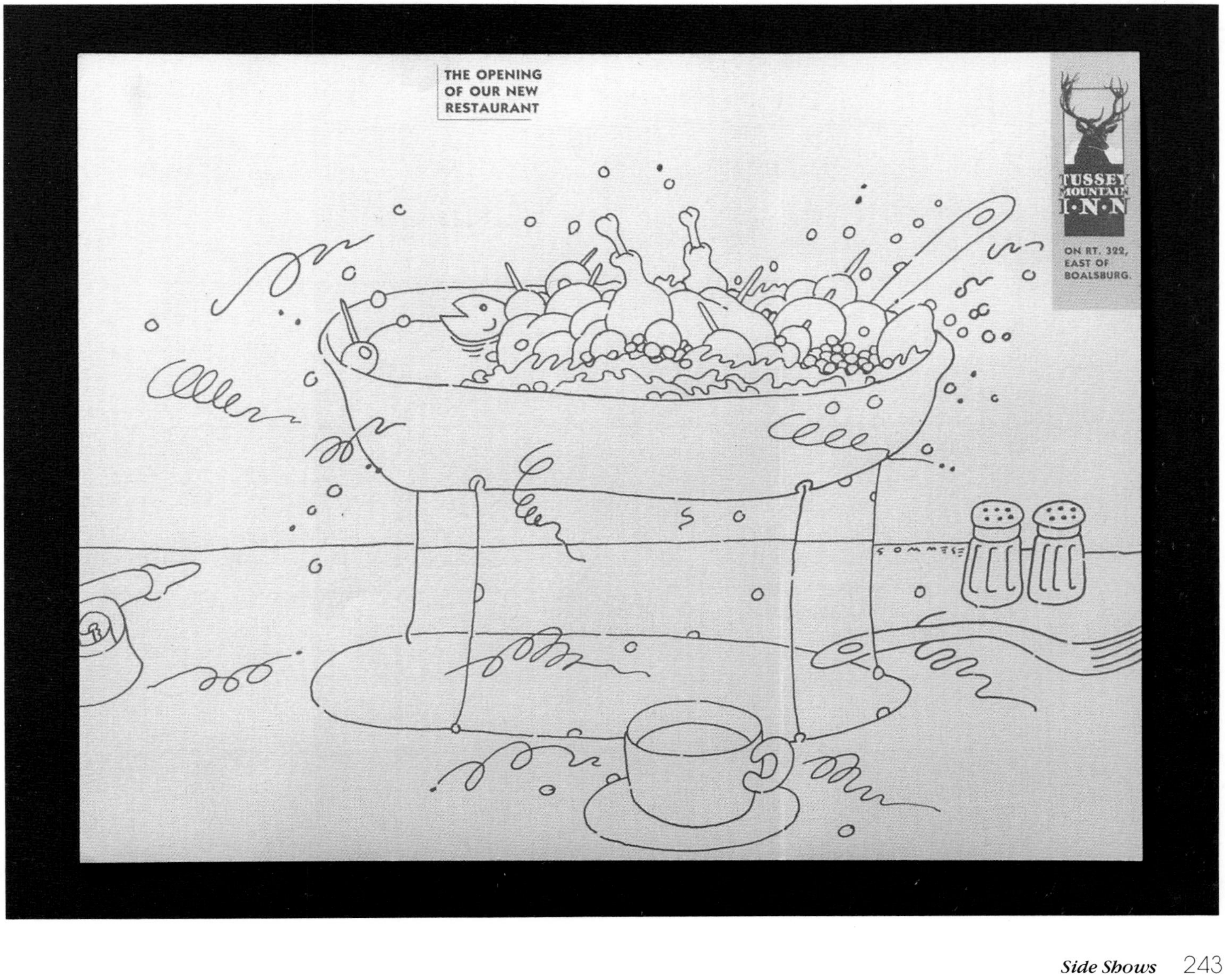

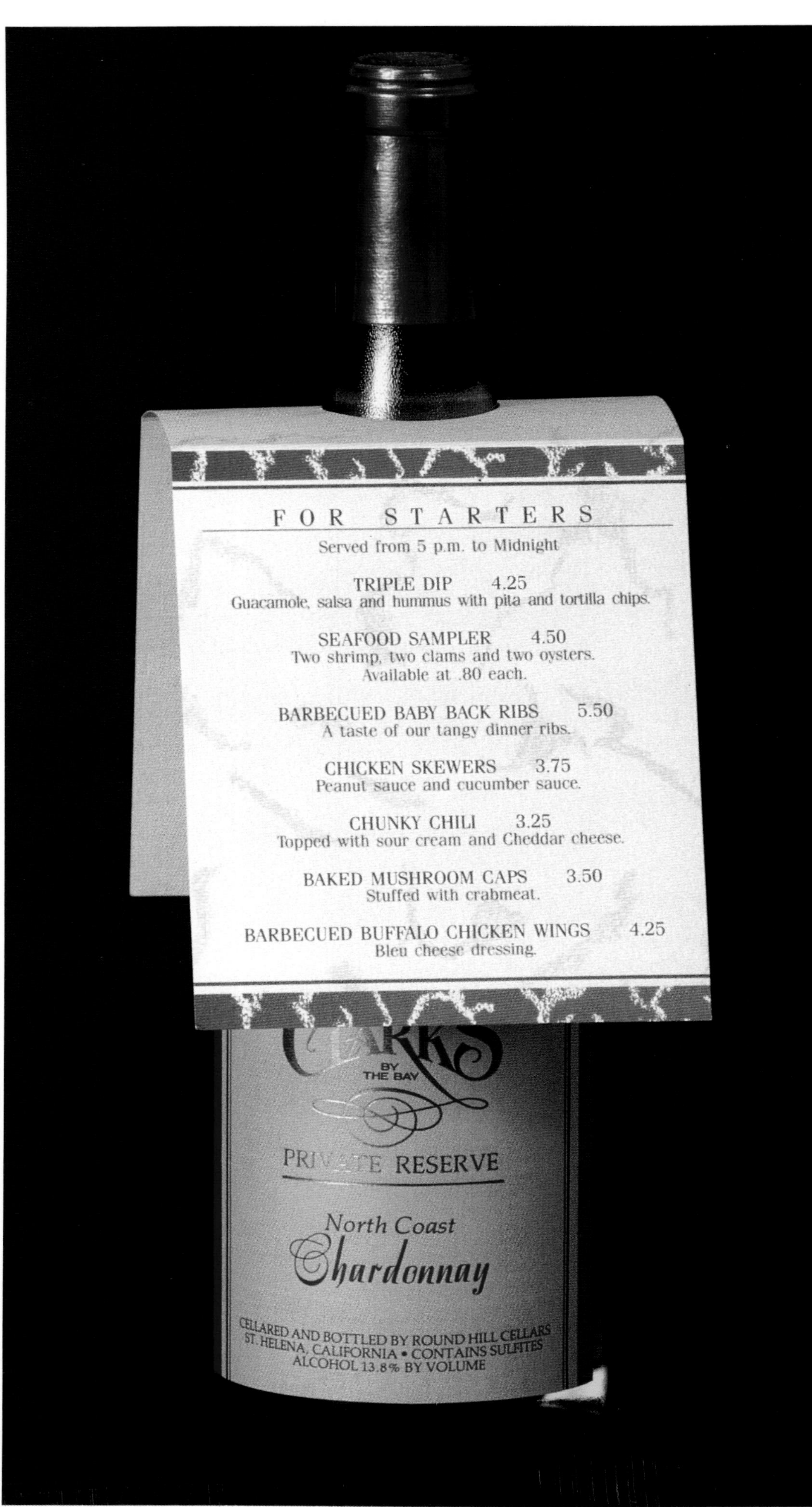

FOR STARTERS
Served from 5 p.m. to Midnight
TRIPLE DIP 4.25
Guacamole, salsa and hummus with pita and tortilla chips.
SEAFOOD SAMPLER 4.50
Two shrimp, two clams and two oysters.
Available at .80 each.
BARBECUED BABY BACK RIBS 5.50
A taste of our tangy dinner ribs.
CHICKEN SKEWERS 3.75
Peanut sauce and cucumber sauce.
CHUNKY CHILI 3.25
Topped with sour cream and Cheddar cheese.
BAKED MUSHROOM CAPS 3.50
Stuffed with crabmeat.
BARBECUED BUFFALO CHICKEN WINGS 4.25
Bleu cheese dressing.
BY THE BAY
RESERVE
North Coast
Chardonnay
CELLARED AND BOTTLED BY ROUND HILL CELLARS
ST. HELENA, CALIFORNIA • CONTAINS SULFITES
ALCOHOL 13.8% BY VOLUME


**Designer:** *Greg Border*
*Associates Printing Service, Inc.*

**Restaurant:** *Table Tent*
*10 Huntington Bar & Grill*
*Westin Hotel Copley Plaza*
*Boston, MA*

This piece is less a table tent than a wine bottle pinafore. Designed to fit over the neck of a 750 ml wine bottle, it promotes snacks on one, pre-printed side. The other side is designed to accommodate a hand-printed list of daily selections of wines by-the-glass.

The marble-look background screen, using only two colors, lends a note of elegance to the otherwise simple presentation.

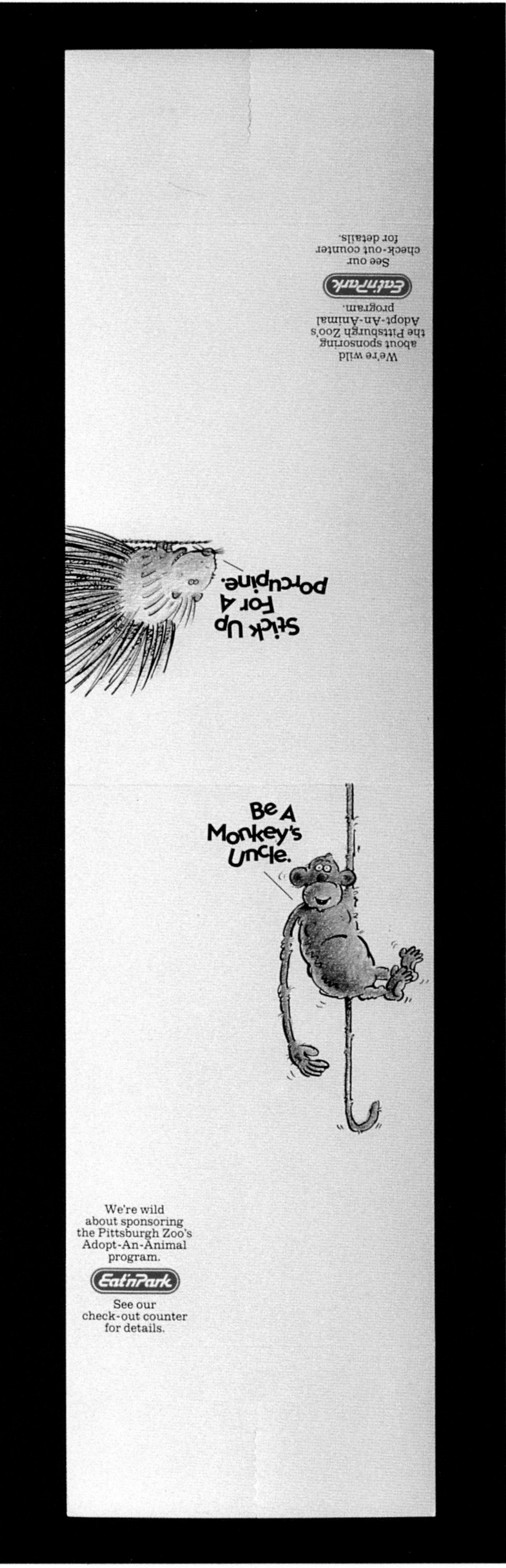


Designer: *Craig Otto*
*Ketchum Communications*
Restaurant: *Table Tents*
*Eat 'n Park Restaurants, Inc.*
*Pittsburgh, PA*

**1987 N.R.A. GREAT MENUS CONTEST WINNER: THIRD PLACE, SPECIALTY**

The restaurant chain has cleverly entertwined its charitable contributions and its marketing efforts via these entertaining table tents. Though few businesses acknowledge it, charity is one way to keep one's name — and the associated memories — in the public view.

Both imaginative illustrations and idealized photography have been brought to bear on the designs of these table tents. In the one advertising a new bakery addition, a die-cut rolling pin adds interest. All the table tents discreetly incorporate the restaurant logo and feature novel copywriting.

# PESO'S

## MEXICAN GRILL

329 Sixth Avenue
(at 3rd Street)
New York, N.Y. 10014

**675-0101**

Hours: Monday–Thursday, 11 AM–11 PM
Friday–Saturday, 11 AM–2 AM
Sunday, 12 PM–10 PM

102 East 25th Street
(at Park Ave. South)
New York, N.Y. 10010

**674-PESO**

Hours: Monday–Friday, 11 AM–10 PM
Saturday, 11 AM–9 PM

**FREE DELIVERY**

AUTHENTIC MEXICAN FOOD
WITH MADE FOR AMERICA TASTE.

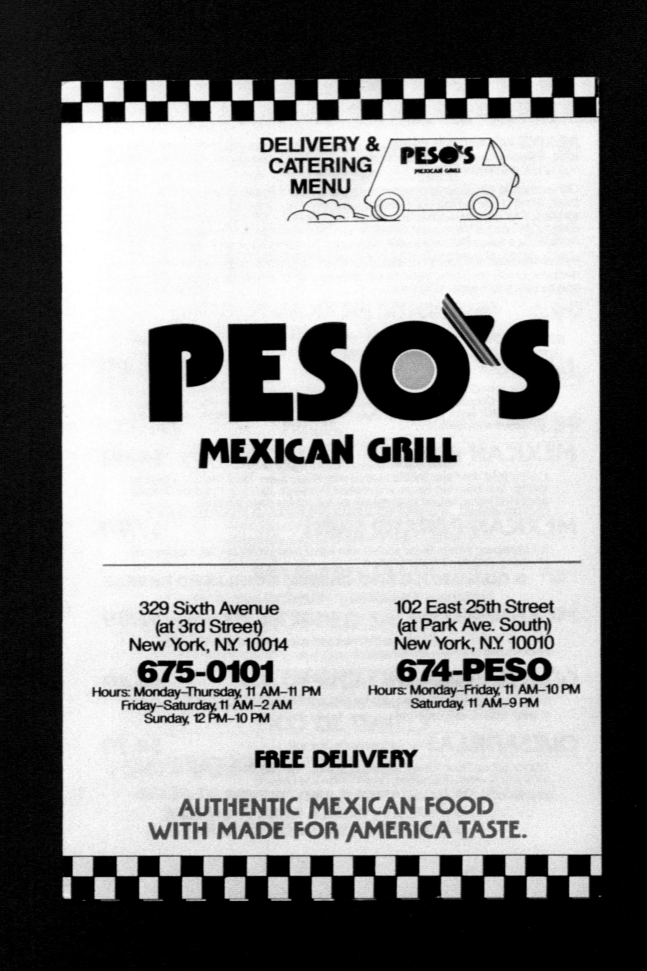

Designer: *Horatio Marketing*
Restaurant: *Delivery & Catering Menu*
*Peso's Mexican Grill*
*New York, NY*

**1987 N.R.A. GREAT MENUS CONTEST WINNER: SECOND PLACE, UNDER $5**

The excitement of Mexico is captured on this catering and delivery menu. Printed three colors over two on inexpensive paper, it is nonetheless effective. The logo of a speeding delivery truck lends a sense of urgency to the cover design. The black and white checkerboard pattern makes it "high style."

In addition to serving as a menu, the piece is designed as a self-mailer to accommodate the needs of busy executives and party planners in New York City.

**PESO'S MEXICAN GRILL** is a dazzling new concept in gourmet Mexican food. It's designed for Americans on the move who insist on fine quality food that's nutritious, convenient, and rich in flavor.

Our authentic Mexican entrees featuring marinated Steak, breast of Chicken and fresh Shrimp are grilled right before your eyes and served sizzling hot on fresh tortillas. Our special appetizers are all large enough for two, and are smothered with 100% natural Wisconsin Cheddar and Monterey Jack Cheese. And, at Peso's we feature a Salsa Bar so you can spice up your dish to suit your special taste.

Peso's Mexican Grill uses no added salt, lard or artificial ingredients in any of our recipes. Once you sink your teeth into any of our freshly prepared Mexican specialties, you'll experience our...

**AUTHENTIC MEXICAN FOOD WITH MADE FOR AMERICA TASTE.**

**NACHOS** Regular **$2.49** Grande **$3.99**

REGULAR—Crispy Corn Tortillas smothered with Melted Monterey Jack and Cheddar Cheese, sprinkled with Jalapeno slices: GRANDE—Regular Nachos layered with Beef, Beans and Guacamole, garnished with chopped scallions, tomatoes and olives.

**MEXICAN PIZZA** (6") **$2.79** (10") **$4.49**

Lightly fried, flat Flour Tortilla layered with Black Beans and Cheese, a second tortilla, Mexican Red Sauce and melted Monterey Jack and Cheddar Cheese, garnished with chopped scallions, olives and freshly diced tomatoes.

**MEXICAN POTATO SKINS** **$2.99**

Six seasoned Potato Skins stuffed with either Guacamole or Chili, topped with Monterey Jack or Cheddar Cheese.

CHOOSE ONE: ● **GUACAMOLE AND CHEESE** ● **CHILI AND CHEESE**

**MEXI-WINGS** 6 Piece **$2.29** 9 Piece **$2.99**

Fiery hot chicken wings, prepared in a hot and spicy marinade, served on a luscious bed of lettuce and tomato.

**GUACAMOLE AND CHIPS** **$4.49**

Fresh Avocado, Cilantro and Onion blended in a delicate puree, served on a bed of crisp lettuce, accompanied by warm Tortilla Chips.

**QUESADILLAS** **$4.79**

Lightly grilled Flour Tortilla filled with Guacamole and Cheese, Tomato, Green Chili and Cheese, or Chicken, Green Onion and Cheese.

CHOOSE ONE:
- **GUACAMOLE AND CHEESE**
- **TOMATO, GREEN CHILI & CHEESE**
- **CHICKEN, GREEN ONION & CHEESE**

**BURRITOS** **$1.99**

Soft Flour Tortilla rolled with Beef, Bean and Cheese or Black Beans and Cheese.

CHOOSE ONE:
- **BEEF, BEAN AND CHEESE**
- **BEAN AND CHEESE**

**BURRITOS** Grande **$4.49**

Soft flour Tortilla stuffed with Chicken and Cheese or Charbroiled Steak and Cheese, served with lettuce and tomato.

CHOOSE ONE:
- **CHARBROILED STEAK AND CHEESE**
- **CHARBROILED CHICKEN AND CHEESE**

**SOFT SHELL TACOS** **$4.79**

Marinated, charbroiled Chicken, Steak, Guacamole or Shrimp served open-faced on two soft Flour Tortillas, garnished with lettuce, tomato, grilled scallion and lime, accompanied by mild or spicy homemade Salsa.

CHOOSE ONE:
- **CHARBROILED CHICKEN**
- **CHARBROILED STEAK**
- **CHARBROILED SHRIMP**
- **GUACAMOLE**

**TACO SALADS** **$4.79**

Crispy Flour Tortilla shaped in a basket, layered with beans, shredded lettuce and tomato, Beef, Chicken, or Guacamole; sprinkled with grated Cheddar Cheese, scallions, olives.

CHOOSE ONE:
- **BEEF**
- **CHICKEN**
- **GUACAMOLE**

**PLATTERS** Regular **$5.49** Grande **$7.49**

REGULAR—Any entree served with Rice and Beans; GRANDE—Includes Regular Nachos or Mexican Potato Skins, as an appetizer.

CHOOSE ONE:
- **TACO**
- **BURRITO**

**CHILI** **$4.79**

Chunks of Beef, Beans and fresh Chiles simmered in a spicy tomato sauce, topped with shredded Cheddar Cheese and Onions, served with Tortilla Chips.

**CATERING**

Peso's Mexican Grill proudly introduces its catering service. It's designed for busy executives and party-givers who insist on fine quality food that is delivered hot to your door. Our catering staff will deliver and set up your meeting/party with plates, napkins, placemats, and all your favorite Mexican dishes. All orders must be placed 12 hours in advance of delivery. We deliver anywhere in Manhattan!

**CALL 675-0101**

**"MEXI-LITE" LUNCH** **$7.50** PER PERSON
Minimum Order: 8 people

- Guacamole and Chips
- Assorted Quesadilla Platter
- Taco Salad (1 per person)
  Beef, Chicken or Guacamole
- Flan
- Assortment of Homemade Salsas

**"MEXI-CALE" LUNCH** **$8.50** PER PERSON
Minimum Order: 8 people

- Regular Nachos
- Assorted Potato Skins Platter
- Burritos (1 per person)
  Beef, Chicken or Bean
- Mexican Side Salad
- Pesitos
- Assortment of Homemade Salsas
- Tortilla Chips

**"FIESTA" PLATTER** **$8.00** PER PERSON
Minimum Order: 8 people

MIXED APPETIZERS, AN ASSORTMENT OF:
- Deluxe Nachos
- Guacamole and Chips
- Assorted Quesadilla Platter
- Mexican Pizza
- Assorted Potato Skins Platter
- Assortment of Homemade Salsas

● **RESTAURANT AVAILABLE FOR PARTIES** ●
● **ASK ABOUT OUR CHARGE ACCOUNTS** ●

Designer: *Jack Biesek*
*Biesek Design*
Restaurant: *Dessert Menu*
*Jeremiah's*
*12 locations from Palm Springs to Houston*

This coated menu uses stylized illustrations and creative copywriting to sell desserts, coffees, teas and coffee- and tea-based after dinner drinks.

A granite-look background provides the base for a pastel menu. Clear, readable type makes the menu easy to follow. The coating makes it durable. The luscious illustrations make it hard on the diet.

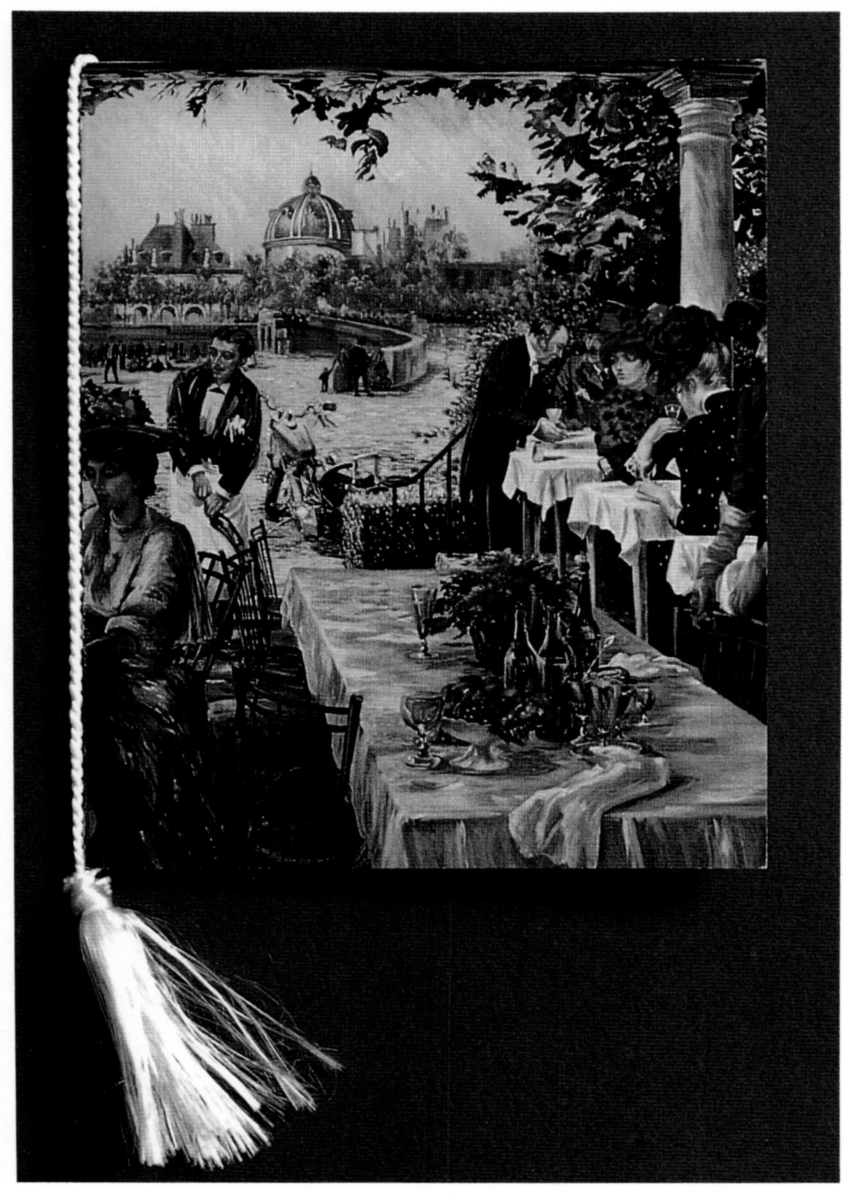

| | |
|---|---|
| Designer: | *Allen Eisbrenner* |
| | *Associates Printing Service, Inc.* |
| Restaurant: | *"Les Celebrités"* |
| | *Hotel Nikko* |
| | *Chicago, IL* |

This elegant little wine list uses a wraparound illustration of nineteenth century Paris as its cover. The simple insert, imprinted in two colors, features a limited but well-chosen selection. Held in place with a fabric cord, the insert can be inexpensively reprinted to reflect the changing contents of the wine cellar.

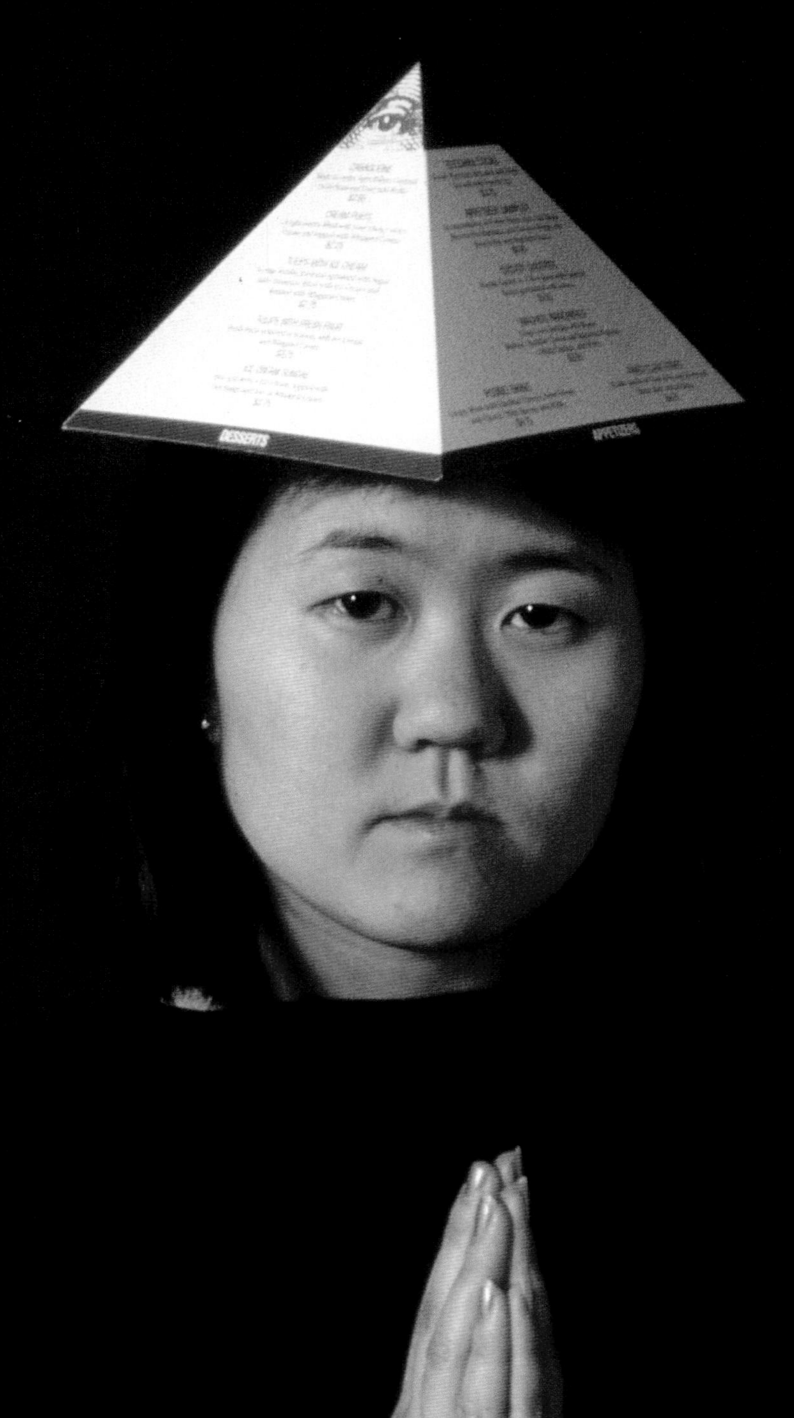
DESSERTS
APPETIZERS

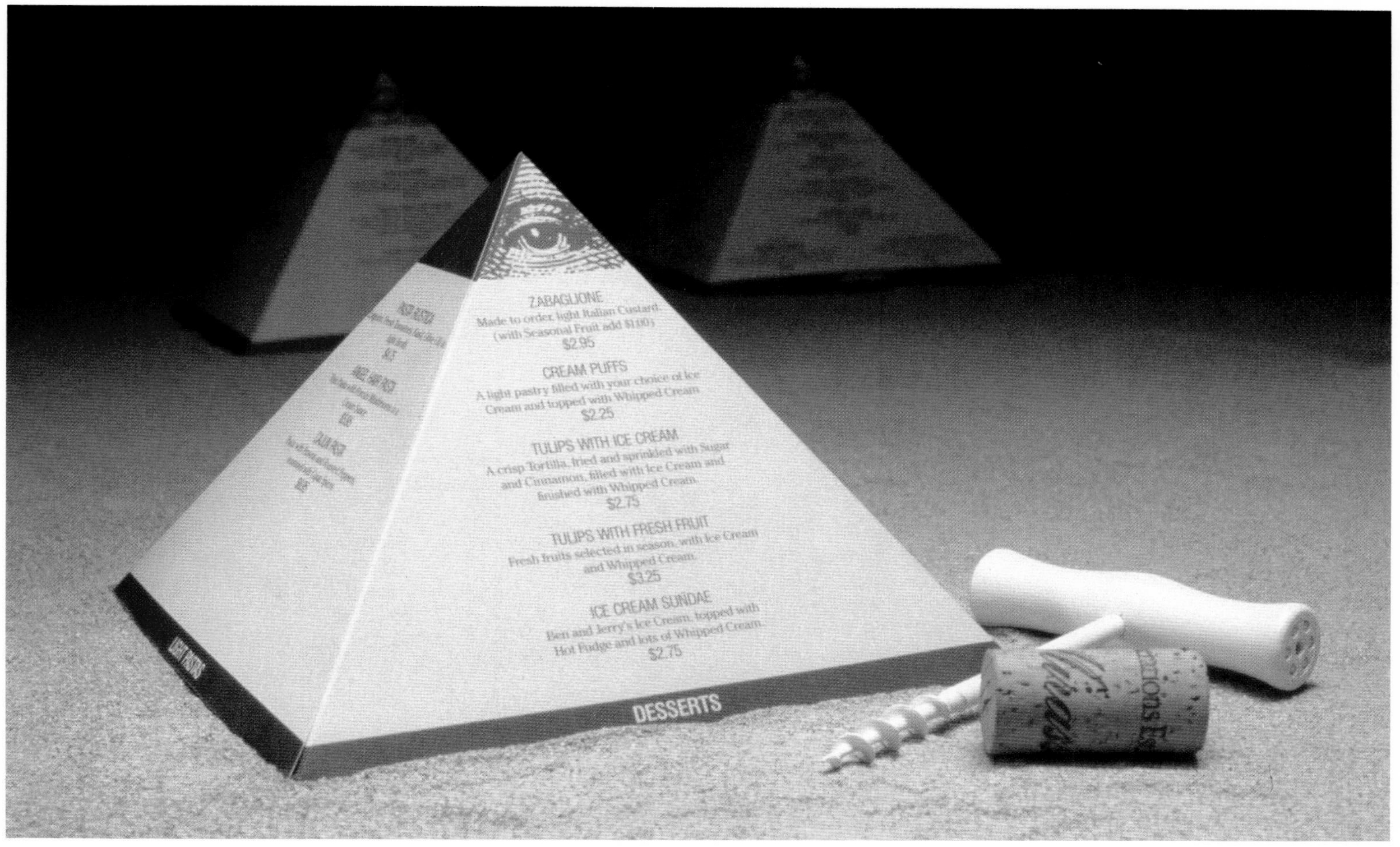

ZABAGLIONE
Made to order, light Italian Custard.
(with Seasonal Fruit add $1.00)
$2.95
CREAM PUFFS
A light pastry filled with your choice of Ice
Cream and topped with Whipped Cream
$2.25
TULIPS WITH ICE CREAM
A crisp Tortilla, fried and sprinkled with Sugar
and Cinnamon, filled with Ice Cream and
finished with Whipped Cream.
$2.75
TULIPS WITH FRESH FRUIT
Fresh fruits selected in season, with Ice Cream
and Whipped Cream.
$3.25
ICE CREAM SUNDAE
Ben and Jerry's Ice Cream, topped with
Hot Fudge and lots of Whipped Cream.
$2.75
DESSERTS


**Designer:** *Rick Tharp*
*Tharp Did It*
**Restaurant:** *Table Tent*
*Eli McFly's*
*Cupertino, CA*

This little pyramid (complete with eye) is a creative way to market light meals, appetizers and desserts.

The menu, printed in three colors, uses a very clean typeface for maximum legibility in low light situations.

The choice of a pyrimidal shape is both eye-catching and practical. Using a shape that is broader at its base than its top means that the light available will most likely strike the object flatly, without casting unpleasant shadows. This is particularly important in bars, where lighting is often dim.

WARM UP
Steamer's Style
WHITE NUN
Brandy, Kahlua, and steamed milk
STEAMED HOG
Haagen-Dazs liqueur and steamed milk
HOUSE CAP
Brandy, Kahlua, espresso, and cream
HOLLAND EXPRESS
Haagen-Dazs liqueur and espresso
ITALIAN COFFEE
Tuaca, Dark Cacao, coffee, and coco cream
APPLE PIE
Apple cider and Rock n'Rye
CALYPSO COFFEE
Jamaican Rum, Dark Cacao, coffee, and cream
TENNESSEE MUD
Jack Daniels, Amaretto, coffee, and cream
KLONDIKE COFFEE
Yukon Jack, Dark Cacao, coffee, and coco cream
JAMAICAN COFFEE
Tia Maria, coffee, and cream
Est. 1854


Designer: *Rick Tharp*
*Tharp Did It*
Restaurant: *Table Tent*
*Steamer's, Fish Again & Pasta Too!*
*Los Gatos, CA*

Originally conceived as a promotion for Mirassou Vineyards, the oversize cork eventually became the holder for this playful drink card.

Only one color of ink has been used in the card's execution but a vibrant feeling has been obtained by reversing the ink on one side of the card. The illustration of a fish, complete with muffler and stocking cap, both pays tribute to the seafood theme of the restaurant and reinforces the idea of warming drinks in the wintertime.

| | |
|---|---|
| Designer: | *Ron Bergner* |
| | *Howlett-Bergner and Associates* |
| Restaurant: | *Table Tents* |
| | *El Torito* |
| | *Irvine, CA* |

Designed as part of a drink promotion, these table tents are well-suited to the Mexican theme of these restaurants. The toucan fits into an existing table tent holder. The various drink promotions can be easily slipped into his beak.

The bright colors impart a cheerful, festive feeling to the whole promotion. All are printed on one side only. Scoring, die cuts and slots permit easy assembly of each piece.

# Appendix *Manufacturing Information*

*In Order Of Appearance*

**Corona Bar & Grill** *Finished size:* 10″x16″, 8 1/2″x11″, 2″x3 1/2″. *Paper stock and weight:* 12 pt. Spring Hill cover. *Finishing techniques:* 4/c process blue; die cut; copper foil; laminated. *Printer:* Fong & Fong Printing, Sacramento, CA.

**Royal Viking Line/Wine Menu** *Finished size:* 10 3/4″x6 1/2″. *Paper stock and weight:* Sundance Natural 65 lb. cover. *Finishing techniques:* Foil stamp. *Printer:* Goff & Associates, San Francisco, CA.

**Royal Viking Line/Gala Bon Voyage** *Finished size:* 12″x4 1/4″. *Paper stock and weight:* Vintage Gloss White 80 lb. cover.

**Royal Viking Line/Grand Circle Pacific** *Finished size:* 9″x12″. *Paper stock and weight:* Currency Gold Cover, Strathmore, Grand Balboa Blue, 80 lb. cover. *Finishing techniques:* Foil stamp; Actual menus are imprinted on board, on parchment and inserted into covers with gold elastic cord.

**Arrowhead Hilton** *Finished size:* 16″ Beach Ball. *Finishing techniques:* Silkscreened.

**Captain Streeter's Outdoor Cafe** *Finished size:* 5″x7″. *Paper stock and weight:* Starwhite Vicksburg 120 lb. *Finishing techniques:* Laminated.

**Hiway Pizza Pub** *Paper stock and weight:* 10 pt. kromecote. *Finishing techniques:* Score and Accordion fold, 2 color. *Printer:* Nittany Valley Offset, State College, PA.

**Pogocha** *Finished size:* 5 1/2″x7″. *Paper stock and weight:* Productolith 80 lb. offset. *Printer:* The Litho House, Seattle, WA.

**California Place/Table Tents** *Finished size:* 4 5/8″x9 1/2″. *Paper stock and weight:* 2/65 Bright White Rhododendron. *Finishing techniques:* Double marcoated. *Printer:* Kenyon Press, Los Angeles, CA.

**Bennigan's** *Finished size:* 6″x12 1/2″. *Paper stock and weight:* Kimdura 250 FP6. *Finishing techniques:* 4/color process, 2 pms colors, tint varnish. *Printer:* Hicks Printing, Garland, TX.

**Tokyo Hilton International/Marble Lounge (Lobby Lounge)** *Menu size:* 20 cm x 18 cm. *Paper:* Coated two-sided paper and art paper. *Printer:* Design Studio, Ltd., Tokyo, Japan.

**Dante's Restaurants Inc./Calling Card** *Finished size:* (w) 2″ x (h) 3 3/4″ folded. *Paper stock and weight:* Strathmore 65 lb. cover. *Finishing techniques:* Score & Fold. *Printer:* Commercial Printing, State College, PA.

**La Fiesta** *Finished size:* 9 1/2″x14″. *Paper stock and weight:* Art Gloss 12 pt. *Finishing techniques:* 1/2 mill lamination.

**San Francisco Grill/Dessert Menu** *Finished size:* 50 cm x 37 cm. *Paper stock and weight: Cover*—440 GSM Belgian. 2 sides, *Kromekote*—high gloss white. *Insert*—250 GSM Shogun Premium. Matte artboard. *Finishing techniques:* Four-color printed with hot stamping in matte white, and embossed. *Printer:* Star Condor Press, St. Peter's, New South Wales.

**Tycoons/Lunch** *Finished size:* 12″x18″. *Paper stock and weight:* 80 lb. mattecoated cover. *Finishing techniques: Lamination*—3 mil Five cover (30 process) over two cover masters 1 cover imprint/2 sides. *Printer:* Boca Raton Printing Co., Boca Raton, FL.

**Grisanti's Casual Italian Restaurant** *Finished size:* 4 3/4″(w) x 12 1/2″ (h). *Paper stock and weight:* Artemis Sandstone 80 lb. cover—line illustration. *Finishing techniques:* 4 panel scored with gatefold and single fold 1.5 mil lamination. *Paper stock and weight:* for 4-color illustration version Artemis Ivory 80 lb. cover. *Printer:* Lipps-National Corp., New Albany, IN.

**Jim's of Austin-Frontier Enterprises** *Finished size:* 9″x14″. *Paper stock and weight:* Lustro Dull cover 100 lb. *Printer:* Communications Specialists.

**MVPs** *Finished size:* 6 1/2″x11″. *Paper stock and weight:* Color dividers—12 pt. Kromecote cover—2 sides coated. *Finishing techniques:* Menu sheets—80 lb. Paloma. Covers—Customcote, President Finishes. *Printer:* Color by Blake Printery (menu sheet—Canterbury Graphics), San Luis Obispo, CA.

**Space Needle/Specialty Menus** *Finished size:* 9″x9″. *Paper stock and weight:* 60 lb. Book. *Finishing techniques:* 4-color. *Printer:* Frank Potter & Associates, Seattle, WA.

**Space Needle/Fine Dining** *Paper stock and weight:* Coated cover with riblaid interior insets. *Finishing techniques:* Laminated cover for wear and cord design for seasonal flexibility. *Printer:* Frank Potter & Associates, Seattle, WA.

**Rose Room/Menu Programs** *Finished size:* Wine—7 1/2″x10 1/4″ vert./Table check holder—4 1/2″x10″ vert./Menu—7 1/2″x10 1/2″ vert. *Paper stock and weight:* 100 lb. w/uv paper on menu. *Printer:* VCS (Visual Communications Systems, Inc.), Woodinville, WA.

**Key West Grill/Daily Menus** *Finished size:* 7 1/8″x12 3/4″. *Paper stock and weight:* 70 lb. Speckletone Cover. *Finishing techniques:* Menu was laminated to make it more durable. Fluorescent inks were used on cover to enhance sunset colors. *Printer:* Republic Press, Dallas, TX.

**El Torito Restaurants/Luncheon Menu** *Finished size:* 7 3/4″x13″. *Paper stock and weight:* Kromecote 12 pt. *Finishing techniques:* Laminated 1/2 mill. *Printer:* Phoenix Press, Irvine, CA.

**Tussey Mountain Inn** *Finished size:* Letterhead set (standard size)/Menu folder—9″x12″ folded. *Paper stock and weight:* Strathmore writing (for letterhead) and 65 lb. cover (for menu folder). *Finishing techniques:* 1 color fold. *Printer:* Commercial Printing, State College, PA.

**Rick's Cafe American** *Finished size:* 9″x14″. *Paper stock and weight:* Kromecote 12 pt. *Printer:* Associates Printing Service Inc., Glenview, IL.

**Macy's Cellar Grill/Daily Menus** *Finished size:* 11″x19″ (22″x19″ tall-opened). *Printer:* Alvin Menu Co., NJ.

**Nut Tree—Winter Enchantment Menu** *Finished size:* 8 1/2″x11″. *Paper stock and weight:* Simpson Gainsborough 80 & 100 lb. cover. *Finishing techniques:* Scorch & emboss cover by apex die and dull coat cover lamination by graphic coating. Cover and inside cover are laminated after printing, allowing for no interference (by way of cover emboss) on inside cover image. All Ms. Dicker's (the artist) originals were exhibited in the Dining Room Gallery for 14 week life of menu. *Printer:* Vlatis Creek Printing, Vacaville, CA.

**Nut Tree—Autumn Lunch** *Finished size:* 8 1/2″x11″. *Paper stock and weight:* Champion Kromekote 12 pt. cover, Simpson Gainsborough 80 lb. text. *Finishing techniques:* Gloss laminate cover 2 sides for durability. *Other:* Menu headings in longhand by illustrator Earl Hollander. This special seasonal menu is in service mid-September to Thanksgiving. *Printer:* Vlatis Creek Printing, Vacaville, CA.

**Nut Tree—Our Favorite Things—Holiday Menu** *Finished size:* 8 1/2″x11″. *Paper stock and weight:* 12 pt. Kromekote glossy 2 sides. *Finishing techniques:* 6 colors solid gloss laminate cover, 2 sides original banner designed by Don Birrell of Nut Tree Des. acted as basis. *Printer:* Vlatis Creek Printing, Vacaville, CA.

**Left Bank** *Finished size:* 5 1/2″x10 1/2″ and 4 1/2″x9 3/4″ (folded). *Paper stock and weight:* Strathmore American (Ivory white) 80 lb. cover; thermographed logo (lunch/dinner); laminated (lounge). *Printer:* Metropolitan Printing, Bloomington, IN.

**Palio** *Printer:* Enterprise Press, New York City, NY.

**Toscana Ristorante** *Printer:* LS Graphics, New York City, NY.

**The '21' Club** *Finished size:* 8 1/2″x11″ and Monarch size. *Paper stock and weight:* Cranes Distaff Linen, sub. 24 Antique wove. *Printer:* Sterling Roman Press, New York City, NY.

**The '21' Club** *Finished size:* 6″x9″. *Paper stock and weight:* Gainsborough text & cover, spiced ivory. *Printer:* Sterling Roman Press, New York City, NY.

**Il Bistro** *Printer:* Combine Graphics, New York City, NY.

**Squash Blossom/Breakfast Menu** *Finished size:* 9″x16″. *Paper stock and weight:* Neenah Classic Linen 130 lb. *Printer:* Associates Printing Services, Inc., Glenview, IL.

**Squash Blossom/Wine List** *Finished size:* 7″x13 1/2″. *Paper stock and weight:* Strathmore Rhododendron 130 lb. D.T. cover. *Finishing techniques:* Die cut, laminated. *Printer:* Associates Printing Services, Inc., Glenview, IL.

**Hyatt Regency Scottsdale/In Room Dining** *Finished size:* 9″x12″. *Paper stock and weight: cover*—Kromecote 12 pt. cover *insert*—Kromecote 10 pt. cover. *Finishing techniques:* die cut, glued. *Printer:* Associates Printing Services, Inc., Glenview, IL.

**Khakis' Raw Bar & Grill** *Finished size:* 6″x10″ inserts triple fold clear vinyl cover. *Paper stock and weight:* Colorado SST 80 lb. cover brite-white four flat colors one side. *Printer:* Boca Raton Printing Co., Boca Raton, FL.

**Squash Blossom/Guest Check Presenter** *Finished size:* 5″x10 5/8″. *Paper stock and weight:* Strathmore Rhododendron 80 lb. cover. *Finishing techniques:* Die cut, glued. *Printer:* Associates Printing Services, Inc., Glenview, IL.

**Brookside Cafe/Children's Menus** *Printer:* Bayshore Press, Santa Cruz, CA.

**Jeremiah's** *Printer:* Blake Printery, San Luis Obispo, CA.

**Cafe Greco** *Finished size:* 8 1/2″x11″. *Paper stock and weight:* 60 lb. cover—Carolina coated. *Finishing techniques:* Napkin ring is die cut for closure. *Printer:* Print Technical Corporation, New York City, NY.

**701 East West** *Finished size:* 8 1/2″x14″. *Paper stock and weight:* Centura 80 lb. cover. *Finishing techniques:* Clearview cafe cover take out box and can wrap. *Printer:* The Litho House, Seattle, WA.

**Kid Shelleen's** *Finished size:* 6″x13″ (dinner) and 11″x14″ (lunch) 4.5″x5.5″. *Paper stock and weight:* Simpson Gainsborough 80 lb. cover; screens of the two colors were used throughout. *Printer:* Charles Printing, Wilmington, DE.

**Little City** *Finished size:* 2″x1 7/8″. *Paper stock and weight:* 10 pt. Kromecote white; hand colored red match. *Printer:* Pageant Match & Creed, San Francisco, CA.

**Butler's** *Paper stock and weight:* Esprit white cover. An extra quantity of full-color covers were printed and cropped for different uses; imprinting was in black (special events, mailers, gift certificates). *Printer:* Technigraphics, San Francisco, CA.

**Andrea's** *Finished size:* 8 1/2″x14″. *Paper stock and weight:* Classic crest 24 lb. writing. *Fabricated Menu Holder*—menu fit in word processor for daily listings to be printed on it. *Printer:* Associates Printing Services, Inc., Glenview, IL.

**Fletcher's American Grill & Cafe** *Finished size:* 7 1/4″x10 3/4″. *Paper stock and weight: Inserts and folder*—Champion Linen cover, rose & ice, white. *Finishing techniques:* cover—Silkscreen on Plexiglass; folder—Offset. *Printer:* Andersen Screen Processes and The Bonsett Press.

**Squash Blossom Lunch/Daily Menu** *Finished size:* 9 1/2″x16 3/4″. *Paper stock and weight:* Strathmore Rhododendron 130 lb. cover. *Finishing techniques:* Die cut, glue; easily changeable menus. *Printer:* Associates Printing Services, Inc., Glenview, IL.

**Westchester Country Club** *Finished size:* 8 1/2″x12 1/2″. *Paper stock and weight:* Strathmore American Ivory 80 lb. cover. *Inserts*—Nechah classic laid text weight, die cut, fold glue. *Printer:* Brody Printing, Bridgeport, CT.

**Mrs. O'Leary's** *Finished size:* 12″x14″. *Paper stock and weight:* Gainsborough 70 lb. text. *Finishing techniques:* to be imprinted daily, using a laser printer. *Printer:* Associates Printing Services, Inc., Glenview, IL.

**Brasserie** *Finished size:* 10″x14″ *Paper stock and weight:* 80 lb. offset (text weight). *Printer:* Brody Printing, Bridgeport, CT.

**Suan Saranrom Garden Restaurant/Hilton International (Thailand)** *Menu size (folded):* 5 1/2″x13″. *Paper:* Silk paper 150 grams.

**Royal Viking Sky** *Finished size:* 7″x11″. *Paper stock and weight:* Silver Gainsborough—80 lb. cover. *Finishing techniques:* debossed, foil stamped. *Printer:* Graphic Reproduction, San Francisco, CA/Apex Die, San Carlos, CA.

**Hyatt Regency Chicago/All Outlets Hyatt Chicago/Special Events Menu** *Finished size:* 10″x10″. *Paper stock and weight:* Starwhite Vilksburg 100 lb. cover. *Printer:* Associates Printing Service, Inc., Glenview, IL.

**Hyatt Regency Chicago/All Outlets/Special Events Menu** *Finished size:* 4 3/4″x7 1/2″. *Paper stock and weight:* 12 pt. Kromecote four-color; 2 sides. *Printer:* Associates Printing Service, Inc., Glenview, IL.

**Westchester Country Club** *Finished size:* 8 1/2″x11 3/4″ when folded. *Paper stock and weight:* 80 lb. coated cover.. *Finishing techniques:* score and fold. *Printer:* Fidelity Press, Milford, CT.

**The University Club, New York City** *Finished size:* 4 3/4″x6 1/4″ when folded. *Paper stock and weight:* 80 lb. glossy coated cover. *Printer:* Brody Printing, Bridgeport, CT.

**American Institute of Wine & Food** *Finished size:* 8″x11″. *Paper stock and weight:* 80 lb. Gainsborough Silver Text. *Printer:* Lithography by Design, Petaluma, CA.

**Les Celebrities—Breakfast, Lunch, Dinner** *Finished size:* 8 1/2″x14″. *Paper stock and weight:* cover—Strathmore Rhododendron; insert—Strathmore Rhododendron—past-on menu illustration—Kromecote. *Finishing techniques:* Embossing, die cut, glue. *Printer:* Associates Printing Service, Inc., Glenview, IL.

**Chardonnay** *Paper stock and weight:* Gainsborough, cover, confetti. *Printer:* Goetz Printing Co., Springfield, VA.

**Hamilton's** *Finished size:* 8 1/2″x14″. *Paper stock and weight:* Strathmore Rhododendron; cover—130 lb. cover; insert—65 lb. cover. *Finishing techniques:* die cut, glue. *Printer:* Associates Printing Service, Inc., Glenview, IL.

**Royal Viking Star** *Finished size:* 7″x12″. *Paper stock and weight:* Speckletone cordtone finish; cream cover. *Printer:* Speedway Printing, San Francisco, CA.

**Regency Ballroom/Wine List** *Finished size:* 6 1/4″x9 3/4″. *Paper stock and weight:* Kromecote 12 pt. *Printer:* Associates Printing Service, Inc., Glenview, IL.

**Waiters on Wheels** *Finished size:* 3 1/2″x5″/folded to 3 1/2″x2 1/2″. *Paper stock and weight:* 10 pt. caste coat. *Finishing techniques:* Masters printed first, then individual restaurant logo printed thermographically. *Printer:* Pacific Coast Concepts, Danville, CA.

**La Tour** *Finished size:* 9″x14″. *Paper stock and weight:* Kromecote 12 pt. *Finishing techniques:* Paste-on embossed illustration—die supplied by customer. *Printer:* Associates Printing Service, Inc., Glenview, IL.

**Platters** *Finished size:* 12″x12″. *Paper stock and weight:* Cornwall 12 pt. *Printer:* Baker, Gurney & McLaren Press Ltd., Toronto, Canada.

**Steak & Ale** *Finished size:* 7 1/4″x13″. *Paper stock and weight:* 65 lb. Irish Cream Cover. *Finishing techniques:* Hard bound with debossed illustrated label, lined with printed marble paper; menus insert into carrier and may be changed. *Printer:* Heritage Press, Dallas, TX.

**Dynasty Restaurant (Osaka Hilton International)** *Menu size:* folded 26″x40″. *Printer:* Verokv Printing.

**Cortlands** *Finished size:* 10″x10″. *Paper stock and weight:* 80 lb. cover Curtis Flannel. *Finishing techniques:* laminated to blind embossed with gold stamping. Gold tassel around sample stitched binding UY2 inside fly sheet. *Printer:* Beasley Printing Co., Houston, TX.

**The Boat House** *Finished size:* 16″x14 1/2″ (folded) 16″x24″ (flat). *Paper stock and weight:* Warren. *Finishing techniques:* die cut and folded. *Other:* Printing 1 side of sheet. *Printer:* Fry & Smith, San Diego, CA.

**Mirabean Restaurant/Lunch** *Finished size:* Cover—Gainsborough. *Paper stock and weight:* Inside—Gainsborough. *Finishing techniques:* Gold foil. *Printer:* The Litho House, Seattle, WA.

**Royal Viking Sky** *Finished size:* 8″x9 3/4″. *Paper stock and weight:* 80 lb. white Teton cover. *Finishing techniques:* embossed, gold-stamped, die cut. *Printer:* Craft Press, San Francisco, CA.

**Carlos Murphy** *Finished size:* 21″x30″ (flat size). *Paper stock and weight:* Super Tuft 100 lb. *Finishing techniques:* Varnish; turn wheel at top of menu to reveal food selections. *Printer:* Fry & Smith, San Diego, CA.

**The Deli** *Finished size:* 8″x18 1/2″ folded. *Paper stock and weight:* 10 pt. Kromecote. *Finishing techniques:* Score (deliver flat) 2 colors, trim angle on top. Size of menu was determined so that 2 could be cut of paper sheet also collar edges were trimmed at angle. *Printer:* Nittany Valley Offset, State College, PA.

**Elephant Bar & Restaurant** *Finished size:* 6″x3 1/2″x4″. *Paper stock and weight:* 10 pt. Carolina. *Finishing techniques:* 4/c process. *Printer:* Republic Printing, Newport Beach, CA.

**Max & Erma's Restaurant, Inc.** *Finished size:* 6 1/4″x8 7/8″. *Paper stock and weight:* 10 pt. coated cover. *Finishing techniques:* 2-color equipment perfected & varnished. *Printer:* Hick's Printing, Canal Winchester, OH.

**El Torito (Texas unit)** *Finished size:* 10 1/2″x5″. *Paper stock and weight:* Sundance Felt 65 lb. cover. *Finishing techniques:* die-cut, 3 color. *Printer:* Green Printing, Long Beach, CA.

**Images** *Finished size:* 4 1/2″x6″. *Paper stock and weight:* cover—Lustrecote 10 pt.; insert—Scott offset 80 lb. *Printer:* Associates Printing Service, Inc., Glenview, IL.

**Phirajak's Thai Kitchen** *Finished size:* 11″x18″. *Finishing techniques:* Hand pasted-on fan. *Printer:* Blair Graphics, Santa Monica, CA.

**Darryl's** *Finished size:* 16″x10″ folded. *Paper stock and weight:* cover—12 pt. Carolina Cover; insert—9 pt. Carolina Varnished. *Printer:* Graphix Associates, Inc., Leawood, KS.

**Fillets Inc.** *Finished size:* 10″x10″ folded to 5″x5″. *Paper stock and weight:* Hammermill vellum—Ivory 60 lb. *Finishing techniques:* Offset printed. *Printer:* Lewis Printing, Paseagonla, MS.

**St. Francis Memorial Hospital** *Finished size:* 17″x14″ folded to 8 1/2″x14″. *Paper stock and weight:* cover—100 lb. w/lustrogloss; inside—15 lb. w/country cream—Sundance cover. *Finishing techniques:* 4 color process plus PMS 423 and then full flood varnish; 2 PMS 425 plus 174 original artwork scanned as a duotone. Test—1 color, 2 sides. *Printer:* Fong & Fong, Sacramento, CA.

**St. John's Regional Medical Center** *Finished size:* 12″x18″. *Printer:* Vincent Graphics, Ojai, CA.

**Brigham & Women's Hospital** *Finished size:* 7 3/4″x12 1/4″. *Paper stock and weight:* 80 lb. cover vintage velvet, 80 lb. text Mohawk Supervine Ivory. *Finishing techniques:* 7-color cover; 3-color text. *Printer:* Nimrod Press, Boston, MA.

**St. Joseph's Hospital Center** *Finished size:* 8 1/2″x5 1/2″. *Paper stock and weight:* Silver Currency 10 pt. *Finishing techniques:* Die cut and embossed, saddle stitch, color—burgundy. *Printer:* G & Q Printing, Detroit, MI.

**Westours McKinley Explorer** *Finished size:* 8″x11″. *Paper stock and weight:* 100 lb. Producto Litho cover. *Finishing techniques:* Silver foil stamp—brunch; coating—ultra coat, dinner. *Paper inserts:* Taped in ;with menu tape. 4-color process from airbrush art.

**Mariner Corporation** *Finished size:* 5 1/2″x13″. *Paper stock and weight:* Starwhite Vicksburg 120 lb. *Finishing techniques:* Die cut. *Printer:* Associates Printing Service, Inc., Glenview, IL.

**Baptist Memorial Hospital** *Finished size:* 10″x11 7/8″ folded (cover varnished). *Paper stock and weight:* 10 pt. Kromecote text: 80 lb. L.O.E. *Printer:* Lithograph Printing, Co., Memphis, TN.

**The Union Club Restaurant.** *Finished size:* 8 1/2″x11″. *Paper stock and weight:* 70 lb. cover matte coated. *Finishing techniques:* LOE Cream; printed both sides, 3 PMS colors, plus copper & varnished. *Printer:* Fabe Litho, Tucson, AZ.

**Traveler's Inn** *Finished size:* 7″x12″. *Paper stock and weight:* Ventura 80 lb. cover. *Finishing techniques:* 2-color. *Printer:* The Litho House, Seattle, WA.

**Juliana's Supperclub** *Finished size:* 220 mm x 190 mm. *Paper stock and weight:* Encore Super Gloss artboard 350 GSM. *Finishing techniques:* Four-color printed on reversal and double sided celloglazing. *Printer:* Stratagem, Alexandria, New South Wales.

**El Torito Table Tent** *Finished size:* 5″x8″ *Paper stock and weight:* 12 pt. Carolina C1S. *Finishing techniques:* Die cut; seven different fruit pieces fit into bird's beak. *Printer:* Lithograph , Anaheim, CA.

**10 Huntington Bar & Grill** *Finished size:* 4″x4 3/4″. *Paper stock and weight:* Strathmore Rhododendron 80 lb. cover. *Finishing techniques:* Die cut to fit over small wine bottle on table to promote daily wine bar and snacks. *Printer:* Associates Printing Service, Inc., Glenview, IL.

**Eat'n Park Restaurant, Inc.** *Finished size:* 7″x5″ (folded). *Paper stock and weight:* 12 pt. Kromekote, C1S. *Printer:* Superior Litho, Pittsburgh, PA.

**Eat'n Park Restaurant (Box menu—children's)** *Finished size:* 3 1/2″x2 3/4″ folded. *Paper stock and weight:* 12 pt. C2S. *Finishing techniques:* Die cut, perforated and hand folded. *Printer:* Geyer Printing, Pittsburgh, PA.

**Eat & Park Flip Books** *Finished size:* 3 1/4″x2″. *Paper stock and weight:* Williamsburg High bulk, Frankote cover. *Finishing techniques:* Perfect bound. *Printer:* Geyer Printing, Pittsburgh, PA.

**Lyon's Restaurant/Children's menu** *Finished size:* 6 1/4″x8 1/2″. *Paper stock and weight:* Starcote 8 pt. cover. *Printer:* King Menus, Hayward, CA.

**Squash Blossom/Children's menu** *Finished size:* 7 1/4″x13″. *Paper stock and weight:* Neenah Classic Crest 80 lb. cover. *Printer:* Associates Printing Service, Inc., Glenview, IL.

**Coco's Japan** *Finished size:* 10″x12″. *Finishing techniques:* Laminated. *Printer:* Robin Hood KK, Ken, Japan.

**Jojo's/Coco's** *Finished size:* 7″x10″. *Paper stock and weight:* 12 pt. Springfield coated. *Finishing techniques:* Varnish; die cut with elastic string to wear as visor. *Printer:* Ink Spot, Ontario, Canada.

**Hyatt Regency—Chicago/All Outlets** *Finished size:* 5″x7″. *Paper stock and weight:* Kromecote 12 pt. (Table top promotion for February and March). *Printer:* Associates Printing Service, Inc., Glenview, IL.

**Les Celebrites** *Finished size:* 4 1/2″x5 1/2″. *Paper stock and weight:* cover—Strathmore Rhododendron 130 lb. cover. insert—Strathmore Rhododendron 80 lb. text. *Finishing techniques:* Held with menu cord. *Printer:* Associates Printing Service, Inc., Glenview, IL.

**Hyatt Hotels Corporation** *Finished size:* 5″x8″. *Paper stock and weight:* 12 pt. Kromecote C2S. *Finishing techniques:* Overall varnish. Tabletop drink/appetizer menu for all hotels in chain. *Printer:* Associates Printing Service, Inc., Glenview, IL.

**Tussey Mountain Inn** *Finished size:* 7 1/2″x8 5/8″ folded. *Paper stock and weight:* Strathmore 80 lb. text. *Finishing techniques:* 1 color fold; careful attention paid to registration. *Printer:* Commercial Printing, State College, PA.

**Raddison Park Terrace Hotel/Room Service—Express Breakfast** *Paper stock and weight:* Curtis Linen white, cover weight. *Finishing techniques:* Light blue silk tassel cord; matching PMS blue. *Printer:* Combined Graphics, Inc., Burtonsville, MD.

# Index

## Design Firms



## Designers